Eros

Eros

The Myth of Ancient Greek Sexuality

Bruce S. Thornton

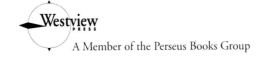
Westview PRESS
A Member of the Perseus Books Group

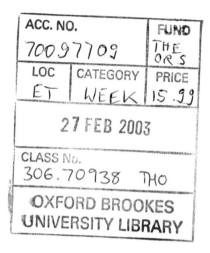
Copyright © 1997 by Westview Press, A Member of the Perseus Books Group

Published in 1997 in the United States of America by Westview Press, 5500 Central Avenue, Boulder,
Colorado 80301-2877, and in the United Kingdom by Westview Press, 12 Hid's Copse Road, Cumnor
Hill, Oxford OX2 9JJ

Library of Congress Cataloging-in-Publication Data
Thornton, Bruce S.
  Eros: the myth of ancient Greek sexuality / Bruce Thornton.
    p. cm.
  Includes bibliographical references and index.
  ISBN 0-8133-3225-7.—ISBN 0-8133-3226-5
  1. Sex customs—Greece—History. I. Title.
HQ13.T46   1997
392'.6'0938—dc20   96-36786
                                                                          CIP

The paper used in this publication meets the requirements of the American National Standard for Per-
manence of Paper for Printed Library Materials Z39.48-1984.

PERSEUS
POD
ON DEMAND

10   9   8   7   6   5

I dedicate this book with love and gratitude
to my wife, Jacalyn,
and my boys, Isaac and Cole,
who have given me a reason to believe that it all has a point.

Oh Plato! Plato! you have paved the way
With your confounded fantasies, to more
Immoral conduct by the fancied sway
Your system feigns o'er the controlless core
Of human hearts, than all the long array
Of poets and romancers:—You're a bore,
A charlatan, a coxcomb—and have been,
At best, no better than a go-between.

—*Don Juan*, I.116

Contents

PART TWO
The "Fancied Sway"

Preface

THE LITTLE WE KNOW about everyday life and behavior in ancient Greece is dwarfed by how much we don't know. We simply lack the evidence, and what evidence we do have is fragmentary. The spectacular excellence of those few surviving monuments—the *Iliad*, the *Oresteia*, Plato's Dialogues—often obscures for us the magnitude of the loss. But a few examples can remind us just how much has disappeared. Of the approximately 1,000 tragedies that were produced in Athens during a little more than a century, thirty-three have survived. The rest exist, if at all, as titles or authors or snippets of texts culled by ancient grammarians and pedants. Or take the case of Sappho, Byron's "sage blue-stocking," Plato's tenth muse. Out of her nine papyrus-roll books of poetry attested by the ancients, only *one* complete poem survives. Imagine what our estimation of Shakespeare's poetry, let alone his life, would be if only one play—and that not necessarily his best—had survived.

But finding out what the Greeks may have thought about sex in their day-to-day lives is difficult not just because of the dearth of evidence. What literary evidence we do have is virtually all "public" speech: that is, writing subject to the conventions and formal strictures of various genres—poetical, oratorical, or historical. We do not have from ancient Greece the journals, diaries, and private letters, not to mention a genre like the novel of social and psychological realism, that open a window into the private lives of more recent societies. And even the more "objective" prose writers, Thucydides, say, or Aristotle, whom we might expect to provide us with more "factual" information, are limited by their choice of subject matter—the public political, diplomatic, or military activities of an elite—or by their own conservative points of view. How representative of the "average Greek" can we assume are Aristotle's misogynistic fulminations? And who is the "average Greek"? Athenian? Dorian? Theban oligarch? A Euboean hardscrabble farmer? From what polis does he come, what social class, what tribe, what linguistic group, what moment from the several hundred years of Greek history? And, of course, when the writing is literary, the problem of the voice's wider representativeness is compounded. Even the lyric "I" can't be uncritically taken as evidence of the poet's own life. Sometimes Greek poets say what they say because the conventions of the tradition in which they are working require them to. The most passionate of poets may be chaste in his private life; as the Roman poet Catullus said, "The pious poet ought to be chaste, but not necessarily his verses." This is not to repeat the formalist fallacy that poetic speech is wholly divorced from life. But if art is the mirror of nature, it is often a fun-house mirror, distorting as much as it reflects.

The claim, then, of some recent fashionable scholars to be doing Classical "history from below," to be recovering, based on this scanty evidence stretching over several centuries, "the everyday functioning of the community"[1] that counters "the values or pretensions of [the] hegemonic group,"[2] that is, the tiny elite that created most of the public documents that have survived, is a self-serving chimera. Nor are such claims buttressed by the use of so-called nonprivileged data, the curse-tablets, dream-books, archaeological remnants, graffiti, or vase-paintings that somehow are supposed to be more representative of the everyday life of the "average" nonelite Greek. We still lack what Lionel Trilling called the "buzz of implication,"[3] the psychological *contexts* of such evidence, let alone its production and use, to generalize safely about everyday life. A scene on a vase, even leaving aside the fact that vase-painting itself reflected formal conventions of subject and execution, may not tell us any more about a middling Athenian than a Wedgwood china pattern tells us about a Victorian hackney driver.

"Everyday life," then, and the beliefs and attitudes of the "average" person are simply too amorphous, shifting, quirky, and mutable to be recovered without an abundance of evidence of the sort lacking from ancient Greece. And when something as fluid, as subjective, as various as attitudes toward sex is at issue, the difficulty in finding out what "really" went on is nearly prohibitive. As Peter Green has said, sex in literature usually is "the image of a minority—often a minority of one. . . . Any resemblance between that image and practical reality is not only coincidental, but in most cases quite impossible to detect."[4] And too much of the Greeks' "practical reality" is utterly different from our own. Bernard Knox recently has emphasized the strangeness, for us moderns, of sacrifice in ancient Greece—the public slaughtering of animals with all the attendant blood and flies and handling of viscera.[5] I would note too the prevalence of military experience and violence, the oddity of aristocratic consciousness, and the quotidian experience of slavery as other social realities difficult for a modern middle-class academic to understand. How can the modern professor of Greek tragedy who has never fought in a war and fancies himself a pacifist "really" understand the motives behind the epitaph Aeschylus wrote for himself, which ignores his ninety tragedies and mentions only that he fought at Marathon? How can the feminist professor of gender studies "really" understand the mind or values, apart from these as provisionally evidenced in her fragments, of a poet like Sappho, whose aristocratic clan mentality, more than her gender or homosexual proclivities, makes her in some ways as strange to us as a Samurai warrior? As Louis MacNeice said, "It was all so unimaginably different / And all so long ago."

This book, then, is not about what the Greeks "really" thought or felt or did about sex. It is about what the literary remains from 700–100 B.C. say about sex, for it is those remains that most influenced subsequent Western culture. This means, first, that vase-paintings, inscriptions, statuary, and archaeological ruins will not be talked about. Second, the book is aimed at the "common reader," the intelligent person who takes pleasure in reading nonfiction more challenging than the latest sex manual or celebrity exposé. Hence the focus will be on primary texts, and references to secondary texts will be from those works in English that avoid for the most part the Charybdis of fashionable theoretical cant and the Scylla of specialized technical pedantry, and so are accessible to this "common reader" who has, as Maynard Mack put it recently, "prudently lost interest in the tribal wars and Byzantine pedantries that now balkanize professional students of literature into new-critics, new-historicists, neo-marxists, feminists, structuralists, psychoanalysts, deconstructionists, and other cells of the elect."[6] Too often these days in Classics, I would add, those ideas are accompanied by the whine of ideological axes being ground. However, in the Critical Bibliography I also direct the reader to some Classical scholarship influenced by these critical fashions, since they have dominated of late most work on ancient sexuality.

The time span chosen is somewhat arbitrary, since significant works of Greek literature fall this side of 100 B.C. But a problem with looking at literary fragments is a tendency to ignore the shifting historical contexts. This isn't as much of an issue when the focus, as it is here, is on describing a literary inheritance that influences later cultures. After all, Virgil, say, may not have known as much about Homer's world, late Dark Age Greece, as we do, but that doesn't affect his literary dialogue with Homer. Still, I will try to avoid such disembodied formalism as much as possible when appropriate, though descriptions of historical changes within this period will necessarily be brief and general. The end date of 100 B.C. will help, since by that time—after Pydna, after the sacks of Carthage and Corinth—the Mediterranean is a Roman lake around which the Greeks sit like frogs, and so any discussion of Greek culture or literature in the Roman period must take into account the Romans—a project, perhaps, for a subsequent volume.

If we can't learn that much about what the Greeks "really" thought about sex, how they "really" experienced it in their daily lives, what is the value of studying these fragments? First, most of the writing on ancient sexuality these days grinds the evidence in the mill of an "advocacy agenda" supported by some fashionable theory that says more about the crisis of Western rationalism than it does about ancient Greece. Thus we are told that the Greeks saw nothing inherently wrong with sodomy between males as long as certain "protocols" of age, social status, and position were honored, an interpretation maintained despite the abundance of evidence, detailed below in Chapter 4, that the Greeks—including pederastic apologists like Plato—were horrified and disgusted by the idea of a male being anally penetrated by another male and called such behavior "against nature." One purpose here is to get back to what the Greeks actually say without burying it in polysyllabic sludge.

But, more important, the attitudes discovered in the ancient literary evidence contain the seeds of later Western thinking about sex. Remember, these literary remains influenced immeasurably the Romans, and through the Romans became part of the Western cultural tradition, at first refracted through the lens of Christianity, then "reborn" in the Renaissance and Enlightenment, and so part of our cultural cargo today—the fragments that generation after generation in the West has shored against their ruin, the tesserae of that vast mosaic of Western civilization it is fashionable these days to denigrate even as it is being plundered. Even if we can't discover, then, what the Greeks "actually" experienced in their sexual lives, understanding what they *wrote* about sex can help us understand some of the roots of our own sexual attitudes. And it can show us an understanding of sex that sees it, as the Greeks saw everything, "steadily and whole," without the idealizations, whether Enlightenment or Romantic, with which we moderns hide its terrible power.

Bruce S. Thornton
Fresno, California

Acknowledgments

T HE KINDNESS OF BOTH friends and strangers made this book possible. "Strangers" first: Adam Bellow read an early draft and gave some good advice. Martin Kilmer carefully read the manuscript and saved me from various infelicities: Those that remain are due to my own stubbornness. Peter Kracht at Westview has been encouraging and helpful throughout. Jon Taylor Howard's copyediting was exemplary. And Camille Paglia continues to provide a model of intellectual integrity and pizzazz.

As for friends: My colleagues in the Foreign Language Department at California State University, Fresno, voted me a sabbatical for the fall semester of 1994, providing a respite from a four-course-per-semester teaching load so I could finish. Victor Davis Hanson is the literal sine qua non of this and much else: I owe him an immense debt of gratitude. Padraic Emparan helped check references. He was not paid enough to be responsible for any mistakes.

B.S.T.

A Note on Translation

U<small>NLESS NOTED OTHERWISE</small>, translations of Greek in this book are my own. I have tried to render the Greek as literally as possible. This means occasionally I resort to the inelegant expedient of multiple English words, separated by slashes, to translate Greek words for which no one English word suffices.

I have tried to keep transliterations of Greeks words to a minimum. However, I think it is important that the reader see the consistent appearance of key terms or phrases; this requires providing the term or phrase in the original. The reader may notice that the same word sometimes has a different spelling. Ancient Greek is an inflected language; its nouns and adjectives change form depending on their function in the sentence. When transliterating, I have kept the original form of the Greek word. Hence the same word in English translation will appear transliterated in its different Greek forms.

Unless noted otherwise, all dates are B.C.

Introduction:
"Custom the King of All"

Custom is king of all things.
—Pindar Fr. 169S

H ERODOTUS, the fifth-century amalgam of historian, anthropologist, and gossip, tells the story of an experiment conducted by Darius, king of the Persians, when some Greeks and Indians were visiting his court. He asked the Greeks how much money they would take to eat the corpses of their parents. Not for all the money in the world, was their answer. He then asked the Indians how much they would take to burn the bodies of their parents—the point being, of course, that the Indians ate their parental dead and the Greeks burned theirs. The Indians "uttered a cry of horror and forbade him to mention such a dreadful thing. One can see by this what custom can do, and Pindar, in my opinion, was right when he called it 'king of all.'"[1]

This anecdote reveals Herodotus's—and Darius's—awareness of one of the most important intellectual questions in Greece during the fifth century: the relationship between and definitions of "custom/law" and "nature," or in Greek, *nomos* and *phusis*, the ancestors of our "heredity and environment" or "nature and nurture" contrasts. These two concepts and their uneasy relation to one another repeatedly crop up in Greek literature, from the asides of comic and tragic writers to the speculations of historians and philosophers. Does good character result from an innate disposition or from education? The comic writer Eupolis asserts in a fragment that nature creates character, but Euripides' Hecuba, the *mater dolorosa* of the ancient world, views the wreckage of Troy and her captive daughters waiting to sail to Greece to be concubines and isn't so sure. She takes time out of her litany of grief to wonder philosophically if goodness "is in our blood" or if it is "something we acquire." Thucydides in his history of the Peloponnesian War broods constantly over the fragility of law and its restraint when faced with the

1

imperatives of appetite and passion, witnessing as he had the self-destruction of Athens, a city whose cultural brilliance still dazzles after twenty-five centuries. Describing the horrors of the civil war in Corcyra during the war, Thucydides remarks that such disorder will always occur "as long as the nature of mankind remains the same," its customs and laws fragile in the face of "imperious necessities." Antiphon the Sophist, one of those thinkers during the late fifth century who focused intensely on the relations of nature to culture and law, claims justice arises from obeying both the laws of one's society and nature's laws—a difficult proposition, since the two kinds of law often conflict, those of society being artificial, those of nature compulsory. Or, as a character in a fragment of Euripides succinctly puts it, Nature wills it, nature who cares nothing for law.[2]

Clearly, these two ideas were on everybody's mind, and culture and nature have a long and complicated history in Greece. Also, the terms shift meaning, their relations to one another change, depending on the time and the thinker. The problem of definition is compounded by the habit all people have of "naturalizing" what is conventional, that is, attributing to nature what is actually a result of culture and history. Is there a "natural" order our laws can reflect? Or is nature a realm of chaos and disorder? The answer depends on whether you ask a tragedian or a philosopher, an Epicurean or a Stoic. "For some think," Cicero's Balbus summarizes, "that nature is a certain irrational force inducing necessary motions in bodies; others that it is a force participating in reason and order, proceeding methodically . . . whose skill no art, no hand, no craftsman could reproduce or imitate, [and Epicureans think that] nature refers to the whole of existence."[3] Despite this confusion, though, a definition of these concepts (that is, of nature and culture) can be deduced from Greek literature—a necessary task, for understanding what Greek literary remains say about sex depends on seeing it in the context of the tension between these two forces as they converge to create human identity. Understanding sex, then, in Greek terms is understanding who and what we are.

Generally, *nomos* means "law," "custom," "habit," everything conventional and historical that humans communally agree to recognize as regulating and limiting their behavior, and that I will use the word "culture" to denote. It is the realm of society, language, technology, the mind and its order. *Phusis* comes from the word *phuô*, "grow," "spring up," and refers to the organic world of material growth and decay, the givens of our bodies with their appetites and passions, and the earth and its forces, the ahistorical realm of necessity and chance, the raw material upon which custom and law—more comprehensively, "culture"—act. *Nomos* is order. Nature is, as Critias and pseudo-Demosthenes say, *ataktos*, "irregular," "disorderly," "lawless," containing within it, according to Plato in the *Timaeus*, an "errant cause," an unpredictable necessary source of disorder.[4] Human identity is possible because the mind and its projections—laws, customs, institutions—impose order upon this welter of chaotic forces, carve out a niche for humans between the serene lives of the gods, "all breathing human passion far above," and the brute necessity of the beasts.[5]

To the modern reader, this view of nature probably sounds reactionary, a reflex of the "Eurocentric" arrogance that now threatens to destroy the planet. But we must remember how much our view of nature results from two modern movements, the Enlightenment and Romanticism. The triumphs of reason, science, and technology liberated us from the chaos of nature that humans before our time—and those today in the Third World—dealt with every day. Only a few of us now grow food, the activity where nature's destructive recalcitrance shows itself most acutely. We forget that before the twentieth century more than nine-tenths of humanity spent most of its time wresting nutrition from a fickle nature and that a failure to do so meant literal starvation for many people. And many of us in the West, urban jungles aside, do not experience cruelty and violence on a daily basis, as did premodern societies, who could witness casually man's infinite capacity to inflict pain on his fellows. Modern medicine has freed us from many fatal and disfiguring diseases, as well as reducing death in childbirth and infant mortality. Technology protects us from the elements and the backbreaking labor that Hesiod and Vergil saw as our only salvation. In short, for us moderns, nature is, as Conrad's Marlow put it, "the shackled form of a conquered monster."

Freed as we citizens of advanced societies are from all but the most spectacular of nature's disorder—earthquakes, floods, fires, hurricanes—it is easy for us to indulge the Romantic idealization of nature that makes "natural" for us a term of the highest approbation, and thus the word of choice on as many products as possible. We only see, as Henry Adams said, "the sugar-coating that she [nature] shows to youth." So we have today what can be called "romantic ecology," the popular idea that the earth and its creatures are all one big interconnected, mutually dependent, happy family—or at least were until the wicked Europeans set about alienating us from this once-happy paradise and destroying the planet. Such ideas are, of course, possible only because that same wicked science has liberated people from hunger, relentless labor, and early mortality—that is, from the daily examples of nature's destructive indifference, giving them the leisure and comfort in which to idealize nature.

The assertion, moreover, that with our technology we are destroying the planet is a reflex of the same anthropomorphic arrogance the romantic ecologist is so quick to criticize. A Greek thinker transported to the twentieth century who familiarized himself with our world might respond that we can't destroy the earth—we can only make it uninhabitable for, say, mammals. But from *nature's* point of view, so what? Does nature mourn the passing of the dinosaurs? Will nature mourn if mammals go the same way? Maybe it's the turn of insects to rule. Nature cares nothing for us or any of the numerous other species that are extinct, a group that includes 90 percent of all the species that ever existed. Nature is a sheer relentless process of creation and, as Keats says, "a fierce eternal destruction," and it is utterly indifferent to the forms of life that are thrown up by random mutations. This particular transient order of mutually interdependent species is no more valuable to nature than the numerous others that preceded it and have disappeared. No one species or life-form is more valuable than any other—the HIV virus and the Bengal tiger are equal in the eyes of nature, prized only for their ability to hand on their genetic package to the next generation. It is only to *us* moral agents, who can *choose* to destroy or preserve, that there is a difference.

Nature, then, and its order are amoral and inhuman, as the Greeks, particularly the poets, understood, though the philosophers, particularly the Stoics, dreamed of a nature defined as the projection of a providential rational order. But nature and its order care nothing for the individual, and we do. We care very much for this species of one—our own self—that will disappear, never again to return. That recognition by the Greeks of the inhuman chaos of nature, the impersonal cruelty of its order, accounts for the lack of a wholesale idealization of nature in Greek literature such as one finds in the Romantic poets. Descriptions of lovely landscapes filled with flowers and other natural charms do appear, but time after time they are the scene of a destructive encounter with the force of the divine "other," that reality beyond the human space that nonetheless often brutally impinges on it. The crags and rocks and streams and woods that delight the modern city-dweller were the home of Pan, the goat-footed and goat-horned god of unbridled lust, a dangerous manifestation of nature's irrational power, hence the inducer of "panic." If you muddied his pristine spring by washing your feet in it, he would sodomize you—unless you liked "such punishment"; then he'd break your head with his club. Calypso's island in the *Odyssey* is a natural paradise, with soft meadows of blooming violets and parsley and an Edenic four springs, but Odysseus wants nothing more than to escape his divine paramour, whom he views with suspicion and distrust, even after seven years of sexual cohabitation. In the *Hymn to Demeter*, the "soft meadow" filled with roses, crocuses, violets, irises, hyacinths, and narcissus is a *dolon*, a trap or snare, the scene of Persephone's rape by Hades, king of the dead.[6]

It is no coincidence that beautiful landscapes in Greek literature are also scenes of sexual violence. In the *Catalogue of Women* attributed to Hesiod, Zeus beguiles Europa with a crocus he breathes from his mouth as she gathers flowers in a meadow. Similarly Creusa, in Euripides' *Ion*, describes her rape by Apollo as she was picking crocuses. A poem by Ibycus appears to be a hymn to nature's beauty, describing the flourishing quince-trees, the flowing rivers, the shaded vine-blossoms, but once more the emphasis falls on the destructiveness of a sexual passion compared to the "Thracian north wind blazing with lightning." Even so-called pastoral poetry, that Hellenistic genre often cited as the most extensive Greek idealization of nature, consistently links a beautiful landscape to some destructive natural force. In Theocritus's fifth *Idyll*, a shepherd brags about "defiling" his boy among the flowers. In the thirteenth, Heracles' buddy Hylas is drowned by enamored nymphs as he draws water from a spring in a hollow surrounded by flowers and herbs. Aeschylus neatly compacts all these associations into one phrase when he calls Helen, the original femme fatale, a "heart-eating flower of love."[7]

But the best example of the Greek suspicion of nature's duplicitous beauty is in Euripides' brilliant last tragedy, the *Bacchae*, about the god Dionysus's vengeance on his mother's family, who has rejected his divinity and worship. The young ruler Pentheus has sent an army to bring back forcibly the Theban women who, maddened by the god, have joined his devotees in celebrating his rites in the wilds beyond the city. But things go horribly wrong, and a messenger returns to tell the tale. He describes at first the Theban Maenads awaking from their sleep in the forest, an idyllic scene of unity with nature, all culture and civilization cast aside. Snakes fasten the women's fawn-skins and lick their cheeks, new mothers nurse gazelles and young wolves, women strike the earth with their thyrsuses—a wand wrapped in ivy and vine leaves and topped with a pinecone—and wine and milk and water and honey come bubbling up from the earth. It is a scene of a lovely reunion with nature, without the alienating restraints of civilization.

But this Golden Age dream turns to nightmare when the Maenads catch sight of the herdsmen who attempt to bring them back to the city. The women fall upon the animals and tear them apart with their bare hands, scattering the bloody scraps throughout the forest. They attack and ravage two cities, pillaging and destroying, immune to the defenders' iron and fire. The wands that recently had drawn life-giving fluids from the earth now draw blood, and the snakes now lick the blood of the slain from the women's cheeks. In an instant nature's beauty and harmony turn to inhuman chaos and destruction.[8]

What we notice about these few examples is that even a beautiful nature is the scene of fatal encounters for humans with the numinous inhuman powers filling the cosmos—and one of the most potent and destructive of those powers is sex. We must not, then, think of "nature" in our terms but in the Greeks', in which nature is the collection of chaotic forces and processes in the teeth of which humans create their orders of identity. From Homer on, this is exactly how human order is perceived: as the triumph of the mind and culture over the brute forces of nature. Book 9 of the *Odyssey* stands perhaps as the most representative passage of Greek literature embodying this idea. Polyphemus, the monstrous Cyclops, is pure nature: Like the other Cyclopses, he has no laws, institutions, technology—no agriculture, no shipbuilding. He lives in a cave, like an animal, and is compared to "a forested peak of high mountains." And he does not respect the most important cultural institution in the *Odyssey*, hospitality, the ritualized treatment of the stranger-guest that acknowledges his common human identity predicated on both the (natural) need to eat and the ordering of that need through the (cultural) ritual itself. So Polyphemus *eats* his guests instead of feeding them—he is *agrion*, "wild," "savage," like nature.

Clearly brute strength is futile against this monster, and Odysseus overcomes him not with force but with guile, his mind that can think up a *metis*, a "plan," "craft," "skill." First Odysseus sharpens the olive-wood stake and tempers its point in the fire—a technical re-forming of natural raw material. Then he gets

Polyphemus drunk on powerful unmixed wine. Notice the presence of two of the Greeks' most important agricultural products, the olive and the grape. Finally, before the monster passes out, Odysseus tells him his name is Outis, "Noman," a linguistic trick that will keep the other Cyclopses from interfering. Then while Polyphemus snores in besotted sleep, Odysseus and his men ram the stake into his eye, twirling it like a carpenter drilling a hole in a ship's timber, and the scorched ball sizzles and hisses like an ax or adze dipped hot into water. As Homer's similes from the important technologies of shipbuilding and metallurgy make clear, the wounding of Polyphemus is like the conquest of nature through technology. Nature may be bigger, monstrous, more powerful, but the cunning mind of man can alter the material of nature, harness its forces, and overcome it.[9]

Again and again in Greek literature human identity is linked to the human mind's reordering of the raw material of nature, its survival dependent on the order it projects onto the world in the form of culture and technology. In Aeschylus's trilogy the *Oresteia* this idea is developed in terms of progress from the dark, sexually dysfunctional world of Mycenean prehistory, with its monarchy and incest and cannibalism and adultery and blood-revenge, all embodied in the monstrous pre-Olympian Furies, earthborn forces of murder and fertility, keepers of the blood of birth, sex, and death; to the sun-drenched world of the fifth-century polis, a democratic order of laws and institutions, of the mind and word, rhetoric and persuasion, its patron deities Athena and Apollo, Olympian culture-gods. Moreover, this progress results not from the banishment of the Furies and what they represent, but rather from their appropriation into the order of the polis, the exploiting of their necessary fertilizing force for the good of the city-state; as Athena sings to the Furies, now renamed the Eumenides, the "well-wishers": "Make the waft of gentle gales / wash over the country in full sunlight, and the seed / and stream of the soil's yield and of the grazing beasts / be strong and never fail."[10]

Or consider the same poet's *Prometheus Bound*. There humans in a state of nature were on the brink of destruction by Zeus, for without natural advantages (Epimetheus, when all the animals were created, didn't save a gift—that is, a natural advantage like speed or flight or fangs—for humans), people end up somewhat of a botched job, unfit to survive in a harsh natural world. But Prometheus saves the human race by giving it, as he boasts even while fettered to the crag, fire as the natural energy source and the "use of their wits," making them "masters of their minds." Harnessing the energy of fire, the mind then creates the saving culture and technologies Prometheus goes on to enumerate: building, astronomy, arithmetic, language, agriculture, sailing, medicine, religion, metallurgy. The "Promethean mind of man" creates through culture and technology its unique identity, what makes it, as the Chorus in Sophocles' *Antigone* says, a *deinon* thing, not "wonderful," as often translated, but "terrible," "awesome," "strange," "clever" all at once, a creature unlike any other because of its "unnatural" mind.[11]

The view we have been sketching is, of course, the optimistic one. Not everyone agreed that the mind and its orders could control the forces of nature without and passion within. Many of the tragedies of Euripides make precisely the opposite point. Jason, Phaedra, Pentheus are all destroyed by the power of the irrational, particularly sex and anger, both akin to the forces of nature such as the sea. In the *Bacchae*, our final scene is not the sunlit polis of Aeschylus's *Eumenides* but rather the smoking ruins of Thebes, its citizens exiled, its queen cradling the head of the son she helped to dismember. Nature, Shelley's "preserver and destroyer," is the inhuman smile of Dionysus, against whose power the polis, the mind, and their orders are helpless. But whether optimistic or pessimistic, Greek thought returns again and again to the uneasy relationship of culture and nature, and it is here we must locate the Greeks' attitudes about sex.

Part 1 of this book will trace the depiction of sex and sexual desire as the "controlless core," a natural force within humans and without in nature, an energy source necessary for the continuation of life human, animal, and vegetable. Chapter 1 describes the imagery of fire, disease, war, insanity, and death that is used everywhere in Greek literature to characterize eros and its power and that locates it in the realm of destructive nature. In Chapter 2 we will take a look at the goddess of sex, Aphrodite, one of Henry Adams's "animated dynamos." She too will be characterized in terms of nature and its dangerous beauty, linked to the sea and the cunning mind serving passion rather than controlling it. In Chapter 3 we will analyze the Greek distrust and fear of women arising out of their sexual power, a creative force too closely akin to the rhythmic fertilizing processes of the natural world. Figures such as Pandora, Helen, and Klytaimestra all reveal the female's subordination to the irrational, particularly sex. Finally, Part 1 ends with an analysis of homosexuality, particularly the passive homosexual who represents the frightening specter of the mind wholly dominated by passion and compulsive pleasure, and thus easily prey to other appetites—political power, money—inimical to the wellbeing of the polis.

Part 1 describes the volatile, chaotic power of sex. Part 2 analyzes the "fancied sway," the various "technologies" the Greeks invented simultaneously to control and exploit this energy, just as agriculture orders and appropriates the fertile power of the earth, or metalworking the energy contained in fire, or a ship the forces of wind and wave. This is the sense in which this book uses the word technology: as a rational reworking or control of natural material or energy in order to exploit the power of nature. Hence ancient ritual and worship are important "technologies," for they attempt to control for the practitioner's benefit the numinous power embodied in the god or goddess.

In the sense that it organizes and controls an inchoate experience by making it orderly and meaningful, reason can be considered a "technology." Thus Chapter 5 will show the attempt by Empedocles and other philosophers conceptually to tame eros by making it the creative attractive force of the cosmos, its rhythmic dance with strife responsible for all creation. On the individual level, philosophy will give us an idealized Reason as the limiting order of the soul checking the potential excesses and disorders of passion as the charioteer reins in his recalcitrant horse. Chapter 6 shifts to culture and its institutions, particularly religious cult, as the means of tapping into the fertilizing power of nature and the gods. One model here will be agriculture, another of the mind's creations that rearrange nature in order to maximize its energy. Marriage will be our next concern (in Chapter 7), the social order that channels human sexuality—particularly female—so that the community benefits by its products, the legitimate children that ensure the continuity of society. Here Penelope, Alcestis, a rehabilitated Helen, will be presented as exemplary wives, their sexuality subordinated to the household's order and to mental virtues considered by the Greeks more typically "male." And last, in Chapter 8, the strange institution of "Greek love," pederasty, will show us another attempt to exploit sexual energy, this time for the moral and political development of the ruling elite.

The phrases taken from *Don Juan*—the "controlless core" and the "fancied sway"—reveal, of course, a bias. Like the poets and tragedians, I believe that the chaotic power of sex resists more often than not our rational or cultural or idealizing orders. Nothing in history argues otherwise, nothing in our own dismal conjunction of clinical sexual athleticism and mawkish sentimentality can make sense of the predatory sexuality, teen pregnancies, dehumanizing pop-cultural images of sex, commodified eroticism, and venereal plagues that pollute our own sexual environment. But in these fragments passed down generation after generation we can find if not the solution to our problems at least an awareness of the roots of our own attitudes, a critical understanding of our culture's depiction of this most terrible and beautiful power, this "curious way . . . of clothing souls in clay."

PART ONE

The "Controlless Core"

ONE

The "Tyrant of Gods and Men"

L ET'S START WITH a famous "love story" from ancient Greece, as told by Apollonius of Rhodes in his *Voyage of the Argo* (ca. 250 B.C.).

The handsome young hero Jason has been sent on a quest for the Golden Fleece by his wicked uncle Pelias, who hopes Jason will never return from such a perilous journey. After many dangerous adventures, Jason and his Argonauts, the flower of Greek heroism who accompany him, reach the exotic land of Colchis, whose king, Aeetes, understandably is loath to part with the fabulous fleece. At this point the goddesses Hera and Athena enlist the aid of Aphrodite, who bribes her roguish young son Eros to make the beautiful daughter of Aeetes, the enchantress Medea, "fall in love" with Jason. Overwhelmed by "love," Medea uses her magic knowledge to help Jason overcome the impossible tasks her father has set for him—yoking fire-breathing bulls and conquering the "earthborn men" who spring from the plowed soil—and to charm the serpent guarding the fleece. They make their escape with the fleece and, after further adventures, return to Greece as husband and wife. Once again, "love" has conquered all.

Told in this fashion, the story of Jason and Medea is easily understandable in terms of our modern assumptions about love and sex. We find it admirable that Medea would give up her father and country for love. Our sexual idealism tells us that such intense sexual passion is a good, perhaps *the* Good, in comparison to which all other goods become insignificant, and for the attainment of which any sacrifice is justified. For the ultimate fulfillment of the individual can happen only when he loses himself in a sexual relationship whose intensity signifies the depth and meaning of the essence of a person, his spirit or soul or "true self," a self defined in opposition to society and its rules and institutions. And the unique, magical nature of passion is reinforced by the fabulous details and locales, the exotic lands and monstrous serpents and fire-breathing bulls. Hence we approve of Medea because she lives up to the Romance Paradigm, like Juliet or Iseult or Guinevere or their thousands of descendants populating countless novels, films, plays, advertisements, and popular songs. "Deny thy father and refuse thy name"—this is our Romantic credo when it comes to sexual passion.

But our sexual idealism has little or nothing to do with what's going on in Apollonius's story, and an understanding of Jason and Medea's relationship in the misleading terms I have sketched it would miss completely its import for an ancient Greek. Not that Apollonius of Rhodes does not reflect certain conditions similar to those that nourish Romantic Love—that's why it's so easy to fit Jason and Medea into a modern romantic mold, as did the screenwriters of the film *Jason and the Argonauts*, which ends with the couple kissing safely on their getaway boat. Apollonius, after all, wrote in the mid–third century B.C., in that new world we call Hellenistic, created in the aftermath of Alexander the Great's spectacular carnage. In this new world Aristotle's old "polis-dwelling animals," men who had defined themselves as parts of the polis whole that encompassed the religious, social, political, and artistic dimensions of their existence, had begun to transform into individualists, people and poets for whom the private and the everyday cohabited with the exotic and recherché. For them the quality of personal emotional experience and sensibility—including of course sex and love—was more important than the donkeylike braying of grand political and epic themes rendered moot anyway by the imperial bureaucratic machines of Alexander's successors. But despite an individualistic social and cultural milieu conducive to the obsessive concern with sex and to an erotic sensibility that are the fertile soil of sexual idealism, Apollonius's story and erotic imagery are understandable only in terms of a long Greek tradition of thinking about eros as an inhuman force of nature destructive and chaotic, overthrowing the mind and orders of civilization.

A closer look at the details and imagery in Apollonius recovers for us that tradition and its complexity, for his poem is a storehouse of traditional Greek erotic metaphors. Take Eros, for instance, the little scamp who wounds Medea with his bow. In Apollonius we first meet him playing knucklebones, an ancient form of dice, with Zeus's boy-love Ganymede, and cheating him blind—a naughty, greedy little boy easily bribed with some new toy, scolded by his mother Aphrodite, whom he easily gets around. The whole scene is redolent of middle-class domesticity and familial psychology, and our own Eros or, more frequently, Cupid—the chubby putto that adorns a million Valentine's Day cards—is easily recognizable in Apollonius's spoiled brat. But this view of Eros as Aphrodite's cute but troublesome son is a late one, and when we begin to inquire into his lineage we find something very different from our greeting-card Cupid, something more frightening and monstrous, something closer to what Medea experiences when the boy leaves the serene, blissful halls of Olympus and enters our world of chaos and death.[1]

Hesiod places the birth of Eros very early in the story of creation: He simply appears with Tartarus and Earth out of Chaos, the mysterious "chasm" filled with darkness. This parentage makes Eros a force of nature, one of the fundamental primal building blocks of the cosmos. Variations on his descent give him the same inhuman identity. Acusilaus, a little-known writer of the early fifth century who presumed to correct Hesiod, makes Night and Erebus, Homer's underworld, Eros's mother and father. Sappho has him born of Heaven and Earth, and Alcaeus of Iris and Zephyr, the rainbow and the west wind, certainly a more romantic mother and father to our sensibilities, though we should always remember that the gods and nature, no matter how beautiful, remain for the Greeks alien inhuman forces. Even the more famous anthropomorphic parents of Eros first given him by Simonides, Aphrodite and Ares, are redolent of disorder and violence, for Ares of course is the god of war, most hateful of the gods, and he passes on to his son some of his martial destructiveness. What these various antecedents show us is an Eros as elemental stuff of existence and one of the primal forces of nature, far removed from Apollonius's cute rogue, let alone Watteau's rosy-bummed cherubs.[2]

Eros, though, is not just a boylike god. He is sexual desire, and when Apollonius's Eros reaches earth, he leaves behind the domestic serenity of Olympus and becomes a concrete embodiment of sexual desire, a representation of how sex attacks the mind, something simultaneously out there in nature and inside us. Hence Eros/eros has a double life in Greek literature: an anthropomorphic god, but also the inhuman force of sexual attraction inherent in every living creature, "the race of mountain-dwelling and sea-dwelling whelps, as many creatures as the earth rears and the sun looks upon," as the Chorus of the *Hippolytus* sings as it witnesses the destruction of prim Phaedra's sanity by forbidden sexual desire for her priggish stepson Hippolytus. Human beings also are not exempt from this defining force that is "seated in the souls of men," according to Xenophon, or as Plato puts it, is one of the "puppet's strings" that make our bodies dance. And Eros/eros rules the gods too. Even Zeus, king of the gods and embodiment of cosmic order, must obey this "most unconquerable" god, as Euripides calls him, this "tyrant of gods and men." Everything that moves and breathes is under the sway of this necessary power.[3]

The power of eros, moreover, is magnified and given wider scope by being implicated in all the other desires and appetites in the human soul. In ancient Greek the noun or verb forms of eros occur in contexts not explicitly sexual and usually imply a desire destructively excessive, something like our use of the word "lust" to describe a powerful desire for something other than sex. In Homer eros sometimes is used to mean simple desire, as in the delightful formula used after one of those Homeric feasts of broiled beef-chines and baskets of bread: "When they had set aside their eros for food and drink," or in Priam's cry to his wife Hecuba, trying to dissuade him from his journey to beg the mangled body of Hector from Achilles, that he would just as soon die once he had held his son in his arms and "set aside his eros for lamentation."[4]

But usually the implication of destructive excess, of overwhelming desire sexual in its intensity, colors the use of eros in what are not sexual situations, creating an effect nearly impossible to duplicate in English. In Aeschylus's *Agamemnon*, Klytaimestra, having heard of the sack of Troy and the imminent homecoming of Agamemnon, hopes that "no eros to violate what they shouldn't fall upon the army"—a lie, of course, since she's planning the assassination of her husband to avenge the sacrifice of their daughter Iphigeneia for a fair wind to Troy and to give the kingdom to her lover Aegisthus. Ironically, the "eros to violate what one shouldn't" describes Klytaimestra's own excessive sexual passion and violence, her own various confused "lusts." Euripides exploits the same complex richness of the word eros in his *Bacchae*. The straight-laced Pentheus, his own sexual ambivalence soon to be exposed by the god Dionysus, whom Pentheus has been trying to drive from the city, says he will pay anything to witness the orgies of the Maenads, which he imagines are filled with sexual riot. Dionysus reveals his intuition of the real motive of the prince, sexual obsession, when he asks Pentheus, "Why have you fallen on this great eros?"—indeed, Pentheus will fall, literally and metaphorically, from the pine tree he climbs to gratify voyeuristically the eros within him he has failed to control, that has led him to the humiliation of dressing up as a woman.[5]

Prose writers use eros in the same way to indicate desires whose near-sexual intensity leads to a destructive excess. Herodotus says that the Spartan Pausanias, commander of the combined Greek forces that defeated the Persians at Plataea in 479, had an "eros" to be a tyrant over all of Greece, a desire that led him to marry a Persian princess. Once again, sex is found implicated in other irrational and destructive desires, here the lust for political power beyond the accepted bounds of the city-state whether oligarchic or democratic. Even the "objective" Thucydides can take advantage of these connotations of the word. He communicates the mindless enthusiasm of the Athenians for the attack on the rich, powerful, distant city-state of Syracuse—one of the world's greatest military disasters, undertaken for seemingly no logical purpose whatsoever—when he says that "eros" for the expedition "attacked" the Athenians (the identical phrase, by the way, that the orator Isocrates later uses to describe another famous armada, the Greek attack on Troy). The Athenians didn't just *want* to attack Syracuse, they *lusted* for it, were attacked as if from without by a powerful force that blinded them to the prophetic warnings of the general Nicias, who tried to dissuade them.[6]

So much for that cute boy cheating Ganymede at dice. Eros is much more sinister than our etiolated Hallmark Cupid—it is a force of nature, a window into the irrational where swarm myriad other desires whose excess leads to our destruction, something very different from our "love," and that is why to say Medea "falls in love" with Jason is to distort and trivialize her experience, as though eros were a mud puddle passively awaiting the unwary. Greek eros rather is something that actively conquers, that tames and breaks and subdues. We can see this characterization of sexual desire in a verb frequently used with eros, *damazo*, "tame," "break," "overpower," "conquer," "kill." Zeus, seduced by his sister-wife Hera so that he forgets about the fighting between the Greeks and Trojans, thus giving the Greeks a respite from Hector's carnage, says to her, "Never yet has eros for a goddess or a woman so encompassed and conquered the heart in my breast" and goes on to enumerate by name, with a male tactlessness only the king of the gods could get away with, all the other nymphs and mortal women he had seduced.[7]

But "conquers" here doesn't adequately communicate the full range of meanings contained in the Greek. Elsewhere in Homer this same verb is used to describe the breaking of a horse, a warrior killing another, and the sexual subjection of a young girl to her husband;[8] thus a wife is a *damar*, a "thing conquered/ tamed/broken/subdued," and an unmarried girl is *admês*, "unwed," "untamed," "wild," as Homer calls the ingenue Nausicaa, the pert Phaiacian maiden who boldly confronts a naked and sea-battered Odysseus, who has washed ashore on her island, and craftily flirts with him all the way to the city. Sappho plays on these various shades of meaning in this word when she describes the young girl's confession to her mother that she can't weave her web because she is "conquered with desire" for a young boy. Weaving, the training for the young girl's proper role as a wife "subdued" by her husband, is here interrupted by her subjection to an illicit sexual passion. Eros doesn't just "conquer" the heart, it attacks the mind, breaks the will like a horse-tamer breaking a horse, lays low the soul like death.[9]

This is precisely the effect that Apollonius's Eros, once he leaves the trivial serenity of Olympus, has on the unfortunate Medea, as can be seen in the traditional images and metaphors Apollonius uses to describe the impact of Eros. Consider the scene in which he shoots Medea with an arrow, an image for us that is the dullest of clichés:

> *Meantime Eros passed unseen through the grey mist,*
> *causing confusion, as when against grazing heifers*
> *rises the gadfly, which oxherds call the breese. And*
> *quickly beneath the lintel in the porch he strung*
> *his bow and took from the quiver an arrow*
> *unshot before, messenger of pain. . . . Gliding*
> *close by Aeson's son [Jason] he laid the arrow*
> *notch on the cord in the center, and drawing wide*
> *apart with both hands he shot at Medea; and speechless*
> *amazement seized her soul. . . . And the bolt burnt deep*
> *down in the maiden's heart, like a flame; and ever she*
> *kept darting bright glances straight up at Aeson's son,*
> *and within her breast her heart panted fast through*
> *anguish, and her soul melted with the sweet pain. . . .*
> *So, coiling around her heart, burnt secretly Love the*
> *destroyer; and the hue of her soft cheeks went and came;*
> *now pale, now red, in her soul's distraction.*[10]

Consider the wealth of images and metaphors Apollonius uses here: the familiar bow and arrow, from war; the gadfly and the snake ("coiling"), from nature; fire, in the bolt burning like a flame; disease, in the elevated heartbeat and the pain; insanity, in the "speechless amazement" and the distracted soul or mind. These images come from a long tradition of Greek literary depictions of Eros and present us with a description of Eros's impact on Medea much more sinister and serious than the modern reader might realize. In the following sections of this chapter we will look more closely at this tradition of imagery that Apollonius self-consciously manipulates and exploits and that despite the poet's literary self-consciousness and slightly ironic manipulation suffuses his scene with an awareness of eros's destructive power that we moderns have sugarcoated with our Romantic idealism.

But when we look at this imagery from disease, madness, arrows, or fire, we have to remember that these metaphors are effectively dead for us, used so much for 2,500 years that they have little specific direct impact. When we hear Elvis sing of a "hunk of burning love," Patsy Cline call herself "crazy," Hank Williams complain of the "lovesick blues," or Sam Cooke ask Cupid to "draw back his bow," the metaphors, dulled by repetition, can't conjure concrete images that really move us, that as Keats says we can "feel on our pulses." Remember too that these images for the Greeks related more directly to their everyday experience. We don't depend daily on fire for our energy, and so are not as subjected to its power. But ancient peoples had to use fire every day, and the widespread use of wood as a building material meant that accidental fires were frequent, the damage extensive, the resultant injuries excruciatingly painful. Thus the impact of Homer's simile comparing the Trojan warriors' attack on the beleaguered Greeks to a "savage fire attacking a city of men, suddenly kindled, blazing, and houses are destroyed in the great blaze."[11]

Or how many of us have experienced arrow wounds, one of the most dangerous and painful of all injuries? Seven decades ago, Hemingway could give his Count Mippipopolous an anachronistic exotic cachet by having him display the scar from an arrow wound. Or how many of us outside the ghetto killing fields have suffered any kind of wound, for that matter, from any sort of weapon, now that war is the business of professionals and the wounds we can look forward to will most likely result from a car accident or a spill from a jet ski? As for disease, though of course we still get sick and shudder at the specter of necrotizing cancer or AIDS, we have been liberated from numerous diseases and plagues that shortened life and made what life there was miserable, leaving victims to incredible pain unalleviated by our modern panoply of painkillers and other palliatives. And though we still go crazy, insanity for us is a challenge for therapy and chemical treatment, something still frightening, yet ever more controllable. In short, the triumph of science and technology has left us relatively indifferent to these destructive forces of nature, at least as compared to ancient peoples or Third World people today, for whom fire, disease, madness, and violence were not unusual catastrophic intrusions into an otherwise safe and orderly world, but rather nonnegotiable everyday experiences of that world, the necessities that defined it and the place of humans in it. So when we discuss such imagery from Greek literature, we have to project ourselves imaginatively into a world more directly and frequently subject to nature's power than is ours.

Madness and the Irrational

Although we still trade in the debased imagery of madness to describe our feelings and condition when we are in love, we don't really believe in any fundamental connection between mental derangement and erotic passion, despite the daily reports of women stalked and murdered by estranged and deranged husbands and boyfriends. The Romantic idealization of the irrational, moreover, the positive charge it gave to madness as a creative and expressive state liberated from the shackles of bourgeois convention, reduces any serious or threatening import in our assertions that we are "crazy" about someone or "mad" about her. Indeed, such assertions are a warrant of sincerity, a testimony to the transforming power of the attraction. When madness and the erotic do mingle, as in the film *Fatal Attraction*, the erotic obsession is simply the form the madness takes, rather than expressing itself in pyromania or kleptomania. There is no link between the *essential* nature of sexual passion and of madness.

But for the Greeks, madness is not just a metaphor for describing what sexual passion does to the consciousness. Excessive passion *is* fundamentally a form of insanity, a destruction of the rational mind's control over the body, a suspension of reason's power that allows the soul to be overwhelmed by the chaos of the natural appetites and emotions. As the fifth-century Sophist Prodicus put it, "Desire doubled is love, love doubled is madness." The imagery of madness, then, in Greek literature is more than just imagery: It is the revelation of the true nature of eros.[12]

This fundamental connection between sex and madness underlies the character of Phaedra in Euripides' *Hippolytus*. Phaedra, as Aphrodite herself tells us, has been stricken by the goddess with sexual passion for her stepson Hippolytus. He, though, is a celibate, a worshiper of the virgin goddess Artemis, a devotee of the hunt, a prim, insufferably superior control freak horrified by the messy world of sex and women. That's why Aphrodite is going to destroy him—he doesn't acknowledge her power, and so implies that he is something more than mortal. In describing Phaedra's passion, Euripides doesn't say that she is "like" someone insane because of her desire for this smug prig. She literally *is* insane, "*astounded* out of her mind," the word one used frequently to describe someone out of control because of fear. Thus Phaedra is described in terms of total mental derangement. The Chorus speculates that perhaps she is possessed by a god, Pan or Hecate or Cybele, the Great Mother, goddess of the earth and fertility. When Phaedra is brought outside, she orders her maids to loosen her hair—a breach of feminine decorum no respectable Greek woman in her right mind would indulge—and raves in fantasies of hunting and horseback riding, all patently sexual. The shocked Nurse begs her to stop "hurling words riding on madness" and questions the fantasies she cries out while "deranged." When Phaedra comes back to her senses, she says simply, "I was mad."[13]

Sexual attraction as madness recurs throughout Greek literature. Pindar, the early-fifth-century celebrator of aristocratic athletic prowess, tells the story of Ixion, who conceived in his "maddened mind" the idea of sleeping with Hera, queen of the gods. Zeus, though, substituted a cloud for Hera, and Ixion spends eternity spinning on a fiery wheel in Hades, an image of lust as apt as Dante's whirlwind. Theocritus, the third-century poet whose slice-of-life short poems about shepherds and suburban housewives reflect the typical Hellenistic relish for the everyday and the outré, in his second *Idyll* shows us the jealous demimondaine Thystelis resorting to magic to drive insane Delphis, the boy who jilted her, and to send him raving like a mare that has eaten the maddening herb hippomanes, a word that in Aristotle denotes the discharge from the vagina of a stud-crazy mare. A few lines later, the despondent Thystelis will decry the "evil madness" of eros that turns the new bride into an adulteress and causes the virgin to lose her virginity. Anacreon's adjective "sex-mad," then, isn't a metaphor, it's a diagnosis.[14]

Our minds, our reason, our mental awareness, the very order of our souls are all vulnerable to the obliterating power of eros that induces us to acts and behaviors literally destructive to ourselves and others. As well as linking sex to a generalized madness, Greek literature is filled with more specific variations on the power of sex to alter the mind and destroy its perceptions and awareness. One word frequently used with eros is *atê* and its related verb, which denote a more particular kind of mental derangement, a ruinous "infatuation" or "delusion" brought about by the convergence of an external force and some internal flaw of passion. Agamemnon, trying to explain his dishonor of Achilles that leads to the near annihilation of the Greeks, says that *atê* and Zeus "stole [his] brains," *atê* that ruins all things.[15]

Such insanity can be brought about by any excessive passion, especially eros. Pindar tells the story of Coronis, who was the lover of Apollo. Despite being pregnant with the god's son, the future mythic doctor Asclepius, she slept with Ischys because of a "great ruinous infatuation" and thought she could get away with cuckolding the god. But he sent his sister Artemis to kill her, himself snatching the fetus of his son from the funeral pyre. A related compound word is used by Theognis, the late-sixth-century sullen antidemocrat, to describe the mental derangement, the "blind folly" and "recklessness" of passion, that overcame the "lesser" Ajax and induced him to try to rape the Trojan princess and ineffectual prophetess Kassandra in the temple of Athena. This violation of the virgin goddess's shrine, and the upsetting of a cult statue to which Kassandra was clinging in supplication, so enraged the goddess that she destroyed the Greek fleet as it was returning home, despite the Greeks' own attempt to stone the offender. Here the disorder of violence, the battle-rage Homer so graphically describes overtaking men when they are crazed with shedding blood, is compounded by the force of eros, both passions deluding or blinding the mind of Ajax and so bringing a retributive destruction on him and the other Greeks.[16]

This is the same mental condition that Apollonius describes Medea as suffering. The literally lovesick girl, agonizing over whether she should help Jason face the fire-breathing bulls or kill herself instead, cries out in her indecision, "Oh, for my reckless folly [atês]!" When she finally decides to help Jason and abandon her home, the moon-goddess, looking down on the girl hastening toward Jason, exults in Medea's "reckless folly," for often the moon was driven away by Medea's spells, control of the moon being a typical power of the ancient magician. This characterization of Medea's mental state in terms of *atê* climaxes in Medea's cold description of herself as "deluded by folly" for running away with Jason, just at the moment that she reveals her plot to help Jason murder her brother Apsyrtus—her first error, the result of sexual passion, makes easier the deadly crime of murdering a family member. In an alternative tradition Medea's crime is even more heinous: Apsyrtus is an infant whom Medea cuts up, throwing the pieces into the sea so that her pursuing father must slow down to pick up the *disiecta membra* for burial. As with Coronis and Ajax, Medea's sexual passion creates a state of mental blindness and delusion that ignores the limits placed on human passion, making possible crimes of destructive violence.[17]

The loss of mental control and awareness inherent in the condition of *atê* also characterizes erotic imagery taken from magic, the realm of charms and enchantments that exploit an occult power to destroy someone's rational control. Often the purpose of wielding such power would be to possess another sexually, as the existence of numerous magical papyri and curse-tablets from the ancient world attests, filled with various grotesque charms for securing erotic reciprocity from an indifferent object of desire, or at least causing him or her very real physical and mental suffering for *not* reciprocating. Our concern here is with imagery and metaphor, and a common word used in erotic contexts is *thelgein*, to "enchant" or "bewitch," the condition of the mind taken over by an alien and often hostile force. This metaphor used erotically is dead for us, of course; no one shivers with fear at being erotically "bewitched, bothered, and bewildered." The title of a popular sitcom in the sixties about a real-life witch married to a mortal could count on our benign, even positive response to being sexually "bewitched." But for the Greeks, living in a world of occult forces continually attacking the frail orders of human identity, the idea of "bewitchment" or "enchantment" retained the frightening sense of an alien power possessing one's mind and will for its own destructive purposes.

"Bewitch" is the word Circe uses to describe what the Sirens in the *Odyssey* do to unwary sailors—"bewitching" them with their song of knowledge as they sit in their meadow surrounded by a "great pile of bones of rotting men." Later Homer uses the same word for the erotic effect Penelope has on the suitors, "bewitching with passion" their hearts as they heed her temporizing siren song, until

Odysseus returns and visits on them a destruction as savage as that of the Sirens. Eros is a "mind-charmer," as Euripides calls him in the *Bacchae*, a "sorcerer" to an unknown Hellenistic poet. Likewise the messenger in Sophocles' *Trachiniae*, which tells the story of Heracles' sack of the city Oechalia to possess the princess Iole, says to Heracles' long-suffering wife Deianira, "Only Eros bewitched him into this war." And that is precisely what Apollonius's Hera and Athena want Aphrodite's saucy boy Eros to do to Medea—"bewitch" her with his shafts.[18]

As I said, the imagery of enchantment was powerful for the Greeks because various magic charms, formulae, and procedures were widely used. Literature gives us a few glimpses into this subworld where the power of black magic is tapped in order to harness another equally mysterious and frightening power, that of eros. The same Deianira mentioned a moment ago, faced with a younger rival in the person of Iole, tries to win back her husband with a love-charm, this one concocted from the blood of the centaur Nessus, who tried to rape Deianira while he was giving her a lift over a stream. Heracles shot him with an arrow, and the dying centaur told the girl to save some of his blood to use as a charm if ever she lost Heracles' love (in some traditions, the centaur told her to mingle his semen with the blood). The dark side of erotic magic, lost to us with our "ol' black magic," is obvious in the details of this story—sexual violence and literal violence, semen and blood, mingle with disastrous results, for when Heracles puts on the shirt anointed with the centaur's blood, he dies in horrible agony, as we will see soon when we come to the topic of erotic disease.[19]

Another erotic charm mentioned in literary sources is the *iunx*, the "magic wheel of love that seizes its victim," as Euripides calls it. This device consisted of a bird, the wryneck—chosen perhaps because of the odd writhing movements of its neck during the mating season—tied by its legs and wings to a wheel that was then spun. The "maddening bird" was invented, according to Pindar, by Aphrodite to help Jason's seduction of Medea, and its power was attractive: In the words of an anonymous Hellenistic poet, it can "drag a man over the sea and boys from their rooms."[20]

The *iunx* figures prominently in Theocritus's second *Idyll*, a poem from the third century B.C. that indulges the Hellenistic fascination with urban exotica and the psychology of passion. A young woman, Simaetha, has been having an affair with a man named Delphis, who used to sleep with her every day but hasn't been around for over a week. Simaetha has confirmed a rumor that he's been unfaithful, and the poem describes the magical procedure she uses to try to rekindle his sexual attraction for her. The details of this spell reveal for us the sinister seriousness of erotic "enchantment," for each step of sympathetic magic, separated from the next by an address to the whirling *iunx*, is intended to inflict erotic pain on the wayward Delphis—she doesn't care if he suffers, as long as he wants to sleep with her again. So she burns some barley, and prays to burn Delphis's bones; burns laurel, and prays for Delphis's flesh to perish; melts wax, and prays for his heart to melt; whirls the *iunx*, and prays for Delphis to whirl before her door; throws the herb hippomanes, which we've already met, on the fire, and prays for him to go mad. The implications of violence and suffering lurking in this erotic ritual become obvious when Simaetha says that if this charm doesn't work, she has others that will kill him. Simaetha's passion isn't the suburban adoration of a nose-twitching witch—it is a deadly force, linked to violence and pain and the primal forces of nature represented in the poem by Hecate, goddess of moon and earth and underworld, associated with ghosts and magic, visible only to dogs who "shiver as she goes among the tombs and black blood of the dead." It is as priestess of Hecate, by the way, that Medea has learned the occult skills and charms with which she helps Jason and later, in Euripides' play, destroys his new bride and father-in-law.[21]

In addition to imagery of madness and enchantment, the destructive effects of eros on the mind are also described in terms of melting and violent movement. Melting, combining as it does warmth and moisture, depicts both the physical experience of sexual arousal and the way passion dissolves rational awareness, causing the mind to lose coherence and form. Pindar, praising the beauty of the boy Theoxenus, says that when he looks at "the limbs of blossoming boys," he "melts like the wax of holy bees" in the sun. The image in Greek is not quite so precious, though, for the verb for "melt" also means "waste away." Hamlet's suicidal wish that his flesh "would melt, / Thaw, and resolve itself into a dew" covers the connotations of the word in Greek—not just liquefaction but also dissolution, a wasting-away into nothingness, as could happen with a disease. Theocritus in his first *Idyll* literalizes the connotations of sickness in his description of the shepherd Daphnis, who is "melting/wasting away," literally dying because he swore an oath of chastity and then fell in love. The impact of eros on the mind correlates with an attack on the body, shading into the imagery of disease we will discuss in a moment. Apollonius exploits the same image of melting: When Medea gives Jason the charms that will protect him from the fire-breathing bulls, his glowing beauty "warms and melts her mind just as the dew melts around roses when warmed by the morning sun." Once again Apollonius skillfully contrasts the preciosity of the lovely image from nature with its darker undertones, the implications of madness and disease that the later behavior of Medea will confirm.[22]

Another cluster of images focuses on the fluttering or agitation of the mind when it is dominated by sexual passion, the violent motion that makes it impossible to think clearly and apprehend rationally one's situation. In the *Odyssey* Athena, the goddess watching over Odysseus and his household while the hero plots the death of the suitors, puts it in Penelope's mind to appear before them and "set their hearts aflutter" with passion for her, making sure they stick around so Odysseus can kill them. The suitors' destruction is ensured by their own recklessness brought about by their blinding desire for Penelope as well as by their lust for Odysseus's wealth and political power. And if any ageists think Penelope, having a twenty-one-year-old son, would be too old to incite such passion, they should note that she could be as young as her mid-thirties, just at the height of her sexual beauty. The implications of violence contained in this imagery can also be seen in Aeschylus's *Agamemnon*. The captive Trojan princess Kassandra, brought home by Agamemnon as his concubine, is explaining to the Chorus of Greek women how she got the power of ineffectual prophecy, the ability to foresee the future but without anybody believing her: Apollo desired her, she promised to give herself to him for the gift of prophecy, then she reneged on the deal. The Chorus responds, a bit incredulously, "Sure a god was not stricken with desire," using a word Homer frequently uses of a warrior's blow. As with the image of melting, metaphors of striking and fluttering suggest to the Greek ear implications of violence and madness lost in our modern dull clichés. Who senses any threat in Elvis's complaint that he's "all shook up"?[23]

Another way to describe the mind-altering effects of sexual passion is to link them to drunkenness, a natural combination since sex and drinking have a long and intimate relation, and Aphrodite and Bacchus frequently revel together. Euripides' priggish Pentheus, outraged that the women of Thebes have left the city to celebrate the rites of Dionysus, speculates with a little too much interested fervor that the Maenads, the devotees of the god, quaff their brimming wine-cups then sneak off into the forest to "serve the beds of men," worshipping Dionysus as a pretext for worshipping Aphrodite. Girls getting pregnant at festivals, when the normal social inhibitions would be relaxed and the celebration of fertility would act as inducement, seem to have been a common occurrence. Ion, the young servant and son of Apollo, mistakenly believes his mother's husband Xuthus fathered him when he happened upon a drunk Maenad at a festival. "Because of the pleasures of Bacchus" Ion was conceived, Xuthus tells him. The Hellenistic playwright Menander uses the same device in his play the *Arbitrants*, whose plot centers around a baby born to a young girl violated at a festival. With that disregard of probability typical of romantic comedy down through the ages, Menander has the girl unwittingly marry the young man who fathered the child she tried to expose out of shame.[24]

The repercussions of impregnating a woman while drunk are more serious for Laius, father of Oedipus. Warned by an oracle that his son would destroy him, he nevertheless "sows a child while drunk and full of lust." Laius's rational awareness of a future truth is here overcome by two forces, eros and wine, both of which attack the mind. The results, of course, are the murder of Laius by Oedipus, the incestuous marriage of Oedipus and his mother Jocasta, the plague that nearly annihilates Thebes, the deaths of his brother-sons Polyneices and Eteocles, and the suicide of his sister-daughter Antigone—a chain of sexual disorder and violence that threatens to destroy a civilization. This intimate link between drunkenness and sexual arousal makes possible a common erotic metaphor. Remember the old pop-song refrain, "a double-shot of my baby's love"? The image is twenty-five centuries old. The sixth-century poet Anacreon, who created a long-lived and oft-imitated tradition of poetry about the pleasures of sex and wine, has a fragment in which the speaker, perhaps Sappho, climbs a cliff to commit suicide because he or she is "drunk on love." As the Wife of Bath put it, "A lickerish mouth must have a lecherous tail."[25]

Madness, delusion, enchantment, mental dissolution and agitation, drunkenness—eros is allied with a vast array of natural forces that attack the mind and weaken its tenuous control over the body's destructive passions. This loss of control frightened the Greeks, whereas to our Romantic sensibilities it is what we seek. We long to love "to the depth and breadth and height [our] souls might seek," so that our erotic selves might find fulfillment without hindrance or check.

Death, Violence, War

Although we link sex and violence when we complain about the debasement of television, we see them as stark opposites, with sex clearly the less dangerous of the two. As Lenny Bruce used to say when satirizing the suppression of pornography, the pillow was the only potentially lethal weapon that ever turned up in a porno film. But violence to us means blood and death and the urban crime that terrifies the middle classes today, despite the relatively low odds that their members will be the victim of a violent crime. Only raving fundamentalists and radical feminists, strange bedfellows indeed, complain these days about depictions of explicit sex. Most everybody else, armed with our modern sexual idealism, considers the expression of our sexual identities a good thing, as long as the unpleasant consequences—teen pregnancy, venereal disease, injured self-esteem—are avoided with counseling and prophylactics and everybody involved is nice to one another afterward. So it is that the extensive erotic imagery derived from the experience of war and violence is for us moderns utterly drained of affective force, the most banal of clichés fit only for the cheap sentimentality of the greeting card.

The Greeks knew better. They saw sex and violence as two sides of the same irrational coin, each interpenetrating and intensifying the other, creating a violent sex and sexual violence that exploded into profound destruction and disorder, a double chaotic energy threatening the foundations of human culture and identity. There are several obvious reasons for the connection of sex and war. In the Dark Ages, between the twelfth and eighth centuries, wife- and bride-stealing was no doubt frequently the cause of disputes. Sexual pursuit and conquest parallels the activity of war, calling forth many of the same skills, and the phallic shape of many weapons invites obvious comparison. As the Roman poet Ovid said, just as generals like a night attack, so does the lover "move his weapons" while the enemy sleeps. Also, the loss of rational awareness during orgasm has invited comparisons with death. The Elizabethans called an orgasm a "little death," and to this day in criminal and pop argot to "do" someone can mean either to have sex with him or to kill him. But it is the Greeks' recognition of the conflict between a controlling reason and culture on one side and a chaotic natural world of passions, including sex and violence, on the other that explains their mingling of the two and that

gives a serious import to their erotic imagery derived from violence, war, and ultimately death. They knew that Eros, rather than being the cute tyke we disregard,
was a "commander and a general," one "unconquered in battle."[26]

Take the Greeks' most famous war, the expedition against Troy. The casus belli,
of course, was the seduction of Helen by Paris. But the sexual roots of the violence at Troy run deeper than that. Paris won Helen because of Aphrodite, who
bribed the Trojan prince with the most sexually beautiful woman in the world so
that she could win the golden apple inscribed "To the fairest." Eris, the goddess of
discord, revealed the apple at a wedding feast to which, understandably, she had
not been invited—the wedding of Peleus and Thetis, whose famous issue would
be the great warrior Achilles. But Peleus was marrying Thetis simply because
Zeus was hot to possess the nymph but was frightened off by the prophecy that
she would bear a son greater than his father. The bloodshed of Troy has its source
in sexual intrigue and betrayal.

The disasters of the *Iliad*, moreover, also have a sexual dimension in their origins. The quarrel between Achilles and Agamemnon starts over two girls. One is
the daughter of Chryses, priest of Apollo, whom Agamemnon has won as a prize
of honor and is forced to return to her father after Apollo visits a plague on the
Greeks for not giving her back the first time his priest asked. Agamemnon then
takes Achilles' prize of honor, the girl Briseis, precipitating Achilles' withdrawal
from the battle and the near annihilation of the Greeks at the hands of Hector.
Now, both Agamemnon and Achilles are concerned with heroic honor, the be-
smirchment of their public reputations that follows when a prize signifying their
status is taken from them. But the girls are important too. Agamemnon says that he
prefers the daughter of Chryses to his wife Klytaimestra, "for she [the girl] is not
inferior to her in beauty, figure, mind, and domestic works." And Achilles calls Briseis his "wife" and had planned to marry her when he returned home, at least according to his best friend Patroklos.[27]

Whatever other ingredients go into a quarrel, sex is often the leaven. Klytaimestra desires to murder her husband Agamemnon for sacrificing their daughter Iphigeneia, but her revenge is also fueled by her own illicit affair with Agamemnon's
cousin Aegisthus. The Chorus of Sophocles' *Electra* certainly sees it that way:
"Eros was the killer" of Agamemnon, it says, and his daughter Electra agrees, not
allowing her mother any motive other than her uncontrolled sexual appetite. But
Agamemnon's passion for his concubine Kassandra, publicly paraded by the king
with the same tactless disregard for his wife he displayed at Troy, also contributes
to the avenging rage of Klytaimestra, and after she kills the girl she boasts, with a
chilling culinary metaphor, that the murder "will give relish" to her sex with
Aegisthus, a statement that reveals perhaps more than any other the Greek understanding of how violence becomes sexualized and hence worsened.[28]

This insight into the intermingling of our sundry irrational forces is not confined to poets. Herodotus reports the Persian historians' explanation for the origins
of the Greek wars with Persia of the early fifth century: It was just one more inci-

dent in a whole series of conflicts between east and west driven by the theft and countertheft of women. First the Phoenicians steal Io, then the Greeks carried off Europa and Medea, then the "oriental" Paris absconds with Helen. According to the Persians, the Greeks overreacted to some insignificant wife-stealing, and this started the whole war. A later historian, Duris, explaining the origins of the fourth-century Sacred War between Phocis and Thebes over the sacred precinct of Delphi, lays it at the feet of a Theban woman, Theano, who left her husband and ran off with a Phocian. Aristophanes parodies this sort of historical analysis in the *Acharnians* when Dicaeopolis, the simple farmer sick of the Peloponnesian War between Athens and Sparta, gives his take on the war's origins—some drunken Athenians stole a courtesan, Simaetha, from Megara, an ally of Sparta. The Megarians in turn kidnapped two whores belonging to Aspasia, the famous mistress of the war's architect, Pericles. As Aristophanes knew, the real origin of the quarrel was Pericles' shutting the Megarians out of the lucrative Athenian market, but here he is making fun of what must have been Greek received wisdom about violence—it always involves sex and a woman, or as the higher-toned Plato put it, there is no cause of battles and wars and civil strifes other than the lusts of the body.[29]

This connection between sex and war receives its most extended comic treatment in Aristophanes' *Lysistrata*, also about the disaffection felt by many Greeks with the costly, drawn-out conflict with Sparta. The Athenian Lysistrata summons the wives of all the men on both sides of the fight and proposes that the older wives seize the Acropolis—the fortified hill in Athens where the money reserves were kept—so the men can't finance their war, while the younger wives seductively tease their husbands yet withhold their sexual favors until the men agree to peace. When the Chorus of old men come to take back the Acropolis by force, Aristophanes laces the dialogue with sexual double entendres based on the analogy of sex and war. Lysistrata's buddy Kleonike worries about the men coming to take back the citadel, but Lysistrata retorts, "They can't force us to open these gates," meaning not just the gates to the citadel but their vaginas too. Likewise the logs of olive wood the old men drag up the hill to use as fuel for a fire to smoke the women out have obvious phallic significance. The chain of images climaxes when the Proboulos, a magistrate whose job was to look after the city's finances, calls for battering rams to force open the women's "gates." "Stop your ramming!" Lysistrata says, as she comes out. "We need some brains, not rams!" Aristophanes deftly conflates here male martial with male sexual aggression to make the serious point that both kinds of excessive passion have culminated in the irrational chaos of the war.[30]

This sexualization of violence humorously exploited by Aristophanes takes a grotesque turn in the story of Achilles and the Amazon Penthesileia, who had come to Troy to fight the Greeks, either to win glory so she could consort with a man, apparently an Amazonian sexual prerequisite, or to flee the murder of a relative. After Achilles kills her, he falls in love with her corpse when he removes her helmet. Apparently he falls so hard that he kills the ugly, foul-mouthed Thersites, the baseborn fool of the epic world, for stabbing the queen's eye,[31] but ancient commentators knew of a tradition in which Thersites' crime was mocking Achilles' necrophilia. At any rate, the mingling of sex and violence, like Klytaimestra's finding added sexual enjoyment from the murder of Kassandra, reinforces the destructiveness of sexual passion, its link to that other lust in the human soul, the lust to kill.

So it is that martial imagery, particularly derived from the great Greek poet of war, Homer, is frequently used to describe the effects of sexual passion on the mind. The first surviving lyric poet in the West and one of its first individualists, Archilochus, a late-seventh-century mercenary unashamed to write a poem bragging about how he threw away his shield during a battle and ran away, has a fragment in which Homeric death imagery serves to communicate the experience of passion: "For such was the eros for lovemaking that twisted itself beneath my heart and poured a thick mist over my eyes, stealing the tender wits from my body." Any reader of Homer will recognize the striking formula describing the experience of death for a warrior—when the obscure Meriones kills Acamas, Homer says "over his eyes the mist was shed." The warrior Archilochus, as familiar with the violence and fear of war as he is with Homer, recognizes the link between sex and violence: Both experiences are antirational and hence inimical to the conscious awareness that defines human life. And though Apollonius was a litterateur rather than a warrior, he and his audience were familiar enough with Homer and the vast slaughters of Alexander and his successors to invest with intimations of mortality his description of Jason's effect on the lovesick Medea: "Her heart fell from her chest, mist darkened her eyes, and a hot blush seized her cheeks."[32]

The similarities between the loss of rational control experienced during overwhelming sexual passion and that associated with death makes another famous Homeric expression, "loosening the limbs or knees," a useful metaphor for describing the effects of eros. Every reader of Homer remembers the striking phrase, as when Paris and Hector's brother Deiphobus stabbed the cannon-fodder Hypsenor in the liver and "loosened his knees." The joints of the limbs and the knees are seen as repositories of the life-force, and the latter perhaps are displacements for the testicles, making the phrase's appropriation for erotic purposes even more intriguing—loss of consciousness and manhood as well as death all implied as erotic repercussions. Thus when Penelope shows herself to the suitors to intensify their sexual attraction to her, standing by the doorpost and holding before her face the shining veil, "straightway their knees were loosened and their hearts bewitched with love." Homer emphasizes the fatal seriousness of the metaphor when a few lines later, Telemachus prays to Zeus that he wishes Odysseus would return home and "loosen the limbs of each" suitor—a rhetorical prayer, so to speak, since Telemachus knows that Odysseus is already home, disguised as the beggar who has just beaten up the suitors' lackey. The loss of rational awareness, of knowledge of just how outrageously they are behaving, caused by the suitors' passion results in the permanent mental darkness of death. Homer makes this

connection between eros and death even more explicit earlier, when the trusty
swineherd Eumaeus, with whom Odysseus first takes shelter on his return to
Ithaca, says that the beautiful Helen "loosened the knees of many men." Indeed
she did: first when all the great Greek heroes desired to possess her, and then when
the Greeks and Trojans died at Troy for her adultery.[33]

Following Homer's literary example, poets use the related adjective "limb-loosening" to describe the power of eros. Homer uses the same adjective to describe
sleep, but the interconnections among sleep, death, and sex, all experiences in
which the mind is conquered, are well known: Alexander the Great said that sleep
and sex reminded him of his mortality. So Hesiod, in his description of the begin-
nings of the cosmos, calls Eros "the most beautiful of all the gods, the limb-
loosener, [who] conquers the mind and shrewd thoughts of all the gods and
men." As in Homer, the emphasis is on the way eros attacks our rational powers,
creating the conditions for the excess that destroys us. The adjective becomes a
commonplace for describing eros. Sappho has a fragment that brings out the full
range of sinister implications suggested by "limb-loosening": "Once again Eros
the limb-loosener shakes me, that bittersweet irresistible creature." These two lines
resonate with the destructiveness of eros: the physical disturbance of "shakes," the
mental derangement and death implied in "limb-loosening," the ambiguity of that
by now worn-out expression, "bittersweet," perhaps Sappho's own invention. And
this onslaught is specifically identified as the effects of a *natural* force: The word
translated "irresistible" means literally "a thing against which are no devices," no
technology or contrivances, and the word for "creature," derived from the verb
"creep," signifies a beast on all fours or a reptile. Sappho's fragment links the mind-
dissolving power of eros to the chaotic forces of the natural world.[34]

Several other expressions describe the effects of eros in terms of the experiences of war and violence. When Alcaeus, the sixth-century poet from Lesbos, says
that he "fell at the hands of Aphrodite," his verb is one Homer frequently uses of a
warrior slain by another. Ibycus, sixth-century poet from Greek Italy, habitué of
the courts of tyrants, writes of his fear of eros in his old age: "How I fear his attack, just as a prize-winning horse, bearing the yoke for all his old age, unwilling
goes with the swift chariot to the race," the word translated "attack" being
Homer's term for the onset of an army. As usual, Aristophanes can turn this serious imagery to humor. In his *Women at the Assembly*, a fantasy about what would
happen if women ruled the state, a young man about to be appropriated by a
crone under the new law that gives old ugly women dibs on the handsome young
men croons to his young girlfriend that "he longs to be embattled between [her]
buttocks." But more often, this militaristic imagery, meaningless for us but forceful
for the Greeks who invented and frequently experienced the terrifying face-to-
face clash of armored men with edged weapons, carries a dark and threatening
import in Greek literature. The Chorus of the *Hippolytus*, witnesses of the chaos
sexual desire creates in the household of Phaedra and Theseus, describes Eros
"marching against" his victims and "laying them waste," imagery that was a reality

for the Athenian audience of 428: Herded within the Long Walls linking Athens to its port Piraeus, they had watched the Spartans "march against" the Athenian countryside and "lay waste" the farms and crops.[35]

The most famous, and by now worn-out, military metaphor for sexual passion is the arrow. Arrows and other missiles make suitable images of the effects of sexual attraction because they do their damage from a distance and often catch their victim by surprise. For the Greeks, though, the arrow has richer connotations that broaden its metaphoric range and intensify the negative dimensions it gives to sex in ways lost to us, for whom the arrow is a quaint relic of our frontier past. First, arrows are unheroic, since they allow a warrior to kill at a distance; they are, as a character in Euripides says, "the coward's weapon, useful for running away." This is true in Homer, where the personal duel with edged weapons is the method of choice for dispatching the enemy, and later after the sixth century, when the hoplite, the armored infantryman fighting with spear and sword shield-to-shield and chest-to-chest with the enemy, was the martial ideal, bowmen, slingers, and other missile-throwers being relegated to skirmishing. Thus bowmen in the *Iliad* carry with them an aroma of unmasculine treachery that also characterizes eros. Paris, the ladies' man whose libido starts the whole war, is a bowman—it is he who will bring down the Greek champion Achilles with a poisoned arrow to his vulnerable heel. But when it comes time to face the cuckolded Menelaus in a duel to settle who gets Helen, he starts to tremble and turns pale, like a man seeing a snake, and only enters the fight after his brother Hector berates him for his good looks and lyre-playing and "woman-madness." After Menelaus bests Paris in the fight and Aphrodite rescues her favorite, the truce between the Greeks and Trojans is broken by another bowman with erotic associations, Pandarus, later to find eternal fame as Troilus and Cressida's go-between—hence our word "pander." He hides behind some shields and wounds Menelaus with an arrow, breaking the truce and starting the fighting up again.[36]

The same disdain for missiles characterized the fifth century also. A Spartan captured at Sphacteria—a critical island battle during the Peloponnesian War in which the Athenians captured nearly 200 Spartiates, the cream of the Spartan crop, and which the Athenians won mainly because of their archers and slingers—defended an imputation of cowardice on his part by snorting, "The arrow would be worth a lot if it could distinguish the brave." Arrows and rocks are anonymous random methods of killing, without the bravery and honor the up-close and personal duel with spear or sword requires. One of the characteristics of Odysseus that set him apart from the other Greek heroes and make him the antithesis of the aristocratic heroic exemplar Achilles is his skill with the bow. That perhaps is why Sophocles, in a fragment from his lost play *The Lovers of Achilles*, about the youthful hero's male admirers, speaks of his powers of sexual attraction in terms of the more heroic spear cast from the eyes, rather than the suspect arrow.[37]

But more important, an arrow wound was one of the worst a soldier could experience, since arrowheads were designed with barbs that made pulling them out excruciatingly painful, if not impossible. Often an arrow would have to be cut out, as had to be done to Alexander after a battle in India. He had taken a arrow through his breastplate into his ribs, and after the shaft was sawed off and his cuirass removed, the head, three fingers broad and four long, had to be cut out from between his ribs. Hippocrates, the ancient Greek father of medicine, has left a portrait of an arrow wound and its treatment even more detailed and graphic than Plutarch's description: "Aristippos was hit high in the abdomen by a powerful and dangerous arrow. Terrible belly pains. Soon there was inflammation. He did not void from below; he retched; dark bile; and when he vomited he seemed relieved; but a little later the terrible pains returned. Abdomen like in ileus [*intestinal paralysis*]; heat, thirst. He died within the seven days." Even a minor arrow wound could be fatal: Another victim described by Hippocrates goes into convulsions and suffers lockjaw, dying in two days. The dangers of an arrow wound explain why Agamemnon, when he sees that his brother Menelaus has been wounded by Pandarus's arrow, shudders and nearly faints, "but when he saw that the sinew [which fastens the head to the shaft] and the barbs were outside the flesh, the spirit was gathered back again into his breast." The trauma of arrow wounds has long been a matter of indifference to us, so we must not think of our Valentine's Day chubby babes with their "weak, childish bows," as Shakespeare puts it, when we encounter arrow imagery in Greek literature. Imagine instead Eros brandishing an Uzi like some sexual Rambo or diapered Terminator, and we might get closer to the impact of the image for the Greeks, even in the late Hellenistic period when a professionalized literary self-consciousness and the decline of citizen-soldiers divorced the image from reality for many poets.[38]

The mercenary Archilochus again leads the way in appropriating the experience of war to describe the sufferings of sexual attraction: "Wretched I lie soulless with desire, pierced through my bones by the bitter pains of the gods." Once more the phrasing and imagery are Homeric. Homer, telling of the time the bowman Heracles shot Hades during some shadowy dispute perhaps arising out of Heracles' filching of the infernal watchdog Cerberus, uses a similar expression, "pierced with pains," to describe the god's suffering from his arrow wound. Literary references, though, serve to communicate better the experiences of life. Archilochus's reference to bones being pierced recalls for us Alexander's wound and suggests that the poet's metaphor reflected a common painful reality for ancient warriors. His description of sexual desire in these terms, then, would reveal a much more serious and frightening dimension to destructive sexual passion than the image can have for us moderns.[39]

That same seriousness defines other uses of the arrow imagery. Old Danaus, counseling his fifty virgin daughters who are fleeing the beds of their fifty cousins, warns them to be careful of the "enchanted arrows" their nubile beauty incites from the eyes of men "conquered by desire." The lost sequels to the play reveal the destructive consequences of the Egyptian cousins' desire—all but one are slaughtered by their brides on their wedding night. Euripides in the *Medea* adds a twist to the image by making the arrows poisoned. "Not against me," the Chorus sings to Aphrodite, "send from your golden bows the unerring arrow anointed with desire"—even as they speak they are witnessing the eros of Medea poisoned by jealousy and slighted honor. The same poet gives us the ancestor of the notorious two arrows—the one golden, the other lead—that a later, less threatening Eros will use to confuse mortals and amuse himself by shooting one person with the golden arrow of attraction, then wounding the object of the first victim's desire with the lead arrow of repulsion, creating an erotic perpetual motion machine. In Euripides the two arrows are distinguished differently. The Chorus of the *Iphigeneia at Aulis*, contemplating the imminent sacrifice of Agamemnon's daughter (ultimately caused by the sexual excess of Paris and Helen), marvels at the "two arrows of desire," the one bringing happiness, the other ruin. Sophocles in his story of the death of Heracles, as he does with the metaphor of madness touched on earlier, literalizes as well the arrow image to expose the destructive reality of eros it communicates. As we saw earlier, Heracles dies horribly when he puts on a shirt dipped in the blood of the centaur Nessus. Nessus, remember, was shot by Heracles' arrow as he tried to rape Deianira. Just as the arrow of the centaur's desire becomes a literal arrow that kills him, so the arrow of Heracles' lust for Iole, which leads Deianira to try and win him back with the charm made from the centaur's blood, ends the hero's life. He is killed ultimately by his own "arrow," that is, his and the centaur's lust and violence.[40]

By the fourth century the arrow image starts to become more self-conscious and stylized, though it still retains its aura of danger and suffering. Alcibiades was the dazzling extravagant satyr who dominated the politics of Athens during the last quarter of the fifth century, a sexual omnivore who had a gold and ivory shield on which was depicted Eros brandishing a thunderbolt. In his famous description of a youthful fruitless attempt to seduce Socrates, he says that after he "let fly his arrows, as it were" and thought that he had "wounded" the philosopher, he wrapped his cloak around them both and lay all night in his arms—chastely. The "as it were" in Greek often apologizes for a metaphor, but Alcibiades' image certainly wasn't dead for him or for Socrates: Both had fought in key battles of the Peloponnesian War, Socrates saving Alcibiades' life at Potidaea, Alcibiades returning the favor at Delium. They knew firsthand what arrows could do to human flesh. And though the Hellenistic poets may not have experienced battle directly, there was enough killing going on by the ambitious and ruthless successors of Alexander—it was the age of antipersonnel artillery—to invest the poets' weapon imagery with effective immediacy for all their self-conscious literary stylization. Theocritus's twenty-third *Idyll* tells the story of a handsome, proud boy scorning the attentions of a male admirer, who warns him to beware of the "bitter arrows" of Eros. The boy, though, pays him no mind, and after the miserable suitor hangs himself, the comely lad is crushed to death by a statue of Eros. Apollonius, remember, makes the wounding of Medea by an arrow the central image of her falling in lust with Jason and, like Archilochus, calls on Homeric phrasing to heighten the violent implications of her desire: The adjective Apollonius uses to describe the arrow, "messenger of pain" or more literally "fraught with groanings," is one Homer uses of an arrow. Now we can see how a whole tradition linking sexual passion to the pain and violence of war stands behind Apollonius's scene, far removing it from the banal cuteness with which we might invest it.[41]

The arrow image proliferates throughout the poetry of the Hellenistic age. One favorite variation is the fiery arrow, a weapon used frequently during sieges and sea battles. Apollonius uses it: The arrow that Eros shoots into Medea "burns deep in her heart . . . like a flame." But it is the last poet of our period, the early-first-century epigrammatist from Palestine, Meleager, who brings out every possible nuance of the image. In his poems we find "fire-breathing arrows" and the "barbed arrows of desire dipped in the fire," among many others. The arrow of fire is particularly useful for describing the destructiveness of eros because it combines the violence of war with the danger of fire, itself a frequent metaphor for passion that we will talk about next.[42]

War, violence, arrows, and wounds are all, like madness, dead metaphors for us when used to describe sexual passion. "When Cupid shot his dart, he shot it at your heart," Buddy Holly sings, and we feel not the slightest frisson of terror. So we don't acknowledge the sharp pain sexual passion can inflict, a pain the Greeks, who *had* seen and felt the agony sharpened iron creates, equated with the suffering of wounded flesh.

"*Thermos Eros*"

As a metaphor for sexual passion, fire is more accessible to us than the arrows and other ancient weapons of war. Human sexual arousal is accompanied by a rise in body temperature, which no doubt accounts for the common connection of fire, heat, and sex, what Shakespeare called the "fire in the blood." Certainly our popular music, the best repository of contemporary worn-out sexual imagery, uses fire more frequently than any other image, from Cole Porter's "too hot not to cool down" to the Doors' "Light My Fire." But the image for the Greeks had a much deeper and more serious import than it has for us. Fire was central to ancient civilization, not imprisoned behind ornamental glass. Cooking, metalworking, sacrifice to the gods were all impossible without fire. Remember the myth of Prometheus: What makes us human are the gods' two gifts, the mind with its "unnatural" cultural and technological projections into the world, and fire, the natural energy source the mind exploits to alter the natural world and create civilization. Fire, then, is a particularly significant image for sex, for the latter too is an energy source, the force of natural procreativity and fertility that must be exploited so that crops, herds, and people reproduce and flourish. But fire is also destructive and hence ambiguous, easily out of control, used in war to annihilate the enemy's city. Likewise with eros, equally dangerous, equally liable to rage uncontrollably and destroy household and city. Helen and Paris's passion isn't just *like* a fire: It *is* the fire that burns the towers of Troy. This is the threatening dimension to erotic fire imagery lost to us, making fire a harmless bit of atmosphere in our romantic iconography. Nobody feels a threat in the improbably numerous candles or the fireplaces with which moviemakers like to decorate their love scenes.

Fire, moreover, combines with other erotic images, as we just saw with the fiery arrow, what Aeschylus's Io, victim of Zeus's lust, called the "heated arrow of desire." The imagery of disease (which we will look at in a moment) also naturally blends with fire, for many diseases are accompanied by fever. Sappho's poem detailing with almost scientific thoroughness the symptoms of her desire for a girl she sees speaking with a young man lists the "delicate fire running beneath the skin." So it is with fire that Apollonius elaborates his description of Eros's impact on Medea: "Coiling round her heart secretly burned Eros the destroyer." Like the fire-breathing bulls Jason must yoke, like the serpent guarding the fleece, Eros is a monster, a "destroyer," a word Apollonius borrows from Homer, who uses it to describe the god of war, Ares.[43]

As with other erotic imagery, the metaphor of fire is elaborated on to almost baroque lengths by the Hellenistic poets, especially by Meleager, indicating perhaps that the imagery is tiring after several hundred years. In one poem, the eyes of the boy Heraclitus say, "I can set afire the thunderbolt-smiting fire of Zeus." The breast of Diodorus counters, "I can melt even a stone warmed by my body." "Wretched the man," Meleager sighs, "who takes the torch from the eyes of one, and from the other a sweet fire smouldering with longing." Another poem combines the lightning image with the Prometheus myth, perhaps reflecting speculation at the time that the use of fire was discovered from lightning. The boy Myiscus, "fighting with the thunderbolt" like Zeus, "hurls flames from his eyes," a second Prometheus bearing to mortals the "rays of desire."[44]

The intimacy of sex with wine we noted earlier is attributed by Meleager to the circumstances of the god of wine Dionysus's birth. Semele, Dionysus's mortal mother, tricked by the ever-jealous Hera, made her lover Zeus swear one of those disastrous irrevocable oaths the supposedly omniscient gods are always falling for, to come to her bed as he does to his wife Hera's, with thunder and lightning. Semele of course is incinerated, with Zeus snatching the fetus of Dionysus from the flames and sewing it into his thigh, from which it is later born. Meleager connects Zeus's erotic lightning to the fire metaphor to explain why sex and wine go so well together: "Born in fire he loves the flame in love." And the poet from Palestine reveals his knowledge of the sort of "barbarian" exotica that delighted the Hellenistic poets when he wonders who now embraces his girlfriend Demo—even if he's a Jew, it won't lessen their passion: "Love is hot even on the cold Sabbath." Jewish custom, of course, forbade lighting fires on the Sabbath.[45]

"Love is fire," Elizabeth Barrett Browning wrote, but her Romantic sensibility made its fire a transfiguring one, a revelation of the soul "glorified aright." To the Greeks eros was no such thing. It was instead a potential conflagration that could burn whole cities and obliterate whole civilizations. No lovemaking lit by fire-light occurs in Greek literature, no cozy candlelight dinners, though oil lamps occasionally illumine sexual trysts. We use those romantic props only because the fire trucks are down the street and the telephone nearby, technology warranting our casual handling of fire just as romantic idealism allows us to trivialize sex. But just as every day people are incinerated because they disrespect the power of fire, so every day even more people are psychically burned and scarred by sexual conflagrations.

Erotic Disease

The most popular hero of the Greeks, and probably the most well-known today, was Heracles, the Arnold Schwarzenegger of the ancient world whose twelve labors cleared the space for culture out of the monstrous chaos of nature. But Heracles also embodied the excess of natural appetite, the overindulgence in sensual pleasures like fine clothes and hot baths and food and sex that made him the glutton and buffoon of the Attic stage—eat, drink, and be merry, he tells the grieving Admetus, whose wife Alcestis has just died in his place, and honor Aphrodite most of all. Heracles followed his own advice, especially the injunction to celebrate Aphrodite, for he married many women and secretly fathered children on many virgins. Indeed, according to the late-sixth-century historian Herodorus, he deflowered fifty daughters of a certain Thestius in five days. The figure of Heracles magnifies the basic human contradiction, man defined as destructive passions and appetites subordinated to the work of culture and the control of the mind, a tense conjunction threatening to explode at any minute.[46]

The circumstances surrounding Heracles' death highlight the power of passion, in the hero's case sexual passion, to overthrow the order and control of the mind. Sophocles' version of the hero's death, the *Trachiniae*, like Apollonius's *Argonautica*, is a compendium of erotic imagery, as we have already had occasion to notice. But the dominant imagery is of disease, a disease that afflicts the mind, a disease that burns like fire, all erotic metaphors that become literalized and destroy the hero.

Heracles lusts for Iole, the daughter of Eurytos, and when the father refuses to give her to him sacks the city of Oechalia and slays all of Eurytos's sons—as the messenger tells Heracles' wife Deianira in a military metaphor, the whole city was conquered by desire, and Eros sacked it. As we have seen, Deianira, desperate to keep her household intact, resorts to a love potion made from the blood of the centaur Nessus, which she smears on a robe she sends to Heracles. The poisoned robe eats away the hero's flesh, consuming him in a fiery, horrible pain that drives him insane. He finally builds a pyre and burns himself to death.[47]

Even in this bald summary the destructive violence of eros's power is obvious, but Sophocles locates this power in the natural world through the image of disease, nature's disorder that attacks and destroys the healthy order of the body and the mind: the disease of his lust for Iole that becomes the necrosis eating away his flesh. Heracles' wife Deianira calls his passion a "sickness" and excuses him because of it. When his son Hyllus describes what happened when Heracles put on the robe, the metaphor of erotic disease becomes literal: "Sweat broke out on his skin, . . . a convulsive itching of the bones came upon him"; the poison consumes him and he yells and screams, the pain dragging him to the ground, then hurling him back into the air. The disease of Heracles' lust, the disease of the centaur's lust, the violence of the hero's death, all mingle to form a powerful image of destructive eros that "eats the flesh" of the hero, sucks the air from his lungs, and drinks his blood.[48]

Sophocles in the *Trachiniae* exploits a long tradition of erotic disease imagery. Two centuries earlier, in her one complete surviving poem Sappho prays to Aphrodite to be freed from the "anguish" and "surfeit" of erotic desire, the latter word one found in the medical writers. Sappho identifies two symptoms of erotic disease: the anguish of desire's lack of its object, and the painful surfeit of its gratification, Keats's burning forehead and cloyed heart. Another fragment, the one mentioned earlier that describes the effects on the speaker of seeing a desired girl talking with a young man, gives us an almost clinical rundown of erotic symptoms: her heart pounds, tongue grows numb, eyes go blind, skin burns with fever, ears ring, sweat pours, and trembling seizes her. Simaetha, the lovelorn young woman whom we met earlier trying to recover her boyfriend through magic, likewise gives us an erotic symptomatology: The first time she saw Delphis, her heart was shaken, her beauty withered, she lay in bed ten days with a fever, she grew sallow, her hair fell out, and she lost weight until she was "nothing but skin and bones." And the first time he visited her room and had sex with her, she went cold as ice, sweat dripped from her brow, she couldn't speak, and all her fair skin froze as stiff as a puppet's.[49]

Sexual desire as disease informs also Euripides' depiction of Phaedra's suffering as she fights her unnatural desire for her stepson Hippolytus. One symptom of her condition, as we have seen, is madness, a loss of mental control manifested in sexual hallucinations. But the madness is a result of the erotic disease killing Phaedra, a virus that wastes her away in a "diseased bed," a "terrible disease" that will ultimately drive her to suicide.[50]

This conception of sexual desire as a disease is not confined to the imagery of poets. Plato's Diotima, the shadowy woman who instructs Socrates on the mysteries of eros, says that the drive to sexually reproduce is a sickness that afflicts all living things. Later in the *Laws* Plato will further define this disease as one among those bodily lusts and pleasures "endless and insatiate of evils." And in the *Timaeus*, sex is termed the "disease of the soul"—a literal one, as Plato goes on to explain in his account of the physiology of sex. The sexual organs are joined by a passage to the spinal column that transmits marrow—the "universal seed-stuff" from which semen is concocted—to the genitals, in which the increasing pressure of the marrow creates an "enlivening desire for emission." Since this marrow ultimately derives from the head, the man whose seed increases abundantly in his marrow becomes mad, his soul "diseased and mindless" because of the pressure to emit the built-up "marrow." Reinforcing his famous belief that knowledge is virtue and no one does evil voluntarily, Socrates concludes that the sexual incontinent is literally diseased, unable rationally to see the destructive consequences of his erotic excess. This idea of sexual desire as a diseased condition sucking marrow from the brain survived in the Victorian belief that excessive masturbation caused blindness and insanity, since it robbed the brain and eyes of sustaining moisture. The French novelist Balzac, after a night of sexual indulgence, cried to a friend, "I just lost a book!"[51]

Such a belief, as quaint and benighted to us as whalebone corsets, would have found sympathy among the Greeks. Our worn-out erotic disease imagery, which survives in pop lyrics like "you give me fever" or in dead metaphors like "lovesick," and whose positive charge ultimately derives from the Romantic idealization of diseases like tuberculosis that supposedly reflected the victim's heightened sensitivity, doesn't begin to capture the seriousness of the Greek metaphor. To the Greeks, sexual desire is a plague, a syndrome like AIDS that attacks the body and mind on several different fronts, ultimately leading, as with Heracles and Phaedra, to death.[52] "Venereal disease" for them is not the unlucky *consequences* of sexual desire, but the necessary, essential nature of it.

Wind, Sea, and Storm

Most of us have little to do with the sea on a daily basis, and when we do venture onto the ocean it's usually in a technologically sophisticated craft that protects us from the fury of wind and wave. Even still, the sea can be frighteningly powerful, as I learned once during a sudden midnight storm while crossing from Crete to Athens on a five-deck ferry packed with Easter vacationers. When the storm hit, that ship suddenly seemed as frail as a twig to be blasted at any moment by the uncomfortably close lightning. Imagine what it must have been like for an ancient Greek sailing his tiny wooden ship on the fickle Aegean, without the comforts of life jackets, diesel engines, radar, or radio.

The geography of Greece, moreover, with its many bays and inlets and islands, made the ancient Greeks dependent on sea travel, and so they were frequent victims of the ravages of storms and shipwreck. Remember too that death at sea was particularly horrible, since the body if unrecovered could not be given a proper burial, leaving the soul to wander in limbo. This old superstition, even during the heyday of Athenian rationalism, cost some admirals their lives: Choosing to pursue the defeated Spartans after the sea battle at Arginusae during the Peloponnesian War instead of picking up the bodies of the slain, they were executed by the angry Athenians. This dependence on and fear of the sea made it, storms, and shipwreck the most common metaphor for chaos and disorder, an image most Greeks could feel in their bones. When Homer wants to communicate the sudden fury of the Trojans as they breach the Greeks' defensive wall, he compares them to a "great wave of the broad-pathed sea [that] descends on the sides of a ship, whenever the force of wind blows hard." Homer's near-contemporary, the dour farmer Hesiod who claims to have boarded a ship only once in his life to cross the narrow stretch of water separating mainland Greece from the island Euboea, considers sea travel the epitome of evil, for it is "terrible to die among the waves." Shipwreck, then, is the harsh punishment of the unjust man, and an absence of sailing the boon of the just. The most famous image deriving from the experience of sea travel is the "ship of state" metaphor, first attested in the seventh-century poet from Lesbos, Alcaeus. This frequent image captures the Greek concern with the intersection of nature and culture in human life, for the ship is a construct projected from the mind and created by its technologies, an alteration of natural materials to make something unnatural, a device that nonetheless must exploit the energy of current and wind in order to function. It makes, then, a powerful image of the mind and culture sub- jected to the destructive forces of nature like eros, forces that it still must exploit and control just as the ship exploits and controls the wind and wave.[53]

Any component of the wind/sea/storm complex can be compared to eros. A fragment of Ibycus works the wind into a rich image that exploits several different metaphors: "Like a Thracian north-wind burning with lightning, darting from Aphrodite with parching madness, murky and fearless, [Eros] mightily, utterly shakes my mind." Several strands of erotic metaphor are woven together in this image: madness, fever, fire, as well as the dominant image of eros as a storm-wind, a Thracian one at that, which intensifies the savagery of sexual desire, the barbar- ian land of Thrace being the epitome of savagery to the Greeks. Most effective, though, are images that combine storm and sea, tapping into the ubiquitous ship- wreck metaphor. Euripides' Phaedra says of her lust-disease for Hippolytus that she is "storm-driven," an image the Chorus picks up on later when it describes her "water-logged with harsh disaster" as she throws a noose around the rafter above her bed and hangs herself. Cercidas, the third-century promoter of Cyni- cism, the philosophy of a "doggy" life lived in accordance with nature, describes two winds of Eros, the one from his left cheek creating excessive love, the "fierce typhoons of passion."[54]

This image captures the idea of eros as an external natural force assailing the "unnatural" ship of the soul. A later Hellenistic poet, the first-century Philode- mus, elaborates on this metaphor in a poem describing a new bridegroom sepa- rated from his bride in the snows of Gaul. The young man prays to Aphrodite, "mother of tempest-footed desires," to save him from the "purple sea" of unre- quited sexual desire upon which he is tossed and guide him to the "harbor" of his new bride Naias. The grumpy aristocrat Theognis also uses a harbor as a symbol of a sexual partner when he advises an old man not to marry a young wife: She doesn't obey the helm, her anchors don't hold, and at night she slips her moorings to find another harbor. Plato adds fire to the sailing/sex image. In an epigram to his aging mistress Archeanassa, on whose very wrinkles yet sits a "fierce love," he pities the wretched men who encountered her on her "maiden voyage": What a conflagration they must have experienced.[55]

Plato's poem exploits another dimension to the sailing image, the way that the motion and rhythm of sailing and rowing mimic those of intercourse. Aristophanes, as usual, gets a joke out of it. When Lysistrata calls together the other Greek women to present them with her plan to end the Peloponnesian War by sexual blackmail, she complains about the absence of the women from the nearby island of Salamis. Calonice assures her they "came early, mounted on their boats"—the word for "boat" also being a word for the sexual position in which the woman bestrides the man and "rows" away, an obscene meaning Aristophanes underlines by using the word "mounted," that is, "sitting astride with legs apart." Apparently people from Salamis were particularly fond of putting the woman on top during sex. In the *Women at the Assembly*, Aristophanes' play about women seizing political power by wearing their husband's clothes and taking their place in the Assembly, one woman says she couldn't steal her husband's clothes because he was "sailing" her all night—he's a Salaminian, she explains. The second-century poet Dioscorides works an amusing variation on this conceit: rather than attempt intercourse with a pregnant woman, which involves "rowing" the "great wave" of her belly and getting tossed about, flip her over and enjoy her "rosy cheeks." The sex-sailing connection is given a serious treatment in Euripides' *Trojan Women*, about the Trojan captive women who have to sail to Greece to be the concubines of Greek soldiers. Their imminent sea voyage prefigures also their sexual subjugation to their Greek masters: "The hand holding the oar already is moving beside the ship," Hecuba warns the Trojan girls. Euripides' verb, also a slang word for "fuck," and the phallic oar prefigure the sexual subjection awaiting the hapless captives.[56]

Once more Meleager is the adept at manipulating this rich tradition of erotic imagery. "Swimming in a sea of boys," he is "storm-driven" by a "heavy gale of desire"—Aphrodite is the captain of his "ship," and Eros holds his soul's rudder. The ship of the soul has been hijacked by alien forces, pirates who sail it at their own pleasure. Another poem complains of the "bitter wave of Eros," the "sleepless winds of jealousy," and the "winter sea of revelry." And he invents, as far as we know, a verb that encapsulates the sex/sailing imagery, "love-sailing": "Sex-loving Asclepias, her blue-gray eyes like a calm sea, persuades all to love-sail." Here the erotic tradition of sex/sailing imagery and the Greek's knowledge of the Mediterranean's deceptive calm lend the faintest hint of menace to this delicate metaphor.[57]

For us that tradition has decayed into cliché; nor do we experience very often the treacherous beauty of the sea. That's why we don't hear even the faintest threat of storm or shipwreck in the pop crooner's invitation to sail with him on the "sea of love." Like fire, the sea is a romantic prop, a dead metaphor making it easier for us to avoid the destructive realities of sexual passion.

The Beasts of Love

Xenophon, the second-most-famous disciple of Socrates, relates a conversation the philosopher had with him about sexual desire. Socrates had just found out that a certain Critobolus had stolen a kiss from the handsome son of Alcibiades, the brilliant rake who had in his own youth attempted to seduce Socrates. Socrates tells Xenophon that such a kiss is as foolhardy as jumping into a fire and would lead to Critobolus's enslavement. When Xenophon protests that a simple kiss could not be so deadly, Socrates responds that spiders by mere contact of the mouth inject a deadly poison into their victims, driving them insane. So it is with erotically attractive people, who also inject a poison. What is worse, they don't even need the contact a spider needs, since they can poison their victim from a distance. He finishes by advising Critobolus to go away for a year.[58]

Such an extreme depiction of sexual desire coming from a "merry Greek" might surprise us moderns, but Socrates' image of the destructiveness of sexual passion is consistent with the Greek idea that eros is a violent force of nature inimical to the mind's order. Eros and the other pleasures and appetites of the body are from the natural side of the human, the side that links us to the beasts and other creatures of nature. Those creatures also have material bodies that experience sexual pleasure—hence excessive hairiness is a sign of lust, on the logic that the person who looks like an animal will behave like one, less able to control his appetites. Those appetites in humans, then, are "slavish and brutish," as Aristotle put it, and so the world of beasts and insects provides a powerful image for communicating the destructive and dehumanizing power of eros. Now we see the significance of Sappho's depiction of eros as a "beast on all fours" or "creeping thing," or the many descriptions of sexual passion "biting" someone, as when Socrates says that the accidental touch of Critobolus's shoulder was like the "bite of a wild animal," or Plato's calling sexual desire a "wild animal": All these images locate eros in the natural world of predators that attack and destroy the settled life of civilization.[59]

But nature in Greek thought is more complicated. It is not just a question of a "wild" nature, the untouched and untamed forests and mountains where the wolf and the lion roam, the "nature red in tooth and claw" constantly encroaching on the cultivated space that humans inhabit. There also is the tamed nature, nature domesticated, its life-giving energy subordinated to the human mind and its technologies, yet always volatile, always ready to erupt into violence and disorder. Eros shares this ambiguity, for it too is out there in the wild but also in the heart of the home and city itself, as well as in the center of the human soul, domesticated it seems, but always ready to explode into chaos.

A long-lived metaphor that captures this ambiguity of eros as well as symbolizing sexual potency involves the horse, another beast humans had to domesticate in order to exploit its energy in war, a technological revolution that altered history as much as gunpowder or the printing press. The mythic Centaurs were creatures composed of various portions of humans and horses; by the fifth century they were usually depicted with the heads and chests of humans but the body and genitals of horses. Thus Centaurs powerfully symbolized the uneasy link of culture and nature in human identity as well as recognizing the destructive power latent in even domesticated animals. Like Nessus, the Centaur who tried to rape Heracles' wife Deianira, Centaurs were notoriously randy. One story in particular sounds all the notes of the culture-nature tension concentrated in the figure of the centaur. At the wedding of Pirithous, buddy of the Athenian founding hero Theseus, the Centaurs got drunk and attempted a wholesale rape of the wedding guests, in some versions including the men. This set off a battle between the Greeks and Centaurs, one of the favorite topics of Greek sculpture, temple-pediments, and vase-paintings, symbolizing as it does the conquest of reason and culture over the natural appetites and passions of humans.[60]

Once more, most of us in the modern urban world have lost contact with the daily experience of horses, and hence horseback riding as a metaphor for sexual intercourse has lost its vividness. The diffusion of pop-Freudian symbology ensures that many people still vaguely connect horses with sex, particularly in the dreams of prepubescent girls astride Black Beauty. But how many younger people get the joke, in the film *Semi-Tough*, of a couple having sex while Gene Autrey croons "Back in the Saddle Again"? How many know that "riding bareback" is slang for sex without a condom? How many have seen horses mate, and so know how violent and sometimes deadly equine intercourse can be? Another long part of human experience—one vivid and familiar to the ancient Greeks—is fading away for us, and with it the literary metaphors deriving from those experiences. The horse as a metaphor for erotic violence, even if we connect the horse with sex, is not going to evoke for us the dangerous interrelation of culture and nature it would for a Greek. At most it will be a clever joke, as in the *Saturday Night Live* skit where the Arnoldesque bodybuilder Franz has a sexual fantasy about Patrick Swayze in which the two ride horseback together.

For the Greeks, though, the metaphor has more serious implications—it signifies the uneasy domination of culture over nature, male over female, even Greek over barbarian, as in this famous poem of Anacreon addressed to a "Thracian filly" that proudly runs away from the speaker: "I could bridle you well, and holding the reins turn you around the goal-post of the race-track. But now you feed in the meadows and lightly bound and play, for you have no skillful horseman to mount you." As well as playing on the obvious image of sexual intercourse as "riding," which Aristophanes summarizes in his word for the female genitals, "the thing one rides horseback," the poem contrasts the cultural artifacts of bridle and reins and racecourse with the natural meadows; the control of sexual energy with the uncontrolled free play of the riderless horse; the dominating skillful human male with the undisciplined equine female; even the Greek, emblem of reason and civilization, with the ultimate in barbarism, the Thracian from the wild north. At the heart of the poem lies the central Greek ideology of nature as a congeries of forces necessitating human rational control.[61]

The same conflict of nature and culture informs another erotic image, one related to the horse—the horse-drawn chariot. The chariot was a military technology as revolutionary as the horse, but by the fifth century the rise of infantry armed with pikes made the chariot insignificant militarily, since horses won't charge leveled spears. But like the ship the chariot metaphor is still a powerful one for the Greeks, for it highlights the dependence both of cultural artifacts on the volatile energy of nature and of the rational mind on the dynamic passions and appetites of the body. Euripides in the *Hippolytus* exploits this symbolism of the chariot in an erotic context. After Hippolytus has been banished by his father Theseus, who believes Phaedra's suicide note claiming Hippolytus raped her, a huge bull sent by Poseidon in answer to Theseus's curse on his son rises from the sea and terrifies the four horses pulling Hippolytus's chariot. The chariot is smashed, the horses "not obeying the hand of their master nor the reins nor the well-fastened car," and Hippolytus is mortally mangled. Both the monstrous bull and the horses signify the sexual power that Hippolytus had tried to deny in himself with the moral "technology" of chastity and rational self-control, the power that now destroys him, heedless of the technology of bits and reins and skill designed to exploit the horses' energy. Euripides' point is that there *isn't* any rational virtue that can ultimately control the chaotic power of eros. Callimachus, the early-third-century Hellenistic poet who was the master of the learned, personal new poetry, likewise uses the chariot overturned by its horses to signify the impact of eros on the soul. Speaking to a friend who apparently is in the first stage of a love affair, he cautions him to "quench the fire he has kindled" and to hold back the "maddened horses" from running, lest they shatter the chariot on the racetrack's turning post and the unfortunate lover be hurled headfirst. Here the imagery of fire and madness reinforces the destructive power of eros on the "chariot" of the soul.[62]

Hunting is another human activity in which violent forces of nature—and of men—are subordinated to the technology and skill of a cultural enterprise. Like sacrifice, ancient hunting ritualized violence, acknowledging the human drive to kill and the necessity of killing while controlling it with the order and quasi-religious ceremony of the hunt. The link of sex to hunting—an obvious and ubiquitous one, given that both involve pursuit, capture, and penetration with a "weapon"—exploits not only the ambiguity of eros, the way it sits on the cusp of culture and nature, but also the violence and death we saw earlier in the erotic imagery derived from war and its weapons. But when we talk about hunting we shouldn't think about it in modern terms. We shouldn't imagine our own suburban weekend warriors, adorned in Wal-Mart camouflage, armed with high-powered rifles sporting scopes, transported via mechanized four-wheel-drive vehicles to game preserves in which their prey is carefully monitored and controlled to provide them with relatively easy targets whose meat will probably be left to rot while the head and horns end up adorning a den.

The typical Greek hunt—like the boar hunt described by Homer in Book 19 of the *Odyssey*—was a much more dangerous affair, one involving greater nerve and skill. Usually, the game would be driven by men and dogs into nets spread in a natural cul-de-sac, where the cornered beast would have to be dispatched with spears, up-close and personal. Odysseus, remember, as a boy suffered a gash on his thigh from a wild boar he killed with a spear—it is the scar of that wound the old Nurse recognizes as she washes her disguised master's feet.[63] Ancient hunting, then, involves not just the violence and the killing, the danger of getting close to a frantic, frightened beast, but also the idea of *compulsion*, of being driven by some external power into a fatal trap. Connected to eros, the hunt and net imagery communicates the power of sex, the way it drives people to destruction against their will.

The idea of overwhelming compulsion informs Ibycus's use of erotic hunting imagery, in the poem we examined earlier comparing the poet to an aged racehorse led unwilling to the race. The first part of that fragment begins, "Again Eros, meltingly gazing at me from beneath his dark eyelids, drives me with all kinds of charms into the endless nets of Aphrodite." Ibycus refines the hunt image by adding the "charms," the victim herded not by force or fear of the dogs but rather by the mind-deceiving sorcery of eros. But the key idea is one of erotic compulsion, which Ibycus seconds in the following image of the reluctant old horse driven by its owner to the race. Xenophon sounds the same note when his Socrates, trying to impress upon the intemperate Aristippus the importance of controlling one's bodily appetites, instances the quail and partridge, creatures of excessive sexual appetite that when they hear the cry of the female are borne along with anticipation and lust and fall into the nets. Hunting as a metaphor for courtship is another frequent variation. The obscure Rhianus, the late-third-century poet and Homeric scholar, complains of losing a "fawn," that is, a boy, he had caught: "I endured countless toils, I set the nets and stakes, and I go away with empty hands. Those who did no work carry off the prey." The predatory nature of ancient literary homosexual courtship is neatly contained in this image. Hunting imagery seems especially common in homosexual erotic poetry, reflecting the aristocratic and militaristic aura of ancient boy-love. Theocritus describes an aloof, unresponsive boy—the one we mentioned earlier who was punished by having a statue of Eros fall on him—as eyeing every man "like a woodland beast suspecting a hunter." And Meleager skillfully compresses the connotations of this imagery into a striking phrase: "Eyes are the hounds of boys." Whether the topic is heterosexual or homosexual desire, though, hunting as erotic metaphor locates sex in the no-man's-land where culture and nature uneasily fraternize and more often try to destroy one another.[64]

Another image from the world of beasts also highlights the compulsive power of eros, as well as locating it in the world of nature. It is the "gadfly," the stinging fly that torments horses and cows and other domesticated beasts. Socrates, during his trial for impiety and corruption of the Athenian youth, called his annoying cross-examination of his fellow citizens a "gadfly" meant to sting the fat lazy horse of Athens into a search for virtue. But in Greek the word for "gadfly" is often translated "goad," for the goad—the stick the herdsman jabs into a beast to move it where he wants it to go—acts on the beast just as the gadfly does, painfully compelling it to movement against its will. Io, object of Zeus's lust, is turned into a heifer by a jealous Hera, who throws in a "sharp-mouthed" gadfly to torment the poor girl with pain and madness—fitting symbol of Zeus's lust responsible for the virgin's misfortune.[65]

Needless to say, most urban moderns have never seen a horse's frenzied attempt to escape a gadfly or have never experienced an animal "kicking" in frustrated anger "against the goads," as Euripides' Dionysus puts it to Pentheus, goaded against his will into surrender to the god (a passage Paul quotes, by the way, when describing his conversion on the road to Damascus). But ancient Greeks had first-hand, daily experience with oxen and cattle and horses, whether on their farms or during the ritual of sacrifice, making the image of gadfly or goad a vivid one for them. For example, a fragment of Simonides, the late-sixth-century poet who wrote the famous epitaph for the 300 Spartans who died to a man fighting the Persians at Thermopylae, talks about how difficult virtue is, for either "greed for profit or the very strong gadfly of wile-weaving Aphrodite or ambition forces a man against his will" to be evil. The appetites, whether for gold or power or sex, drive a man to destructive excess, like something external to him, apart from his rational awareness. Plato speaks of the genitals in these terms in the *Timaeus*, desirous as they are of emitting the "marrow" that swells them. This pressure makes them "autocratic and disobedient, like a creature without a rational mind, attempting to rule because of its desires goaded to madness." To Plato the gist of the "goad/gadfly" image is the absence of rational control that could resist the power of appetite.[66]

Now we see the tradition behind Apollonius's description of Eros's effect on mortals as he leaves Olympus and reaches earth: "Eros passed unseen through the grey mist, causing confusion, as when against grazing heifers rises the gadfly." The heifer, of course, prefigures the virgin Medea, and the impact of Eros's arrow upon her will be like the sting of the gadfly, compelling her against her will to betray her father and murder her brother, just as the heifer is driven in pain across the field. This is not "falling in love." It is rather the experience of being attacked by some natural force heedless of the destruction it causes.[67]

The common thread running through these various images taken from the world of beasts and their interaction with humans is the recognition not just that eros links us to the natural world of irrational beasts, is part of the animal within us, but also that eros is both an internal compulsion and an overwhelming external force, driving the soul to its destruction just as the boar is driven into the nets or the ox is goaded to the sacrifice. No modern American swain would croon that his lover makes him feel like a deer shot through the head, even though the results of eros can be just as destructive. Just ask the numerous wives and girlfriends stalked, hunted, and often butchered by their eros-mad mates.

The "Very God of Evil"

The imagery we've been tracing so far describes eros in terms of the natural world, aligning sexual passion with the forces of nature that impinge on human existence, especially those like fire that humans must control and exploit in order to survive in a harsh natural world. Other areas of Greek life in which the mind must confront and manipulate and control the irrational—the body's physical force or destructive appetites—also provide potent images for the ambiguity of eros. Sports were, of course, a central civic experience of ancient Greek life. Just about every year games were celebrated at one or another of the four Panhellenic religious centers of the Greek world, at Olympia, Isthmia, Delphi, and Nemea. Athletes enjoyed the same adulation and pecuniary rewards we mistakenly think characterize only our debased, commercialized corporate sports. Great political prestige attached to the individual and his city-state successful in the games, and high-priced poets composed choral odes celebrating the victors and flattering their aristocratic clans. One reason for the importance of sports to the Greeks, apart from their seemingly endemic competitiveness, was that the events of the games were metaphors for human existence, activities in which the mind's skill and the body's force had to cooperate to overcome the limiting necessities of weight, distance, time, or the muscles and brain of an opponent. In short, sports is tragic, like life, a pitting of the mind's manipulation of its body's force and passion against the recalcitrant necessity of existence, with clear-cut winners and losers.

Sport as metaphor for sexual desire, then, communicates the struggle the rational soul undergoes when it confronts the force of its own and another's passion. A few fragments of Anacreon, preserved on a papyrus scrap, seem to celebrate the poet's escape from a hard boxing match with Eros: "I was boxing with a harsh opponent, I raise up my head and look up again." Another fragment captures the hope and excitement of embarking on an affair: "Fetch water, boy, fetch wine and garlands of flowers, bring them on, so that I can box against Eros." Boxing was bloodier in ancient Greece than in modern America, since Greek boxers fought with stiff, lead-lined leather strips wrapped around their hands instead of padded gloves. Hence the mingled intimacy and violence of boxing work well as an image of the destructiveness of eros. Deianira, Heracles' wife, forgives her husband's lovesickness for Iole because "he who would stand against Eros as a boxer" isn't thinking straight. Deianira's common sense is pathetic, of course, for there's no stepping out of the ring, no throwing in the towel when Eros is your opponent.[68]

Wrestling, with its clenches and embraces, carries a strong sexual charge, especially for the upper-class Greeks who pursued their homosexual amours in the palaestra, the wrestling school where the boys exercised and wrestled naked. Alcibiades, during the first stages of his attempted seduction of Socrates, exercised and wrestled with him, hoping by fleshly contact to break down the philosopher's self-control. But Eros and Aphrodite are as formidable wrestlers as they are boxers. Sophocles in a fragment says that Aphrodite has thrown all the gods three times, the number of throws needed by a wrestler for victory in the games. In her chilling prologue to Euripides' *Hippolytus*, the same goddess boasts that she "trips up those who think big against me"—meaning of course Hippolytus, the chaste youth defeated by Aphrodite even though he attempts to steer clear of her. That is where the wrestling and boxing metaphors depart from life: You have no choice but to enter the ring against Eros, because it is part of what you are, a necessity of human existence. And Eros always gets the win, losing it seems only to the prodigy Socrates.[69]

Sports metaphors are accessible to us because the experience of the athlete while he competes is the same now as it was in ancient Greece, no matter how different the meanings each culture attributes to sports. But slavery, the everyday experience of human beings owned by other human beings as a piece of property, is utterly alien to us. It doesn't mean as much to us as it did to the Greeks when we call someone a "love-slave." Yet slavery in Greek thought provides a potent image of subjection to the inferior, bestial, irrational side of human identity, since slaves were often barbarians considered more sensually indulgent and passionate, hence "naturally" fit to be ruled by the superior Greeks. Aristotle in the *Politics* makes this idea very explicit when he says that men who differ as much from other men as the soul does from the body and humans from the lower animals are naturally slaves, possessing only enough reason to apprehend but not be fully rational, because like animals they are subservient to their passions. Slaves are ranked with animals and the passionate body on the assumption that they are not as rational, that is, human.[70] Thus the image of enslavement, for more than a century a dead metaphor for us, was vivid for the Greeks, not least because slavery was a very real possibility for people in the ancient world, either through kidnapping by pirates or through the fortunes of war, one of the most profitable enterprises of which was the enslavement of the conquered survivors—the fate the Athenians meted out to the inhabitants of the rebellious island of Melos during the Peloponnesian War.

As a metaphor, then, slavery suggests not just subjection to another's will but also the loss of humanity, the slipping-down into the natural world of irrational beasts. In the fragment of Anacreon we talked about earlier, the boxing image is followed by the poet's relief that he "escaped the chains of Eros made harsh by Aphrodite." The relief of the escaped captive reinforces the relief of the boxer after a tough match, both images communicating the dehumanizing experience of subjection to an irrational lust that controls one's mind and will. This subjection to passion and appetite is continually called slavery in the philosophers, whose fundamental assumption is that humans are rational animals, and so any loss of rational control signifies the loss of human status predicated on the slave, Aristotle's "living tool." Plato's Phaedrus, extolling the rational pleasures of reading and conversation, values them over the "bodily pleasures," which cannot be enjoyed without pain and hence are "justly called slavish."[71]

Xenophon's Socrates goes even further. Discussing the true nature of freedom with Euthydemus, Socrates elicits agreement when he postulates that the incontinent man is totally without freedom, and since the worst form of slavery is subjection to the worst master, the incontinent man suffers the worst slavery, for he is compelled to do what is base and prevented from doing what is noble; that is, he cannot fulfill his human potential any more than a slave can. Even the Cynic Diogenes, the exponent of the "doggy" life who wore only a loincloth, urinated and copulated in public, and believed that the "natural" life was best for a man, nonetheless reinforced the same hierarchy of the human rational mindset over slavish bodily lusts when he said that worthless men obey their lusts as household slaves obey their masters. This denigration of the body and its passions, endemic in Greek thought and powerfully transmitted by the slave metaphor, is one of the most important legacies of Greek thought to the West. When applied to eros, it testifies not only to its compulsive but also to its *dehumanizing* power, the way it robs us of our rational awareness and control, the hallmark of our human identity.[72]

Slavery on the political level is subjection to tyranny. The *turannos* in ancient Greek signifies something different from our "tyrant." Tyrants flourished in the Greek world in the eighth through sixth centuries, important phases in the transition from aristocratic rule to constitutional government, whether democratic or oligarchic. Often a tyrant was an aristocrat who, disaffected with elite clan politics and without hereditary claims to power, championed the cause of the disenfranchised and with their support seized power through force. Historically they accomplished much that was good, their courts contributing to the artistic and cultural flourishing of their cities. But by the fifth century, particularly in city-states like Athens that had liberated themselves from tyrannies, the tyrant came to signify the subjection of law and political institutions to the unbridled ambition and passion of the autocratic strongman. Hence Solon, the Athenian lawgiver and one of the Seven Sages, wrote in a poem that his greatest glory was refusing to become a tyrant, for the autocrat is linked to "ruthless violence." Aristotle defines the tyrant in these terms as one who rules subjects of the same or a better class without check or limit, in order to further his own interests rather than those of the subjects. Aristotle explicitly links such rule to slavery when he comments that "no free man willingly endures such a rule." In literature too, often the tyrant is depicted as lacking self-control, unable to rein in his sexual or violent impulses. Sophocles' Oedipus is the epitome of the tyrant so conceived, quick to violence, ready to impose his will with force. Significantly, Oedipus's two crimes, parricide and incest, represent the extreme destructive manifestations of violence and sexual passion.[73]

To call eros and the other desires tyrants, then, is to link them to lawlessness and excess as well as to characterize them as compulsive forces without check or limit.

This is what Euripides intends in his fragment that calls Eros the "tyrant of gods and men," a tyrant who in the *Hippolytus* is seen also as a conqueror "ravaging and raining ruin" on all the mortals he visits, an autocrat who uses violence to enslave those he conquers. Plato elaborates on the same idea in the *Republic*. Assuming the individual to be a microcosm of the state, Socrates parallels the political servitude of a state subjected to a tyrant to the servility of the individual soul enslaved to the tyranny of desire, the "most maddened part," which like a "gadfly" harries and drives the soul into confusion. On the political level, order in the state derives from rule by law and institutions that check the citizens' excessive ambitions and desires. On the level of the soul, order results from the rational mind that limits and subordinates the excessive appetites and passions, particularly eros, the "indwelling tyrant," as Plato calls it. The breakdown of this order on both levels is called tyranny, a destructive disorder leading to the ruin of state and individual, a condition akin to madness. The aged Sophocles saw it that way. Asked whether he still enjoyed the pleasures of sex, he answered, "I feel as if I had escaped from an insane and furious despot."[74]

In addition to the various metaphors discussed in this chapter, Eros is consistently characterized with epithets signifying destructiveness, suffering, pain, and numerous other frightening disorders, making him what Byron called the "very god of evil." One representative epithet is *schetlion*, "shrinking from no evil." Apollonius apostrophizes Eros with this word, just before he describes Medea and Jason's treacherous murder of her brother Apsyrtus: "Wicked Eros, great plague, great curse to humans, from you come destructive strife and mourning and groans, and countless pains are stirred up by you." We in the modern world with our sentimentalized sexual idealism cannot imagine talking about sexual desire in such terms, or as "terrible," "harsh," "bitter," "violent," "painful," "oppressive," "rough," "cruel," "remorseless," "savage," "sharp," and "man-slaughtering," to mention some typical epithets given to the "God of Love," as we so idealistically call eros.[75]

If we return to Apollonius's story of Jason and Medea, and his description of Eros wounding Medea with an arrow, we can see now that not a shred of sexual idealism, of our elevated notions of "love" and "falling in love," apply to Apollonius's story. Indeed, our survey of the imagery and vocabulary of eros reveals a relentless negative characterization of sexual passion. Eros is a force of nature, doubly dangerous because it permeates the external world and drives the human soul, and hence operates in the shadow-land where culture and nature, the mind and the world, intersect. It is implicated in the other irrational forces of the soul, aligned with violence, fear, and death, and it shares the destructive qualities of other natural phenomena like fire, the sea, storms, and disease. Moreover, this overwhelmingly dark view of sexuality—in our society held only by the most benighted of religious zealots—is not balanced by an optimistic or idealized one, except for conjugal love or Plato's etherialized homosexuality.

Moreover, our own Romantic-inspired idealizations of sexuality as a force of personal liberation and self-fulfillment would strike most Greeks as a dangerous folly and delusion. How else would they regard a statement like the following, from the apostle of "sexual revolution," Norman O. Brown, who as a classicist should have known better: "The life instinct, or sexual instinct, demands activity of a kind that in contrast to our current mode of activity can only be called play. The life instinct also demands a union with others and with the world around us based not on anxiety and aggression but on narcissism and erotic exuberance."[76] Or listen to another proponent of sexual liberation, Herbert Marcuse: "The civilized morality is reversed by harmonizing instinctual freedom and order: liberated from the tyranny of repressive reason, the instincts tend toward free and lasting existential relations—they generate a *new* reality principle."[77] A quarter-century of the consequences of "erotic exuberance" and "instinctual freedom"—illegitimacy, venereal plagues, an expanding divorce rate, the weakening of the nuclear family, the debasement of women, and the trivialization of sexuality in the mass media— has not, unfortunately, invalidated such thinking.

But 2,500 years earlier Euripides wrote the response to Marcuse and Brown in his *Bacchae*, where "liberation of the instincts" leads to horror and destruction, not just for the "repressed" Pentheus but for those like Teiresias and Cadmus who *want* to welcome Dionysus and recognize his power but who end up suffering just the same, marching off into exile at play's end, the ruins of Thebes smoking behind them. Liberating the instincts, especially eros, is like freeing a fire or a wild beast— only destruction will follow. As we shall see later, to the Greeks control and exploitation of the powerful force of eros are necessary so that the orders of mind and civilization can exist. But first we must meet the mother of Eros, "laughter-loving" Aphrodite.

TWO

The Golden Child of the Bloody Foam

THE LATE-EIGHTH-CENTURY *Hymn to Aphrodite* tells the story of how the goddess was stricken with love for the mortal Trojan Anchises, who was tending cattle in the wilds of Mt. Ida. After her attendants, the Graces, perfumed and dressed and decked her with gold, the goddess made her way through the woods to the shelter of the mortal, whom she found playing "thrillingly" on the lyre. Disguised as a demure nubile girl, she told him she was a mortal princess snatched away from home by the god Hermes and brought to Anchises to be his bride. Seized with desire, Anchises took the goddess on his bed strewn with the skins of wild animals. After their lovemaking, Aphrodite revealed herself and told Anchises of the son she would bear him, Aeneas, destined to be a mighty prince of the Trojans and, in the later Roman tradition, founder of Rome.

What mortal man would not desire such sexual dalliance with the Goddess of Love? We moderns can imagine the scene—the handsome, buff young Trojan, the disguised goddess looking like one of Botticelli's blonde Florentines, the soft-focus lovemaking to the rhythms of that faux-Hellenic lyre music from sand-and-sandal Steve Reeves epics. But such a staging of the scene would be wrong: about Aphrodite, and especially about Anchises' experience with her. Consider the mortal's response when Aphrodite reveals her divinity: "He was terrified, and averting his eyes he turned away, covering his handsome face with his cloak. . . . 'I beseech you, do not leave me to live feeble among men, but pity me, since he is no hale man who sleeps with a deathless goddess.' "[1] Why this terror?

This response to Aphrodite is not an archaic remnant of prerational primitivism. The essential ambiguity of the goddess, another name for whom is Kypris, is captured as well in this fragment of a play of Sophocles: "Kypris is not Kypris alone, but is called by many names. She is Death and undecaying life, she is the rage of madness." Euripides too wonders at the dual nature of Aphrodite: "There are many complexities in Aphrodite, for she delights and grieves mortals very much." Even the structure of Euripides' sentence is ambiguous—does the adverb "very much," placed between the two verbs, modify "delights" or "grieves"? Is the essence of Aphrodite the joys of sex or the destructiveness of irrational passion? Or is she like her mother the sea, calm and shining one moment, heaving with wind and wave the next? Like her son Eros, Aphrodite packs a double force: the disorder of sex, the chaos from which Anchises turns his face, but also the pleasures of seduction and lovemaking, the sweet desire that makes Anchises say to the unrevealed goddess, "I would go to Hell, woman like a goddess, once I had mounted your bed."[2]

The fearsome, dangerous power of Aphrodite is revealed in the same attributes we saw given to her son Eros. Like his power hers is cosmic in extent. "Sing me the deeds of much-golden Kyprian Aphrodite," the *Hymn* begins, "who rouses sweet desire in the gods and subdues the tribes of mortal men and sky-hovering birds and all the creatures, all the many the earth rears and the sea—to all these the deeds of richly crowned Cytherea [Aphrodite] are a concern." Aphrodite is not the Goddess of Love, as we call her today, but the goddess of *sex*, the sheer amoral drive of all life to reproduce, "the force that through the green fuse drives the flower," as Dylan Thomas put it. The Nurse in the *Hippolytus*, witnessing the erotic madness of Phaedra, captures this inhuman primal aspect of the goddess when she says, "Kypris is no god, but something greater than a god." And, as the fate of Phaedra and Hippolytus shows, Aphrodite demands recognition of and respect for her power, punishing severely those who in any way slight it, in history as well as myth. Herodotus tells of the rampaging Scythians who were stricken with the mysterious "female disease"—impotence, perhaps, or homosexuality—for plundering her famous temple at Ascalon in Syria. She repays Diomedes for wounding her during the Trojan War by making his wife Aegialeia take numerous lovers and plot against him. For neglecting her honors, the women of Lemnos, victims of Aphrodite's "terrible anger," are driven by jealousy of their husbands' captive concubines to kill every male on the island. Sex is the purview of Aphrodite, and those who, as she says in the *Hippolytus*, "think big" against her are visited with some form of sexual disorder and violence.[3]

Sex, then, not love is the activity that acknowledges Aphrodite's power, is indeed the true "worship" of the goddess. That is why prostitutes were her particular devotees and beneficiaries of her goodwill. The renowned fourth-century hetaira or courtesan Laïs, mistress of both the orator Demosthenes and the Cynic philosopher Diogenes, used to pray to Aphrodite Melaenis, an epithet meaning "of the dark," since that's when her "worship" took place; Pausanias notes a temple to the Black Aphrodite near Mantineia, "black" because men, unlike beasts, copulate at night. After Laïs finished her prayers, the goddess would then appear to the courtesan and reveal the coming of wealthy lovers. Another hetaira, Laïs's rival

Phryne—she was the model for both Apelles' painting *Aphrodite Rising from the Sea* and Praxiteles' statue *Cnidian Aphrodite* and was worshipped after death along with Eros in his temple at Thespiae—purportedly bared her breasts to the jury while being tried on a capital charge, and the (all-male) jury acquitted her because they feared this "attendant and expounder" of Aphrodite.[4]

As well as possessing a volatile power extending from the gods to the beasts, Aphrodite is just as able to subordinate the mind's faculties to the demands of sexual passion as is her son Eros. She herself is a "deceiver," Homer says, "craftyminded." Her *himanta*, the band encircling her neck and crossing between her breasts, the magic erotic accessory Hera in the *Iliad* borrows when she wants to seduce her husband Zeus, is fashioned with charms that can "steal the shrewd mind of even the wise."[5] The Chorus of Euripides' *Andromache*, about the suffering of the Trojan women after their city's destruction, explains Aphrodite's winning of Paris's favorable judgment by referring to this mind-corrupting power; she prevailed with her "crafty/deceitful arguments" whose final result is the ruined towers of Troy and the captive women huddled on the beach, waiting to sail to Greece to be the concubines of their captors. These are not mere literary conceits. Pausanias records a temple to Aphrodite Machanitis, the "Deviser," because she inspires such various speeches and devices for gratifying sexual passion. The ability of passion to exploit language for its own ends made the goddess Peitho, Persuasion, a frequent attendant of Aphrodite. Sappho made Peitho her daughter, and the two goddesses were worshipped together at a shrine on the southwest slope of the Acropolis in Athens.[6]

The ubiquity of her power and its dire effects on the mind make Aphrodite a force as destructive and frightening as her son Eros. Hence she is characterized by many of the same epithets and metaphors. She "subdues/conquers/breaks" her victims, obliterating their will to resist. "Do not break/subdue me," Sappho prays to Aphrodite, "with anguish and surfeit," the twin pains of erotic repletion and lack. She can be "most bitter," as Sappho hopes she will be to the gold-digging prostitute Doricha, a.k.a. Rhodopis, "Rosy-face," who financially ruined the poet's brother. Euripides' Helen, in her reincarnation as chaste wife slandered by the sexual depredations of her phantom double, calls Aphrodite "murderous" and "insatiate of evils."[7] Yet like a bright, placid sea Aphrodite can be lovely, her gifts delightful. "What life, what joy," the sixth-century poet Mimnermus asks, "without golden Aphrodite?"[8] Whereas Eros represents more the force of desire, the painful lack that drives one to destructive excess, Aphrodite often embodies as well the more concrete pleasures and charms of seduction and intercourse.

A fragment from the lost epic the *Cypria*, which told of the events precipitating the Trojan War, describes Aphrodite, on her way to the Judgment of Paris, in terms of the fragrant natural loveliness of sex and desire: "She put on her body the clothes that the Graces and the Seasons made for her and dyed in the springtime flowers, such ones as the Seasons bear—in crocus and hyacinth and flourishing violet and the beautiful blossom of the rose, in its sweet nectar, and in the ambrosial buds of the narcissus and lily." The Graces are goddesses associated with the sexual beauty of youth—they are the "givers of life's bloom," as Pindar says, from whose eyes flows what Hesiod calls "limb-loosening love." Yet even in these descriptions of Aphrodite's beauty, the perfumed sweetness of desire, there lurk intimations of the fierce power that so terrified Anchises. The epithet "limb-loosening," we saw in Chapter 1, is associated with death and the loss of rational control. Likewise in the *Odyssey* Athena anoints Penelope with Aphrodite's "balm," the magic ointment bestowing a sexual loveliness that "loosens the knees" of the suitors—literally, when Odysseus returns and slaughters them all. The greatest mortal beneficiary of Aphrodite's power of sexual beauty was Helen, but as Euripides' Helen laments, her sexual beauty, "gifts of Aphrodite," bore "much blood, much weeping, grief upon grief, tears upon tears." Like the beauty of nature, the flowers in which the Graces dye her clothes, Aphrodite's attractive loveliness conceals the inhuman brutality of sexual power.[9]

Many of the other epithets and images associated with Aphrodite reveal the ambiguity of her sexual charm. The famous compound adjective "laughter-loving," evoking the delightful flirtation of seduction, is very similar in sound and spelling to the more graphic and bestial "penis-loving" or "kin to the penis" (*philommêdea*); that is, the severed organ of Ouranos from which, as we will soon see, she is said to have been born. The epithet Sophocles gives her, "golden-reined," reflects the very common epithet for Aphrodite, "golden," which refers either to the dazzling ornaments on her cult-images—the sixth *Homeric Hymn* refers to her gold crown and necklace and earrings—or to her complexion and hair color, a memory of the tawny early Greeks, as in Ibycus's description of her as "golden-haired." But "reins," of course, are instruments of control, the means by which the horseman compels the horse to do his bidding. The titillating joys of seduction are reflected in another frequent epithet, "glancing-eyed" or "coy-eyed," but duplicity and trickery are suggested as well. Pindar in a fragment proclaims that the man who does not "swell with desire" when he sees the boy Theoxenus is unhonored of "glancing-eyed" Aphrodite. He then goes on, however, to describe how he "wastes away" like wax in the sun whenever he sees the limbs of "blossoming boys." A shifty-eyed Aphrodite conceals the cost of passion, the diseaselike dissolution of the mind stricken with youthful sexual beauty. "Sweet" is an epithet that also evokes the pleasures of seduction and sex; "sweet delight" is Aphrodite's "portion," Hesiod tells us, the realm of experience given to her as her especial purview.[10]

But variations on this common image are more ambiguous. Sappho's invention "bittersweet" is a long-lived economical expression of this ambiguity. Euripides' Heracles, unaware that his buddy Admetus's wife has just died in his place, advises him to honor Aphrodite, "sweetest of the gods," in order to dispel his gloom. But Heracles' jolly hedonism drips with irony, for in the mythic tradition he will later die horribly because of the "sweet gifts" of Aphrodite, his lust for Iole that leads him to sack a city and destroy his own household. All these attributes evoke the pleasures of seduction and sex, the "allurements" and "dalliances" and "beguilement" embroidered on Aphrodite's magic breastband, the "whisperings of maidens" and "smiles" and "deceits" that are her purview. But lurking beneath that beauty lies the "bitterness" of her power, the disorder from which Anchises hides his face.[11]

The duplicitous sexual beauty of Aphrodite has, of course, a much broader dimension, for she is the source of all fertility and procreativity, the universal urge of all creatures to mate and reproduce after their kind. Historically the Greek Aphrodite descends from earlier incarnations of the Earth Mother, the direct line running from Paleolithic fertility goddesses like the Venus of Willendorf or Lespugue, through Near Eastern earth/fertility goddesses like the Sumerian Inanna, the Babylonian Ishtar, and the Phoenician Astarte, with collateral influences from the Minoan "Dove goddess" and the early Indo-European "Dawn goddess." As such, Aphrodite's sexual beauty reflects the important drive of reproduction, the force that makes the flocks and herds and people reproduce, that births the sun each day, that resurrects the spring each year. The positive view of this power will be discussed in Chapter 6. But that cosmic force has its dark side as well—the impersonal brutality of the life process, the fecund womb that is as well a devouring tomb. It is the frightening cruelty of nature itself and its collusion with death. If we turn from history to myth, the origins of Aphrodite reveal the primal violence of an inhuman nature.

Hesiod tells the story. First there was the mysterious Chaos, and just as mysteriously appeared from this primal stuff Earth and Tartarus, the dark world below the earth. Earth by herself bore Ouranos, the Starry Heaven, and the hills and the Ocean, "without sweet lovemaking." Then she lay with her son-consort and bore the Titans, including Cronos "of the crooked mind." And she bore monsters, giants with a hundred arms and fifty heads springing from their shoulders, grotesque creatures of nature hated by Heaven, who by means of continual sex with Earth kept them hidden away in her womb. So Earth enlisted the aid of her son Cronos and fashioned a sickle with which he cut off the erect penis and testicles of Ouranos as he copulated with Earth. The bloody members were flung into the sea, and from the foaming semen and blood was born Aphrodite.[12] The foam-semen drifted past the island Cythera and landed at Cyprus, where the goddess came ashore, giving her the name Kypris, and mythically explaining why that island became one of her most important cult-centers in ancient times.[13]

Incest, castration, deformed monsters, the primal mingling of violence and sex—this grotesque family romance does more than provide a folk etymology for Aphrodite's name from the word *aphros*, "foam." It describes for us as well the essential nature of the goddess: her father the bloody erect penis and testicles and spermy foam, the undifferentiated forces of sex and violence; her mother the sea that as Meleager says, "roars with the savage whip of winds," another volatile yet necessary natural force that humans must learn to navigate but that frequently destroys their fragile orders.[14]

The common connection of Aphrodite with the sea communicates as well her defining ambiguity. We will see in a moment how Euripides brilliantly exploits these connections in the *Hippolytus*. Historically Aphrodite functioned as a maritime deity, for the power of destruction becomes protective if propitiated properly, that is, bribed with gifts and worship. Pausanias records the names of numerous harbors and rocky promontories named after her. At Cnidus, site of Praxiteles' famous statue of her that in ancient times was a popular tourist attraction, she was worshipped as Aphrodite Euploea, "of fair sailing," and at Hermion were temples to an Aphrodite of the Deep and an Aphrodite of the Harbor, covering both her destructive and her protective dimensions. Athenaeus records the story of a sailor caught in a storm who prayed for deliverance to a statuette of the goddess. Suddenly, fresh myrtle—sacred to Aphrodite—grew over the ship, a delightful fragrance arose, and the sea calmed.[15]

The positive force of Aphrodite's maritime functions reflects the attempt of Greek culture to appropriate her power through the "technology" of ritual, as we will see in Chapter 6. Likewise myth reinvents the primal goddess, making her one of the Olympians, those younger anthropomorphic culture-gods who supersede the monstrous, more nature-oriented pre-Olympians and who have subordinated their natural forces to a cultural function. As one of those sophisticated eternal hedonists living the good life on the peaks of snowy Olympus, Aphrodite cannot have such a Southern Gothic ancestry as Hesiod gives her. Thus Homer records her more respectable parentage. Her father now is Zeus, king of the gods, embodiment of cosmic order, and her mother is Dione. But a closer look at Dione reveals the same primal forces more grotesquely imaged in the *Theogony*. According to Hesiod, Dione is the daughter of Oceanus and Tethys, the former the sea that encircles the earth, the latter a daughter of Ouranos, Heaven. We are back to the same natural elements, the sea and the severed penis now replaced by anthropomorphic grandfathers. Dione and Tethys, moreover, are both given the epithet *eratê*, "lovely" or more accurately "sexy," indicating perhaps some ancient connection with sex and fertility. Even Aphrodite's more respectable pedigree in the *Iliad* retains her essential ambiguity, her combination of seductive beauty and terrible power.[16]

Likewise with her Olympian consorts, Hephaistos and Ares—"fire and the sword," as Meleager describes them. Her husband Hephaistos, the misshapen lame blacksmith god, and her lover Ares both represent that intersection of natural force and human culture, Hephaistos fire and metalworking, Ares violence and war. It is significant, though, that her legitimate partner is Hephaistos, the craftsman god, the technician of Olympus, fashioner of Pandora and Achilles' shield and the mechanical watchdogs of the Phaiacians in the *Odyssey*. Hephaistos is closer to the human world of culture than is bloody Ares, so the former is the husband, sharer in the marriage that legitimizes sex, whereas the latter is the adulterer—though an ancient proverb, "Lame men fuck the best," might also explain why the limping Hephaistos is husband to the queen of sex. But even Hephaistos retains his links to one of the most important forces of nature, fire. He may originally have been a fire deity, and often his name is a synonym for fire. The elemental force of Hephaistos is used beautifully by Homer in the *Iliad* when Achilles, about to be swamped and drowned by the angry river-god Xanthos that he has clogged with the corpses of slaughtered Trojans, is rescued by the apocalyptic fire of Hephaistos that scorches the river and burns the bodies. But Hephaistos ultimately represents the control of fire, the exploitation of it by skill and craft. Ares, in contrast, "most hateful of the gods" according to Homer, never moves far from the primal violence of war for which his name is a synonym. He is more like Aphrodite in that the force of violence is doubly chaotic and volatile, for unlike fire but like eros it is *inside* the souls of humans as well as outside in the world of nature, and it is no more easily organized or contained than is sex. As we saw earlier, Simonides makes Ares the father of Eros, but he is given three other children by Aphrodite: Harmonia, Phobos, and Deimos, the latter two Ares' attendants in battle, the one the personified "panic fear" of war, the other "terror."[17]

This link of Aphrodite's sexual power to the fearsome disorder and violence of war embodied in her paramour Ares emphasizes the destructiveness of sex we saw earlier in the imagery and epithets associated with Aphrodite. No surprise, then, that a martial Aphrodite was worshipped throughout Greece—as Areia, the "warlike," at Sparta; as the Armed Aphrodite at Corinth, Sparta, and Cythera; as the Bringer of Victory at Argos.[18] According to Plutarch and Athenaeus, after Laïs was beaten to death with footstools by some jealous women in Aphrodite's temple in Thessaly, the goddess was worshipped as Aphrodite Androphonos, the "man-slaughterer," an epithet Homer gives to Ares. The ancients recognized that sex and violence, our diametric opposites, were forces more intimately implicated with one another, particularly in the emotion of jealousy. Even the "scientist" Aristotle noted that "it wasn't absurd to join together Ares and Aphrodite, for all such [martial] men are inclined to intercourse either with men or with women."[19]

This dual nature of Aphrodite generates the famous distinction between the "Heavenly" Aphrodite and the so-called "Vulgar." Temples to the former are mentioned in Pausanias and in Herodotus, who claims that the one in Ascalon plundered by the Scythians was the oldest. In mythic terms, the significance of the epithet Ourania lies in Aphrodite's sort of once-removed descent from the sky-god Ouranos. Historically it reflects the influence on Aphrodite from Near Eastern goddesses like Inanna and Ishtar, who have astral connections, especially to the dawn and the morning star. Aphrodite Pandemos, or "of all the people," to give the epithet a less loaded translation, was also widely worshipped—at Thebes, Megalopolis, and especially Athens, where the cult was said to have originated. One version of the cult's origins makes the legendary Athenian king Theseus the founder, who established the worship when he organized all the demes or local parishes into one city-state. Presumably Aphrodite of All the People represented the attractive force of social friendship and community that politically united the villages. Thus the worship of Peitho, Persuasion, alongside Aphrodite Pandemos—

a political community's cohesion depends on the ability of citizens to convince one another through language rather than violence. An alternative explanation for the Athenian cult of Aphrodite Pandemos, one favored by the comic writers (e.g., Philemon), says that the early-sixth-century statesman Solon instituted the worship when he organized all the prostitutes, financing the cult from the profits of the brothels.[20]

Although these two cultic versions of Aphrodite did not originally carry the distinctions between bodily and spiritual love that Plato and Xenophon later gave them, the different explanations for their origins point to the development of such a contrast. Images of the two goddesses highlighted the difference between a positive, unifying force of sexual attraction and an earthier, more bestial one. Pausanias describes two statues at Olympia: the one by Phidias, fifth-century creator of monumental statues of Athena and Zeus, was a "chryselephantine" or gold-and-ivory Aphrodite Ourania; the other, by the fourth-century sculptor Scopas, showed Aphrodite Pandemos riding a goat, the animal of unbridled indiscriminate lust. These distinctions reveal the attempt of cult-technology to organize and hence control Aphrodite by distinguishing between her powers of unifying affection and those of sheer physical sex. Another version of Aphrodite's origins attributes them to Harmonia, daughter of Ares and Aphrodite whose name means "joiner." She it was who gave her mother *three* names: the Heavenly, pure and free from bodily lust, the Common, and the Rejector, who rejects unlawful and sinful lust. Married love too was associated with the "purer" Aphrodite, the love of courtesans and prostitutes with the "common." The late-fifth-century comic poet Philetaerus complains in a fragment that everywhere are statues to Aphrodite the Hetaira or mistress, but none to Aphrodite the Married goddess. The chaste wife, a poem of Theocritus says, prays not to Aphrodite Pandemos but to Aphrodite Ourania.[21]

We see here the idealization of erotic power that reaches its fullest realization in Plato's and Xenophon's pederastic ideal in which sexual attraction is used as the energy for the development of the boy's soul. Hence Xenophon's Socrates distinguished between the rituals of Aphrodite Ourania and Pandemos, the latter's "more impure" and linked to "carnal" love, the former's "pure" and expressive of the love of the mind and friendship and noble deeds. Plato's Pausanias in the *Symposium* similarly contrasts the two goddesses: Aphrodite Pandemos is the younger, sprung from Zeus and Dione, chaotic, déclassé, bisexual, bodily, and indiscriminate; Ourania is older, the daughter of Ouranos, homosexual, orderly, intellectual, and aristocratic.[22] We will speak more about this pederastic ideal in Chapter 8. For now note how the development of the two Aphrodites formalizes and resolves the inherent ambiguity of the goddess by distinguishing between a positive creative force and a negative destructive one little acknowledged as such by us moderns.

Poetry generally is more content to let ambiguities lie, and in the following stories about Aphrodite we will see the destructive power lurking beneath her seductive golden beauty.

Aphrodite and Helen

In Book 3 of the *Iliad* Menelaus, husband of Helen, and Paris, her Trojan paramour, fight a duel to decide who gets possession of the most beautiful woman in
the world. Menelaus gets the best of Paris in the fight and is dragging him by the
helmet back to the Greek lines when Aphrodite intervenes—she breaks the helmet's chin strap and whisks Paris in a cloud of mist back to Troy, depositing him
in his bedchamber. Then the goddess disguises herself as an old serving woman of
Helen's and announces to her that Paris is back from the battle, "shining with
beauty and raiment" and presumably in the mood for love.[23]

Why at that particular moment does Aphrodite want Helen and Paris to make
love? Because sex is the activity that recognizes and celebrates her power, the
power she has just used to save Paris's life. Paris understands the reciprocal nature
of his relationship to the goddess. When his brother Hector berates him for
shrinking from the fight with Menelaus, mocking his lyre and beauty and curls
and other "gifts of Aphrodite," Paris responds, "Do not scorn me for the lovely
gifts of golden Aphrodite, not at all should be despised the glorious gifts of the
gods." Those gifts are the manifestations of a power that operates to his benefit.
But he must reciprocate, and that means making love with Helen, for this is the
true worship of her deity.[24]

But Helen balks at Aphrodite's suggestion, and the goddess's subsequent anger
reveals the dark side of that power, its ever-present though latent destructiveness
that like the sea can sweep away the frail mortal who tries to resist it. Helen
quickly recognizes Aphrodite behind the disguise as an old woman, for she sees
her "most beautiful neck and desirable breast and flashing eyes," the sexual beauty
linked to Helen's own erotic power that even the withered old men of Troy, their
voices as thin as those of cicadas, can remark is "strangely like a goddess to look
at" when she mounts the wall before the duel. Yet Helen forgets her dependence
on the goddess and angrily asks her why she wants to deceive her with "guileful
mind" and indignantly reminds the goddess of the shame she has already inflicted
because of Helen's sexual infatuation with Paris. Helen can see the destructive reality behind the sexual beauty of the goddess, the deceiving and beguiling power
that has already led her to abandon her husband and child and instigate the suffering and bloodshed soon to begin again before the walls of Troy.[25]

Confronted with this rejection of her power, the angry goddess reminds Helen
that she survives only because of her sexual beauty, the "gift" of Aphrodite that if
removed would lead to her destruction: "Do not provoke me, wretched girl, lest I
grow angry and desert you, and hate you as much as now I terribly love you, and
devise grievous hatred for you in Greeks and Trojans alike, and you be destroyed
by an evil fate."[26] "Love" means "reciprocate": I have benefited you, Aphrodite reminds Helen, and you must now reciprocate by using your sexual beauty in the
act of sex. For Helen to do otherwise is to reject the power of the goddess and

dishonor her, the act of an enemy that would bring down revenge upon her. Helen is terrified and follows Aphrodite in silence to the bedroom.

There Helen takes out her anger on Paris, berating his cowardice and belittling his fighting ability, trying to shame him. But Paris doesn't care. He is filled with the power of Aphrodite: "Never before has eros so covered over my mind," he tells Helen: "Now I want you and sweet desire has seized me."[27] Shame and dishonor mean nothing now, only the imperative of the flesh, the worship of Aphrodite that drives the two to the bed, where they make love while Helen's husband Menelaus rages up and down the line, searching in vain for the quarry that has slipped his grasp.

Like the later seduction of Zeus it parallels, this scene reveals to us clearly the ambiguous nature of Aphrodite: seductive beauty and the sweet pleasures of sex masking a threatening destructive power that cannot be resisted, that deceives and beguiles and subverts the mind and its consciousness of shame and right. In a sense, Helen's conversation with Aphrodite images her awareness of her own sexual beauty, her erotic power that at times seems alien to her, a force attacking from without, driving her to the shame and pleasure of Paris's bed.

The Seduction of Zeus

It is one of the direst moments of all the war for the Greeks. With their champion Achilles still sulking in his tent, the Trojans have breached the Greek defensive wall, driving them back upon their ships. Hera, on the side of the Greeks ever since the Trojan Paris picked Aphrodite as the fairest goddess, thinks of a plan to provide the Greeks with some breathing space—she will seduce her husband Zeus, take his mind off of the war and the Trojans he is supporting to further the revenge of Achilles against Agamemnon and the other Greeks who dishonored him. So Hera visits Aphrodite and asks for "desire and lovemaking, with which you subdue all the immortals and mortal men." Aphrodite complies and loans Hera her breastband "intricately embroidered, on it fashioned all manner of charms—lovemaking, desire, and alluring dalliance that steals the shrewd mind of even the wise." Armed with this erotic magic, Hera seduces her husband on Mt. Ida, their lengthy lovemaking hidden by a golden cloud, thus allowing the Greeks some time to rally their beleaguered forces.[28]

The charm of this interlude is darkly set off not just by the mortals killing and dying while the gods dally in their Maxfield Parrish cloud, but also by the power of Aphrodite to attack the mind, to beguile it so that the victim—in this case Zeus, king of the gods, upholder of cosmic order—can no longer see or think straight, overwhelmed as he is with sexual passion. "Never before," Zeus pants to his alluring wife, "has eros so subdued/conquered/broken/tamed [*edamassen*] my mind"—and then he tactlessly enumerates his various mortal and immortal paramours. Homer, again using the word that typically describes the effect on the soul of Eros's and Aphrodite's power, emphasizes the impact of lovemaking on Zeus's mind when he describes him as "conquered/subdued/broken by sleep and love-

making"—with the result that Poseidon is unleashed to help the Greeks and delay
Zeus's dispositions of the fate of the Greeks and Trojans. Like his daughter Helen,
Zeus is the victim of Aphrodite's mind-controlling power lurking within the
shining beauty and pleasures of sex.[29]

Fear and Desire on Mt. Ida

We saw earlier in the fifth *Hymn to Aphrodite* the dual nature of the goddess, her
seductive erotic beauty and her destructive power. A closer look at the *Hymn*
shows this power explicitly linked to nature and the wild, the realm of inhuman
forces beyond the civilized space of the city and its cultivated farmlands, the primal powers terrifying to the mortal who encounters them.

The natural landscape of the seduction, Mt. Ida, "mother of wild beasts," locates Anchises' experience far from the city and its institutions. As Aphrodite
moves through the forest, wolves, "fierce lions," bears, and leopards "ravenous for
deer" fawn on her, and "when she saw them she was glad in her heart, and she put
in their breasts desire, and by twos they mated in the shadowy lairs."[30] Aphrodite's
pleasure in the sexuality of predators notorious for attacking men and their domesticated animals reflects one of her historical antecedents, a version of the
Earth Goddess called the Mistress of the Beasts, a type of which was worshipped
on Crete. More important, it shows the connection of Aphrodite with a predatory
nature, the intimacy of its sex and violence reflected as well in some of her epithets and in her adultery with the war-god Ares. The herdsman Anchises is about
to be visited by a force from beyond the human world, one simultaneously
thrilling and terrifying.

Lest he be frightened of that power, Aphrodite disguises herself as a mortal girl,
for the direct force of divine sexuality can be literally destructive. Remember the
fate of Semele, who was incinerated by lightning when she encountered Zeus in
all his divine sexual glory. Yet Aphrodite's mortal disguise still reflects the goddess's
link to the natural world. Her robe was "brighter than the light of fire, and she
wore curved brooches and shining flower-shaped earrings, and around her tender
neck were beautiful necklaces, golden and intricately wrought, and they shone like
the moon over her soft breasts, a marvel to see." Her beauty is the beauty of nature,
of the moon and fire and flowers, alluring yet inhuman, rife with chaos. As soon as
Anchises sees her, "eros seizes" him and he hails her as a goddess—flattery, to be
sure, but also the intuition that such sexual beauty could not be human. So he
promises to build her an altar "on a mountain peak" and sacrifice to her "at all seasons" and asks in return renown among the Trojans and a long happy life. Anchises,
suspecting that he is confronting a divine force, attempts to control it through the
"technology" of ritual that establishes a reciprocal relationship with Aphrodite's
force, for it can be destructive unless bound to one by recognition and offerings.[31]

The goddess, though, continues to deny her divinity and spins out an implausi-
ble tale of being kidnapped by the messenger god Hermes and dropped off on

Mt. Ida because she is destined to be Anchises' bride. After this transparent lie, Aphrodite "puts sweet desire in his heart," just as she had done with the wolves and lions and leopards. And Anchises is just as peremptory as the beasts in gratifying his desire, leading her to his bed upon which were strewn "the skins of bears and deep-roaring lions that he himself had slain in the high mountains."[32] Clearly this sex act is primal, linked to death and the violence of the hunt, that activity in which men become natural predators. Only the thinnest veneer of a cultural order like marriage, invoked by Aphrodite and quickly dismissed by Anchises, overlays this experience. This is not a sex act sanctioned by culture, organized by its institutions. It is the direct, bestial gratification of lust—and as such, to the Greeks, threatening and dangerous to a degree we "enlightened" moderns find only among fundamentalist fanatics.

This danger inspires Anchises' fear we noted at the beginning, when he begs her not to leave him "feeble," a word Homer uses of the dead in Hades. And Aphrodite justifies that fear when she threatens Anchises with destruction by a "smoking thunderbolt" of Zeus if he reveals that he impregnated her, a possible fate she anticipated earlier in her story of Tithonus, paramour of the dawn-goddess Eos, who secured him immortality without also asking for eternal youth for him. Now Tithonus lives a horrible life-in-death, "babbling endlessly," hidden away by the ashamed and disgusted goddess.[33] Contact with the awesome power of sex exposes mortals to the fundamental forces of the cosmos, the sheer energies of life and death, creation and destruction.

Sappho's Aphrodite

The one surviving complete poem of the late-seventh-century poet Sappho, the so-called "Hymn to Aphrodite," like the earlier *Homeric Hymn* reveals the ambiguity of the goddess, the inhuman power lurking behind her beauty. The poem describes as well the mortal's attempt to control that force, as we will see later in Chapter 6. For now Sappho's description of Aphrodite's power is the issue, a description that calls on the traditional imagery of the goddess's destructiveness and her beguiling character. Like Helen in the *Iliad*, like Anchises in the *Homeric Hymn*, Sappho, one of our few female voices from antiquity, confronts that power in fear and trembling.

The poem takes the general form of a "ritual-prayer" designed to enlist the aid of a god. It starts with the poet begging the goddess not to unleash her power: "Do not, I beseech you, conquer/subdue/break my heart with anguish and surfeit," the twin pains of desire's lack and its cloying fulfillment. The poet reminds Aphrodite of times in the past when she asked what Sappho wanted in her "maddened heart," and she begs Aphrodite to liberate her from her present "cruel cares." These effects of sexual desire that shake the soul are, of course, the result of Aphrodite's power—that's why Sappho calls on her, for divine energy, like Achilles' spear, can heal where it wounds. These destructive effects are also linked by Sappho to the nature of the goddess—she is a "weaver of wiles" and "intricate-minded," if we accept the doubtful textual reading *poikilophron*. The word translated as "wile," *dolos*, more specifically means "trap," "trick," anything used to entrap or deceive. *Poikilos* has a wide range of meanings, including "complex," "subtle," "changeful." Even if the more accepted reading *poikilothron'*, "intricately-throned," is used, the implications of the adjective are still linked to the goddess. Both epithets communicate the beguiling, shifting nature of the goddess, the deceptive way the pleasure and beauty of sexual passion conceal its dangerous power.[34]

Sappho, though, recognizes as well the beauty of the goddess in her description of an earlier epiphany: "You came, leaving your father's golden house after you yoked your chariot, and beautiful swift sparrows beating quickly their wings bore you over the black earth down through the midst of the heaven." But the distance between the "golden house" and the "black earth" serves to emphasize the almost inhuman serenity of the goddess as she "smiles with her deathless face" and responds with philosophical detachment to the anguished cry of the mortal.[35] What that answer means we will talk about in Chapter 6. Taken with the earlier emphases on her destructive power, though, the cool beauty of the goddess serves to deepen her awesome mystery. As such Aphrodite must be ritually invoked so that her force benefits rather than injures the poet.

This Sappho does by means of the ritual-prayer. A similar prayer Sappho may be alluding to comes in Book 5 of the *Iliad*. There Diomedes prays to Athena for help in destroying the Trojans. Like the affair of Aphrodite and Ares, the connection of sexual desire with the violence and death of Homer's world asserts the intimate connection of sex and violence, both irrational forces that overthrow the mind. One needs the aid of divine power to survive the disorder both love and war bring in their wake. Thus Sappho asks Aphrodite to be her *summachos*, her "fellow-fighter," which is essentially what Diomedes asks of Athena, and exactly what Athena does when she answers the warrior's prayer and appears at his side.[36] Love is war, Aphrodite a volatile force of destruction that one must get on one's side to avoid annihilation.

Helen, Anchises, and Sappho all confront the ambiguous beauty of Aphrodite and attempt to come to terms with it, Helen by acquiescing in the imperative of sex, the essential act of worship of the goddess, the other two by invoking the technology of ritual. In contrast, Euripides' Hippolytus, denizen of the fifth-century Athenian Enlightenment, will try to counter the goddess with the power of rational virtue, only to suffer the full force of her lethal fury. Pure reason, the Greeks tell us, is no match for desire.

"Something Greater Than a God"

Euripides' *Hippolytus* is perhaps the most significant ancient story for understanding the nature of Aphrodite. All of the attributes and associations we have traced so far are exploited by Euripides to develop the primal inhuman power of the goddess—her link to the forces of nature, particularly the sea, her assault on the orders of civilization and the mind. She is, as the old busybody Nurse says, not a god but "something greater than a god."[37]

Hippolytus is a young man who refuses to worship Aphrodite because he is a devotee of Artemis, chaste goddess of the hunt, and so is himself celibate. As we have seen, sex is how we honor Aphrodite and recognize her power. To refuse sexual intercourse is to slight that power, to imply that one is immune to it. But all humans by definition are sexual. One can no more refuse sex than one can refuse to eat—both are defining necessities of human nature. Aphrodite says as much in her opening speech asserting the extent of her sway: "Mighty among mortals and in heaven, not inglorious, I am called the goddess Kypris. As many as dwell within the Atlantic boundaries of the sea, looking on the sun's light, I honor if they reverence my power. But I trip up those who think big against me."[38] Not only is every mortal subject to Aphrodite's power, but they are obliged to *recognize* it by having sex. If they don't, they will be destroyed. Like all divine forces, sex is inhuman and amoral, destructive if not propitiated by worship.

And Hippolytus indeed "thinks big" against Aphrodite. When the wise old man suggests he acknowledge the goddess, the arrogant youth replies, "I, being pure/chaste, embrace her from a distance," for "no one of the gods who is worshipped at night pleases me." By denying his sexuality, Hippolytus denies an important component of his humanity, the bestial side located in a body subject to time and change. This denial in turn implicitly asserts equality with the gods. So Aphrodite sets out to destroy him and prove the magnitude of her power. This she does by making Hippolytus's stepmother Phaedra sick with "dreadful lust" for the youth. Phaedra's sickness is literal: "Astounded by the goads of lust, the wretched woman wastes away in silence." She will eventually die, but Aphrodite cares nothing for the innocent woman, whose resistance to the goddess and shame over her sexual feelings also by implication belittle Aphrodite's power. To be sure, Phaedra has built a temple to the goddess, attempting to control that force with the "technology" of religion, but the only worship that matters is sex. Aphrodite's cruel indifference to the suffering of Phaedra suggests the inhuman destructiveness of passion, the violence the Chorus sees in other sexual disasters linked to traditional images of violence and fire: the "bloody bridal" of Iole taken by Heracles with "blood, with smoke," the "bloody doom" of Semele in the embrace of Zeus's "flame-girt thunder."[39]

Though like Hippolytus in her rigid moralism, Phaedra differs from him because she is, in her moments of lucidity, conscious of the battle she is waging and losing, and she realizes the uselessness of her moral technology of "shame" that cannot resist the disease devouring her. As the Nurse says, "The self-controlled/chaste unwillingly, yet still lust for evil."[40] So Phaedra gives in to the Nurse's suggestion that Hippolytus be told of his stepmother's desire. The outcome is disaster—Hippolytus explodes in rage, and the listening Phaedra is humiliated by the young man's sexual rejection of her, as well as suspecting that he will use the information to destroy her own children's position in the household. So she hangs herself, leaving behind a suicide note accusing Hippolytus of raping her.

Just as Phaedra's "technology" of religion and shame is useless before Aphrodite's volatile power, so Hippolytus's cultural ideal of rational self-control is a fragile weapon with which to confront the goddess. Hippolytus represents historically a type of smug, noble Athenian current during the last half of the fifth century, the same milieu from which develops the absolutist idealism and antinature philosophy of Plato, a type characterized as class-conscious, antidemocratic, misogynist, and distrustful of the chaos of nature and passion. The concern with an inherited nobility threatened by Athenian democracy leads to a definition of nature in which noble qualities such as virtue are "natural," not to be acquired through study or training. Hence Hippolytus rejects Aphrodite because he believes he is *naturally* celibate. Only those chaste "in nature," he says in his prayer to Artemis, may gather flowers in the "untouched meadow" from which he gathers the garland he dedicates to her image, and which symbolizes for Hippolytus his idealized relationship with Artemis, chaste goddess of the hunt and one of the three goddesses over whom Aphrodite is powerless.[41]

But Hippolytus's delusion is obvious in his own description of the meadow, for it is the realm of nature, bound up in the processes of procreation: "There no shepherd deems it right to feed his flock, nor does iron come, but only the bee roves the undefiled springtime meadow." The meadow *is* undefiled—by culture, represented by the shepherd and the sickle, emblems of agricultural technology. But the bee, the flowers, and the reference to spring, all redolent of sexual fertility, contradict Hippolytus's claim of sexual purity. Later in the play the Chorus will link Aphrodite, "the dread one breathing on all things," to a bee, highlighting these sexual implications.[42] To the Greek *sex* is natural, not chastity, which is as much an artifact of culture and the mind as agriculture is. Hippolytus is blind to his own human nature, necessarily sexual, and so subject to the power of Aphrodite. Moreover, Hippolytus is not as in control of his irrational side as he thinks he is. It is tempting to see his passionate dedication to Artemis and the hunt as a sublimation of sexuality in violence, the expression of one repressed passion through another. Aphrodite certainly reads it that way, using of his association with Artemis words that also mean sexual intercourse. These Freudian speculations aside, the young man's explosions of anger, what the wise old man calls his "vehement innards" when he begs the goddess to forgive the impetuous youth, give the lie to his pretensions of rational self-control, especially during his violent misogynistic tirade. Hippolytus is closer to Phaedra than he thinks.[43]

Throughout the play, in fact, Euripides undercuts Hippolytus's ideal of chastity and self-control by imagistically linking Phaedra's sexual disease to the idealized nature of the meadow and his life as a hunter. The seeming opposition between Hippolytus's celibacy and Phaedra's sexual madness is subverted by subtle similarities between the two mortals and the two goddesses, Aphrodite and Artemis, leaving the significant opposition that between the inhuman forces of the divine and

nature, and the suffering humans with their frail orders. The linkage of the goddesses reflects in part some of Artemis's functions that perhaps are holdovers from
an earlier earth-goddess incarnation. She is a "mistress of the beasts," like the
Aphrodite of the *Homeric Hymn*. Women in labor call on her, the Chorus sings, and
she has sympathy for all young creatures. Like Aphrodite, Artemis is "queen of arrows," and like Aphrodite, Artemis is linked to the sea in the guise of the Artemis
who "roams the waters of the Lake" and travels on the "eddies of the salt sea."[44] In
the ravings of her sexual madness Phaedra fantasizes about the world of Hippolytus and his mistress Artemis, further binding the two goddesses. She calls on the
Artemis of the Lake, dreams of lying in the grassy meadow beneath the poplars,
imagines herself far off in the mountains, hurling the spear at the hind fleeing the
dogs.[45] The idealized nature of Hippolytus and his life spent hunting with Artemis
are infected with the sexual madness of Phaedra, for nature is the realm of violence
and sex, of divine forces callous in their disregard for humans and the fragile controls with which they attempt to come to terms with those forces.

Those controls, of course, are futile. Aphrodite will not forgive the insult to her
power, for she is like the sea and its sudden, deadly violence. To communicate the
destructive power of the goddess, Euripides exploits the traditional link of
Aphrodite to the sea, and the shipwreck imagery that we saw in Chapter 1 is used
to describe erotic disaster. She is designated the "sea-born queen, Kypris," reminding us of her bloody origins in the severed penis of Ouranos, and sea imagery is
used to describe Phaedra's disease of lust visited on her by Aphrodite: "For Kypris is
unbearable when she comes in flood," the Nurse warns Phaedra: "How do you
think to swim to land?"[46] This imagery climaxes in the messenger's speech describing Hippolytus's fatal accident. Banished by his father Theseus because of Phaedra's
incriminating suicide note, Hippolytus is driving his chariot near the shore when a
"supernatural wave rising to sky," sent by Poseidon in answer to Theseus's wish,
hurls onto the shore a "bull, a savage monster" that frightens the horses of Hippolytus. The youth loses control of his animals and the chariot crashes, the horses
mangling their master, "smashing his dear head against the rocks, shattering his
body." In one brilliant image, the destructiveness of eros is linked to the sea and the
savagery of the bull, which in turn unleashes the power of the horses, bull and
horse both sexual animals par excellence. Forces of nature that man attempts to
control—sea, bull, horse—explode in savage chaos, and the emblems of culture and
the mind, the chariot and reins and harness, are overwhelmed and subverted into
the instruments of destruction. Just as Hippolytus's virtue of rational self-control
tripped him up, so now he is "tangled in the reins" and destroyed.[47]

No part of nature, including humans with their passionate bodies, is free from
sexuality, from the power of Aphrodite. "You drive even the unbending minds of
gods and mortals," the Chorus addresses her as the messenger goes to fetch the mangled remains of Hippolytus.[48] The impulses to sex and violence, Aphrodite and
Artemis, are manifestations of the inhuman force of nature that neither Hippolytus
nor Phaedra can resist with their rational cultural ideals of "self-control" or "shame."
Sooner or later, we are all victims of the elemental both within and without us.

Her Cruel Smile

The third-century poet Theocritus's first *Idyll*, with its description of whispering pines and babbling waterfalls harmonizing with the rustic songs of the shepherds, is famous as the first "pastoral" poem in the West, the first extended presentation of nature as an idealized lovely space of freedom and leisure where love and art alike can flourish. But the poem's vision of nature and sex is not that sentimentally simple. The attractive ideal of a nature sympathetic to human art and love is continually undercut in the poem by a recognition of nature's predatory destructiveness. Likewise with Aphrodite, who makes an appearance in the poem, her character rife with the inhuman cruelty she displays to Anchises, Helen, and Hippolytus.

One of the shepherds in the poem, Thyrsis, sings a song about the death of Daphnis, another shepherd who like Hippolytus thought he could resist eros but is now wasting away because of a "bitter love." During this somewhat extended swan song, Aphrodite appears before him to gloat, displaying beneath her charm her cruel power: "And Kypris came to him, laughing sweetly, but laughing treacherously, holding down her grievous anger." Using a wrestling metaphor, she derides the youth for thinking he could "throw" eros but getting himself "thrown" instead. The famous laughter of Aphrodite that gives her the epithet "laughter-loving" is recognized by the dying Daphnis for what it is: the conqueror's cruel indifference to suffering. So he answers her with the epithets that lay bare her destructive nature—"cruel," "vengeful," "hated by mortals." He then alludes to her affairs with Anchises and Adonis, and to her humiliation at the hands of Diomedes in the *Iliad*, all limitations of Aphrodite's power we will talk about in Chapter 6. But here the emphasis is on an Aphrodite like the one in the *Hippolytus*, savagely jealous of her power, willing to destroy in order to prove its force and extent. Like those of nature, the charms of Aphrodite and eros are deceptive, concealing a lethal force that sweeps away any who try to resist them.[49]

Aphrodite Domesticated—Somewhat

The goddess's last major appearance in Greek literature of our period occurs in Apollonius's *Voyage of the Argo*. As we saw in Chapter 1, Hera and Athena pay a visit to Aphrodite to get her to make her son Eros infect Medea with love for Jason so that she will help him filch the Golden Fleece. The Aphrodite of this scene seems different altogether from the cruel avenger of the *Hippolytus*. She comes off rather like some Hellenistic middle-class housewife, idly combing her hair while hubby Hephaistos is off at work. Sensitive to the disapproval of her on the part of the two goddesses, one a virgin, the other queen of marriage, she chides them for not visiting more frequently. Like any mother, she complains about her brat Eros, who won't listen to her and ignores her threats, and then she pouts when Hera and Athena laugh at her. When she goes to fetch him and finds him cheating

Zeus's cupbearer Ganymede at dice, she has to bribe him to do her the favor of making Medea's life miserable.[50] All in all, the ambiance of middle-class domesticity and psychology is all too human, similar to the gossiping housewives of Theocritus's fourteenth *Idyll* or Herodas's *Mimes*, other Hellenistic works reflecting a growing sense of individualism and privacy. In Apollonius the effect continues the contrast throughout the story of epic grandeur with bourgeois sensibility, and it sharpens the suffering of the mortals by juxtaposing it with the serene triviality of the gods, just as Homer does in the *Iliad*.

It is important to remember the erotic suffering of Medea and its destructiveness, for which the chatty housewife Aphrodite is responsible. Apollonius relentlessly documents those effects with all the traditional imagery discussed in Chapter 1. Eros's arrow leaves Medea "speechless" as it burns in her heart "like a flame," her heart races with agony, her soul melts with "sweet pain."[51] This mental and emotional disorder is like a disease eating away at Medea's self-control and sense of shame, until she betrays her father and helps Jason steal the fleece. This madness reaches its horrifying climax during her and Jason's escape. Cornered by the pursuing Colchians led by her brother Apsyrtus, Medea, who is "filled in her mind with abominable madness" by "ruthless Eros, the great bane, the great abomination for humans," lures her brother into a fatal trap by promising to help him recover the fleece. Apsyrtus, trusting his sister, comes as a guest and is cut down by Jason "like a bull." The hero then cuts off the corpse's arms and legs and licks up the blood and spits it out three times, a spell to ward off the retribution for such an evil crime.[52] Another version of Apsyrtus's murder is even more brutal—he is a small child taken hostage by Medea and Jason and then killed and dismembered, the pieces thrown into the sea so that the pursuing Aietes, Medea's father, must slow down to recover the pieces. Horrifying enough, Apollonius's description of the murder of Apsyrtus details graphically the human evil and violence directly resulting from the machinations of smiling Aphrodite and her scamp of a son, Eros.

Aphrodite, however, is kept distant from all this disorder. In Homer or the *Homeric Hymn*, her frightening power is expressed *through* her seductive charm and beauty, is indeed one with it. Four centuries later in Apollonius, though, her ambiguity has been somewhat resolved—she is "humanized" and separated from the disastrous effects of her power, her airy domesticity never tainted by the chaos of Medea's suffering and madness.

The Goddess of Gold and Blood

Aphrodite's primal antecedents take us to the heart of her meaning. The severed phallus and the foaming, bloody sperm graphically image the brutal force of procreation, the sheer drive of all life to reproduce and to destroy, "death and undecaying life," the "rage of madness" that like a stormy sea can sweep away the frail orders of the mind and culture. Yet like the sea the golden goddess can smile, can give "gentle gifts," the sweet joys of seduction and sex, the loveliness of desire.[53] For us mortals the trick is to recognize the inhuman power hidden within the alluring smile, to know when the laughter is the cruel gloating of the conqueror. But blinded by our sexual idealism we see only the "Goddess of Love," and so, like Hippolytus, we slight and trivialize Aphrodite's power, forgetting that sooner or later, she will have her revenge, the chariots of the mind and culture wrecked by the monsters of lust.

THREE

Pandora's "Foul Tribe of Women"

Aᴄᴄᴏʀᴅɪɴɢ ᴛᴏ Hᴇꜱɪᴏᴅ, after Prometheus stole fire from the gods and saved the struggling race of men, Zeus set about his revenge. He had Hephaistos fashion an "evil thing" to balance the good of fire—a woman in the "likeness of a bashful maiden." Athena adorned her with "silvery raiment" and a veil and taught her the housewife's arts of needlework and weaving. Aphrodite gave her grace, Persuasion necklaces of gold, the "rich-haired Seasons" a crown of spring flowers. Zeus named her Pandora, "endowed by all," because all the gods had given her gifts. But the lovely maiden was not all that she seemed. For Aphrodite also gave her the power to arouse "cruel longing and limb-devouring cares," and Hermes, god of thievery and deceit, gave her a "bitch's mind and a deceptive character . . . lies and wily words." And this beautiful, duplicitous creature, this "sheer trap," is the ancestress of the "race of women," the "plague to men who eat bread."[1]

Hesiod's account of the creation of Pandora is usually the first charge in the modern indictment of ancient Greek misogyny. Even those who don't subscribe to the feminist scholar Eva Keuls's reductive thesis of an Athenian "phallocracy" in which women were sequestered, starved, and nameless still acknowledge that the Greeks weren't up to our modern enlightened standards in their estimation of women. True, a survey of quotations from Greek literature of our period can quickly generate an anthology of misogyny like the one Chaucer's Jankin enjoyed reading—until the Wife of Bath tore it up. Hesiod says that women are an "evil thing, the partners of painful works." Semonides, late-seventh-century arch-misogynist, goes Hesiod one better and calls women the "greatest evil." "Plague" is another favorite term for women, the disease eating away at a man's life and livelihood. The works of women are "terrible/awesome/strange," according to Aristophanes, and earn them a good beating. And Menander simply curses Prometheus for creating the "foul tribe of women."[2]

Once we have shaken our heads at the benighted Greeks, though, the question we should ask is why—what is it exactly about women that generates this attitude in Greek literature, almost all of which was written by men? The answer can be found, as numerous scholars have argued, in the Greek definition of woman as a procreative force of nature, more passionate, less rational, hence chaotic and destructive unless subjected to the ordering control of the mind and culture. Yet like Pandora and Aphrodite, woman also is sexually alluring, shining with an erotic beauty promising all the joys and pleasures of eros. Like Aphrodite, like the earth itself, she is doubly dangerous, her deceptive loveliness masking her potent power of sexual attraction and fertility.

The Charybdis of Appetite

When we look more closely at specific Greek complaints against women, it is precisely this inability to control their appetites and passions that makes them so explosive. A woman in Aristophanes' *Women at the Thesmophoria*, about the Athenian women's trial of Euripides for his misogynistic female characters, summarizes the standard complaints against women in her brief against the tragedian: Euripides has publicized that they are "adulteresses, man-lusting, wine-bibbers, betrayers, chatterers, unwholesome, the great evil for men." Each of these failings reflects women's inability to control their emotions and appetites. Talking too much, "chattering," as Hesiod too says, is perhaps the most trivial charge, but one that recurs throughout Greek literature. The fourth century comic poet Xenarchus envied the male cricket, since the female was believed to have no voice.[3] Thus the famous praise of silence in a woman. It is their adornment, the philosopher Democritus says, their "grace," according to Sophocles and Aristotle. The Athenian statesman Pericles, in his funeral oration that praised the unique excellence of Athens, said that for women the greatest glory was not to be talked about for good or ill. But before we accept this as evidence for the "silencing of woman's voice," we should remember that according to Plato, Pericles' speech was written by his girlfriend, the famous courtesan Aspasia. And Plutarch records that after the speech Pericles was garlanded by the women of Athens—no trembling recluses they— and one of them, Elpinice, publicly criticized him for spending Greek lives in the subjection of another Greek city.[4]

In the view of Greek men, women can't control their emotions any more than they can their tongues, another sign of the weakness of their powers of reason. Some of these emotions are good, or at least neutral. The philosopher Empedocles asserts they are "much-lamenting," but this could reflect the fact that life gives them many more opportunities for suffering. Medea plays on this stereotype, simpering to Jason that woman is "born for tears." Jason, who can't see past these inherited clichés about women, will watch his family destroyed by a very unfeminine Medea. Medea also exemplifies another female failing, jealousy, what Hector's widow Andromache calls the "disease of Kypris," one worse than man's philandering and linked to woman's worst appetite, her sexuality. Plato shows himself a product of his cultural milieu when he sniffs that women are "petty and cowardly" and that it is in their nature to display emotion, whereas men remain calm and enduring. That is why in his utopia he will not allow his paragons of reason, the philosopher kings who run the state, to play the role of an impassioned woman on stage, lest imitation lead to habit and the men lose their natural manly self-control. And Plato's mentor Socrates, who used to start each day with a prayer thanking the gods he was born a man instead of a woman, sends away his womenfolk when he drinks the hemlock so that his last minutes on earth aren't filled with their annoying emotional displays. Aristotle sums it all up in terms similar to those used by the woman of Aristophanes' play: Women are more compassionate, moved to tears, jealous, querulous, scolding, violent, despondent, less hopeful, void of shame, false of speech, and deceptive. The only good thing about them is they also need less food.[5]

Given the female tendency to irrational excesses from the trivial annoyance of talking too much to the corrosive sickness of jealousy, it follows for the Greeks that women are untrustworthy, for all virtue is a consequence of the mind's control of the disorderly body. In addition, Pandora's legacy, the deceptive external beauty and sexual charm of women, exacerbates their deceiving nature by hiding it behind their erotic allure. "Write their oaths in water," Sophocles says, using a long-lived popular image for the infidelity of women. Euripides' Hippolytus, in his violent misogynistic tirade triggered by the Nurse's attempt to set him up with Phaedra, asks Zeus why he even made this "counterfeit, fraudulent evil," using the adjective for debased coinage.[6] If women are slaves to appetites and passions that render them untrustworthy, no wonder they make men's lives so miserable. Only two days in a woman's life give pleasure to a man, the sixth-century satirist Hipponax wrote, the day you marry her and the day you bury her, a poetic conceit that would last for over a thousand years.[7]

Women, in short, are such a pain to Greek men because they are like Swift's Yahoos, creatures of "nature" and the body, a source of constant disorder resulting from their uncontrollable appetites. And of all those appetites, the most volatile and troublesome is sex. That is the point of Hesiod's Pandora, one lost on some modern commentators. She is not the ancestress of just woman but *sexually attractive* woman, possessing a power that speaks to the irrational in men and that like the earth's is creative. That's why women are not so easily dismissed. Sometimes her sexuality is subordinated to her other appetites, such as greed. "Don't let a rump-adorning woman cheat your mind," Hesiod advises, "she's after your barn." But more often the emphasis is on the volatile sexual appetite of women who are prone to "all-daring shameless eros," as it's put by the Chorus of Aeschylus's *Libation Bearers*, witnesses of Klytaimestra's sexual fury that makes corpses of

Agamemnon and Kassandra. We will see the tragic consequences of female sexual passion when we examine some famous femmes fatales. But comedy, too, frequently exploits this gender stereotype. In Aristophanes' *Lysistrata*, about the sex-strike waged by the Greek women sick of the Peloponnesian War, the sex-hunger of women recurs throughout. It is the absence of their husbands and lovers, as well as the drying up of the supply of "eight-finger-long dildos" imported from Miletus, that as much as the desire for peace motivates the women to join in on Lysistrata's plot. Throughout the play, the difficulty of keeping the women under sexual control provokes Lysistrata to misogynistic insults worthy of Hesiod. When Lysistrata first explains her plan to the gathered women, and each one adamantly refuses, she snorts, "Oh utterly lewd is our whole race," using a word (*pagkatapu-gon*) untranslatable in English but much more graphic and shameful than "lewd," deriving as it does from the experience of passive homosexuals. After the wives barricade themselves on the Acropolis, Lysistrata finds it harder and harder to control the women and keep them from sneaking off to rendezvous with their men. Like a female Semonides she complains, "The deeds of evil women and the female mind" are what depresses her—they're all "fuck-crazy."[8]

In other comedies, too, woman's lack of sexual self-control provides the opportunity for numerous jokes. That woman in the *Women at the Thesmophoria* we met earlier who chastised Euripides for criticizing her sex's unrestrained appetite later admits she's angry not because he *lied*, but because he publicized the *truth*, alerting heretofore dullard husbands to their wives' sexual escapades and machinations. She goes on to describe how she herself betrayed her husband with an old lover after only three days of marriage and confesses as well women's taste for mule drivers and slaves as sexual partners if nothing better is around. That women are consumed with sexual appetite informs the *Women at the Assembly* as well. When the women do get political power by infiltrating the Assembly, they use it to create an egalitarian sexual utopia in which marriage is abolished and all women are "common and free to sleep with men and to bear children to whomever they want." What's more, the old and ugly women will have first dibs on the handsome young men.[9]

These jokes all depend on the assumption that women love sex more than men do—they just hide the fact, as an anonymous poet stated. The renowned prophet Teiresias was able to confirm this observation. Walking in the woods one day, he espied two snakes copulating and struck them with his staff, whereupon he was turned into a woman. Some time later he saw the same two snakes in the same posture and struck them again, turning himself back into a man. So when Zeus and Hera were arguing about who had more fun during sex, the man or the woman, Teiresias was able to prove Zeus right, adding more precisely that the woman had a ten-to-one advantage in sexual pleasure over the man. Hera in her anger blinded Teiresias, but Zeus in recompense made him a prophet. This male belief in the omnivorous sexual appetite of women is used by Herodas, the third-century author of brief "realist" slices of everyday Hellenistic life, to add verisimilitude to his portrait of a couple of gossiping housewives oohing and ah-hing over some nice, smooth leather dildos acquired from a cobbler. The implica-tion is that women are so addicted to masturbation that one of them, Koritto, would screw the old bald cobbler Kerdo just to get her hands on one. Women's obsession with sex apparently made them the experts at lovemaking—all the at-tested authors of sex manuals in ancient Greece have women's names.[10]

An equally male-dominated philosophy is no more immune from cultural gen-der stereotypes than is comedy. In fact, the equation of women with unbridled sexual appetite makes them for philosophers the natural "objective correlative" of vice and passion. Democritus identifies two things a man should not be a slave to—pleasure and women. Prodicus, a Sophist philosopher contemporary with Socrates, told the famous story of the hero Heracles' encounter with Virtue and Vice, two women each directing the hero to a different road, one steep and ardu-ous, the other smooth and broad. Virtue is dressed in white, "her limbs adorned with purity, her eyes with modesty, her figure with self-control." Vice, in contrast, is a tarted-up, voluptuous hussy, her eyes brazen, her dress arranged to reveal her sexual "bloom." She promises Heracles the life of pure sensual indulgence that her appearance represents. Aristotle likewise in a poem calls virtue a "virgin" and else-where uses the decidedly unvirginal Helen as a metaphor for pleasure.[11]

Plato in the *Timaeus* subtly exploits this same connection of woman with irra-tional appetite when he describes the bodily location of the various parts of the soul: Reason is in the head, joined by the neck to the "spirited element" in the chest, which in turn is divided from the appetites located in the belly and genitals by the diaphragm, just like the wall separating the men's quarters from the women's in the Athenian house. Like Plato, Aristotle constantly equates the male with reason, order, and control, and the female with the irrational. Men, he tells us, are by nature meant to rule women just as free men rule slaves and reason rules the irrational. Men and reason are contrasted with and ranged above women and appetite, everything innately inferior and potentially chaotic and destructive if not subjected to control. This was not just the cranky fulmination of a philosopher, or unrepresentative of typical Greek male attitudes. Athenian law invalidated a will if the testator was proved to be under the influence of madness, senility, drugs, dis-ease—or a woman.[12]

Woman's subjection to the power of sex leaves them vulnerable to other disor-derly appetites, especially wine. Sex and wine are, as we have already seen, frequent companions—wine, Aristophanes says, is the "milk of Aphrodite"—and through-out Greek literature the bibulousness and lustfulness of women are intercon-nected and offered as evidence for their bestial natures. Comedy is filled with jokes about tippling women.[13] Aristophanes exploits this stereotype when Lysis-trata and the other Greek women swear the oath sealing their agreement not to have sex with their husbands and lovers. Instead of sacrificing a lamb to ratify the oath, they "butcher" a jar of Thasian wine, one of the choicest in ancient Greece, taking another oath not to mix the wine with water, as was normally the case. And instead of pouring the wine on the ground, as was usual during sacrifice, the women drink it. Finally, after they swear not to engage in sex or, if forced, not "to spread [their] Persian slippers to the roof" nor "stand like a lioness on a cheese-grater" (that is, with head down and rump in the air), they agree that compliance with the oath will earn them a cup filled with wine, and noncompliance one of water.[14] These stereotypes, by the way, were useful not just for getting a laugh on the comic stage. Pseudo-Demosthenes' blackening of the character of Neaira, a prostitute posing as a legitimate Athenian wife, includes the charges of both dypso- and nymphomania, obviously pandering to the prejudices of the all-male jury.[15]

Most important, women's enslavement to sexual appetite meant that their reason was subordinated to their lust, and so we find, as with Eros and Aphrodite and Pandora, repeated emphasis on women's slyness, craftiness, or trickiness, their rational power and its instrument—language—corrupted by Aphrodite, as Euripides put it. Perhaps this is why Democritus considered it a "terrible/strange thing" for a woman to practice argument, for their minds are sharper than a man's in malign thoughts. This prejudice against woman's intelligence surfaces in Hippolytus's tirade against women. "I hate a wise/clever woman. Never may there live in my halls a woman smarter than she ought to be. For Kypris breeds more evil among the wise/clever females. The stupid woman avoids sexual folly because of her feeble mind." Hippolytus assumes that intelligence in a woman will be put to the service of her lust rather than controlling it. In the *Medea*, Kreon bases his decision to banish Medea on the same assumption. "You are wise/clever," he tells her, "and skilled in many evil things. And you are grieved about being robbed of your husband's bed." Anger and sexual dishonor are the passions that will exploit Medea's intelligence—as Medea herself admits. "You are a woman," she tells herself, "and we women, most resourceless for doing good, are the wisest/cleverest contrivers of all manner of evil deeds." Given this belief in the inherent corruptibility of woman's mind by her passions and appetites, it is not surprising that Menander advises against educating a woman, since that would be like making a snake more venomous.[16]

The craftiness of females is imagistically linked to weaving, the woman's identifying activity that symbolizes as well her ambiguity. Spinning and weaving were among the most important household tasks for Greek women, and their importance in Athens was recognized civically in the procession of the *peplophoria*, the presentation of the new *peplos* or robe to Athena that climaxed the Panathenaea, a week-long festival in late July. During the *peplophoria*, a later term for the "procession of the robe," the goddess Athena's *peplos* or robe, woven by citizen-women aided by girls, was carried through the city and deposited in the Parthenon. Spinning and weaving and the loom, then, represent the woman's proper wifely role in the male order of the household and city, her subjection to culture and technology. As we shall see in Chapter 7, Penelope, paragon of wives, is famous for her weaving. Agamemnon in the *Iliad* asserts the complete subjection to him of his concubine by saying she will grow old "sharing my bed and walking to and fro before my loom." The girl's sexual and muscular energy are both exploited by the household for its benefit, the production of children and of cloth. Herodotus and Sophocles both exemplify the topsy-turvy outlandishness of Egyptian gender roles by noting that in Egypt, the women go out and shop and the men stay home and weave. Euripides in the *Bacchae* exploits the weaving metaphor as the image for the social and cultural subjugation of women, a subjugation that in this instance fails horribly. The women of Thebes, filled with the frenzy of Dionysus, have left their households and the city and gathered in the wild to celebrate the rites of the god along with the Asian Maenads who have accompanied him on his migration to Greece from Phrygia. The young prince Pentheus, emblem of the male order of rationalism and the city-state threatened by the irrational disorder fomented by Dionysus, orders his men to capture the Maenads, whom he will either sell or "keep as slaves at the loom." The failure of this ideal of social control is graphically portrayed when Pentheus's god-intoxicated mother Agave—cradling her son's head that she and the other Theban women tore from his body, thinking him an animal—brags that she "quit the loom and the shuttle," liberated herself to become a hunter, shedding her culturally imposed role.[17]

Weaving, then, is the concrete sign of the legitimate wife whose sexual energy is contained by the household. The woman who plans to control her own sexuality, like the Theban Maenads, rejects the activity concomitant with sexual subservience. Likewise when a girl in a poem by the Hellenistic poet Nicharchus makes up her mind to become a prostitute, she burns all her weaving gear to ratify her decision, since prostitute and legitimate wife are mutually exclusive categories. Aristophanes also links weaving to the sexual role of women. In the *Birds*, Euripides rejects Athena as the patron goddess of the utopian city of Cloudcuckooland, for "how could a state be well-ordered, when a god born a female stands fully armed, and Cleisthenes holds a spindle?" Cleisthenes was a notorious effeminate often accused of passive sodomy. Aristophanes' joke depends on the assumption that being penetrated by men and weaving are both signs of the sexual subordination of women to the order of the city.[18]

But weaving can also signify woman's craftiness, her weaving of plots, her subjection of the mind's power to the demands of the irrational. The guileful Pandora, remember, is given the skill of weaving. Her most famous "daughter," the sexual adventuress Helen, whiles away the time at Troy weaving a tapestry depicting the battles of the Greeks and Trojans caused by her infidelity. Aeschylus in the *Oresteia* plays on the ambiguity of weaving in his development of Klytaimestra, who conceals her murderous rage behind the guise of the good wife. She destroys her husband Agamemnon with the aid of two woven fabrics. One is the rich crimson carpets she orders strewn in his path, inviting him to an act of arrogance. "Thought never conquered by sleep" will see to the rest, she goes on, linking her malign mind and its "woven" plot to the carpets, for "the rest" is the murder of her husband. Likewise with the robe in which she entangles Agamemnon in his bath before she hacks him to death, a "boundless net," a "rich evil of a robe." In the case of the prototypical bad wife, weaving signifies not her proper wifely role but its subversion by passion, leading ultimately to the worst crime of the wife, the murder of her husband. Greek myth is full of femmes fatales linked to weaving and plotting, and often some sort of sexual failing or jealousy fuels the woman's trickiness, her deceptive wiles that destroy her man. Like Sappho's Aphrodite, women are "guile/trap-weavers."[19]

In the mind of the Greek male, women are dangerous and hence frightening because of their greater subjection to the natural appetites, especially sex, that define *all* humans and that must be controlled in order for all of us to exist *as* humans. Ultimately, what disturbs men about women is what disturbs men about *themselves*—the whirlpool of the irrational threatening to overwhelm and sink the craft of the mind. To dismiss these attitudes as "sexist" or "misogynist" is to purchase a cheap moral superiority at the expense of a deeper understanding of the Greek exploration of human identity and its defining contradictions.

The Daughters of Earth and Blood

All these attributes of women—their emotionalism, unbridled sexual appetite, tendency to appetitive excess, treachery, and trickiness—mean that they are closer than the male to the chaotic forces of nature, to the earth and the world of beasts. As such they are more in tune with the forces and cycles of the natural world. "When the artichoke blossoms, and the chirping cicada sits in a tree, pouring down often his shrill song from under his wings in the season of toilsome heat, then goats are fattest and wine the best, and women are most wanton, but men most feeble, for the Dog-Star scorches the head and knees." Women "blossom" sexually when nature does, but that energy is specifically destructive, particularly for men, whose "mind" and vitality are withered by both a malign nature and the sexual appetite of woman. This same link between nature and the sexual woman is clear from another passage of Hesiod that describes the "tender virgin," ignorant of the "works of Aphrodite," who stays indoors with her mother, safe from the north wind that curves the old man like a wheel. The girl innocent of sexuality is divorced from nature's destructiveness, protected by the male order of the household.[20]

A more specific connection of women to nature results from associating them with various animals. This can be as simple as calling them a beast—no beast is more shameful than a woman, the fifth-century comic poet Alexis writes, emphasizing that the failure to control appetite is what qualifies one for bestial status. Slang terms and imagery for female sexuality and genitalia likewise diminish women's humanity by presuming the animality of their indiscriminate sexual appetites. Pigs especially are extensively linked to women in Greek culture from comedy to ritual, partly because of their fecundity, but also because they are sexually wild—according to Aristotle, a sow in heat will even attack humans. A fragment of the fifth-century comic poet Hermippus calls a promiscuous woman a sow. "Sow" and "piggy" are comic favorites for denoting women's genitals, "piggy" usually denoting the hairless pudenda of younger girls, "sow" those of older women. In the *Lysistrata*, the Chorus of old women attacked by the Chorus of old men threaten to "loose [their] sows," that is, their mature "cunts," at their enemies. And in the *Acharnians* Aristophanes develops an extended sequence of double entendres arising out of the tricky Megarian's attempts to sell his daughters for sex by advertising them as "mystery piggies" who will make "most beautiful porkers" for sacrificing to Aphrodite. As well as commenting on the "inhuman" quality of female sexuality, this association of pigs with women points as well to the ambiguity of woman's eros, a force of procreation that must be "domesticated" to serve the household and the state. Hence the role of pigs in important civic religious rites particularly important to women, such as the Thesmophoria (see Chapter 6).[21]

To the late-seventh-century satirist Semonides, though, the failings of women no matter how "domesticated" are all expressions of their bestial appetites and passions, and so in his poem cataloguing the different kinds of destructive female, each is linked to an animal or other natural element. The sow-woman is fat and dirty, "sitting on the dung heap." The vixen is moody and inconsistent. The bitch is a gossip and a chatterer that even a beating can't control. The earth-woman is a stupid, lazy glutton; the sea-woman is given to emotional extremes, laughing and happy one day, raging like a bitch with puppies the next. The she-ass is lazy, gluttonous, and welcomes any sort of companion to her bed. The ferret is malicious and "crazy for sex," sickening the man she sleeps with. The aristocratic mare is finicky, proud, and expensive, and the ape-woman wily, shameless, and vicious. Even in summary form, the various types of woman are all defined by their uncontrollable appetites and emotional instability. What's more, Semonides specifically makes a point of their disorderly minds that can't control their passions and appetites. His first line asserts that Zeus made "the female mind apart," different from man's. So women are either stupid, like the earth-woman who doesn't know bad from good; or duplicitous, like the vixen that calls the bad good and the good bad; or confused, like the sea-woman who thinks with two minds.[22]

All these feminine failings, then, are consequences of their bestial passions and weak minds. And men are subjected to this "unbreakable fetter" because of woman's sexual power—even the woman who seems to have self-control is constantly betraying her husband, who "gapes" after her to the amusement of his neighbors. The Chorus of the *Women at the Thesmophoria* allude to their erotic power when they mock the misogyny of men by asking, "If we truly are an evil thing, why do you marry us?" Their subsequent elaboration detailing their sexual hold over their husbands, who agonize over their whereabouts and sexual behavior, provides the answer—it is their sexual attractiveness that draw men to them despite all the trouble they cause. In Semonides the primacy of sexuality as the source of woman's disorder is made clear by the one creature that symbolizes the good woman, the bee. As well as working hard and producing, as Swift said, "sweetness and light," the bee was also believed to be asexual. Aristotle reported the theory that bees chastely fetched their young from flowers or reeds or the olive. Consequently, bees have an intense disgust for sexual matters. The late-second-century A.D. naturalist Aelian says that a bee will attack a man who has recently come from "excessive intercourse," and Plutarch advises the beekeeper to be faithful to his wife, or he will have to face the anger of the bees. Semonides' bee-woman, then, loves her husband, bears children, and avoids the sexual gossip of other women. Her sexuality has been completely subordinated to the household for which she toils like a bee, and this in turn allows her other appetites and passions to be kept in check.[23]

Greek men didn't have to look far to figure out why women were more bestial and less rational than they, why female sexuality was so problematic. Women's bodies and their functions appear to be more closely linked than do men's to the processes of nature. The particular prevalence of the mysterious vital fluid, blood, in women's critical life-changes—menarche, defloration, menstruation, and parturition—linked them to the chaotic messy realm of primal forces, of formless fluids that threaten to overwhelm the order of the mind, the same lack of a dependable discriminating and identifying form embodied in a female monster like the Empusa, constantly changing its shape. These fluids make the woman moist and cold, as pseudo-Aristotle claims, whereas men are hot and dry. And this moisture specifically "hinders intelligence," according to the fifth-century philosopher Diogenes of Apollonia. The mental weakness of woman is directly linked to the fluids, all sexually related, that throughout her life remind men of her similarity to the mysterious forces of nature.[24]

Menstrual blood is particularly disturbing and accounts for Aristophanes' disgust with a certain Ariphrades, whom Aristophanes fingers as the inventor of cunnilingus: "For he outrages his own tongue with shameful pleasures, in the brothels licking up the spat-out dew, fouling his mustache, stirring up the scabs." As that last distasteful image suggests, menstrual blood is what bothers Aristophanes so much about cunnilingus. As with many cultures worldwide, though, menstrual blood isn't just disgusting to men, but also is given malign powers due to its primal nature—in the ancient world it was believed that it could cloud a metal mirror, dull the edge of steel and the gleam of ivory, rust bronze and iron, destroy beehives, and drive dogs mad. The dark powers of nature, directed specifically against artifacts of culture or domesticated creatures, are somehow contained in menstruation, its flow linked to the mysterious moon.[25]

Superstition wasn't the only place menstrual blood was given destructive powers. The ancient medical writers attribute a whole host of psychological and physiological disorders to the inadequate discharge of menstrual blood, particularly in virgins or women with abnormally narrowed cervixes. When the menses is backed up and can't flow out of the vagina, it flows backwards out of the womb into the heart and mind (the latter located by the Greeks in the chest), thus leading to insanity. The girl can also become fearful, murderous, or suicidal. We have here a more "scientific" explanation for woman's weak intellect—its vulnerability to her reproductive organs and their mysterious processes. The ancient cure for these maladies? Sex and pregnancy, the latter stopping menstruation and its attendant maladies, as well as subjecting the woman and her volatile organs to the social order of marriage.[26]

This dependence of female character and behavior on the woman's reproductive organs reaches perhaps its most bizarre form in the infamous "wandering womb," the ultimate source of our word "hysteria," literally "wombiness." Plato describes this malady in the *Timaeus*. The womb, the "animal" in the woman, is desirous of procreation, but if it does not conceive, it gets angry and wanders throughout the body, blocking the air passages and causing all sorts of diseases. According to Hippocrates, this peripatetic womb can cause suffocation, torpor, and foaming of the mouth if it moves toward the head and must be lured back to its proper place with aromatic vaginal suppositories—that is, symbolic intercourse.[27]

Given that woman is disturbingly close to the chaotic forces of nature, subject to her mysterious reproductive processes, vulnerable to the irrational, particularly eros, it makes sense that men see women as inferior and themselves as superior because they are not *as* subjected to nature. If women are more than half-natural, men are more than half-cultural, that is, more human. Thus women are, as Aristotle put it, "as it were mutilated," a "departure from the type," the passive earthlike "matter" in which the active male "form" engenders life. And if men are naturally superior, then it follows that they should rule, and that rule by women is a perverse reversal of the natural order of things, the "ultimate outrage," as Democritus put it.[28] Sophocles in the *Antigone*, about the maid Antigone's refusal to obey her uncle Kreon's order not to bury her brother Polyneices, makes this traditional aversion to female authority an expression of Kreon's insecurity and weakness. The tyrant defines masculinity as the power to enforce authority: If Antigone gets away with flouting his rule, Kreon reasons, "I am not the man, but she is the man." As the girl persists in her resistance, publicly throwing it in Kreon's teeth, he explodes as he condemns her to death, "No woman will rule me while I am alive." Sophocles, of course, is laying bare the inadequacy of such sex-role stereotypes, since it is *Kreon's* passionate anger and lack of self-control—feminine failings that presumably justify the exclusion of women from political authority—that bring about his own arrogant blindness to what is right, causing the deaths of his son and his wife as well as Antigone. But Kreon, remember, is a *turannos*, a type of political male defined by his womanlike readiness to indulge his appetites.[29]

What happens when women do rule, whether in comedy, history, or myth, is a degeneration of the political order that threatens the basis of human identity itself. We have mentioned already Aristophanes' *Women at the Assembly*, where the Athenian wives seize control of the Assembly and refashion the state into an egalitarian sexual utopia, in which sex and marriage serve the appetites of women rather than the social order. Aristotle apparently follows the same logic in the *Politics* when discussing Sparta. The relatively greater freedom allowed to Spartan women has been "harmful" to the state, for they "live luxuriously and intemperately in regard to all manner of licentiousness," leading to a greater regard for wealth than was good for the state.[30]

The myth of the Amazons, though, expresses the dire effects thought to result from reversing the natural order of things and letting women rule. Everything about Amazonian life reverses the Greek social and cultural order: Rather than living in a household with men, Amazons live outside without men; rather than spinning and weaving at home, they wear armor and fight, cutting off one breast to facilitate drawing the bow, weapon of effeminacy and cowardice, hence the name "Amazon," "breastless"; rather than identifying offspring through the father, they don't recognize paternity at all; and rather than conceiving legitimate children at home, they couple randomly in the mountains, like animals. In short, they represent barbarism and savagery, the absence of the defining Greek orders that make human identity possible and separate it from beasts. Thus the defeat of the Amazons, whether in battle or by having one sexually conquered by a Greek hero, was a popular theme for sculpture and painting as well as literature. The mythic founder of Athens, Theseus, kidnaps the Amazon queen Antiope (or Hippolyte). The Amazons retaliate by invading Attica and besieging the Acropolis, sacrificing to Ares on the nearby hill, henceforth called the Areopagos or "hill of Ares." In other versions the queen falls in love with Theseus and fights by his side when the Amazons attack to punish her for betraying their laws. Either way, they are defeated, the Greek men reinforcing their sexual and military superiority over these outlandish females. In fact, every Greek hero—Heracles, Achilles, Bellerophontes—has his "Amazonomachy" or "battle with the Amazons," for the defeat of the Amazons represents the triumph of Greek civilization, embodied in these heroes, over monstrous alternatives.[31]

The women of Lemnos are another society of women without men, for the women murdered all the males on the island in a fit of jealousy over some Thracian concubines, the innocent killed with the guilty so they couldn't take vengeance. But despite their finding it easier to plow and wear armor than to perform their household tasks—that is, despite their preference for the man's role—they are terrified by the fear of avengers from Thrace and are advised by an old woman that without husbands they will die off in one generation and that without children to tend them they will find old age unbearable. So they mate with the Argonauts on their way to Colchis and try to persuade them to stay with them and be their husbands. The point is not just that women are emotionally volatile, but that a society without men is impossible, for human life is defined by marriage and the household, where legitimate children are born and reared. The subordination of women to men is part of a larger social order in which human sexuality is controlled and exploited, men's as well as women's. After all, it is the Lemnian *men* whose sexual appetites bring on their destruction. Still, the plot depends on an assumption of chaotic female sexuality that must be controlled by the superior male. Hence "Lemnian" passes into Greek as an adjective describing crimes of particular heinousness. The attack on the husband is an attack on culture and ultimately on human identity itself.[32]

Given this persistent male characterization of women as always potentially destructive because of their greater subjection to nature and the irrational, it is no surprise that Greek literature is filled with femmes who are literally fatales, women charged with a sexual power akin to the primal forces of nature. In the following sections we will look at the most famous from Hesiod and Homer to fifth-century tragedy and see how their stories revolve around just this conception of woman as force of nature always threatening to destroy the cultural orders of household and city.

The Mother of Them All

We have already seen that Pandora is the mythic progenitor of destructive woman, occupying in the Greek male mind the place that Eve does in the Judeo-Christian—the destroyer of paradise and source of all the evils afflicting men in a harsh natural world. But Pandora must be understood not just as first woman but in the larger context of what characterizes *all* human life: a double existence comprising the bestial passions and natural necessities, on the one hand, and the cultural practices that try to control and make sense of those forces on the other. Women, especially sexually attractive women, are an intensified expression of this universal ambiguity, their reproductive power close to the primal processes of nature, their erotic allure attractive yet duplicitous. Both powers must be subordinated to marriage and the household so that children can be born who will carry the society into the next generation. But women always remain ambiguous and dangerous, their beautiful exterior hiding their volatile sexual power.

A closer look at Hesiod's details of Pandora's creation reveals that she is part of a hostile natural world against which men must struggle to exist. The famous story of Pandora's jar—only later a box—makes the first woman the cause of nature's hostility to humans. When Zeus delivered Pandora to Prometheus's thick-headed brother Epimetheus ("Hindsight"), she came with a jar filled with "countless evils." The first thing she did, of course, was to take the lid off the jar and release these miseries and banes. Before this men had lived "free from evils and harsh labor and grievous diseases." This is the Golden Age Hesiod goes on to describe, a time defined by a benevolent and benign nature, when men lived without technology and culture. But the arrival of Pandora brings this Edenic life to an end. Now is the Iron Age, when nature is harsh and hostile and man must use technology to survive. Women, then, are like nature, their sexual beauty reminiscent of the lost paradise whose transient beauty returns each spring, but their passions destructive like nature's inhuman forces, necessitating the "technology" of marriage in order to control them.[33]

Hesiod's description of Pandora confirms this characterization of her. She is fashioned from earth and water, nature's primal stuff. Athena adorns her head with garlands made from the "flowers of fresh-budding plants" and with a golden crown on which are engraved "wild creatures, as many as the earth and sea nurture." But this thing of nature linked to earth and water, flowers and wild animals, is given the "beautiful shape of a maiden" and the "appearance of a bashful maid," along with the grace and weaving skills bestowed on her by Aphrodite and Athena. Her beauty, however, is deceiving, like the beauty of nature, for it is explicitly sexual, the power to arouse "cruel longing and limb-devouring cares," the destructive force of eros permeating the cosmos. Hence the human mind within her is subordinated to passion—Hermes puts in Pandora "lies and wily words and a thievish character." As is the case with Aphrodite, Eros, and women in general, Pandora's mind is corrupted by the demands of appetite. And that ultimately is what makes Pandora and women and sex so dangerous—all are not just evil but, like Pandora, a *beautiful* evil, a "sheer snare/trap" whose promise of joy and pleasure, whose lovely human appearance conceal a force of nature volatile and chaotic.[34]

Two more of Hesiod's details about Pandora confirm her function as a particularly intense female example of that uneasy conjunction of culture and nature that defines human existence and identity. The first is the "bitch mind" that Hermes gives her. Like eros, dogs represent the uneasy union of the natural world with human culture. They are the domestic beasts most intimate with human life, capable of loyal service, like the ancient Argos, the faithful hound of Odysseus lying forlorn and flearidden on the dung heap, using his last ounce of life to wag his tail when he recognizes the hero beneath his beggar's rags. But they also represent unbridled appetite, particularly the female that mates frequently and indiscriminately—the dog is, as the fourth-century historian Clearchus puts it, "all-devouring." Hence words derived from "dog" signify a "shamelessness" resulting from a failure to control appetite. Dogs are linked with scavenging birds as devourers of corpses, as in the common Homeric formula describing the unburied dead as "a feast for dogs and birds." Priam, trying to convince his son Hector to avoid battle with Achilles by retreating inside the walls of Troy, signifies the horror of the city's destruction and his own death by describing the dogs nourished at his table shamelessly tearing and devouring his head and chin and genitals. Likening someone to a bitch or dog thus indicates not only indiscriminate appetite but a betrayal of the social norms and controls that make human community possible. In the *Odyssey*, the wicked maid Melantho is called "bitch-faced" to denote her shamelessness about betraying her household by sleeping with the suitor Eurymachus. As we shall soon see, this same epithet is a favorite for signifying Helen's and Klytaimestra's sex-linked crimes. When used of Pandora and women it communicates the destructiveness of a sexuality that must be brought into the house, where it remains a constant threat.[35]

The other detail of the myth reinforcing Pandora's ambiguity is the role of fire in her story. Pandora is specifically an evil sent by Zeus "in the place of fire" stolen by Prometheus for the benefit of humans. Fire makes human civilization possible, for it is the natural energy source the mind exploits to work metal, cook food, and worship the gods, all the things animals don't do. But fire too is destructive unless handled properly, and as we saw in Chapter 1 it is a favorite metaphor for the destructive potential of eros. Fire, though, is more manageable than women, much simpler than the complex deceptive creature with the "voice and force of a human being." So Zeus balances one natural energy source with another, the female whose sexuality is more volatile and deceptive than fire, but ultimately just as necessary.[36]

That female sexuality and fecundity are central to Hesiod's misogyny is clear from his specific complaints about "Pandora's daughters." They "dwell as a plague among men, companions in wealth, not in destructive poverty," the drones that feed off the work of others. But women are also necessary, for from their wombs come the sons who will tend the father in his "deadly old age." The malevolent Iron Age means that men are vulnerable when old, prey to other men and a hostile nature and ultimately to death. Sons protect the father and bury his body, as well as inheriting his property, this transference of name and property being the only immortality humans can hope for. Now we see another dimension to Pandora's "jar"—it is the woman's womb from which swarm the evils of female eros. But clinging beneath the rim of the jar is "expectation," the hope for the future embodied in the next generation who will carry on the father's identity.[37]

The story of Pandora, then, is to the Greeks the story of human existence. The harsh natural world in which they lived meant that they had to work and endure suffering, their labor and pain mitigated by both the technologies fueled by fire and the "technology" of marriage, the order that harnesses woman's procreative power but that always remains vulnerable to the disorder lurking beneath the glittering veil of woman's erotic beauty. For us modern Westerners, energy is easily acquired with the flip of a switch or the turn of a key, and woman's procreative power has been subjected to the chemical and technological control of science. No wonder nature has been reduced to pleasant scenery or an object of sentimental compassion, no wonder *our* Pandoras have been trivialized into trophy-consorts or whining victims, their natural sexual power either camouflaged by sexual idealism or turned into a commodity.

The "Memorial of Disasters"

More so perhaps than even Pandora, Helen represents the essential ambiguity of woman and the sexual beauty divinely embodied in her patroness Aphrodite, and equally as destructive as hers. So it is that Byron calls her "the Greek Eve," the source of masculine Greece's "fall." Like Aphrodite's, like Pandora's, Helen's sexual beauty is preternaturally powerful. Yet that same beauty is the source of myriad calamities, the violence and bloodshed of Troy whose "topless towers" she burned. Helen is the best mythic example not just of the destructiveness of female eros, the chaos of nature and passion, but of its *attractive* power, its ability to enslave men and drive them to overthrow the orders they create to survive in a world riven with explosive natural energies. Thus Semonides sums up his tirade against women, "the greatest evil," by making Helen, not Pandora, the origin of the "bond of an unbreakable shackle" first imposed on men when the heroes died fighting for a woman, the creature most intimate and most necessary to men. Helen, woman, is indeed, as the late-fifth-century Sophist Gorgias put it, the "memorial of disasters."[38]

The ambiguity of female sexual beauty that Helen represents is apparent in her origins, like Aphrodite's a confusion of the divine and elemental, the cosmic order embodied in Zeus coupling with the chaos of the natural world. Homer first calls her "daughter of Zeus," the only mortal so named, a lineage that implies certain privileges and indulgences, as we will see in Chapter 7. That blue-chip pedigree no doubt explains Menelaus's forgiveness of his straying wife—as he brags to a visiting Telemachus, he knows from the shape-shifter Proteus that he will not die but live forever in the Elysian Fields, the hero's heaven, because he had married Helen and so was the son-in-law of Zeus. Her mother is the mortal Leda, whom Zeus raped in the form of a swan, and who hatched Helen out of a hyacinth-colored egg that according to Pausanias could still be seen at Sparta. This bestial detail of Helen's birth links her to the natural world, as does another variation of her origins that makes her the daughter of a "daughter of Ocean," and hence a relative of sorts to Aphrodite. Still another variation makes Helen the daughter of Nemesis, who personifies the force of divine retribution and vengeance. Nemesis hounds and destroys those whose excessive passion drives them beyond the cosmic limits of human action. Zeus pursued Nemesis in the form of a swan or a goose, and the goddess turned into a fish and other "dread beasts" in order to escape him, for she was ashamed of lying in love with her own father. All of these various antecedents for Helen locate her and her sexual beauty in the realm of violent inhuman forces, whether bestial or divine, that impinge on mortal lives, forces either chaotic or serving some cosmic purpose to which the sufferings of humans, those "generations of leaves," are of little or no account.[39]

Such a lineage also throws light on the power of Helen. She is not just the "most beautiful woman in the world"—she is the most *sexually* beautiful woman in the world, an erotic as well as aesthetic force of awesome, godlike power. We saw earlier the old men of Troy still stunned by her beauty "strangely like a god's to look on." A fragment of the *Eoiae*, an Archaic poem celebrating women who married gods, specifically says her beauty was that of "golden Aphrodite," her eyes the eyes of the Graces, Aphrodite's attendants. No wonder, then, that all the Greek heroes, "evil-minded, marriage-mad," lusted to marry her, and all promised to kill one another if they didn't get to. Fearing a violent abduction on the part of one or more of her disappointed suitors that would follow his choice, Helen's "father" Tyndareus made them all swear an oath (in one tradition over a dismembered horse), that they would collectively punish the man who carried her off by force. That oath is why, of course, they all end up at Troy, "summoned to arms" by Helen's beauty.[40]

After Troy is destroyed and Helen recovered, ten years have not diminished the force of that beauty a bit. When Menelaus first encounters his wayward wife, he intends to kill her. In Euripides' *Trojan Women*, set in the direct aftermath of the sack of the city, Helen is dragged out and handed over to her angry husband, who claims he will stone her when they return to Greece: "The evil woman will evilly die," he claims, as a lesson to other women to be chaste. In another tradition, Menelaus intends to kill her on the spot but drops his sword when he catches a glimpse of her naked breasts.[41] Ibycus places this scene appropriately enough in the temple of Aphrodite to which Helen had fled for refuge during the fight for the city. Stesichorus's variation has all the Greek soldiers about to stone her when they are stricken by her incredible loveliness. Perhaps the failure of "swords" and "stones" has some phallic or testicular significance, the overpowering of man's sexual violence by Helen's erotic beauty. That's certainly the point of a joke in Euripides' satyr play the *Cyclops*, where a satyr asks Odysseus if all the Greeks didn't "pierce"—the verb can mean "stab" or "fuck"—Helen since she had already screwed so many men.[42]

Like Pandora's, Helen's beauty is a deceptive veil for the power of her sexuality, destructive because it is uncontrollable by men. She must have been adept at lovemaking, for her maid Astyanassa—on whom, apparently, nothing was lost—would later be reputed the inventor of sex manuals, including one entitled *On the Postures for Intercourse*. Helen's promiscuity, her inability to be satisfied with one man, was said to result from Aphrodite's anger, either because Helen's father Tyndareus neglected the goddess once while sacrificing, or because the goddess was jealous of the beauty of his three daughters, Helen, Klytaimestra, and Timandra. Either way, Aphrodite saw to it that Tyndareus's daughters were "twice-wed and thrice-wed and husband deserters," Helen's three husbands being the king of Sparta, Menelaus; the Trojan prince Paris; and his brother Deiphobus, whom she married after Paris's death. No wonder Tyndareus was said to have dedicated a wish-fulfilling statue of a fettered Aphrodite, and in Euripides' *Orestes* won't even speak about his daughter, whom he calls Menelaus's "evil wife."[43] Helen's shameless hunger for men makes "bitch" imagery a favorite for describing her. Twice in Homer she calls herself "bitch-faced" or a "bitch," once adding the adjective "evil-plotting," highlighting the link of woman's deviousness to her uncontrollable sexual appetite, the same connection implied by Pandora's "bitch's mind."[44]

But Helen's three husbands aren't the whole story of her man-hunger. She is, as the Hellenistic poet Lycophron puts it in his bizarre poem recording Kassandra's unheeded prophecies, the "five-times-married possessed woman," the latter adjective one typically used of a Bacchant, the devotee of Dionysus. As well as being carried off by Paris, she was first stolen by the ubiquitously randy Theseus—when she was at the tender age of seven, according to the historian Hellanikos.[45] Theseus was fifty at the time and made off with the girl while she was dancing in the temple of the virgin goddess Artemis. Another tradition has Theseus preserve the girl's virginity—presumably she's a bit older—by having intercourse with her anally, thus making Helen a coinventor of sodomy. But this last detail may just reflect the traditional association of Sparta with buggery, for Spartan young men reputedly enjoyed their girlfriends this way before marriage, as well as being saturated in a martial culture of pederasty. At any rate, Helen's precocious sexual beauty touches off a war, just as it does later when she is mature. Her famous brothers, Castor and Polydeuces, invaded Attica and sacked Athens and the nearby village of Aphidnae, kidnapping Theseus's mother. Even in girlhood, Helen's sexuality is the instigator of violence and destruction.[46]

Theseus makes four "husbands," so who's number five? Achilles, best of the Achaeans, was too young to woo Helen, otherwise she would have chosen him. After he grows up and comes to Troy, though, Aphrodite and Achilles' mother Thetis get the two together, according to the *Cypria*. Perhaps this is why Achilles stays on at Troy after he withdraws from the fighting to avenge himself on Agamemnon's insult—Lycophron tells us that Helen made Achilles pine away, "whirled in his dreams by her perfect body." Though they could meet only once in life, Helen and Achilles spend eternity together, according to Pausanias, living together on the White Island at the mouth of the Danube, the epitome of martial power wed for eternity to the epitome of sexual.[47]

By this point we begin to notice a strong resemblance between Aphrodite and Helen—in their mixed origins, their "golden" beauty, their adultery. Helen eventually becomes a tutelary deity for sailors, like Aphrodite. Even Helen's afterlife marriage to the warrior Achilles parallels Aphrodite's affair with the war-god Ares. Clearly part of Helen's meaning resides in her embodiment, on the human level, of the sexual power Aphrodite represents on the cosmic. But Helen is also, like Pandora, representative woman, as Semonides recognizes when he makes her the origin of female depravity. Hence she shares many of the negative characteristics we have seen attributed to the female "tribe," particularly those associated with woman's subjection to eros. Like all women, she obviously cannot control her sexual appetite, which overcomes her consciousness of shame, as we saw in her confrontation with Aphrodite in the *Iliad*. Sappho too, though more sympathetic to the power of erotic beauty, uses Helen as the best example of how sexual attraction confers on the loved one an obsessive value to the detriment of all other obligations, including household and family: "For she who far outstripped all humans in beauty, Helen, leaving behind the best of all husbands sailed off to Troy, not at all mindful of her child and her dear parents." She herself, both during the war in Troy and back in Sparta and reconciled to Menelaus, calls her behavior a case of *atê*, that "blind sin" born of excess and frequently linked to eros.[48]

Since her mind is controlled by her sexual appetite, Helen displays all the trickiness and duplicity of the female, the "lies and wily words" Hermes gives to Pandora. Homer brings out this aspect of her character in the *Odyssey*, when Odysseus's son Telemachus visits Helen and Menelaus in his search for information about his father. The couple seem happily reconciled as they entertain the youth. After some tearful reminiscences and a glass of wine doctored by Helen with a mood-altering drug, she tells a story about Odysseus, about how he disguised himself as a beggar and came to Troy to spy. Helen says she alone recognized Odysseus, and swore not to expose him. Odysseus revealed to her the plans of the Greeks, then escaped back to the ships, slaying many Trojans on the way. But Helen was glad, for she "regretted the blind folly [*atên*] that Aphrodite" had given her, forcing her to abandon her home and husband.[49]

Helen's story, while praising Odysseus for Telemachus's benefit, manages to protest as well her own loyalty to Menelaus and the Greeks, laying the blame for her folly on Aphrodite. But Menelaus will not let her get away with her revisionist history. He tells another story, one from the last night of the war, when the Trojans had dragged the wooden horse filled with Greek warriors into the city. Visiting the horse with her new husband Deiphobus, Helen three times circled the horse, "feeling the hollow ambush," and she named aloud all the Greek chieftains, "likening [her] voice to the wives of all the Argives." Menelaus and Diomedes and Anticlus started to answer back, but Odysseus, himself the master of trickery, held them back, closing the mouth of Anticlus with his hand. Telemachus tactfully changes the subject, and we hear no more from Helen. Menelaus has subtly exposed his wife's clever attempt to resolve the ambiguity of her behavior in Troy.[50]

Euripides too makes this clever rationalization part of his Helen's character in the *Trojan Women*. Dragged before Menelaus, who as we saw earlier is ready to kill her on the spot, Helen spins out a speech blaming everybody except herself for her behavior. First Hecuba, Paris's mother, is to blame for birthing him. Then Priam is at fault for not killing the infant even though Hecuba had dreamed that she bore a torch that would burn Troy. Aphrodite, of course, is indicted for making Helen the bribe inducing Paris to choose Aphrodite as the recipient of the Golden Apple—a good thing, too, since if he had chosen Athena, his reward would have been the lordship of Asia over Greece. Helen's adultery kept Greece free. And, in an ancient precursor of "blaming the victim," she chides Menelaus for sailing off to Crete when Paris was a guest at Sparta, finishing up with the claim that many times she had tried to escape. The captive Trojan women who overhear this performance, eager to see the cause of their misery destroyed, pronounce this speech a *deinon* thing, "terrible/clever/strange," the adjective consistently used during the late fifth century to describe the deceptive eloquence and cleverness of Sophistic rhetoric, the power to distort the truth and make "the worse argument the better."[51]

With her sexual beauty, her uncontrolled appetite, her deviousness, and her dangerous ambiguity, Helen is an exaggerated example of all women, like the Pandora whom she resembles. But her similarity to Aphrodite shows that she is as well a conduit for the cosmic sexual force, the link between women and Aphrodite that establishes a continuum of destructive female sexuality. And we all know just how destructive Helen's beauty was, if only from Marlowe's lines, "Was this the face that launched a thousand ships, / And burnt the topless towers of Ilium?" Throughout Greek literature Helen is made the cause of Troy's destruction. She "loosed the knees of many men," Odysseus's swineherd Eumaios says, the image capturing both the attractiveness and destructiveness of her sexual beauty. Alcaeus, the early-sixth-century poet from Lesbos, sings that "bitter grief" came to Priam and his sons from Helen's "evil deeds." Aeschylus creates a memorable pun capturing her power to destroy. Exploiting the similarity in the sounds of "Helen" and a word that means "destroy," he says that she was "Hell on ships, hell on men, hell on the city." Not only do Greek and Trojan soldiers die because of her, but Iphigeneia—in some traditions her own daughter—is sacrificed for a wind to Troy. Her own mother, Leda, and her brothers Castor and Polydeuces commit suicide out of shame for her sexual sin. And the Greeks do not like her any more than do the Trojans. In Euripides' version of Orestes' murder of his mother and her lover, Orestes' accomplice Pylades wants to kill Helen too, in vengeance for all the Greeks "whose fathers she killed, whose children she destroyed, whose brides she made widowed of their yoke-mates." From Helen and Paris's lovemaking the violence, suffering, and bloodshed unfold geometrically and exponentially.[52]

Obviously, Helen is seen as the direct cause of the manifold sufferings brought about by the Trojan War. Hence just as Eros and Aphrodite are linked to death and violence, so too is this exemplar of female sexual beauty, as can be seen in the variety of negative epithets and images ascribed to her, a vocabulary of intense disgust and horror surprising to us with our idealized vision of the "most beautiful woman in the world." In Homer she is "dreadful/loathsome/hateful," a word etymologically related to the name Styx, the famous underworld river; "chilling/horrible," a word used elsewhere of war; "making one shudder," an adjective also used of a lion. Later she is called a "plague," "bitter and ill-starred," "to be spat upon," "hated," "without justice, a betrayer, faithless, godless," "hated by the gods," a "she-dragon," and a "viper."[53] Most of these epithets are from Euripides' Trojan plays and reflect the anger of the Trojan War's victims. Yet many of these same epithets we saw were given to Eros and Aphrodite as well and reflect the seriousness with which the force of sexuality is taken, particularly the duplicitous erotic beauty of woman, containing beneath its shimmering surface the primal inhuman powers of nature. One cannot imagine giving such violent epithets to Monroe, Loren, Bardot, our modern Helens who usually arrive wrapped in the gauze of our sexual idealism, promising desire and joy but never exacting the price Helen inflicted on the Greeks.

Helen, then, concentrates and intensifies all the disastrous, violent consequences of eros, particularly as this force is embodied in women, who to the Greeks have even less of the intellectual control over passion that in men is so fragile and tenuous. She is the focal point for all that is seductive and destructive in Eros, Aphrodite, woman, and nature, and this I think accounts for her power as a literary figure: In her converge all the problematic forces of *human* existence with which both male and female are riven. Helen's larger significance beyond the issue of woman's eros can be seen in the characterization of her partner in crime, Paris, he of the effeminate curls and unheroic bow, who is given many of the same epithets. He, like Helen, is hated—his own brother Hector berates him in terms evocative of Helen's trickiness and duplicitous beauty and uncontrolled passion: "Evil Paris, most noble in appearance, woman-mad, beguiler, would that you were unborn and had died unwed." He shares with Helen the blame for the destruction brought to Troy, as the Chorus of the *Andromache* sing, as they witness the sufferings of Hector's wife, now the concubine of Achilles' son. They wish that Hecuba had heeded Kassandra's prophecy and slain the infant Paris, the "great ruin of Priam's city." And if Helen in Lycophron is a "she-dragon" and a "viper," Paris is the "wolf" and the "pirate of Kypris," emblem of lawless indiscriminate appetite. Like his paramour, Paris represents the disorder wrought by the failure to control one's sexuality, the consequences for society of unbridled sexual nature. The problem is a human one, the tragic result of unconstrained passion. But in women—given their greater subjection to nature's reproductive forces, given their seductive beauty linked to that procreative power—the problem is magnified.[54]

But the destructiveness of Helen is not her whole story. As her origins attest, ambiguity lies at the heart of her, and her end shows the same double quality. According to Pausanias, after the death of Menelaus she was driven out of Sparta by his sons Nicostratus and Megapenthes, the former her child too, the latter a bastard. She flees to Rhodes, where she is ultimately hanged by Polyxo in revenge for Tlepolemus, the colonizer of Rhodes who was killed at Troy by Sarpedon.[55] So one of her victims achieves revenge at last. But as we have seen, the daughter of Zeus ultimately wins godhead—worshipped at Rhodes as the "Hanged Goddess," worshipped at Sparta, worshipped by sailors, living on forever with Achilles on the White Island. But Helen's rehabilitation must wait until Part 2. Now we must meet her sister Klytaimestra.

The Lion in the House

There can be no redeeming eternity for Klytaimestra. On the surface she and her half-sister Helen are similar examples of destructive female passion. Odysseus pairs them that way when he commiserates with the butchered shade of Agamemnon in the underworld: "Many of us were destroyed because of Helen, and Klytaimestra spread a snare for you while you were away." But Helen's half-sister had a human father, Tyndareus, and so her sexual beauty is merely mortal, unleavened by the divinity that makes Helen transcend the suffering and violence she causes. Hence Klytaimestra's destructiveness is at once less cosmic in scope but more immediate and intimate, working out its violence in the very heart of the household. The old men of Troy can understand why their city suffers for the godlike beauty of Helen, but no one would ever say the horrors wrought by Klytaimestra were an acceptable price to pay for her mere mortal beauty. If Helen represents the ambiguity of female sexual loveliness, Klytaimestra embodies the relentless havoc of unleashed female passion that attacks from within the orders of household and state. She is, as much as Helen, in Aeschylus's words the lion raised as a pet in the house, "child-loving and a joy to the old" while young, but ultimately defiling the house with blood, a "priest of destruction" when its savage nature surfaces.[56]

The variety of images and epithets predicated on Klytaimestra all revolve around the ruinous characteristics of women, Aphrodite, and Eros we have been tracking—the bestial inability to control the sexual appetite, a devious mind given to plotting, the betrayal of the household and state. In short, she is a monstrous creature of nature ravaging from within the orders of culture, as the lion metaphor shows. Other images play on the same recognition of the inherent bestiality of female eros. Like Helen, Klytaimestra in Homer is also "bitch-faced," as Agamemnon in the Underworld calls her while describing her cruel refusal to close his dying mouth and eyes, after she has cut him down at a feast. "So it is there is nothing more dreaded or more bitch-like than a woman who puts such deeds in her mind," he comments, linking Klytaimestra's sexual crime to her corrupted mind. Aeschylus too plays on the bitch image, when the guileful Klytaimestra tells the Chorus that she has been a "trusty wife in the halls," a "watchdog of the house faithful" to Agamemnon—a lie, of course, since she has already plotted his destruction along with her lover Aegisthus. "Bitch of the house" is what she *really* means. Kassandra later recognizes Klytaimestra's duplicity with the same image when she describes her as the "hateful bitch, licking him with her tongue, stretching her ears in gladness." Like Priam's dogs nurtured at his table but eating his dead flesh, Klytaimestra is driven by the instincts of nature that overcome her "domestication."[57]

The other creatures associated with Klytaimestra make the same point. What should such an inhuman woman be called, Kassandra wonders. The "amphisbaena," a double-headed snake that moves backwards and forwards, a monstrous creature linked to the earth and the primal powers below it, like the snake-haired Furies, pre-Olympian forces of blood-vengeance? Or Scylla, the monster of the shore-rocks feeding on passing sailors, her vagina ringed with the barking heads of dogs? Scylla is particularly appropriate, a graphic image of destructive female sexuality linked to the treachery of the bitch. Elsewhere in Aeschylus Klytaimestra is the spider, a "weaver" of snares, and the viper, a creature believed to bite its mate through the neck during intercourse. And she is the lion, one that mates with the wolf, the usurper and tyrant Aegisthus, who also is driven by sexual appetite and the lust for power. Both wolf and lion are predators that attack the flocks and herds, the domesticated animals of human culture; they are savage forces of nature like the poisonous snake, viper, and spider, like Klytaimestra the denizens of a raw, inhuman natural world.[58]

The main reason women are closer to animals than are men, we have seen, is because the minds of women are controlled by their appetites, and so Klytaimestra's motives for murdering Agamemnon are ambiguously mixed. Pindar asks, "Did Iphigeneia, slaughtered at the Euripus, far from her homeland, stir her to raise a heavy-handed wrath? Or did nightly couplings lead her astray, subdued by another husband?" According to her, the murder of Agamemnon is the "exacted justice for [her] child" Iphigeneia, sacrificed by her father for a favorable wind. But Klytaimestra's motives are also sexual—her passion for Aegisthus, who rules Mycenae with her after the murder, and her jealousy of Kassandra, the Trojan princess whom Agamemnon brings home as a concubine. For if justice for her daughter was her motive, why kill the innocent Kassandra, a murder that she chillingly admits "adds a dainty to my bed"? In that phrase violence and sex commingle, anger and eros intensifying each other, unleashing the destructive force of the irrational that makes Klytaimestra "all-daring," unrestrained by any rational, social, or cultural limits.[59]

Dominated as she is by her passions, Klytaimestra's mind is corrupted to their service—she is "black-minded" and "evil-minded," reason's power now furthering the destructive ends of anger and eros. Her murder is premeditated, the culmination of a plot, a "snare/trap" laid for the unwary Agamemnon. As we saw earlier, the imagery of weaving usually signifying the good wife is used to symbolize the trap she weaves, from the scarlet carpet upon which she induces Agamemnon to tread to the robe with which she immobilizes him before she hacks him to death in his bath. Ultimately it is Klytaimestra herself, as Kassandra sees in her horrifying vision of the crime, who is the "hunting net, she who is the bed-sharer, she who is the joint-cause of murder." Like Aphrodite, like eros, like nature, woman is a trap, an alluring fatal net into which man is driven by his own passion.[60]

All of these traditional attributes of women and eros enrich the character of Klytaimestra in her most sustained literary appearances, Aeschylus's *Agamemnon* and *Libation Bearers*. But in those plays Klytaimestra goes beyond the role of typical woman subjected via her sexuality to the chaotic forces of nature that destroy the order of society. The Watchman speaks of her "man-minded heart," signaling that physical sex is not the whole story. Kassandra in her vision of the murder describes the "craftily devised horn," the sword with which the "bull" Klytaimestra murders her mate, collapsing together bestiality and trickiness with phallic power, imaging a force more numinous and frightening than just a passion-driven woman, as bad as that is. There's a horrific, heroic grandeur to Klytaimestra when, realizing her son Orestes has returned to kill her, she yells, "Someone hurry and give me a man-killing ax—let's find out if we conquer or are conquered!" Transcending her female humanity, Klytaimestra becomes masculine and heroic, as magnificently destructive as an Achilles or an Ajax, like them a force of nature ultimately representing not just women or their sex but human passion itself, the source of our crime but also our greatness, the daring the Chorus of the *Libation Bearers* regards as the most dangerous of the "many things reared by the earth, things terrible, monstrously fearful"—the "overbold thought/will of man" and the "all-daring eros" of women, man's will-driven mind and woman's sexual passion colluding to bring about the destruction of human order.[61]

The Child-Killer

Like Klytaimestra, Medea is driven by the female's most potent force, a sexual energy intensified by a heroic anger itself kindled by injustice and dishonor. And like Klytaimestra's, Medea's violent passion transforms her from a woman into a divine and bestial power, a destructive force transcending any semblance of humanity.

But Medea is unique in several respects, particularly in Euripides' version of her story. First, it should be remembered that she is not Greek but a barbarian, one of those non-Greek-speaking, outlandish races who rather than speaking Greek bray something that sounds like "bar-bar-bar," people considered by the Greeks to be more prone to appetite and passion than even a woman is. "There is no Greek woman who would have dared" to murder her sons, a broken Jason cries to Medea as she looks down on him from the Chariot of the Sun, the bodies of her murdered children at her feet. Second, in Medea the motive energies of the female and the hero are taken to an extreme that does not allow for any resolution in cultural terms. Klytaimestra's crime, horrible though it may be, in Aeschylus's trilogy is one episode in the unfolding progress of culture and its institutions, celebrated at the end of the final play in the sunlit triumph of Orestes' exoneration by the rational order of language and law. But Medea gets away with murder, the sanctuary given to her by Athens making a mockery of those institutions.[62]

Another difference between Medea and other femmes fatales is that the pernicious cleverness attributed to women in Medea is a dominant characteristic, reinforcing and worsening her intense violent passion. She is the niece, remember, of Circe, the divine enchantress who turned Odysseus's men into swine. More than the garden-variety female cleverness, Medea's powers are supernatural. She is a devotee of Hecate, grim goddess of night, crossroads, and black magic, knowledgeable about poison, visiting graveyards for the body parts and herbs from which she concocts charms and drugs. With her powers she can quench flames, stay the course of rivers, and stop the moon and stars in their paths. In one tradition she rejuvenated Jason by boiling him. The cleverness of the eros-dominated woman in Medea has become infinitely more powerful and frightening.[63]

Given the extremism that marks her passionate barbarian nature and her dark knowledge, Medea represents in its most intense and destructive form the essential danger of female sexuality and human passionate anger, both directed specifically against the household that exists to contain and harness woman's procreative energy.

In Chapter 1 we heard the first part of Medea's story, her betrayal of her home and country, her murder of her brother Apsyrtus. Writing two centuries before Apollonius, Euripides picks up the tale after Jason and Medea have settled in Corinth. There Jason, an ambitious opportunist, arranges to marry the daughter of the king Kreon. Jason is no older man grown tired of his dutiful wife and seeking excitement and renewed manhood with a younger woman—he explains to Medea that he "wasn't stricken with desire for a fresh bride."[64] His motives are coldly mercenary, the desire for money and prestige. He is a fifth-century yuppie, compromising a personal relationship in order to further his career, shedding past idealism and commitments for a comfortable and secure middle age. And he completely underestimates Medea, thinking her anger is over his sexual rejection of her. The inherited stereotypes about woman's passion blind Jason to the true depths of Medea's wrath that leads her to destroy Kreon and Jason's new bride, as well as her own sons, in order to achieve revenge on Jason.

Eros and excessive passion are important forces in Medea's character throughout the tradition from Pindar to Apollonius, whatever the variations developed by individual authors. We saw in Apollonius the whole repertoire of erotic imagery exploited to detail the impact of eros on her soul. Pindar too spoke of her "burning heart lashed with the whip of Persuasion." Medea's nurse likewise describes her as "stricken in her mind with eros" when she ran off with Jason, and Medea herself, her miseries worsened by Kreon's banishment of her, laments, "How great an evil love is to mortals." Jason thinks Medea's current anger is a consequence of that passion now challenged by his new marriage: "You women have reached such a state that if your bed is happy, you think you have everything. But if there is some mishap regarding the bed/marriage, you are most warlike against the best and fairest circumstances." The Chorus too sees Medea as an object lesson in the destructiveness of excessive sexual passion. But eros is not the whole story of Medea. Her sexuality is part of an already violently passionate nature. That's why Jason is blind to think she can be comprehended with his gender stereotypes, for her anger is heroic in its intensity. Repeatedly in her story the intensity and volatility of her wrath are emphasized. Her nurse, who ought to know, speaks of her "grievous mind," her "wild character and hateful nature." The Chorus also fears her "heavy-hearted wrath" that will lead her to a deed of "dread/terrible daring."[65]

This anger is not just a response to the current crisis. Apollonius describes how the young Medea, thinking Jason during their escape was planning to send her back to her father in exchange for keeping the fleece, "seethed with a heavy/grievous anger" and wanted to burn and hack apart the ships and throw herself into the fire. Jason manages to mollify her, but her history records the other times she acted on her violent nature. We've seen already that she murders her brother Apsyrtus, either as an infant she subsequently dismembers or as a youth she lures into an ambush where he is cut down by Jason. She dispatched as well Pelias, Jason's uncle who usurped his throne and tried to get rid of him by sending him on the suicide mission to get the fleece, by tricking Pelias's remarkably gullible daughters into cutting him up and boiling the pieces in order to rejuvenate him. In Euripides' play she horribly kills her rival, Glauke, and the king Kreon with a poisoned robe and crown that eat away their flesh, and her violence culminates in the murder of her two sons, what she herself calls a "most unholy deed."[66]

But her violence does not end with those crimes. Given sanctuary by the king of Athens, Aegeus, she later attempts to destroy Theseus, who Aegeus doesn't know is his own son, first by sending him off to capture the deadly Marathonian bull and then, when that fails, by trying to poison him. In some traditions it is she, not Helen, who ends up the eternal consort of Achilles in the Elysian Fields, a union that recognizes the heroic scale of her passionate anger and violence. The destructive anger of the epic and tragic hero, of an Achilles or an Oedipus, is in Medea intensified by the ruinous power of female eros, a power akin to the inhuman forces of nature, especially the predatory violence of beasts. Hence Medea is called "rock" and "iron" and compared to a lion and a bull and a tiger. And like

Klytaimestra, she is compared to the sexual monster Scylla; in fact, her nature is "wilder" than the creature with the twelve feet and six heads and the triple row of teeth. As Medea herself says, passion—the irrational forces of sex and anger—is stronger than the mind and is the cause of mankind's greatest evils.[67]

Medea, then, exemplifies not just woman's destructive eros, but ultimately the *human* condition, the power of the irrational to destroy the fragile orders the mind and culture create. The role and problems of woman are quickly rejected by Medea in Euripides' play, though at first she is presented as a typical female, weeping over her husband's rejection, trying to starve herself, wishing she could die. But her aristocratic jealousy of honor, as well as her violent and passionate nature, quickly propels her beyond her identity as woman. Her famous speech on the tribulations of women, a favorite of suffragettes and modern feminists alike, is part of her calculated attempt to enlist the sympathy and silence of the Chorus of Corinthian women, who *are* typical women. Most of the evils of arranged marriage Medea describes reflect *their* experience. But Medea married for passion. As Pindar says, "In opposition to her father Medea decided on her own marriage." And unlike the Corinthian women, who have their city and their fathers' houses and their network of friends and family to supplement their married life, she is isolated, possessing nothing but her own passionate wrath to take vengeance for the dishonor inflicted on her—the injury Jason gave her in exchange for her benefits to him. She is like an epic hero, "not worthless or weak or gentle, but of different character, grievous to my enemies and kind to my friends. For the life of such people is most glorious." Achilles couldn't have articulated better the heroic ethos—its rage against dishonor, its thirst for glory. The difference between Medea and an Achilles is that Medea's wrath is radically intensified by eros, the destructiveness of an Achillean "baneful wrath" doubled and redoubled by feminine eros.[68]

Medea is not just a woman. That is a role she plays with the dense men she must deal with, all of whom—Kreon, Jason, Aegeus—are blinded by their gender stereotypes, which she cleverly manipulates to further her ends. Thus her simpering indulgence of Jason's prejudices when she feigns an apology for an earlier violent outburst by saying, "We are such—I won't say evil, but women," as if the word "women" contains the idea of "evil," as it does in the misogynistic tradition starting with Hesiod.[69] But Medea is not a "mere" woman, and we must not limit our understanding of her by seeing her as a representative victim of patriarchy. Medea is the powerful force of human passion, heroic anger exponentially intensified by eros. Through her Euripides seems to say that if you add eros to epic violence, a force will be unleashed that sweeps away marriage, family, city, human identity itself.

Phaedra

Phaedra is a more typical female than is Medea or Klytaimestra. She is a victim of Aphrodite who recognizes the struggle within her between an alien passion and her sense of shame. In her is starkly figured the vulnerability of women to the force of sex, and the fragility of the cultural orders created to control that force. But like Medea and Klytaimestra, Phaedra is also concerned with honor and dishonor, and the suffering that she causes is evidence not just of female sexual disorder but of the aristocratic obsession with honor and vengeance against the enemy who dishonors one. As in the *Medea*, Euripides is concerned with the irresistible power of the irrational, how the woman's greater vulnerability to erotic disorders worsens the effects of the aristocrat's passionate need for honor. Once again we see the Greeks putting the problem of human identity, the struggle between passion and order, in the context not just of gender but of politics, specifically the ongoing fifth-century contest between democratic and aristocratic values.

The story of Phaedra, wife of Theseus, king of Athens, and her "diseased" love for her celibate stepson, Hippolytus, was told in Chapter 2. A closer look at Phaedra herself reveals a woman who, much like Hippolytus, has believed in the cultural orders meant to control sexuality, especially the household and the ethical value of shame. Phaedra is as much a puritan as Hippolytus, as much disgusted by the sexual depravity of women. When Phaedra comes to after her sexually charged hallucination in which she hunts the stag alongside Hippolytus, she is mortified: "Cover again my head, for I am shamed by what I've said. Hide me— the tears fall from my eyes, my eyes are turned to shame." Later she makes her case to the Chorus, explaining how at first she tried to control her disease, "conquering through self-control," but failed. Then she decided to die, "so that I never be caught shaming my husband." The thought of sexual sin horrifies her. As vehemently as Hippolytus she condemns the erring wife: "May she utterly perish, whoever first began to shame the bed with strangers!" But Phaedra's "technology" of shame cannot resist the force of sexuality, and ultimately she gives in to the Nurse's misguided attempt to cure her by arranging an assignation with Hippolytus. In the struggle of Phaedra we see most closely the central problem of human, not just female, identity—the weakness of our cultural and social orders before the relentless power of the sensual and the irrational.[70]

When the Nurse's plot blows up and Phaedra overhears Hippolytus's brutal, shaming condemnation of her as an "evil woman plotting evil"—that is, characterizing her as the typical duplicitous woman she had thought herself *not* to be— she decides to kill herself and destroy Hippolytus in the bargain, for as she tells the Chorus, "By dying I will become an evil to that other man, lest he be proud about my sufferings."[71] As with Medea, the destructiveness of female sexuality compounds the passion for honor, the irrational desire to uphold one's public reputation and destroy the man who besmirches it, thus recuperating some honor from the shame. As with an epic hero like Achilles or Ajax, not only does "shame" fail to keep passion in line, but it becomes a force of destruction in itself.

This passion for honor, whose destructiveness is a constant theme in epic and tragedy, is intensified by the chaos of woman's sexuality. Women are slaves to eros, creatures of appetites, but then so are men. After all, Hippolytus's violent outburst is as much a cause of his destruction as is Phaedra's sickness. Phaedra reveals her understanding of Hippolytus's character when she wants him to die so that "having a share in my disease he will learn to have self-control," the virtue he fancied himself to possess by nature.[72] Heroic anger and female sexuality are both natural energies cultural order must try to control. Whether or not they *can* be controlled, either by marriage and the household or democratic institutions, was one of the key questions the Greeks asked.

"Man-Slaughterer"

Deianira, whose name means "man-slaughterer," was the wife of the strongman Heracles. In Sophocles' play about the death of Heracles, she is the good wife, motivated not just by sexual jealousy over Iole, the concubine Heracles is bringing home, but by the desire to protect the integrity of her household. The fragility of all such cultural orders is a lesson of Deianira's fate, particularly because her husband Heracles is the greatest culture-hero of the Greeks, his twelve labors representing the imposition of order on a monstrous, chaotic natural world. Yet Heracles as we have seen is also the embodiment of appetite, particularly sexual. For all his labors to create order, he cannot control his own eros, which is what destroys him. Once again we see that woman's erotic disorder is so dangerous because it is implicated with and intensifies the chaotic passion of *all* humans, the nature within as well as without that must be tamed, like the monsters and dragons and beasts Heracles destroys.

This contrast of natural disorder and cultural order defines the story of Deianira throughout. Heracles had to win her for his bride, defeating the monstrous Achelous, the shape-shifting river-god who appears as a bull, then a snake, then a half-man, half-bull. But the natural disorder and violence Achelous represents is in Heracles himself, in the disease of erotic appetite, the "dread desire" that drives him to destroy the town of Oechalia and its king Eurytos so that he might possess the princess Iole. Up to this point Deianira has lived the role of the "good wife," miserable because of her husband's absence, concerned for his well-being and the safety of her household. But the arrival of the younger Iole awakens within Deianira both jealousy and the fear of losing her position in the household, her recompense, she bitterly complains, for her "keeping safe the home."[73]

So Deianira uses the potion the centaur Nessus gave her, made from his blood, which she smears on a robe and sends to Heracles. Now the stereotypical "plotting" of women, evoked by the woven garment Deianira poisons, defines her character as the "guileful" one who "weaves" the trap destroying Heracles in a fiery madness that brings to vivid life all the metaphors of a destructive eros. The violence of eros is apparent as well in the potion, for as we saw earlier Nessus was shot by Heracles as the centaur tried to rape Deianira. As he lay dying, he advised the girl to save his blood, and in some traditions it was mixed with his semen. Thus the potion functions as a powerful graphic metaphor for sex—its provenance in the monstrous world of primal nature, its violence and power to destroy.

And it locates the origins of Heracles' horrible death in the chain of passion, the interwoven sex and violence of Nessus's rape, Heracles' killing of him, Heracles' destruction of Oechalia, his lust for Iole, and Deianira's insecurity and jealousy. Heracles ultimately is killed by his own passion. The woman's eros is merely the last instrumental link in the chain, the force unleashed when the integrity of the household is weakened. As is usual in tragedy, the hero of order like Heracles cannot control his own chaotic passions, let alone the more volatile eros of woman his order is supposed to control.[74]

The Power of Pandora's Tribe

As our survey has shown, women in Greek literature, with the exception of those "good" women like Alcestis and Penelope, embody more intensely and destructively the basic duality of the human condition—natural passions and drives and appetites that cultural order attempts to control and subordinate. This common theme characterizes four centuries of literary expression and remains constant regardless of the individual author's own purposes and needs. For women, their closeness to nature, the greater power of their appetites, and the weakness of their minds' control over them sharpen this duality, particularly when eros is the issue. This is so because the need to procreate, to keep the race going beyond one generation, as well as the allure of female sexual beauty subject men to the power of women. And when they respond to that beauty they open themselves to the force of their own eros, which is to say to the power of nature. Moreover, their response to female sexual beauty reminds them of their own dependence on nature's creative energy that they must exploit and limit. Hence women are interesting to Greek literature because in them this fundamental human problem, this conflict between nature's chaos and culture's order, is magnified—as are the consequences of the failure of those orders. Medea, Phaedra, Deianira—all *try* to be good wives, to subject themselves to the household's order, but the weakness of their husbands' control over *their* passions compromises that order, unleashing the volatile forces of violent eros.

If women in Greek literature are understood in these terms then we can see the weakness of a popular, but by no means universal, interpretation of Greek women as powerless, cowering victims of a misogynistic patriarchy. Such a view renders meaningless Pandora, Helen, Klytaimestra, Medea, Lysistrata—all those women whose magnificence depends on a recognition that men are vulnerable to, and hence *fear*, the sexual power of women. One does not fear what one perceives to be powerless. And I suspect this was the case in history as well as myth. After all, the largest monument in Athens was built by the late-fourth-century embezzler Harpalus for his mistress Pythionice. And why, as the early-fourth-century proto-Cynic Antisthenes asked, would adulterers run such risks, including death, when gratification was available for a pittance? The sexual power of woman is a force of nature *and* history, as much as climate or economics or war. To deny women that elemental power is as much a sexist diminishment of them as relegating them to second-class political and social status.[75]

The modern reductive view of Greek woman as oppressed victim tells us very little about antiquity yet quite a lot about the late-twentieth-century politics of victimhood and the liberal-democratic assumption that all power resides in political rights and institutions. It reflects as well the loss in our popular imaginations of the sexually powerful woman, the popular icon of female fecundity once embodied in someone like Marilyn Monroe. Even while blowsy and overweight, she exudes more sexual energy in the film *Some Like It Hot* than do all of the models in all of the Victoria's Secret catalogs and *Sports Illustrated* swimsuit issues put together. These women, mere "tits on a stick," with their masklike faces and boyish hips, their womanhood reduced to gender-signifying breasts, represent not creative sexual power but *commodifying* power—sex as consumer object, standardized, sleek, industrialized, as shiny and flawless as a new BMW. Likewise with Madonna, whose hard metallic brilliance communicates not sex but the rationalized *idea* of sex, a commodity totally divorced from the natural, procreative reality of eros. Given the modern trivialization of woman's sexuality, it's understandable why some scholars these days miss completely the Greeks' wary respect for woman's power.

But the Greeks, and most humans before our smug twentieth century, knew that the power of woman was the power of eros, and the power of eros was the creative and destructive power of nature itself, the forces that both men and women must strive to order and control for civilization—and human beings—to exist. And they knew the consequences of that energy when unleashed: suffering, violence, the obliteration of all order, the descent back into the primal chaos. It is this fear of an omnivorous appetitive power as embodied in the *kinaidos*, the passive homosexual, that we will explore next.

FOUR

Monsters of Appetite

In Plato's dialogue the *Gorgias*, Socrates is probing the hedonistic philosophy of Callicles, one of those radical fifth-century Sophists who believed, like Hamlet, that "nothing's good or bad, but thinking makes it so." Callicles asserts that "it is necessary for the man living rightly to allow his desires to be as powerful as possible and not to check them, and when they are as powerful as possible he ought to be able to serve them through his manliness and intelligence." To Socrates this is a dangerous inversion of what *should* be the order of the human soul—the bestial passions and appetites controlled and minimized by, rather than ruling, the rational mind. So he sets out to refute Callicles by exposing the absurdity of his belief. If maximizing pleasure creates happiness, Socrates conjectures, the man who spends his life scratching an itch is happy. Callicles agrees. Then Socrates springs the trap. But what about "the life of passive homosexuals [*kinaidôn*], isn't it awful and shameful and wretched? Or will you have the audacity to say that they are happy, if they have enough of the things they need?" "Aren't you ashamed," a shocked Callicles replies, "at leading the discussion to such topics?"[1]

Socrates' contemptuous description of the passive homosexual, Callicles' shocked disgust at such a creature even being mentioned in a philosophical discussion, should give us pause. Aren't these men Greeks, those enthusiasts of pederasty, the liberated icons of "Greek Love"? Even the modern semiliterate knows that any joke about the Greeks and sex leads to a punch line about sodomy. Isn't Socrates himself an ardent admirer of young males? When he "catches fire" at a glimpse of the chest of the youthful Charmides, he nearly passes out. And doesn't he spend all his time at the wrestling school and the gymnasium, admiring the boys as they exercise naked, bodies glistening with olive oil? Or is Socrates' and Callicles' disgust reserved, as some modern commentators argue, for the adult homosexual, whereas buggery inflicted on youths, the future citizens of the polis, is perfectly acceptable? In this chapter and in Chapter 8 we will try to sort out these contradictions of a practice Pausanias, a speaker in Plato's *Symposium*, calls *poikilos,* "complex/intricate/complicated" and "not easy to understand."[2]

Part of the problem is that homosexuality, contemporary as well as ancient, is no easier for us so-called moderns to understand than it was for the Greeks. One of our difficulties when reading about ancient Greece is that the most common manifestation of homosexuality in the evidence concerns pederasty, the quasi-rit-ualized, transient, physical and emotional relationship between an older male and a youth, an activity we view as criminal.[3] Very little, if *any*, evidence from ancient Greece survives that shows adult males (or females) as "couples" involved in an ongoing, reciprocal sexual and emotional relationship in which sex with women (or men) is moot and the age difference is no more significant than it is in hetero-sexual relationships. Thus the evidence from ancient Greece involves either man-youth homosexuality (the idealized social relationship we will discuss in Chapter 8), or the precisely defined passive homosexual or *kinaidos*, the adult male who perversely enjoys being penetrated by other males and who has sex with women only because of societal pressure. These two categories, as we will see, are not as mutually exclusive as they might appear, which accounts for the anxiety tingeing even the most enthusiastic ancient celebrators of pederasty.

Another major impediment to understanding homosexuality for both ancients and moderns is the confusion of nature and culture in explaining it. Thanks to science we know today that homosexual men may have "interstitial nuclei of the anterior hypothalamus"—a region of the brain responsible for "regulation of male-typical sexual behavior"—two to three times smaller than heterosexual men. Yet we're still not much farther along in discovering the biological roots of ho-mosexuality than Victorian adventurer Richard Francis Burton, who theorized about a "sotadic [homosexual] zone," a geographical band precisely located be-tween 30 and 43 degrees northern latitude in which people are prone to homo-sexuality.[4] The issue is further confused by careless use of the word "natural." If one believes, as did many Greek philosophers from Heraclitus on, that the cosmos reflects some sort of rational order, then "natural" would denote behavior consis-tent with that order. One could then act "unnaturally" by indulging in behavior that subverted that order and its purpose. The "rational" and "natural" purpose of sex, then, is procreation, as the Stoic spokesman Balbus in Cicero points out, and homosexuality is "unnatural" because it does not serve that end.[5] Of course, logi-cal consistency would demand that *all* sexual acts, heterosexual or homosexual, that do not lead to procreation be deemed "unnatural," a view we will see Plato take in the *Laws* and that later Christian philosophers endorse, like Jerome when he condemns excessive conjugal sexual pleasure as fornication.

But if we remember the alternative Greek view of nature described in the In-troduction, that it is like Homer's Polyphemus, savage and monstrous and inhu-man, then "natural" carries a different, more negative force. In these terms eros is, as we have seen, a natural energy flowing out from humans onto *any* object, whether same-sex paramour, child, relative, or beast, as evidenced by the many Greek myths involving incest and bestiality. There is no qualitatively distinct category of "homosexual" or "heterosexual," for eros is by definition indiscriminate. Thus a Greek would not categorize as "homosexual" a man who has penetrated another. Any limitations of eros arise not from the inherent *nature* of sexual activity that directs itself toward one object or another, but from the literally *unnatural* codes, laws, customs, and institutions of society that define the proper and improper objects and occasions of sexual activity. As Glaukon says in Plato's *Republic*, without the fear of "law and custom" every man would pursue his myriad desires, including having sex with whomever he could. Likewise the speaker in an oration of Lysias, charged with physically attacking his rival for the love of a boy, apologizes to the jury for his unseemly behavior by appealing to the common assumption that "desire is in all humans." The defendant is counting on the jurymen's sympathetic understanding that the force of eros is indiscriminate and powerful and hence capable of befuddling the mind. Given such a definition of eros, "homosexual" and "heterosexual" would then be cultural, not natural categories, together whose function is to control and limit the force of eros both to minimize its destructiveness and, as we will see in Chapters 7 and 8, to exploit its creative energies.[6]

Both of these explanations of homosexuality—as either an "unnatural" perversion of sex or an excessive expression of its essential nature—can be found in ancient Greek literary remains. Choosing one of the two to the exclusion of the other, which is often the practice among modern scholars, oversimplifies the complexity of attitudes attested in the evidence. Our purpose in this chapter is not to impose an artificial coherence on this muddled picture, but to examine what sorts of *meanings* are given to the *kinaidos*, the passive homosexual whose inability to control his appetite, his "itch" for sexual pleasure, induces him to forsake his masculinity and submit to anal penetration. What we find is the *kinaidos* as emblem of unrestrained compulsive sexual appetite, of surrender to the chaos of natural passion that threatens civilized order, a traitor to his sex, a particularly offensive manifestation of eros's power over the masculine mind that is responsible for creating and maintaining that order in the face of nature's chaos. Thus Callicles' disgust: The *kinaidos* is like a woman, only worse. At least the woman's sexual appetite is also a procreative energy that in the order of marriage produces citizens and the mothers of citizens. But in nearly every genre of Greek literature the *kinaidos*'s appetite is sterile, useless, good only for pleasure, rendering the male prone to other appetites, for money or power, that also threaten culture and its discriminating categories, particularly if he is a citizen responsible in some measure for the political functioning of the city.

Culture or Nature?

The ambiguity and complexity of Greek attitudes toward homosexuality can be seen first in the various speculations about its origins, which oscillate between the poles of culture and nature. Whatever its source, though, habitual passive homosexuality is clearly considered an aberration, a disorder linked to violence and disease, even in the supposedly accepted institution of pederasty.

Both myth and history imply a time when homosexuality did not exist, at least not in the most typical and frequently referred-to manifestation of it, pederasty. One would think, if there was a period when there was no homosexuality, that its origins would lie not in nature but in a historically conditioned cultural innovation, but the matter is not so clear-cut. The myth of Chrysippus reflects this confusion, at least in what we know about it from the handful of surviving references. According to the shadowy Peisandros and Euripides in his lost play the *Chrysippus*, Chrysippus was a son of Pelops—hence uncle to Agamemnon and Menelaus—whom Laius, father of Oedipus, kidnapped and raped. Chrysippus then killed himself because of "shame" (*aischunês*), and Hera—goddess of marriage—sent the Sphinx to Thebes as punishment. Another punishment for this act was the death of Laius at his son Oedipus's hands.[7]

The story is confused—is Laius the *originator* of homosexual desire or just the first to act on it? But Plato at least understood the myth to finger Laius as the inventor of homosexuality. In the *Laws*, the Athenian Stranger, tackling the difficult problem of regulating sexual passion, "the cause of myriad evils both for the individual and whole states," says that "following nature" legislators should make the law as it was "before Laius," when sex with men and youths as though they were women (a reference no doubt to sodomy) was forbidden on the model of animals, which Plato mistakenly believed restricted sex to procreation. Plato sees the state of nature as one in which homosexuality does not exist, sex between males thus being an unnatural innovation whose origin is Laius. This would be consistent with Peisandros, who calls Laius's passion a "lawless eros," "lawless" in the sense of "contrary to natural law," an interpretation supported by another epithet Peisandros uses, *athemiton*, which means "lawless" in the sense of "contrary to established customs," the unwritten laws handed down by the gods before history, not those legislated by men. Nor is Plato's view of homosexuality as "unnatural" merely a consequence of his cranky old age. In the earlier *Phaedrus*, one of the great encomia to pederasty, he likewise calls same-sex physical gratification "lawless" and criticizes the lesser soul that cannot see the form of beauty in a handsome boy and so "is not ashamed to pursue pleasure against nature."[8]

Homosexuality, then, to the Greeks is a historical innovation, a result of the depraved human imagination and vulnerability to pleasure. In Euripides, though, Laius is made to rationalize his crime by saying, "Nature drove me on."[9] We see here the difference between the philosopher and the tragedian, between the view of nature as an order with which man's laws should be consistent and nature as a congeries of destructive forces overthrowing reason and law. In the latter view homosexuality is one of those forces, Laius's crime initiating a chain reaction of erotic disorder culminating in the incest and parricide of Oedipus, the blight of Thebes blasting the newborn life of humans, herds, and grain alike. In contrast to Plato, then, Euripides sees homosexual eros as a constant of human nature.

Whether the origins of homosexuality are to be found in nature or history, though, it clearly is problematic, even in its presumably accepted form of pederasty, a phenomenon needing to be accounted for mythically in the crime of Laius.

Another origin for homosexuality is located among the Dorians, those more warlike Greeks like the Spartans, who purportedly swept through Greece toward the end of the second millennium and ultimately occupied most of the Peloponnese and Crete. In the Athenian imagination, the Dorians and Spartans functioned like the Bulgarians in Voltaire's *Candide*, enthusiasts of buggery who made the best butts of sodomy jokes.[10] Most stereotypes, however, contain a kernel of truth, and the highly militarized and hence masculine nature of Spartan society no doubt fostered homosexuality, particularly pederasty, the romance of the barracks. The pederastic milieu of the gymnasium, where the young men exercised naked, was considered a Spartan invention, along with the innovation of rubbing olive oil on the body before exercising, to protect the skin but also no doubt to increase the athletes' erotic allure.[11] Plato's Athenian Stranger indulges these cultural stereotypes when he holds the Dorians responsible for "corrupt[ing] the pleasures of sex which are according to nature, not just for men but for beasts." Again Plato sees homosexuality as a historical phenomenon, an "enormity" arising out of the "inability to control a pleasure" defined as "against nature" because it is its own end rather than serving the goal of procreation. Later in the *Laws* he again condemns homosexuality, along with adultery and heterosexual sodomy, on the grounds of being "not according to nature" because it does not lead to procreation. Plato's distaste for homosexuality is shared by his contemporary Xenophon, a great admirer of the Spartans who is anxious to absolve them of their traditional responsibility for legitimizing homosexuality. The mythical lawgiver of Sparta, Lycurgus, Xenophon tells us, forbade physical intimacy between the boy and his admirer, categorizing homosexuality with other crimes like incest. Like Plato, Xenophon considers sexual relations between men a depravity that all right-thinking men should abhor as much as they would incest.[12]

Aristotle also attributes homosexuality to the Dorians, though he never tells us, as he promises to, whether he thinks it is bad or not. And his speculations about why such an institution should arise focus not on the lure of pleasure but on the more practical need to control population, which accounts as well for the segregation of women. Sodomy as a means of controlling pregnancy may explain an anecdote in Herodotus that at first glance appears to designate sodomy as "lawless." Pisistratus, the sixth-century tyrant of Athens, had intercourse with his wife, the daughter of Megacles, "not according to law/custom" because he feared a curse that would be fulfilled through his children. Megacles becomes angry when he finds out that his son-in-law is "dishonoring" him by sodomizing (presumably) his daughter, but why? Because of a horror of sodomy, or because Pisistratus was not ratifying the marriage by impregnating his wife? Childlessness could be an excuse for getting rid of a wife, as even an enraged Medea admits. The "law/custom" Herodotus refers to, then, might be the one that says husbands should get their wives pregnant, not that they should be restricted to pe-nile-vaginal intercourse. Though this passage doesn't help much in determining what Herodotus thought about sodomy and perforce homosexuality, elsewhere he remarks that the Persians learned pederasty from the Greeks, implying again a cultural rather than a natural phenomenon, at least for this particular subspecies of homosexuality.[13]

In the later fourth century, the culture-versus-nature debate that frames specu-lations on the origins of homosexuality led to a sort of "back-to-nature" philoso-phy advocating the rejection of artificial social conventions. The founder of Sto-icism, Zeno, started out as a follower of Cynicism, the philosophical sect that preached the most extreme form of "natural" life, the "doggy"—that is, "cynical" in Greek—life exemplified by the famous Diogenes, who claimed there was noth-ing wrong with masturbating in public and scorned most other social conventions as unnatural vanities. Similarly Zeno once asserted that it is a matter of indiffer-ence whether one "spreads the thighs" of a loved or an unloved boy, or of a man or a woman, since the act is the same. But even this apparent endorsement of ho-mosexuality on the basis of its "naturalness" still marks it off as deviant—Zeno goes on to advocate as well cannibalism and incest. It is the assumed widespread *disapproval* of homosexuality, similar to the horror of cannibalism and incest, that makes Zeno endorse it in order to shock his conventional fellow Greeks. But Zeno ultimately is striving for an effect, not promoting a radical naturalism. The historian of philosophy Sextus Empiricus assures us that Zeno lived as conven-tionally as everybody else.[14]

Although Aristotle, as we saw, implies the Dorians invented homosexuality, else-where he recognizes that homosexuals can be born as well as made. Either way, though, they are a deviation from the norm. While discussing in the *Nichomachean Ethics* why some unpleasant or disgusting practices are pleasurable, he says that some "diseased things" result from "nature" or "habit," and he instances pulling out one's hair, nailbiting, eating coals or earth, and "sex between males." The lat-ter, he notes, often results from childhood sexual abuse. Such persons are no more "unrestrained" in their sexual behavior than is a woman, whether they are made that way by nature or the "disease" of habit. Despite Aristotle's tolerant and objec-tive tone, homosexuality is still characterized as a "disease" (*nosêmatôdeis*), a com-pulsive, unpleasant, and destructive behavior akin to manias like eating dirt or chewing one's fingernails. Even pederasty, that supposedly accepted institution of the city-state, is here seen as possibly contributing to what Aristotle considers a morbid condition. Today's *kinaidos* is yesterday's *eromenos* or "boy-favorite."[15]

The Aristotelian corpus offers other evidence for the belief that homosexuality results from a physiological deformity brought about by either nature or habit. A bizarre passage from the *Problems* explains why a man would find pleasure in being anally penetrated—obviously in the Greek mind a disturbing anomaly needing some explanation. Starting from the assumption that every form of excretion has a region in the body from which it is secreted, the writer explains that the passive homosexual, due to some damage to the ducts that takes the semen to the testicles and penis, is "unnaturally constituted" and so has semen collect in his anus. This damage could be the result of an inborn deformity or childhood sexual abuse. The collected fluid creates friction caused by desire, a desire that cannot be gratified because there is no way to discharge the accumulated semen. Hence the catamite seeks out anal intercourse in order to relieve the swelling. The writer goes on to note that boys subjected to anal intercourse will become habituated to it, thus associating pleasure with the act. Environment and childhood experience play a major role in creating the passive homosexual by deforming the body.[16] The pseudo-Aristotelian *Physiognomy* similarly describes the effects passive homosexuality has on the body: The effeminate man is drooping-eyed, knock-kneed, his head hanging on one shoulder, his hands carried upturned and flabby. He wriggles his loins as he walks, or tries not to, and he looks around furtively.[17] Both these passages, like the ones in Plato, see homosexuality as a deformed condition brought about either by a natural disorder or by habit—something, in short, "abnormal," not quite the practice "accepted by and fully integrated into society" that some modern scholars believe it to be.[18]

Finally, the most famous and straightforward instance of the ancient Greek belief that homosexuals are born and not made can be found in Aristophanes' myth of human sexual origins in Plato's *Symposium*. Aristophanes describes the first humans as round double creatures with two faces, two sets of genitals, four arms, and four legs. They locomoted by doing cartwheels and came in three kinds: male, female, and "hermaphrodite," male-female. Out of their arrogance they conspired against the gods, so Zeus had Apollo split them in two and sew them up, our navels the scars of that ancient tailoring. Descendants of those split from the all-male creatures are homosexuals, from the female are lesbian, and from the "hermaphrodite" heterosexual. Thus we always search for our lost half, and this explains the power of eros—our desire to restore our lost unity. Aristophanes' fairy tale, at the same time it humorously punctures the pretentious rhetoric of his fellow banqueters, clearly reflects the commonsense view that some people are born lovers of their own sex. These people, Aristophanes explains, marry and have children because of custom (*nomou*) rather than nature (*phusei*). Additionally, Aristophanes reinforces Pausanias's earlier distinction between the worshipers of the "Vulgar" Aphrodite, who love women as well as boys, and those who honor the "Heavenly" Aphrodite, who love only boys, which implies the existence of exclusive homosexuals. Indeed, Aristophanes identifies two of his fellow banqueters, Agathon and Pausanias, as examples of exclusive male-lovers.[19]

Whether created by history or nature, childhood sexual abuse or deformed seminal ducts, the man who enjoys anal penetration by another man is an aberration, a volatile locus of potential social disorder that like the woman he resembles must be dealt with.

The Heterosexual Paradigm

Another argument against the unqualified acceptance by the Greeks of homosexuality is the prevalence of the male-female sexual pattern in the references to same-sex relations, which suggests that the heterosexual paradigm is the "natural" one that homosexual relations mimic and pattern themselves after. As Aristotle says, "The affection between man and woman appears to happen according to nature, for humans by nature are disposed to live in pairs more than in political communities." Thus the passive homosexual is assimilated to the woman's role, which accounts for the traditional animosity between women and *kinaidoi*—the latter are poaching on a female preserve. The fifth-century comic poet Cratinus attributed homosexuality to hatred of women, and another comedian, Timocles, in a burlesque of a scene from Aeschylus's *Eumenides*, showed the notorious pederast Autocleides as Orestes, with courtesans as the vengeful Furies sleeping around him.[20]

This tailoring of homosexual relations to the heterosexual pattern can be seen in the assimilation of the passive partner, whether boy-love or adult *kinaidos*, to the woman's role and appearance. In the case of boy-love there appears to have been a historical development of taste, with the sixth and early fifth centuries preferring more masculine types and the fourth century going for the girlish look. But these generalizations have to admit exceptions. Plato, writing in the early fourth century, says in the *Republic* that the boy-lover finds *every* type of boy attractive, from the manly swarthy boy to the delicate pale one, since irrational passion is indiscriminate. And a Hellenistic poet, during the supposed heyday of the taste for girlish boys, talks of kissing a "blood-dabbled" boy just after he's won a boxing match. But most of the evidence characterizes the desirable boy in feminine terms, even during the supposedly more macho-inclined sixth century. The Archaic poet Theognis—assuming the lines are his and not a later imitator's—praises the "smooth cheek" and "smooth skin" of a boy, using the same word (*hapalochroos*) as the Hellenistic poet Meleager 400 years later, a word often used to describe a maiden.[21] Another Hellenistic poet, Polystratus, calls a boy "delicate/dainty" (*habron*), the adjective again one used elsewhere of women. Anacreon more explicitly links the boy to the girl when he mentions the "maidenly glance" of an indifferent boy. This frequent praise of boys in terms more appropriate for girls elucidates the courtesan Glycera's remark that men like boys only as long as they look like women.[22]

The praise of boys' softness is linked to the distaste for facial and body hair, the onset of the beard supposedly marking the end of the boy's desirability. That's why the fourth-century historian Theopompus is shocked to record that the Macedonians bugger boys even after their beards have come in. Likewise the unnamed friend of Socrates in the *Protagoras* tweaks him for still being attracted to Alcibiades after his beard has begun to show. The presence of hair on a boy would be a sign that his homoerotic phase had ended and that he should be pursuing women. The Hellenistic poet Phanias notes that the hair on the boy Pamphilus's thighs and face means that desire will now lead him to a "different madness," the love of women. A common theme in Hellenistic pederastic poetry is the vengeful glee of boy-lovers at seeing once-haughty boy-loves brought down to earth by their hair. Alcaeus warns the snooty Nicander he'd better not let his ass get as hairy as his leg, or else he'll lose all his admirers. Likewise Meleager says that the boy Heraclitus's buttocks, a "Nemesis" or "retribution" growing on them, repels "behind-mounters," and in another poem he sneers that "hairy-assed" boys are fit only for "goat-mounting" herdsmen, who are accustomed to hirsute paramours. The veiled reference to depilation and the explicit reference to sodomy show the boy-love shading into the adult *kinaidos* who, as we will see, artificially cultivates the girlish look.[23]

What is desirable in the boy, though, is disgusting in the grown man who plays the passive part during sex and demonstrates this role in his effeminate appearance and character. Hence the universal disdain for the idea of men being penetrated by other men. Usually the penetrated man is the object of opprobrium, though there are occasional negative references to the active partner. The personified Vice in Prodicus's allegory is accused by Virtue of "using men like women"; active homosexuality here made a defining characteristic of vice in general. But most of the contempt is reserved for the man who forsakes his masculinity and feminizes himself, not just in appearance but also in behavior. Plato in the *Laws* assumes the passive homosexual will be a coward, on the following logic: Women are cowardly, the pathic is penetrated like a woman, ergo the pathic will be a coward. So it is that one of the most deadly insults one can inflict on a man is to accuse him of effeminacy, which always carries the implication that he allows himself to be buggered by other men.[24]

This predilection for the woman's role during sex leads the *kinaidos* to attempt to duplicate the woman's appearance. Thus the effeminate is always described as clean-shaven and depilated, including his anus, and "soft," like the girlish boys described above. Conversely, being "hairy-rumped" and "hard" are signs of masculinity. The Chorus of old men in the *Lysistrata* flash their rumps at the Chorus of old women, saying that the mid-fifth-century general Myronides, victor over the Corinthians and the Boeotians, was similarly "harsh and hairy-assed to all his enemies." Masculinity means as well taking the active penetrating role in sex. The fifth-century comic poet Alexis says that the man who is shaved or depilated with pitch intends to do things inconsistent with a beard, that is, with the man's active sexual role.[25] Aristophanes repeatedly exploits this association of hairlessness and softness with effeminacy, always with the implication that such a man is a passive homosexual. In the *Clouds*, his play savaging Socrates and the new philosophy that Aristophanes blames for the degeneration of Athenian virtue, he stages a debate between Just Logic, the old-fashioned values that made Athens great, and Unjust Logic, the newfangled Sophistic rationalizations for unbridled indulgence of appetite. Just Logic condemns as a sign of the corrupt present the young boys who make their voices "soft" (*malakên*) for their admirers, the adjective one typically used to describe moral "softness" and sexual degeneracy—and cognate even today to the pejorative modern Greek word for passive homosexual (*malaka*, a deadly insult). Thus Aristotle defines sexual incontinence as a "kind of softness," and Plato condemns democracy's materialistic self-indulgence as evidenced in the younger generation, "too soft to rule over pleasures and pains." Likewise Aristophanes in the *Wasps*, another comedy contrasting the corrupt present with the doughty generation that defeated the Persians at Marathon, signals that corruption by describing the mincing, "daintily soft" young catamite of a public prosecutor who bullies the old jurymen, veterans of Marathon, before he pockets his bribe. We see here a constant motif of Aristophanic comedy—the linkage of political corruption to the passive homosexual, both signs of a breakdown of public values and the subsequent unleashing of unbounded appetite.[26]

In Aristophanes this linking of hairlessness and softness to the effeminate pathic informs the poet's characterization of two of his favorite targets, Agathon and Cleisthenes. Agathon was the fifth-century tragedian for whom it is said Euripides, stricken by his beauty, wrote the *Chrysippus*; Agathon's victory party for winning a prize for his first tragedy in 416 was the scene for Plato's *Symposium*. It is clear in Plato that Aristophanes assumes Agathon, about thirty years old, is the homosexual lover, not just the "boy-love," of Pausanias—he specifically points them out as examples of his "males by nature," descendants of the all-male double protohumans who seek physical and emotional gratification exclusively from males and who marry and bear children only because of the force of "custom." Certainly in his comedies Aristophanes derides Agathon as an effeminate passive homosexual. In the *Women at the Thesmophoria*, when Agathon makes his entrance in the special-effects crane used to elevate actors above the stage, Mnesilochus says, "I see no man there, but I see Cyrene," the name of a woman notorious for her promiscuity. A few lines later he notes Agathon's "saffron-colored robe," a woman's garment dyed in a color typical of women, and his "woman's hair net." The character of Euripides in the play makes Agathon's effeminacy explicit: Agathon is "fair of face, white, clean-shaven, woman-voiced, soft, pretty." And when Euripides wants to dress Mnesilochus as a woman so that he can infiltrate the women's festival, he shaves him with a razor he borrows from Agathon and singes off his hair "below," not only because women removed their pubic hair but because *kinaidoi* like Agathon depilated their anuses. Agathon himself gets out of playing the spy for Euripides by admitting, "I appear to steal the night-thrusting works of women, and to filch the female's Aphrodite." The link between effeminacy and sodomy is made more explicit by the coarse Mnesilochus, who several times refers to Agathon getting "fucked." When Agathon refuses to help Euripides with the angry women, saying misfortune must be met with "endurance," literally "things suffered," Mnesilochus puns on the same word and says, "Yeah, and you, oh sodomite, are wide-assed not with words, but with the things you've suffered." Aristophanes, at least, has no doubts that the man who *looks* like a woman will sexually *perform* like a woman, which is to say endure penetration by a man.[27]

Cleisthenes is more obscure than Agathon, but no less pilloried by Aristophanes for being a passive homosexual. In the *Acharnians* the poet accuses him of shaving his "hot-tempered anus," an insult Aristophanes also inflicts on his old enemy, the demagogue Kleon, who has the "asshole of a furnace." In the *Frogs* Cleisthenes is described "plucking the hairs from his anus among the tombs," graveyards and public privies being favorite spots for homosexual trysting. The lack of hair on his face likewise occasions Aristophanes' mockery. He appears before the ladies of the *Women at the Thesmophoria* to protest his solidarity with them, offering his unshaven cheeks as evidence that he is "of like kind" with them. As with Agathon, this effeminacy is the sign of passive sodomy. In the *Lysistrata*, the sexually desperate Athenian tells the Spartan ambassador that if they don't settle with the women soon, they'll have "to fuck Cleisthenes," suggesting that the supposedly gender-indifferent Greeks considered the penetration of other men as a sexual act of last resort.[28]

Many other unfortunate Greek men besides Agathon and Cleisthenes are attacked in comedy for being effeminate and perforce pathics. There is Amynon, awesome in his knowledge of anuses, and so the man to call for a tough case of constipation. A certain Aristodemus is such an enthusiastic pathic that his name becomes a synonym for "anus." The fourth-century politician Callistratus has his name given as the answer to a riddle describing the anus: "There is a thing that speaks though it's tongueless, the female the same as the male, steward of its own winds, shaggy, elsewhere smooth, speaking nonsense to the sensible, drawing melody from melody, one and many, and though wounded is unwounded." The references to "wounded" and "smooth," sodomy and depilation, indicate why Callistratus can be a synonym for the anus. Clearly the comic writers, like Aristotle, see the willingness to endure penetration by another man, the evidence for which is the effeminacy of the pathic, as a sign of "unnatural" degeneration from masculine identity.[29]

The assimilation of the *kinaidos* and the boy-love to the appearance and role of the woman creates a link between the two, as Aristotle saw in his explanation of homosexuality as resulting from childhood sexual abuse. This suspicion that pederasty can lead to adult homosexuality partly explains the consistent defensive anxiety about pederasty that runs throughout even the most enthusiastic panegyrists. Consider Socrates in the *Phaedrus*, who says that the lover interested only in physical gratification will prefer a boy who is "soft," pale from spending all his time in the shade, accustomed to an "unmanly and delicate way of life," using makeup and indulging in sexual misbehavior Socrates won't even mention.[30] In short, the boy already embodies all the disgusting qualities of the pathic who abandons his masculinity for the identity of woman: softness, white skin, effeminacy, and a predilection for unnatural sexual gratification. The male-female pattern is the norm, in which the two sexes are distinguished by external signals as well as sexual roles defined in terms of active penetration and passive receptivity. Anyone who deviates from that norm, as do the *kinaidos* and the boy-love who submits to anal penetration, is a target for disgust, mockery, and anxiety. In short, there is no evidence in Greek literature for the current fashionable supposition that the Greeks viewed the penetration of both women and men in the same light.

Outrage and Shame

The Greek antipathy for the penetrated *kinaidos*, which we have already seen in our discussion of homosexuality's origins and its deviance from the heterosexual norm, can also be found in the rich vocabulary of abuse centered on buggery, including a consistent association of passive homosexuality with "shame" and "outrage."

Ancient Greek has several insulting epithets that derive their force from the disgust felt toward those who allow themselves to be sodomized. Indeed, for a society considered tolerant of a wide spectrum of sexual behavior, the ancient Greeks possessed a much *wider* public vocabulary of homosexual disparagement, outside the public rest room, than a sexually uptight America can call on. Two of those epithets from ancient Greece—*euruprôktos*, "wide-anused," and *katapugôn*, "passive homosexual, lecher"—are compounds built around the words *pugê*, "rump," and *prôktos*, "anus." This obsession with the anus reflects the Greek contempt for the man who endures anal penetration. Other insults originating in the disgust sodomy provokes include "cistern-assed," "gaping-assed," and "gapers," alluding to the stretched-out anuses of pathics. Moreover, it does not lessen the homoerotic force of these words to argue, as some modern scholars do, that these words are sometimes used of women or in contexts not explicitly sexual.[31] Whatever context they are used in, these words are insults because they link excessive destructive behavior to what is seen as the premier standard of degeneracy, the *kinaidos*. "Motherfucker" is a powerful insult even when sex with mothers is not the issue, for the behavior of the person given the epithet is characterized as the sort that someone who *would* have sex with his mother engages in, mother-son incest considered the absolute worst sexual crime. Try insulting someone by calling him a "fatherfucker." Or consider "cocksucker," another term of debasement—it is so only because the spectacle of men performing fellatio is seen by most men as inherently revolting. No man, even a homosexual, will get very upset by being called a "clitsucker." These ancient Greek epithets are so deadly because they characterize the recipient of them as a creature of unrestrained appetite who sacrifices his humanity to the lure of bestial pleasure.

The use of these epithets, then, serves to identify those whose excessive appetites pose a threat to civilized order. The old veterans of Marathon in Aristophanes' *Wasps*, who defended Athens against the Persians, proclaim, "How I esteem my old age, better than the ringlets and fashion and wide-anuses of today's youths," the orators and rhetoricians who have never held an oar or a spear but who squander the wealth the veterans won from the Persians. The bribe-taking, "soft" public prosecutor we met earlier from the same play is also called *katapugôn*, "lecherous" specifically in the manner of a pathic. Likewise in the *Acharnians*, where Aristophanes calls on the Athenians to ignore the lying sophistries of the corrupt orators and so keep from becoming a "city of gapers." As we will soon see, these terms of abuse link a generalized political and social corruption, resulting from the lust for power or money, to the compulsive sexual activity of the pathic, the worst example of the failure to control the natural forces of the body.[32]

Passive homosexuality is also denigrated by being linked to defecation, for obvious reasons. As we noted earlier, outdoor privies were favorite spots for homosexual assignations. Cratinus mentions the ruins of a shrine to the Athenian Cimon as a popular venue for both crapping and buggering. Certain words derived from *kopros*, "shit," often suggest buggery. "I'll cover you in shit" is the Sausage-Seller's threat to bugger and humiliate Kleon in Aristophanes' *Knights*. The Spartan ambassador in the *Lysistrata* reflects the national predilection for anal intercourse by wishing "to carry dung" in answer to the horny Athenian's desire "to plow the field," the latter a stereotypical metaphor for marital sex. Other jokes work by taking for granted a connection between sodomy and excrement. The servant in the *Peace*, feeding the giant dung beetle on which his master will ride to heaven, tells the other servant to fetch the stools of a boy-love, since such are nicely "rubbed" or "smoothed" or "kneaded," the latter sense conveying aptly the rhythmic motions of buggery. When the beetle gets to heaven it will dine on "Ganymede's ambrosia," the turds of Zeus's catamite and cupbearer. The Sausage-Seller in the *Knights*, parodying, in a passage filled with thinly veiled allusions to sodomy, the folk belief that a sneeze was a good omen, interprets the fart of a pathic as a good sign. Presumably the anus of a *kinaidos*, widened and loosened by buggery, produced propitious tones. And in the *Women at the Assembly*, the defecating Blepyrus describes the constipated stool "banging at his gate" in terms that suggest buggery and wonders which pathic (*kataprôktôn*) he should call for help, since they obviously are experts at moving stools.[33]

The main purpose of these jokes, of course, is to get a laugh. Scatology serves the leveling intent of comedy by focusing on the great natural egalitarian functions of shitting, pissing, and farting. But the tarring of passive homosexuality with the brush of defecation locates the *kinaidos* in the realm of a chaotic, destructive nature and its primal processes that remind us of our own contingent and mortal flesh. Hence this comic contempt for the pathic corresponds to a more serious and pervasive characterization of it as "shameful." Shame is an important social construct for a culture like the ancient Greeks', in which more of life was lived before the eyes of others than in our society, and so public estimation was more important than private. Aristotle defines shame (*aischunê*) as a "pain or disturbance in regard to bad things . . . which seem likely to involve us in discredit, and shamelessness [*anaischuntia*] as contempt or indifference in regard to these same bad things." These "bad things" are those behaviors that the community as a whole agrees are to be avoided and that involve the excessive indulgence of appetites and passions. Among the latter Aristotle includes "carnal intercourse with forbidden persons."[34] The idea that passive homosexuality is "shameful" dominates the literary remains, including even apologists for pederasty, whose anxiety about shame reveals the uncomfortable propinquity of the boy-love to the pathic. Remember that Chrysippus, the boy raped by Laius, kills himself out of "shame" (*aischunês*).

From the comic poets to the orators and philosophers, "shame" dominates the characterization of the *kinaidos*. Aristophanes' Just Logic in the *Clouds* calls Unjust Logic, the exponent of unbridled gratification of all desires, a "shameless sodomite" (*katapugôn ei kanaischuntos*), reinforcing the insult derived from buggery with the idea of shamelessness.[35] This doesn't surprise us, coming from a comic writer who finds the effeminate pathic an easy target. Yet the same concern with shamelessness shows up in contexts that also display an approval of high-toned "spiritual" pederasty. Socrates in Xenophon's *Symposium*, sanctioning the supposedly chaste attraction of Callias for the beautiful athlete Autolycus, calls physical gratification in such a homoerotic relationship "the most thoroughly shameful things" (*eponeidistotata*), the prefix *ep-* and the superlative redoubling the already negative force of the word. A little later, alluding to the older male's pedagogical rationale for chasing the boy, he says the lover cannot improve the boy-love if he exhibits "shamelessness and incontinence" (*anaischuntian kai akrasian*), specifically defining the former in terms of physical gratification. And in reference to the idea, voiced by Pausanias in Plato's *Symposium*, that an army of lovers would be the bravest, since they would be prohibited by shame from deserting each other, Socrates snorts that men "wallowing in incontinence" would be habituated to shameful behavior and so would not be "ashamed to do anything shameful" (*aischunountai aischron ti poiein*). In fact, he goes on, that's why the Thebans and Eleans, notoriously laissez-faire regarding homosexuality, pair their lovers—to keep an eye on them and make sure they don't run off. The Spartans, the world's greatest infantrymen, fight just as bravely alongside foreigners, for they are impelled by duty, not the shameful bond of physical pleasure. Plato in the *Laws* agrees with Xenophon's Socrates, denying that homosexuality promotes bravery and asserting that the man who yields to irrational pleasure will yield as well to fear—especially, but not exclusively, the one who plays the woman's part.[36]

The categorizing of passive homosexuality as shameful is so pervasive in Greek thought that even pederastic enthusiasts like Plato's Pausanias must admit this widespread estimation and the unsavory odor it lends to the sort of high-minded pederasty he endorses, in which physical gratification is justified by the improvement the lover brings to the boy's soul and character. This "good" lover, Pausanias argues, is inspired by the "Heavenly" Aphrodite and is exclusive and permanent, whereas the canaille are incited by the "Vulgar" Aphrodite and hence are lovers of the body only; it is *they* who are responsible for "some" saying that it is "shameful [*aischron*] to gratify a lover." Clearly the existence of these "some" bespeaks a disapproval of even idealized pederasty serious enough for Pausanias to feel compelled to engage it, which he does by rationalizing that gratification is shameful only if it is given to a worthless man. In the same dialogue Aristophanes, tongue firmly in cheek, reflects the same public opinion when he admits that the "natural" male-lovers are called by some "shameless" (*anaischuntous*). Likewise Socrates in the *Phaedrus* speaks of the soul attracted to the beauty of the boy's body as "not ashamed [*aischunetai*] to pursue pleasure in violation of nature." Apparently a significant number of Athenians saw no difference between the adult passive homosexual and the presumed physical gratification the boy bestows on his admirer, since both involved anal penetration by another male. It is this opinion that compels pederastic apologists to make these fine distinctions between the boy gratefully acknowledging his lover-mentor's improving instruction and the shameful *kinaidos* merely scratching his lustful itch.[37]

The orators reflect the same common characterization of same-sex activity as something the community as a whole considers disreputable, whether the context is pederasty or adult homosexuality. The author of the *Erotic Essay*, attributed to the fourth-century statesman Demosthenes, is careful to preface his praise of the beautiful young Epicrates with assertions of his elevated intent, since such pederastic praises "attach shame [*aischunên*]" to the recipients, apparently because people will think sexual favors will be given in exchange. Thus he has been careful to avoid even the slightest imputation of physical gratification, since a "just lover" would neither do nor request anything "shameful." This dichotomy between the "just lover," the one who "associates chastely" with his favorite and bestows on him the benefits of "love without shame" (*chôris aischunês*), in contrast to the others who want mere physical gratification, runs throughout the essay and will be discussed in more detail in Chapter 8. The anxiety about shame makes its avoidance one of the most important qualities the boy-love can possess. Hence the author praises Epicrates for handling his admirers in such a way that not one of them can even hope for "such things as result in shame [*aischunên*]," which is to say physical gratification. All this defensive elaboration would not be necessary if pederasty and same-sex relations were not looked upon with disapproval. Just like Pausanias, the author of the *Erotic Essay* must take pains to address and counter the common belief that pederasty is a pretentious rationale for buggery, a sex act considered inherently disgusting *in any context*.[38]

The fourth-century orator Aeschines' prosecution against Timarchos for prostitution exploits to the hilt the widely accepted view of passive homosexuality as shameful. The case arose out of a complex web of political intrigue and vengeance. In 346 Aeschines had been an envoy to the court of the Macedonian Phillip II, where a peace treaty was signed. The Athenians grew unhappy with the terms of the treaty and with Phillip's subsequent behavior. Under the lead of the famous Demosthenes, Phillip's inveterate enemy, they went after the envoys, including Aeschines, threatening them with prosecution in court and possible execution. Timarchos was probably the lead prosecutor. To head off the attack, Aeschines in turn prosecuted Timarchos for accepting money for sex in his youth, a crime of "outrage" that barred the perpetrator from holding office or addressing the assembly or prosecuting a citizen.[39] Aeschines won his case and so postponed the attack on himself.

From beginning to end of his prosecution, Aeschines attacks Timarchos with the club of "shame," which Timarchos deserves because he "lives shamefully [*aischrôs*]," allowing other men to penetrate him and taking money for it. That Timarchos's uncontrolled appetites, rather than the mere fact that he occasionally prostituted himself, are the source of his shame is clear later when Aeschines says that Timarchos was "slave to the most shameful pleasures [*aischistais hêdonais*]" including gluttony, heterosexual excess, and gambling as well as passive homosexuality. The point is that Timarchos's inability to control his appetites leads to a whole range of sensual indulgences, the worst of which is passive buggery, and it is this lack of control that "shames" him—the taking of money for it the insult added to the injury. This emphasis on the lack of self-control that defines the pathic is made explicit when Aeschines refers to Timarchos's "disgusting and unholy nature" and his "excessive incontinence," charges that have nothing to do with taking money. Thus "shame" becomes the leitmotif of the speech. Timarchos "shamed himself" by having sex with a public slave, he is driven by "shameful pleasures," and he is charged with "the most shameful activities." And Aeschines makes clear the nature of these shameful "pleasures" and "activities"—not taking money but committing a "woman's sins," allowing himself to be penetrated and thus "outraging his own body contrary to nature [*para phusin*]."[40]

Just as in Xenophon, Plato, and pseudo-Demosthenes, it is passive homosexuality that is seen as unnatural and shameful, the worst in a continuum of appetitive excess that delivers a man to the destructive forces of the irrational, compromising his reason and hence his humanity. Mark Aeschines' repeated use of the word "beastly" in reference to Timarchos. Such "beastly excesses" forfeit his humanity, thus rendering him unfit to participate in the political and social life that Aristotle says is the essence of human identity.[41]

Like shame, "outrage" (*hubris*) is another important term that communicates the idea of excess, particularly the excess of passion and appetite that leads one to injure and hence "shame" or dishonor another. Sexual crimes including rape, seduction, and pedophilia all would be characterized as hubris, as would sexually using a man like a woman, which is to say penetrating him anally. Sodomizing a man, then, just as today in American prisons, humiliates and shames him, as in the fifth *Idyll* of Theocritus, where the shepherd Comatas asserts his power over Lacon by reminding him how he "taught him as a child" by buggering him until he was sore. Likewise in Aristophanes' *Knights*, where the Sausage-Seller threatens to "fuck [Kleon's] asshole like a sausage-case," one of many examples in Aristophanes of buggery used to humiliate and shame.[42]

Once again the idea of irrational excess and the destructive behavior that follows it define passive homosexuality. Aristotle, in that passage from the *Nichomachean Ethics* explaining the origins of "sex with males," says some men indulge in such behavior because they were "outraged [*hubrizomenois*] from child-

hood." Plato in the *Phaedrus* likewise calls the "bad horse" of the soul, the one desiring physical gratification from a beloved boy, the "comrade of outrage [*hubreôs*]."
And Aeschines uses the same word to describe Timarchos's behavior, quoting the
law against sexual "outrage," which he believes covers Timarchos's transgressions,
since he defines his sexual crimes as an "outrage [*hubrin*] against his own body," an
outrage "contrary to nature." Like the association of buggery with defecation, the
ideas of "shame" and "outrage" locate passive homosexuality in the realm of destructive appetites and excessive passions, excrement and gender confusion, indiscriminate forces of nature threatening the orders of the mind and the city.[43]

The Itch of Appetite

In Xenophon's *Memorabilia*, Socrates notices that Critias, later to be infamous as
one of the thirty thugs the Spartans installed after their victory over Athens, desires a certain Euthydemus and is trying to use him sexually. When Critias ignores
Socrates' protestations, the philosopher remarks that Critias "has the sensibility of
a pig, desiring as he does to rub up against Euthydemus like pigs rubbing themselves against stones."[44] This coarse image, like Socrates' description in the *Gorgias*
of homosexual desire as an "itch," takes us to the heart of what passive homosexual eros means in ancient Greek literary remains: The worst example of the destructiveness of eros, it is a compulsive bestial power controlling the mind, an omnivorous force that stands synechdochically for all the natural greedy appetites that
threaten civilized order.

This link of greed and homosexuality crops up in complaints about both mercenary boys and pathics, the former because they were wooed with gifts and so
could mask their greed in the ritual of pederasty, the latter because their overwhelming desire to be buggered reinforced *all* their lusts, including the lust for
money, leading to prostitution as a means of gratifying both desires. Pederasts constantly complain about gold-digging boys—the "handsome boy sells everything
for money," Callimachus sniffs. Similarly the Hellenistic poet Dioscorides advises
the "boy-raven" to approach the beautiful Hermogenes with a "full hand," for the
"expensive pathic" feels neither pity nor shame. The reference to shame and the
vulgar noun—the word translated "pathic" literally means "screw" in the sense of
"fuck"—indicate a blurring of the line separating the boy-love from the despised
kinaidos. Aristophanes makes their connection explicit in the *Wealth*. When Cario,
testifying to the power of money, says that boy-loves, like prostitutes, favor only
wealthy lovers, Chremylus, parodying the high-flown distinctions of a pederastic
enthusiast like Pausanias, responds that only the "base" ones ask for cash—the
"noble" ones settle for a good horse or hunting dogs. As Cario says, because they
are ashamed (*aischunomenoi*) they "disguise their depravity with a name." The
common denominator of the depraved boy-love, the pathic, and the prostitute is
an omnivorous greed also displayed in their submission to sodomy.[45]

The assumption that the man who submits to anal penetration is a Charybdis of greed dominates Aeschines' attack on Timarchos, whose sexual irregularities, the "reckless pleasures of the body," are linked to a more generalized greed, the belief that "nothing is enough," the twin motives of the robber, the pirate, the assassin, and the tyrant. Since the prosecutor must play to the prejudices of the several hundred jurymen, this assumption that the passive homosexual was also mercenary in order to finance his debauchery must have been widespread. Comedy generally reflects popular prejudice as well. The third-century playwright Menander gets a laugh by referring to a certain Ctessipus, a dyed and depilated pathic who sold the stones of his father's grave monument in order to pay for his unusual sexual proclivities. Whether by the boy-love or the pathic, the submission to the worst of bodily pleasures, anal penetration, leaves the soul vulnerable to *all* forms of greed, leading ultimately to the use of any means, no matter how lawless or shameful, to gratify the body's imperious desires.[46]

It is in the comedies of Aristophanes, though, that this connection of a corrupting greed with sexual excess is most thoroughly developed in order to characterize the decline of Athenian society in the latter decades of the fifth century. Continually Aristophanes contrasts the "good old days" of early-fifth-century Athens, when the hardy hoplites and rowers defeated the Persians, with the corrupt present of the Athenian Empire, a time dominated by ambition, careerism, opportunism, and greed; a time when, as John Donne would say of his own time, "New philosophy calls all in doubt," when smooth-talking orators gull the citizenry torpid with wealth, and clever Sophists, the spin doctors of the ancient world, make "the shameful noble and the noble shameful," as Just Logic in the *Clouds* puts it. All of these unwholesome innovations culminate in the destructive war with Sparta, a war motivated by ambition and imperial greed. This is clearly how Lysistrata understands the origins of the war when she says that all the strife of the city, including the war with Sparta, arises to give the politicians an opportunity for stealing. Aristophanes uses sexual excess, particularly the unnatural lust of the pathic, as a concrete image for *all* these destructive appetites, and he merges the pathic with the type of the "new man": the smooth-talking orator and Sophist, the lupine careerist and ambitious demagogue, the "laconizing"—pro-Spartan—snooty aristocrat, all of whom promote the war and weaken the fabric of society for private gain and the gratification of appetite.[47]

Throughout Aristophanes' plays political and social corruption is presented in the context of unrestrained appetite, and the lust for power and money is always attended by sexual lust both hetero- and homosexual. In the *Knights* the vulgar Sausage-Seller's rise to political preeminence is the result of his unabashed omnivorous sexuality: The willingness to screw and be screwed is the necessary condition for success in a corrupt Athens. Thus he is first lured into the political life by the promise that he will be able to "fuck in the Prytaneum," the state-run Council Hall where the steering committee for the Council, distinguished visitors, and Olympic athletes could eat for free. Sex and politics, "screwing" both literally and metaphorically, here converge. In the *Wasps*, Aristophanes used Philocleon to portray the intellectual corruption of the radical Sophists, with their extolling of nature and unrestrained desires and their dismissal of the arbitrary conventions of society. Philocleon is the "natural" man who once he is freed of society's conventions immediately gets drunk, trashes a drinking party, kidnaps and attempts to rape a flute girl, destroys a baker's goods, assaults another man, and tries to rationalize his behavior with a buffoonish parody of the hedonism of a Callicles or Thrasymachus, Sophists who preached the doctrine of unrestrained pleasure as the greatest good. Likewise the shade of Aeschylus in the *Frogs* explicitly links the corruption of Athens by deceiving politicians to the scenes of sexual irregularity staged by Euripides in his plays—"pimps, women giving birth in temples, women screwing their brothers," with the result that Athens "is filled full of clerks and vulgarians and mob-monkeys deceiving the people." Political, philosophical, and theatrical corruption all share a common denominator—sexual excess.[48]

This depiction of political decay in terms of a generalized sexual unrestraint is perhaps best seen in the debate between Just Logic and Unjust Logic in the *Clouds*. The two Logics are struggling for the soul of Pheidippides, a young fop whose father has sent him off to Socrates to learn how to use clever argumentation to get out of paying the bills the old man has run up financing his son's aristocratic pretensions. Just Logic warns Pheidippides that if he follows the hedonistic relativism of Unjust Logic, gratifying all his appetites and rationalizing them with clever speaking, he will end up with a "wide asshole" (*euruprôktos*), either from being buggered or from having a radish stuck up his ass, the traditional punishment for adultery. Giving in to indiscriminate sexual appetite leads to passive homosexuality or seducing other men's wives, both seen as crimes of "outrage" violating the cultural order. Unjust Logic shrugs, So what? The whole city is filled with men with "wide assholes"—the politicians, the tragic poets, the orators; even the members of the whole audience have "wide assholes" because they are controlled by a sexual appetite so powerful it compels them to be sodomized or to seduce other men's wives. At this point a despairing Just Logic admits defeat, for the whole city *is*, he admits, made of "fucked ones," all corrupted by social and political institutions that exist only to gratify without restraint their appetites and passions rather than limiting and controlling them. So it is that references to the big erect penis in Aristophanes' plays signifies the surrender to a destructive excess and greed, since the organ presumably is oversized from overuse. If you follow Unjust Logic, Just Logic warns Pheidippides, you will have just such a "big cock." Likewise in the *Knights* the Sausage-Seller tells Demos, the personified people of Athens, that if they listen to Kleon, Aristophanes' type of the corrupt politician, they will be "completely hard," pure unrestrained appetite.[49]

Passive homosexuality, though, most frequently characterizes the corruption of the city by greed and ambition, for as we have seen, to the Greeks homosexual eros is unredeemed by procreation and hence exists solely to indulge sexual appetite. The rivalry of the Sausage-Seller and Kleon for control of the city in the

Knights is presented through an imagery of buggery, for they are really competing to see who gets to "sodomize" Demos, the personified citizenry, which is to say use it for their own private pleasures and aggrandizement. Aristophanes seems to be saying that things are so bad in Athens that the shameless pursuit of all appetites, including active and passive homosexuality, is the most important qualification for a politician.

The Sausage-Seller tells a story about himself that demonstrates his political promise in these terms. Once when he was a boy he stole a piece of meat and got away by hiding it between his buttocks. An orator who noticed this obvious image of passive sodomy proclaimed that the Sausage-Seller would some day be a leader of the people—he's a thief and he's willing to get screwed. Later the Sausage-Seller confirms the sexual meaning of the anecdote when he says that he sold sausages and "was fucked" for money in the marketplace. His rival Kleon, the "Paphlagonian," has the same qualifications. Demosthenes, one of Demos's slaves, tells us Kleon's anus lies "among the Gapers," those whose anuses are stretched out from continual buggery. When Kleon claims that he benefited the city by stopping the "fucked ones," the pathics, the Sausage-Seller exploits the connection between buggery and a political career by saying Kleon was just trying to cut down on the number of both his sexual and his political rivals.[50]

This imagery culminates in both men presenting themselves as rival pederastic lovers (*erastês, anterastês*) of Demos, once more obliterating the distinction between the pathic and the supposedly accepted "boy-love." Parodying the rhetoric of the pederastic apologist, the Sausage-Seller chides Demos that he "acts like the boys with their lovers. [He] doesn't accept the noble and good men, giving [himself] instead to lantern-sellers, cobblers, shoemakers, and leather-sellers." The Sausage-Seller is mimicking the antidemocratic and pederastic biases of someone like Socrates, who at least according to Plato didn't believe tradesmen and craftsmen were qualified to deliberate and decide on the fate of the city. The irony, of course, is that the Sausage-Seller is a much lower form of riffraff than a cobbler. He is manipulating pederastic rhetoric to mask his real desire—to "fuck" the city. Such dishonest political rhetoric is like the sophistries of pederasty, rationalizations for the indulgence of private appetite and ambition—and these are the forces corrupting Athenian society.[51]

The interconnection of effeminacy, passive homosexuality, and political and social corruption recurs throughout Aristophanes' plays. In the *Clouds*, Just Logic links the city's corruption to the effeminacy of modern youth, who "make their voices soft/effeminate [*malakên*] for a lover, marching around pimping themselves." This contrasts with the good old days, when the modest boys sat with their legs crossed tight and smoothed the sand so that not even an imprint of their genitals could be seen. If Pheidippides follows Just Logic, he continues, he will "hate the agora"—the public space where the politicians and Sophists idle—and "avoid the baths and be ashamed at shameful things." But if he follows Unjust Logic, he will end up looking like the effeminate pathic, with "pallid skin, thin arms, weak chest, fat tongue, tiny ass, a big cock": the tongue fat from practicing oratory, the ass withered by buggery, the big cock, as we have seen, the sign of unbridled appetite. Likewise the Chorus of Marathon veterans in the *Wasps* derides the "curls" and fashions of modern youth with their "wide assholes," the aristocratic and pro-Spartan pretensions destroying the democracy, the effeminacy seen in the "soft, mincing sodomite" of a public prosecutor who takes bribes and cheats the city.[52]

The orators particularly come under attack as the source of the city's ills since they manipulate a deceptive rhetoric to sway the Assembly and exploit it for their own aggrandizement. They were perceived to be the creatures of the Sophists, who taught them how to disregard truth and "make the worse argument the better," as Socrates puts it in defending himself against the misperception that he was one of their tribe. When coupled with the extreme relativism and hedonism of the more radical Sophists, the ability to manipulate language was seen as an instrument for gratifying appetite and indulging passion. Hence the frequent link of oratory and the study of rhetoric to effeminacy and buggery, the newfangled sophistries that serve to rationalize greed and ambition. The comic poet Plato said that pathics necessarily become orators—that's why there are so many of them. Just Logic, as we just saw, contrasts athletic prowess and military exercising with "chattering in the agora" and bringing lawsuits, the practice of rhetorical skill that leaves the tongue fat and the buttocks weakened not just from inactivity but from buggery. The same contrast between manly physical activity and effeminate rhetorical practice crops up in the *Frogs*, where the shade of Aeschylus complains that the mania for prattling and chattering has "emptied the wrestling schools and worn out the asses of the chattering young men." And Praxagora in the *Women at the Assembly*, assuring her fellow conspirators that they will have no problem speaking in the Assembly once they have disguised themselves as men and infiltrated it, says that the young men "fucked the most" make the best speakers. Since being penetrated comes naturally to women, public speaking ought to also.[53]

For Aristophanes, the dissolution of the political, social, and cultural order of Athens is driven by the forces of irrational appetites, the lust for money and power whose best image is sexual lust, particularly the "unnatural" sterile "itch" of the pathic to be sodomized. The destructiveness of eros we have been tracing so far finds its worst manifestation in passive homosexuality, a chaotic force attacking those civilized orders that allow humans to exist as humans and not slip back into bestial savagery. As do women, *kinaidoi* magnify the central problem of human identity: the need to limit and control, through the mind and culture, the natural forces of the body's passions. But as a male the pathic is worse than a woman, for the male is supposed to represent the order of the mind and culture that contains the chaos of nature. By submitting to the compulsive and socially useless desire to be penetrated, the pathic abandons his masculine identity, and so can represent *all* the ways that civilized order is threatened by the irrational, a monster of appetite that ultimately threatens the very basis of human identity itself.

The Controlless Core

Like fire and storm, disease and death, the Greeks' eros is a force of nature, indiscriminate, chaotic, relentlessly attacking civilization and its orders—the mind and its projections onto the world, the political and social structures that clear the space for human identity. Embodied in golden, laughter-loving Aphrodite, the sexual drive deceives with its joy and beauty that, like a calm sea, veil its destructive powers. Like the goddess, woman too is deceptively beautiful and lurks on the frontier of nature and culture: She is tied to the cycles and blood and passions of the earth and its primal forces, yet her procreative power is necessary for the survival of the city and its institutions. Then there is the *kinaidos*, the creature of a sterile pleasure—anal penetration—that abandons to the vortex of desire not just his own rational control over his passions but also the masculine order enshrined in the political and social institutions of the city, subjecting them to the corrosive acid of all appetites, all lusts.

But this picture of the woman and the pathic is ultimately an exaggeration of the central *human* predicament, the subjection of all of us to the natural "controlless core" constantly encroaching on the mind and its constructs, the soul's eternal dialectic between its appetites and its reason, its body and its soul, chaos and order. What forms that order takes, what mechanisms of control the Greeks imagined could organize the disorder of eros, what "fancied sway" they created to tame the beasts of nature, will be found in Part 2.

PART TWO

The "Fancied Sway"

FIVE

Taming the Beasts

BEFORE SOCRATES in the *Republic* can make the case that injustice is always damaging to its perpetrator as well as to its victim, he must first describe the essential nature of the human soul by means of a "likeness in speech." The human soul is a composite creature, Socrates says, like the Chimera or Scylla or the three-headed, snake-tailed watchdog of Hades, Cerberus.[1] It comprises a "many-headed and intricate beast, having in a ring the heads of tame and wild beasts, able to metamorphose and make grow from itself all these things." Joined to this monster are a lion and a man, all hidden from view by the human shape that contains them.

If this is the true nature of the soul, then to say that injustice is a good is to affirm that it is beneficial to feed and strengthen the "multiform beast" and the lion and allow them to control the man and ultimately "to bite and fight and eat" each other, in the end destroying the soul. But the philosopher who says that justice is the good affirms that everything we do should be directed toward what Emerson called "aw[ing] the beast"—the "man" in the soul should have the most power over the composite soul and "manage the many-headed beast, like a farmer nurturing and domesticating the tame plants, but keeping the wild ones from growing. And the man should make an ally of the nature of the lion, and caring for all the beasts in common make them friends to one another and to himself, and thus he will nurture them."[2]

Plato's image embodies one of the most significant and enduring ideas the Greeks bequeathed to the West, one so pervasive that it is part of the mental furniture of all Westerners whether they know it or not: the picture of human identity as a composite formed of the truly human and humanizing essence, reason; the monstrous, ever-changing, bestial appetites and passions; and the potentially positive emotions like courage or indignation. Equally important is the relationship among these three, for reason is supposed to control, domesticate, manage, and tame the "lion" and the passions and appetites that left uncontrolled will literally devour the soul and destroy the man. Note too how Socrates' simile from farming links reason's dominance to the technology of agriculture, another "unnatural" human activity that imposes order on nature to exploit its creative energy, just as reason should "domesticate" the passions and reconcile them to one another and the man, so that they are creative rather than destructive. And of all those passions and appetites, sex is perhaps the most powerful and volatile, the most in need of control and order for the soul to function harmoniously and not be swept away by the chaos of sex.

This hierarchical dualism consisting of a humanizing and immaterial reason set above the bestial material body and its appetites is not, of course, peculiar to Plato or even invented by him. It recurs throughout Greek philosophy in a variety of images in which the mind is superior to the body, the rational to the irrational, the immaterial to the material. The late-fifth-century philosopher Philolaus reformulated the old Orphic and Pythagorean image of the body as the "tomb" of the soul. The idea that the body, being material and subject to change and decay, is a mere superficial transient home for the immortal soul can likewise be seen in Empedocles' notion of the body as the "clothes" of the soul. And the idea that the body is inimical to the soul turns up in Xenophon's image of the body as a net in which the soul is caught. All of these implications following from the body's presumed inferiority to the rational soul occur over and over in Plato's various metaphors describing the body as an oyster shell, a vehicle, or a prison—that is, something the soul is trapped in or uses, mere matter ultimately unrelated to the true nature of human identity. Throughout Greek thought, from the earliest pre-Socratics to the Epicureans, these various images reinforce both the superiority of reason to the irrational and the need for the mind to control, order, and limit the passions of a body that in Plato's words is "mortal and multiform and irrational and dissoluble and changeable," too much akin to a chaotic natural world continually threatening human identity and order.[3]

As we have seen in Part 1, eros is a powerful force of that world, as well as residing within the souls of humans. Our first "technology," then, that attempts to exert a "fancied sway" over eros is the rational control of it by the soul. On the cosmic level, this control is part of a view of eros as a physical natural force somewhat like gravity or electromagnetism, conceptually subordinated to the human mind and hence more tolerable, even if still beyond any human attempt to change or manipulate it. On the individual level, eros and its bestial pleasures are subject to the truly human mind and its rational virtues that allow the orderly soul to function harmoniously and to avoid the pain and disorder that all the passions and appetites bring in their wake.

Cosmic Love

The earliest speculations on the creation and nature of the cosmos acknowledged the need of a motive force, a "cause that will move things and join them together," as Aristotle put it. The creative force of sexual attraction provided an obvious energy that could be projected onto the universe and so account for the continual creation and variety of new bodies as well as for the movement of those bodies. In Hesiod's seventh-century account of creation, Chaos, Earth, and Tartarus, the regions below the earth, all mysteriously come into being, as does Eros. Eros then becomes the force of further creation through sex. Night, born of Chaos, "mingled in lovemaking" with Tartarus and bore Aether, the upper atmosphere, and Day. The phrase "mingled in lovemaking" is the same one Homer uses of sex, and we see primal creation very early on conceived of as successive sex acts creating the generations of deities whose family romances account for cosmic development and history.[4]

This view of Eros as the cosmic generative force is quite common in Greek philosophy and religion. The Orphics believed the cosmos began as an egg from which emerged Phanes, a principle of generation also called Eros. The early philosopher Pherecydes, from the seventh or early sixth centuries, is reported to have said that Zeus when about to create the cosmos changed first into Eros, bringing the cosmos into harmony and love out of opposites. The idea of order, which is the root meaning of "cosmos" in Greek, is embodied in both "love/friendship" and the figure of Zeus, already in Homer the upholder of universal order. The fifth-century Parmenides makes Eros a creation of the goddess who guides everything, specifically the "cruel mating" of male and female seen as a fundamental principle of order. By the fourth century the speakers in Plato's *Symposium* speak of Eros's cosmic creative role with the casualness of received wisdom.[5]

The early-fifth-century philosopher Empedocles, though, gathers these various perceptions of sexual love as a creative force into a system in which love accounts not just for the creation of the world but its continuing history, as well as for positive human qualities like affection and harmony. Empedocles posited four elements or "roots"—earth, air, fire, and water—and two forces—Love and Strife—to explain the existence of our world. That world and everything in it result from the attractive and repulsive action these two forces arouse in the four elements, causing them continually to combine and separate. This accounts for both the variety of bodies and their movement through time. The force of Love is sometimes called Aphrodite but never Eros, for Empedocles wants an *idealized* force of attraction in which sexual energy is part of a spiritual or psychological bonding as well as a physical bonding. Thus the word *philotês* is used, which embodies both the sexual aspect of love and qualities such as friendship and affection. Empedocles' Love is still the force of sexual attraction, what he calls "adhesive" love permeating all things and "implanted" in mortal bodies. But it is also "friendship" and "affection," the agent through which men "think friendly/affectionate thoughts and perform harmonious deeds." Aristotle understood Empedocles to mean that the good, order, and beauty are all caused by this Love and its still sexual attractive power.[6]

We see here an early example of one of the most pervasive means of controlling eros and lessening its destructive power: the subordination of it to those tender attachments between people that can contain the sexual but are not limited to it. As we will see in later chapters, marriage and pedagogical pederasty will create contexts of affection for ordering eros, and ultimately our modern superstition of Romantic Love is a heightened elaboration of this same idea. Yet in all these sexual relationships erotic love is a constant, and sexual intercourse always provides the basic paradigm for Empedoclean Love. That is because it must be *creative*—the mingling of bodies that creates a new body. From this it follows that Empedoclean Love be literally heterosexual, in the Greek sense of the prefix "hetero," which means "different." Love in Empedocles is not the attraction of like element to like—this is the function of Strife, which causes each of the four elements to stick to its own kind and avoid combining with the other three. Love rather is the attraction of *different* elements. Just as the dissimilar man and woman unite in sex to create a new life, so Love unites different elements to create the complex variety of existence. And these bodies, infused with Love, come together and desire one another in "love/lovemaking/affection," continuing the creative process on a higher level.[7]

Empedocles' idealization of sexuality as a creative and unifying force can be further seen in his theory of the cycle of cosmic history. The world we know is the result of the opposing forces of Love and Strife. It represents an intermediate stage in an eternal alternation between a cosmos dominated completely by Love and one controlled completely by Strife, a "double creation" and a "double decline." In the Love-dominated cosmos, all four elements are so intermingled as to be indistinguishable from one another, united under the power of Love into one ordered whole, a cosmic god divine, harmonious, unified, with no "unseemly war in his limbs." In other words, the Love-dominated cosmos is perfect order, everything that our multiform, mutable, conflict-ridden world is not. *Our* world is the result of the advance of Strife, which initiates the movement of like element to like, an attraction that along with the still-present influence of Love to unite dissimilar elements creates our material world and all its processes of change and alteration. Eventually Strife is triumphant, leading to a world in which all that exists are the four discriminated elements, until the whole process starts over again. We live in the time of Strife's growing ascendancy, and so the war and violence and hatred and disorder that characterize our world. The time when Love was ascendant was the mythic Golden Age, a time of peace and simplicity when nature was kind to man and provided him with sustenance, beasts were tame and friendly to vegetarian humans, and Aphrodite ruled all. Here we clearly see the connection of an idealized sexuality first, in the Love-dominated cosmos, to a divine unity, a perfect order; next, in the Love-ascendant cosmos, to an ideal natural world of peace and harmony with nature. The destructiveness of eros we traced in Chapter 1 has been accounted for, all its disorder not inherent in *it* but due to the necessary rhythmic advance of Strife in its eternal cosmic dance with Love.[8]

The control Empedocles asserts over sexuality is conceptual, not practical. The mind that knows the reality of the cosmos can better tolerate the disorder of this world. The highest human emotions are idealized, yet at the same time they are absolved of any responsibility for improving the disorder made necessary by the cycles of cosmic history, the alternation of Love and Strife. The eros so powerful and destructive elsewhere is thus here elevated into a cosmic principle that creates all our good. And though we have no way to control those forces and that cosmic cycling through the realms of Strife and Love, knowledge is power. Empedocles' Love is a domesticated sexuality, put in its cosmic place, not a mysterious inexplicable force. Finally, it is the source of harmony and affection in our Strife-dominated world, a reminder of the lost paradise in which men and nature were as one.

The "Steersman of the Soul"

In Chapter 1 we described a complex of imagery in which eros was pictured as a force of nature, chaotic and destructive unless subjected to the control of the mind and culture. Images of disease, madness, violence, bestiality, and servility all highlighted the volatile disorder of this natural force. But what makes eros doubly dangerous is the sweet pleasure of desire and gratification, the honey that dupes us into swallowing its bitter gall. This picture of eros and its dangerous pleasure is part of a more general distrust of the body's desires and appetites, their attractive pleasures that blind us both to the pain all pleasure demands as its price and to its corrosive effect on our minds, nailing the soul, as Socrates put it, to a material body subject to decay and death.[9]

The problem with the body's desires and their pleasures is that they are inherently insatiable, blindly demanding gratification with no innate sense of sufficiency. And so they always return to upset the balance of the soul with their excess. That's how Democritus describes the pleasures of eating and sex—they are brief and short-lived, present only when being indulged but bringing after themselves pain, for after the transient enjoyment the desire returns. Even the pleasure that lures us into overindulgence is itself a source of pain once we are sated. Socrates in Xenophon's *Symposium* is made to disapprove of physical sex with a boy-love because the material body and its beauty fade and because "in the use of beauty there is surfeit," just as too much food creates nausea, the disgust with sated pleasure that attends all bodily appetites. Plato too notes that the disorder of pleasure results from its lack of any inherent completion, remaining an open-ended, repetitive process, "infinite . . . and never having in itself a beginning, middle, or end of its own." This absence of a limit, an end in which the agitation and anxiety that desires and their pleasures arouse in us are stilled, is what makes pleasure so uncontrollable and volatile.[10]

Socrates in the *Gorgias*, the dialogue recording his attack on the philosophical hedonism of the radical Sophists, elaborates an image of the "incontinent" (*akolastos*) soul that is based on this recognition of the never-ending demand of desires and their pleasures. First, he refers to a Pythagorean allegory of the incontinent part of the soul as a "jar perforated because of its insatiable desires." This soul after death is condemned to filling its leaky jar with a sieve, the sieve symbolizing the defective rational soul that can't remember the good and so devotes all its powers and energy to the fruitless task of gratifying its desires that never are permanently sated and so constantly demand more and more. When Socrates' interlocutor Callicles persists in his belief that pleasure is the good (and the more the better), Socrates tells of another allegory illustrating the lives of the "self-controlled/temperate" man and the "incontinent." The former's soul is like a man with a number of jars in which are stored various precious products difficult to acquire. When the temperate soul draws its fill, it forgets about the jars and is at peace. But the incontinent soul's jars are "perforated and unsound," and so the soul is compelled to labor night and day to keep the jars filled, thus "suffering extreme pains." The moral is clear: Given the disorder of the appetites and their pleasures, happiness can result only from the rational management of both, that is, the imposition of limits that lessen their potential for destructive excess.[11]

Given the disorderly nature of pleasure, then, it is no surprise to find it consistently characterized with much of the same negative imagery used to describe eros, itself an appetite whose intense pleasure masks its destructive effects. The corrosive power of pleasure on the mind is likened to madness by Antisthenes, who sees pleasure as the worse affliction of the two. The bestial nature of pleasure and appetite are implied by Heraclitus, when he says that if pleasure created true happiness (that is, self-sufficiency), oxen would be happy when they found vetch to eat. Pleasure's lawless destructiveness is communicated by the comic poet and philosopher Epicharmus in his image of pleasure as "unholy pirates" who drown the man they catch. Democritus equates passion with disease, asserting that wisdom frees the soul from passion just as medicine heals the diseases of the body. Thus happiness can come only from avoiding the pleasure of mortal things. And Xenophon uses the potent image of slavery to describe the state of the man who has surrendered his soul to his desires.[12]

Even a cursory survey of Plato's work uncovers similar images locating appetites and their pleasures, including of course sexual pleasure, in the realm of nature, including beasts, madness, disease—all the excessive chaotic forces militating against human order. The tyrant image frequently used of eros also characterizes pleasure, for the tyrant is the Greek political exemplar of unrestrained lawless power and excess: "Excess/outrage [*hubris*] breeds the tyrant," the Chorus of the *Oedipus Rex* sings. Plato in the *Republic* exploits this popular image of the tyrant when he links pleasure to "excess/outrage [*hubrei*] and incontinence," asserting that the man given over to his pleasures is "tyrannized" by them. The same image is used to describe the power of appetite, "the Asiatic king of the soul," in the "oligarchic man," Plato's denizen of a "cash nexus" state, corrupt because it is dominated by wealth and avarice. Elsewhere in the same dialogue the appetites are described as bestial, as we saw in the image of the soul with which we began this chapter, with its multi-headed beast, the "bestial" and "wild/savage" part of our souls.[13]

Other dialogues tap into this same complex of imagery, making Plato our most important source of the long-lived prejudice against the body and its appetites that dominates the philosophy of the West. The truly wise man, who to Plato of course is the philosopher, like the condemned Socrates cares nothing for the pleasures of eating or drinking or sex. He "dishonors the body," treats it with contempt as a thing of no account, because its pleasures are enslaving. Another frequent image is that of disease—intense pleasures and pains are called the "greatest of the soul's diseases" in the *Timaeus*, and in the *Laws* pleasure makes us the victims of a "disease endless and insatiate of evils." All of these images of tyranny, slavery, disease, madness, and bestiality mark a consistent feature of Plato's thought: The body is the wild beast, the thing of material nature that must be tamed, domesticated, subjected to reason's order for humans even to exist as humans and not slip back into an animal existence.[14]

Plato's image from the *Phaedrus* of reason as the "steersman of the soul" evokes the guiding power of the mind as well as linking it to the wider technologies humans create to exploit the energy of nature. In the balanced soul, the mind steers the whole man by using the energy of the passions just as a ship is driven by current and wind. And just as a good steersman avoids the storms that can destroy the ship, so reason should avoid the excesses of passion and appetite, the "fierce windstorms of passion," as Cercidas puts it. But sometimes the relationship between reason and passion is more antagonistic. Often we see imagery taken from war used to describe the incompatibility and hostility between the rational and irrational. "It is hard to battle desire," Democritus says; the brave man conquers not just the enemy, but pleasures. Likewise Socrates, talking about courage with some generals, says that true courage is fighting against "desires and pleasures," either keeping in the ranks of the phalanx or turning against the enemy. Hence the greatest victory is the victory over the self, its desires and appetites. Aristotle too asserts that passion yields only to force, not argument, for the irrational "battles against" the rational principle. Even poets use the same imagery. The Hellenistic poet Posidippus, braving Eros, defies the god by saying he has reason "drawn up in battle order against [Eros]"—as long as the poet is sober.[15]

In this battle between the rational and the irrational, reason must be the victor in order for humans to be truly human and not just clever beasts. Thus all human wisdom, virtue, and happiness can come only from the mind, the godlike immortal part of us through which we can escape the material natural world of change and decay. Two hundred years of Romanticism have made most of us suspicious of what modern pedants call "logocentrism," that Eurocentric prejudice in favor of reason and science as the royal road to truth and earthly bliss. The heart and its "reasons of which reason knows nothing" are to us moderns *our* truly human essence, whereas reason and science—Blake's "tree of death"—that "murder to dissect" only stunt our human identity, creating a mechanistic world in which nature is dead matter to be exploited and humans mere extensions of the machines dehumanizing our lives.

Of course, these attitudes are possible, as we mentioned in the Introduction, only because of the triumph of reason that has created a level of material existence only dreamed of in earlier ages, one in which the perfectibility of humanity appears within reach and the idealization of the irrational is made possible because science gives us the technology to lessen the destructive effects of passion and removes some of the ignorance and superstition that fostered evil. And though the Romantic criticism of rationalism—a criticism whose roots, by the way, go back to the Greeks—has much that is valid, no one perusing the bloodstained history of humanity, with its dismal record of murder, rape, plunder, torture, cruelty, starvation, and slavery, could argue that those crimes resulted from an excess of reason and a stunting of the irrational. Auschwitz represents not the triumph of rationalism but the triumph of the irrational will, the evil of a passionate hate and fear that as reason slept appropriated its power to make more efficient the irrational's monsters.

To the Greeks, though, living as they did in a world in which nature's fury and the murderous passions of men were both everyday realities to an extent that we in America outside the inner city can only imagine, the belief that reason could help us tame the beasts and achieve divinity was a dream too potent to forgo. Hence throughout Greek philosophy the good of human life, happiness, wisdom, and ultimately divinity itself all are made functions of rational activity. Democritus believed happiness came not from the body but from a wisdom that frees the soul from passion and mortal concerns. "To need nothing," Xenophon's Socrates says, "is to be divine," for incontinence excludes wisdom; true pleasure is rational, not tied to bodily pleasures or desires. Plato, of course, is our most influential, if only because he is our most copious, source for this locating of wisdom and happiness in the divinelike life of the mind rather than in the bestial pleasures of the body. The man who indulges his lusts has made himself mortal, Socrates says in the *Timaeus*. But he who "concerns himself with the love of learning and true thinking, exercising these qualities above everything else, must by necessity think things immortal and godlike, if ever he seizes on truth, and as much as human nature can participate in immortality, he must have a share in this." And though later Aristotle seems not to have believed the soul was immortal, and though he was more tolerant of the body's needs and their place in human happiness, he too recognized that the rational and irrational were at odds and that reason should rule. "For by nature the soul has a ruler and a ruled." The "soul rules the body with a despotic rule, and the mind rules the appetites with a constitutional and kingly rule." All of these formulations from various philosophers rest on one fundamental assumption: that the body and its appetites and pleasures are a part of the material natural world of change and disorder and so must be subjected to the controlling, godlike power of the mind. Only that way can a human achieve any measure of happiness, so long as happiness is defined precisely in terms of an absence of excessive passion and pleasure.[16]

But not the absence of pleasure and passion altogether. The Greeks did not share Tennyson's desire to "let the ape and tiger die," for they did not believe that to be possible. Their dichotomy of inferior body and superior mind did not lead to the later Christian ideal, in which the appetites and pleasures of the body are eradicated in a brutal process of purification and refinement. The Greeks rather want to *appropriate* the energy of the irrational, control it so that its creative energy can be exploited but not allowed to rage out of control, just as the master uses the energy of a slave to further his own economic ends. This is what makes the relationship of reason to the irrational so problematic: Reason must harness the energy of passion without being destroyed in the process. In terms of eros, this distinction is critical. The philosophical goal is not to *eliminate* eros, to become a "eunuch for the Kingdom of God's sake," but to *exploit* its creative energy just as the farmer uses the fertile power of the earth, subjecting it to the technology of agriculture.

But how can reason accomplish this task of appropriation and exploitation? What is its energy source, the parallel to fire, the gift of Prometheus that the mind uses to reshape the material world? A look at the pictures of the soul's structure in Plato reveals an irrational part of the soul separate from the appetites and desires and potentially amenable to reason's control, though it can be corrupted by the appetites and made to serve them. This third part of the soul thus acts as a mediating force, a colonized energy available to reason to help it organize and limit the more volatile and stubborn desires.

In the picture of the soul from the *Republic* with which we began, the appetites, remember, were a "many-headed and intricate beast" having a ring of the heads of wild and tame beasts, a thing of nature, bestial and ever-changing and monstrous. But in addition to reason and the beasts the soul has the "lion," a nonrational force that Plato earlier in the dialogue defined as the "spirited element," what makes us capable of experiencing righteous indignation or anger at injustice. Plato likens this "spirited element" to a shepherd's dog, heeding the voice of reason just as the dog obeys its master. The dog is a telling image, for as we saw earlier, as a domesticated beast that serves humans it represents the control and exploitation of nature by man that parallels reason's appropriation of the "spirited element" from the irrational. But just as the dog can turn on its master (as in Priam's vision of the dogs nurtured at his table mangling his corpse), so the "spirited element" or the "lion" can be corrupted by "evil nurturing" to betray reason and serve the appetites. The dog now turns into a wolf that preys on the sheep rather than protecting them. Likewise in the soul of the unjust man the appetites and the "lion" are strengthened at the expense of the "man" in the soul, or reason, with the result that the lion fights with the beasts, creating chaos that ultimately destroys the whole man. That is why, as we saw, the man must make the lion his ally and reconcile the beasts to one another and to the lion in order for the soul to flourish harmoniously. Notice again that one can't *eliminate* the "wild" beasts but only *tame* them, domesticate them so that they serve the soul rather than destroying it.[17]

The *Timaeus* gives us the same tripartite structure during the course of locating each of the soul's parts in the body. Reason, the "immortal principle of the soul," resides in the head, separated by the neck from the "mortal" soul, which is housed in the thorax and contains the "terrible and necessary" passions—pleasure, pain, rashness, fear, anger, hope, "irrational sensation," and "all-daring lust." The thorax is divided by the diaphragm so that the "better part" of the mortal soul, which resides in the chest and partakes of courage like the *Republic*'s "spirited element," can communicate with reason. Together with reason, the "better part" of the mortal soul then helps reason control and subdue with force the unruly "race of desires" exiled on the other side of the diaphragm in the belly and genitals. Once again, the chaotic appetites and desires, including eros, are aligned with the bestial part of us, requiring the control of reason aided by an appropriated irrational energy.[18]

This emphasis on reason's management and control of the appetites and desires based on the structure of the soul also surfaces in Plato's and Aristotle's descriptions of how in practice reason can, at least potentially, bring a *calculating* power to bear on the appetites, rejecting a destructive excess or those appetites that do not serve a necessary function. The ideal man, defined in Plato's *Republic*, would be the one who always subjects the demands of the body to a rationally apprehended good, choosing or rejecting those demands not on the basis of their immediate pleasure but of their usefulness for achieving that good. This man, of course, is the philosopher, the "lover of knowledge," a knowledge that reveals eternal truth rather than the ephemera of the material world of change and decay. Hence the philosopher despises the inferior pleasures of the body and pursues the immaterial pleasure of the rational soul contemplating an abstract absolute Good. The "philosophical natures" are those that "love [*erôsin*] always the knowledge that shows them that essence always existing and not wandering between generation and decay," pursuing the "pleasures of the soul" and "abandoning those of the body." But this is a standard of rational control only a very few can obtain. That is why in Plato's utopia the philosopher kings will be a tiny elite educated for thirty years in the life of the mind and rational activity.[19]

The ordinary mortal, though, must strive for at best something like what Jeremy Bentham called the "felicific calculus," an ability to discriminate among desires, calculating the "cost," that is, the future pain, of gratifying each and rejecting those in which disorder is more expensive than pleasure. Plato doesn't esteem this sort of practical rationalism as much as the pure disinterested higher reason of the philosopher, as can be seen in his sneering portrait of the "oligarchic man" we met earlier. This is a sort of proto-Protestant/Capitalist who controls by force those unnecessary excessive appetites not because his knowledge of the Good directs him to, but because they are too costly. They are the "spendthrift desires," including excessive eros, and these the oligarchic man avoids because they are unnecessary and expensive. He will pursue only the "necessary" desires, those that cannot be avoided but are gratified at their bare functional minimum. In contrast to the philosopher, whose desire is directed toward rationally apprehending the good, the oligarchic man controls his appetites in order to make more efficient the acquisition of wealth.[20]

In the later *Laws* Plato describes this same calculating power of reason in terms of the innate psychological forces of pursuing pleasure and avoiding pain. The "temperate man" will experience "gentle pleasures and gentle pains, mild appetites and loves not partaking of madness." The "licentious man," though, will be violently excessive in his appetites, pleasures, and pains, pursuing a love as "maddening as possible." In this life the pains will outnumber the pleasures, whereas in the temperate life the opposite is true. The orderly life is not one totally devoid of pleasure, but one in which a rational cost-benefit analysis is made and desire indulged only insofar as doing so does not entail a cost in pain greater than the benefit or pleasure experienced. This will mean that most desires will be avoided or minimally indulged, since they by definition are chaotic and destructive, tending to a costly excess. The assumption, of course, is that reason can have this power of coolly assessing profit and loss when confronted with the imperative force of eros, that there can be such a thing as an "eros not partaking of madness."[21]

Aristotle presents us with a somewhat similar view on the calculating and controlling power of reason. All movement in the soul begins in appetite, the desire for something not present that creates the motion to acquire that thing. But appetites can conflict with each other, their blind demand for gratification overinfluenced by the immediate pleasure. Hence thought must decide if the object desired is to be pursued or not, taking into consideration any future consequences that an appetite, besotted with the anticipation of pleasure, cannot see. The man who resists temptations has desires like anyone else but resists them because he follows thought and takes into consideration the long-term costs. As a necessary constituent of the human soul, desire in all its manifestations must be weighed, judged, and ultimately rejected or accepted on the basis of rational analysis. Hence desires such as eros are subjected in the "temperate" man to the calculating control of reason, serving *its* plans and goals at the expense of immediate and potentially disorderly pleasure.[22]

This utilitarian view of reason's relationship to the appetites and desires is most thoroughly developed in the philosophy of Epicurus, the third-century philosopher who believed that all existence is material atoms in motion, that the soul and its processes are material, and that pleasure is the motive force and goal whose acquisition makes for the happy life. Every pleasure is good and every pain is bad, but this does not mean, as it does for a radical Sophist like Callicles or a modern pleasure-seeker, a life of uninhibited hedonism, what most people think of when they hear the adjective "epicurean." For not every pleasure is to be chosen just because it is a pleasure, nor every pain to be avoided. How then do we choose? By a rational analysis of pleasures and pains based on comparative measurement and an examination of all advantages and disadvantages of any pleasure or pain. The pleasure of drunkenness, for example, will be outweighed by the pains of a hangover or disease, whereas the pain of exercise will be offset by the pleasure of bodily health. Thus drinking and carousing and the enjoyment of boys and women do not necessarily make the happy life but rather "sober reasoning" (*nêphôn logismos*), which finds the reason for every choice and avoidance. "Prudent thought" (*phronêsis*) is thus the greatest good, for it helps one calculate how one can maximize the pursuit of pleasure, which ends up being not hedonistic wholesale indulgence of appetites, since these by definition will create pain, but rather the intellectual pleasure of leading an honorable and just life. So we see that even the materialist philosopher who does not believe in an absolute immaterial good and so does not denigrate per se the appetites of the body or their pleasures, still subordinates them to the control of the mind and still assumes the mind *has* such controlling power. Hence Epicureans did not believe the wise man would fall in love or that love was sent by the gods, for "no one was ever improved by sex."[23]

This necessarily cursory sketch of ancient Greek philosophy's hierarchical dualism, in which the body and its desires ought to be subordinated to and controlled by reason, provides an important context for understanding the "fancied sway" meant to control eros, that force of nature that the "unnatural" mind, the godlike faculty no other material creature on earth possesses, must manage. Now we can see eros viewed warily not just because of its destructive effects, but because it is one of the body's appetites and pleasures, *all* of which are deemed bestial and inferior, part of the material natural world of change and decay. And the most important virtue in the rational soul's arsenal with which it fights against eros is *sôphrosunê*, "self-control," "temperance," "chastity," to which we turn next.

The Order of the Soul

That temperance/self-control is a virtue of the mind is clear in the origins of the word *sôphrosunê*. Both Aristotle and Plato derive it from the idea "saving thought/prudence," and the word and its related verb and adjectives carry a strong sense of rational awareness and acuity as well as signifying self-control. This is a major meaning of the word in Homer, where it denotes something like "having common sense." In the *Odyssey*, when Odysseus's old nurse Eurykleia tells Penelope that Odysseus has returned home and slaughtered all the suitors, Penelope responds that the Nurse must be crazy, even though once she was of "sound mind" (*saophrosunês*). The Chorus of old men in the *Lysistrata* exploit both meanings of having a sound mind and self-control when they say they are of "sound mind" (*sôphrones*) because they hate women, like the legendary misogynist Melanion, who fled marriage and lived in the desert. Often the related verb can mean something like "having sense," as when Dionysus in Hades, overseeing the contest between the shades of Aeschylus and Euripides, tells the latter that if he "has any sense" he will seek shelter from the skull-cracking diction of Aeschylus, notorious for his outré imagery and ornate compound adjectives.[24]

Temperance/self-control is clearly a virtue of the mind, of thought and calculation brought to bear on the body's excessive appetites. Socrates was the epitome of the temperate man, as many anecdotes attest. The most telling is the one the stunningly handsome Alcibiades relates in the *Symposium* concerning his youthful attempt to seduce the philosopher. After spending the night with Socrates wrapped in a cloak on a banquet couch, Alcibiades says he awoke the next morning no more "having slept" with Socrates than if he had spent the night with a father or brother, and he marveled at the "self-control/temperance [*sôphrosunên*] and manliness of his nature," a self-control Alcibiades specifically relates to Socrates' "prudence" (*phronêsin*). He goes on to tell of other examples of Socrates' mastery over the body and its needs—going about in the dead of winter barefoot during the campaign at Potidaea in northern Greece during the Peloponnesian War, or standing in one spot for twenty-four hours pondering some philosophical conundrum, or saving the wounded Alcibiades' life, or surviving the disastrous rout of the Athenians at Delium by "keeping his senses" (*emphrôn*) and coolly retreating while the panic-stricken were slaughtered around him. Socrates' life was an embodiment of his statement that temperance and justice are the "order of the soul."[25]

The rational order of temperance/self-control is thus defined in contrast to the chaos of the body, its inherently excessive and unrestrained passions and appetites. To be temperate, Socrates says in the *Republic* and in the *Gorgias*, is to be ruler "over the desires and pleasures of food and drink and sex." There is no "association" between temperance and "excessive pleasure," but there is between pleasure and "outrage [*hubrei*] and licentiousness," the latter (*akolasiai*) being the state directly opposite of temperance, a condition of the soul we earlier saw compared to a leaky jar that the soul must continually fill. The man who is temperate, Socrates says in the *Phaedo*, is not "agitated" by desires but instead cares little for them and acts in an orderly fashion.[26]

Aristotle likewise defines temperance/self-control as a rational virtue specifically concerned with the "slavish and brutish" pleasures of touch and taste, those· that belong to our animal natures like eating and drinking and sex. The temperate man, he says, enjoys pleasure only as "straight/correct rational principle" (*orthos logos*) advises. Developing a more nuanced contrast between temperance and "self-control," Aristotle give us a more extreme definition of temperance when he says the temperate man doesn't just restrain but takes no pleasure in the things the "licentious" (*akolastos*) man enjoys and actively dislikes them. He does not find pleasure in wrong things or in excessive pleasures, and he will not feel pain when these are lacking. He will only enjoy pleasures that are not ignoble or beyond his means. Though his definition of temperance is more radical, like Plato Aristotle defines temperance in contrast to licentiousness (*akolasia*), which is "excess in regards to pleasure," and for Aristotle, too, the licentious man pursues all pleasures in preference to anything else. Temperance, then, is a virtue of the mind directed against the excessive pleasures of the body.[27]

This contrast of temperance with "licentiousness" and "outrage," that injurious behavior resulting from excessive passion, is not peculiar to Plato and Aristotle or to the esoteric speculations of philosophy. The fifth-century Sophist Antiphon says that only the man who fortifies his soul against immediate pleasures and can conquer himself can judge temperance, for whoever wishes to gratify his passion wishes the worse instead of the better. The philosophers reflect the general consensus of Greek public opinion, as can be seen in the orators, who had to flatter the prejudices of the jurymen, who were not legal professionals, and so can be considered good repositories of Athenian received wisdom. Thus Demosthenes contrasts temperance with acts of "outrage" like hiring a citizen for prostitution or debauching a citizen-wife, and Isocrates repeats the philosophers' opposition of temperance to "licentiousness and outrage" (*akolasian kai hubrin*).[28]

As these examples of "excessive" and "outrageous" pleasures show, eros more often than not is the appetite most problematic for the person attempting to be temperate as well as the desire whose excessive indulgence most often brands one "licentious." Aristophanes explicitly contrasts temperance with the worst example of sexual excess in his allusion in the *Clouds* to a lost play in which he brought on stage two characters, Sôphrôn or Temperance and Katapugôn or Lecherous Sodomite, the last word one we saw in Chapter 4 that refers directly to passive anal intercourse, the epitome to the Greeks of unbridled sexual appetite. To Aristophanes the personified appetite that most directly opposes temperance is the erotic, and of erotic appetites the worst is passive buggery. Xenophon too says that it is not easy for someone touched by eros to be temperate, which is why the best example of Socrates' legendary temperance is his resistance to the advances of the beautiful Alcibiades.[29]

It is the poet Euripides, though, acknowledging as he does the awesome power of eros, who explores the confrontation of temperance and moderation with sexuality as well as the difficulty of trying rationally to control an uncontrollable force. Frequently in his plays characters faced with disasters caused by erotic excess praise or yearn for a "temperate" eros. Responding to Agamemnon's horrific decision, ultimately brought about by Helen's sexual crime, to sacrifice his daughter, the Chorus of the *Iphigeneia at Aulis* prays for a "moderate and temperate [*sôphrosunas*] Aphrodite," a sexual passion that avoids the "maddening goads" and arrows of Eros. Or the rehabilitated Helen, exiled in Egypt while a shameless phantom of her commits adultery in Troy, wishes that Aphrodite would be "moderate," for then she would be the kindest of all the gods. The Chorus of the *Medea* likewise prays to be spared from Aphrodite's "unerring arrow poisoned with desire" and hopes for an Aphrodite who comes "just enough," as well as longing for the protection of "temperance" (*sôphrosuna*). The desperation and wish-fulfilling quality of these appeals, none of which is ever answered in the carnage bloodying the stage, reveal Euripides' distrust of the ability of a rational virtue to control the powerful force of sexual passion.[30]

As we said earlier, the point of temperance is not the eradication of desire, but its *control*, which means that the temperate person is not the one who never experiences desire, but the one who can experience it with due measure. Thus the temperate man will have all sorts of desires, but the measure of his temperance will be his ability to withstand them. Antiphon puts it radically when he says that he who has never touched the "shameful" is not temperate, for there is nothing over which he has gained control. The person who doesn't like alcohol anyway shouldn't get any credit for his sobriety. Plato doesn't go as far as the Sophist, but he does agree that temperance means neither starving nor indulging excessively the appetites so that one may put them to sleep and not disturb reason with excessive pleasure or the pain of ungratified desire. Likewise in the *Laws* the Athenian Stranger points out that shielding the youth completely from pleasure makes them all the more vulnerable to even the most shameful desire, once it is armed with the allure of novelty.[31]

This, I believe, is what Euripides in his tragedies objects to: the assumption that reasoned temperance has the power to exercise calculating control over a passion inherently unstable and by definition excessive. The best example of Euripides' pessimism appears in his portrait of radical temperance in the character of Hippolytus, whom we met earlier. Hippolytus, remember, believes he is one of those few men who are *naturally* chaste, that is, who are asexual, never experiencing desire rather than learning to control it. Only those who "have it in their natures to act chastely/temperately [*en têi phusei/to sôphronein*]," he asserts, can gather flowers in the untouched meadow that symbolizes his chastity—but as we saw, the meadow is an image from nature, its flowers and bees bound up in the process of procreation. And Hippolytus's violent anger undercuts as well his claims to innate temperance. Phaedra too is a portrait of temperance and shame overthrown by the power of Aphrodite. "The temperate [*hoi sôphrones*] though unwilling love evil things," the Nurse comments on learning of Phaedra's lust for her stepson.[32]

Hippolytus appears to be a failed example of what Aristotle, having more faith in reason's power than Euripides has, will later define as the truly temperate man, whom he develops in contrast to the merely "self-ruling" one. Though both the temperate and the self-ruled man do nothing against reasoned principle (*para ton logon*) regarding the pleasures of the body, the temperate man has no "base/worthless/bad desires," nor does he take pleasure in such things as are counter to reasoned principle, whereas the self-ruled man *does* experience those desires but won't act on them. Aristotle leaves undefined exactly what "bad desires" are or how they relate to the "bestial and slavish" appetites and desires. Clearly he espouses here a radical view of temperance as the *absence* of certain desires, though no doubt Aristotle would never number sexuality as one of them, as Hippolytus does.[33]

The philosophers' faith in the managing and controlling power of reason and a rational virtue like temperance is certainly not shared by Euripides. Over and over in his plays he shows us people who are devastated by the irrational despite their minds' awareness of the right—and usually eros is the force that destroys them. Laius, the ravisher of Chrysippus, says, "Nature drove me on, even though I had thought/judgment." Phaedra, dying with the disease of lust, slipping in and out of sanity, tries to conquer Aphrodite with "thought/judgment" and "temperance," but as she herself says, rebuking Socrates and anticipating St. Paul, "We know the good and recognize it, but we cannot do it." And Medea, agonizing over her plan to kill her children because of erotic anger and rage at her dishonor, says, "Passion is stronger than my resolutions, and this is the cause of the greatest evils for mortals." Reasoned temperance and self-control, the calculating power of the mind to master the passions and appetites of the body, all are dreams of order that the chaos of the irrational will sweep away. Nevertheless, Euripides never suggests that submission to pleasure and passion, the hidden faith of our modern therapeutic culture, can bring bliss but rather that successful resistance cannot be found in the power of reason alone.[34]

But the wisdom of Euripides is lost on us moderns, steeped as we are in the Enlightenment optimism that itself is a direct descendent of Greek rationalism, even though we are filled too with the Romantic idealization of sex and passion. We gaze upon the sexual chaos surrounding us, the teen pregnancies and venereal plagues, and respond with sex education and condom distribution and posters and jingles and filmstrips. We believe with Socrates that virtue is knowledge, that given the right information rational and positive choices will be calculated by callow teen and jaded lothario alike in that moment when eros shakes the soul like a storm at sea. Twenty-five hundred years later, we still believe in the ideal this chapter has described—that the mind and its controlling, calculating power can hold back the force of eros. Yet paradoxically we continue to cling to a shopworn Romanticism that idealizes sexual passion and justifies abandoning the time-honored social controls—marriage and chastity, guilt and shame—that once helped to prevent sexual excesses from destroying American society. Euripides may have been right that an idealized rational virtue cannot control eros, but he would have been amazed to see a supposedly advanced culture handling sexual passion with all the blithe insouciance of an infant with a loaded gun.

That ideal of rational virtue is the first example of the "fancied sway" some Greeks, philosophers mostly, thought could clip Eros's wings. Whether by the conceptual control bestowed by a picture of the cosmos whose order results from an all-pervasive idealized Love responsible as well for friendship and harmony, or by the reasoned tempering of the appetites to minimize their chaotic effects, the mind creates a stable order in which the natural energy of eros is simultaneously exploited and regulated. In the remaining chapters we will see this order and its key virtue of self-control/temperance as both are manifested in social and cultural institutions, the "technologies" the mind projects onto the disorder of the natural world.

SIX

Erotic Technology

On his way home from Troy, Odysseus had a famous encounter with the Cyclops Polyphemus, the adventure we talked about in the Introduction. But before he tells his Phaiacian hosts the story of his defeat of the man-eating monster, he describes an island near the Cyclopses' land, a passage a modern reader might pass over as epic formulaic padding. But Odysseus's long, detailed description of this uninhabited island is a fascinating window into the Greek attitude toward nature that is to be more fully revealed later in the struggle with the Cyclops Polyphemus. The island, Odysseus says, is without men, untilled and unsown, filled with wild goats—just the way we urban moderns like our nature, pristine and untouched. Our Romantic idealizations of nature have taught us that civilization is an evil, the "shades of the prison house," and that the beautiful natural world from which we have fallen is our real home. That's why we invented national parks, chunks of the wild kept in their natural state—with convenient roads and rescue helicopters to facilitate our communing with nature.[1]

This attitude would have been completely alien to Odysseus, who is annoyed that the island's potential is wasted because of the Cyclopses' savagery and ignorance. As he surveys the island, he notes only its features that could be useful for humans if skill and technology were applied—"well-watered meadows" where vines would grow, "level plow land" where grain would flourish, a good harbor with a spring where ships could be sheltered from the sea. All the island needs is the human technology that the savage Cyclopses lack. Then it would be *euktimenên*, "developed so as to be good to dwell in," a place superior to anything nature on her own can create, for it would be useful for human beings. Like the protocapitalist Robinson Crusoe, Odysseus sees nature only as raw material to be worked on by the human mind to create a sustaining space in which humans can live and flourish.[2]

Eros and Aphrodite represent natural energies that like the Cyclopses' island must be ordered by "technologies" limiting their destructiveness and exploiting their fertilizing power. In Chapter 5 we saw how this works in the "microcosm," the individual soul that must through the "technology" of rational virtue and self-restraint limit the body's passions and appetites. Here and in Chapters 7 and 8 we will examine this same process on the level of the "macrocosm," the way larger social and cultural institutions, both in their literary representations and in what we know of them historically, organize the volatile power of sex just as the technologies of agriculture reorder soil and plants and trees to maximize their productive power.

Flowers, Fruit, Furrows

This continuity between human sex and natural creativity and fertility is obvious, of course, and nature's sexual beauty is the flip side of the destructiveness of eros we chronicled in Part 1. As we saw in Chapter 1, the creation of the cosmos is imagined in terms of sex acts, although in Hesiod the creation of the world results from an act of sexual violence, the continuous rape of Gaia, the earth, by her son-husband Ouranos, the sky, that ends only when Cronos castrates his father, separating sky from earth. Homer, however, sees the cosmic sex act as taking place in the context of marriage, a human institution, and he highlights the beauty of divine fertility rather than the primeval violence of Hesiod's account. When the sky-god Zeus and his wife Hera are making love in the *Iliad*, the "divine earth made new-sprouted grass to grow, and dewy lotus and the crocus and the hyacinth, thick and soft, that raised them up from the ground." The blossoming flowers and the gods' lovemaking are both seen as manifestations of the same procreative power responsible for the sexual loveliness of Hera and the vernal earth. This sex act of the gods is the archetypal fertility ritual, a reenactment, in the context of marriage, of the raw primeval copulation that in Hesiod creates the world and that re-creates it every spring.[3]

   A fragment from Aeschylus's lost play the *Danaides* likewise links cosmic sexuality and fertility to the social institution of marriage. The daughters of Danaus, remember, were virgins whom their fifty Egyptian cousins pursued as brides, the story told in the surviving first play of the trilogy, the *Suppliants*. The third play, the *Danaides*, probably described the slaughter of the bridegrooms by the daughters of Danaus after they had been compelled to marry against their will. One daughter, though, Hypermestra, spared her new husband, an action defended by Aphrodite: "Holy heaven desires to wound the earth, and eros for marriage seizes the earth. The rain falling from her husband the sky fertilizes the earth." The rain is the semen of the sky impregnating the earth during their "moist marriage" in order to bring forth "fodder for herds" and grain, the major food of the ancient world. The importance and sanctity of human marriage, upheld by Hypermestra, are validated and favored by being linked to the cosmic marriage that creates and sustains all earthly life and that is the purview of Aphrodite's sexual power, to whom Hypermestra reportedly dedicated an image. Life on earth, particularly the life of the plants and beasts upon which humans depend for survival, results from a cosmic sexual act, one made meaningful not just in natural terms but in the context of a cultural institution, marriage. Aphrodite's power—and nature's—is subordinated to the control of culture.[4]

As forces of fertility, Eros and Aphrodite create the springtime loveliness of the earth, including the sexual beauty of humans. The connection between nature's beauty and human eros, though, does not serve simply to celebrate the loveliness of sexual attraction and its link to cosmic fertility, as it might for us, liberated as we are from nature's fickleness. For us nature is just scenery. But as we saw in the Introduction, for the Greeks nature's beauty is always fraught with intimations of a destructive primal power, which that beauty ultimately serves, for creation and destruction, beauty and death, are two aspects of the same process of life, the "destroyer and preserver," as Shelley apostrophized it in his brilliant poem, "Ode to the West Wind." Floral imagery captures this essential ambiguity of natural beauty, and the Greeks constantly acknowledged the ambiguous loveliness of sexually blossoming young boys and girls by linking it to flowers. Despite 3,000 years of use, the connection of sex and flowers still works for us for the simple reason that flowers are still an intimate part of our lives in a way that fire or arrows are not, although the greenhouse's gift of year-round flowers lessens the force of their intimations of inevitable decay. Their appearance in spring, "when Eros comes bearing delights," their role in plant reproduction, their beauty, their odor, their androgynous appearance—phallic stems crowned with vaginal petals—make flowers obvious symbols of sexual beauty, attractiveness, and fertility.[5]

The seventh-century lyric poet Mimnermus exploits these sexual connotations of flowers when he calls "secret lovemaking and gentle persuasive gifts and the bed" the "flowers of youth" in a poem that opens with the wonderful rhetorical question, "What life, what joy without golden Aphrodite?" More specifically, floral metaphors highlight the fresh sexual charm of young boys or girls, as well as locating them in the realm of nature, at that sexual peak before they are tamed by culture through citizenship or marriage. Ibycus imagines a boy whom Charis, goddess of grace and charm and attendant of Aphrodite, nurtures among "lovely buds" of flowers, perhaps roses, and the garland the poet wears is fragrant with the same flowers used by the goddess to "anoint" the boy. A long fragment of the early-seventh-century poet Archilochus, discovered this century on a papyrus scrap, tells of the speaker's somewhat botched seduction of a young girl—I say botched, since it appears the poet orgasms a little prematurely. Archilochus uses the flower metaphor twice in the poem. First, when he rejects the girl's older sister Neobule because "the flower of her girlhood has lost its petals." Neobule, by the way, according to legend was so shamed by Archilochus's poetic attacks—including perhaps charges that she performed fellatio on one man while being buggered by another—that she hanged herself. And the sexual act itself, such as it is, takes place outside on a bed of flowers, like Zeus and Hera's lovemaking. The poet makes it clear that just touching the "newly ripe" virginal beauty of the girl makes him jump the gun so that he merely "graz[ed] her golden [pubic] hair" when he "shot off his [white] strength."[6]

Implicit in the flower metaphor, though, is the reality of decay and death, for all flowers fade and die. That inevitable mortality gives floral imagery its poignancy, for the young boys and girls so sexually fresh and blooming now must grow up and enter the world of experience and ultimately death: "The rose-lipt girls are sleeping / In fields where roses fade." Housman's imagery as well as his sentiment has a long ancestry. That same poem of Mimnermus celebrating sex as the flower of youth goes on to lament the "painful old age" that makes the old man an object of contempt to women. Another of his poems also mourns the flowerlike brevity of sexual beauty: "We enjoy the blossoms of youth for a brief time," and beside us stand two evil spirits, the one of old age, the other of death. Sappho, in a fragment from one of her epithalamia, or "wedding songs," evokes the mortality implicit in the flower to capture the fragility of the young girl's sexual beauty destined to be subordinated to a man in marriage: The virgin is "like the hyacinth that the shepherds trample underfoot in the mountains." The natural beauty of nubile girls and boys, so much like the beauty of spring flowers, is fragile and transitory, for humans must live and take their place in the institutions of society. The young are like the Cyclopes' island, useless unless "cultivated," their sexuality subordinated to the needs of the city.[7]

If flowers in general embody the transitory sexual beauty of youth, one flower in particular suggests also its dangers. The association of the rose with sex, particularly female sexuality, is probably a Greek invention and now a commonplace so ubiquitous that years ago Gertrude Stein was moved to snort a "rose is a rose is a rose is a rose." The rose is so symbolically useful because in addition to the beauty and fertility other flowers suggest, the rose adds the thorns, the wounding dangers of sexuality, particularly young female sexuality that social prohibitions gird like the thorn thicket surrounding Sleeping Beauty's castle. Then as now, the gift of a rose was a statement of erotic interest, for as Meleager puts it, the rose is "love-favoring." As an emblem of dangerous sexual beauty, the rose is sacred to Aphrodite, according to Pausanias, reflecting her own ambiguous beauty. The Chorus of the *Medea*, longing in the midst of sexual violence and disaster to return to the Golden Age of unproblematic sexuality, imagines the Aphrodite of that time donning "fragrant garlands of roses." In the Iron Age of the present, though, the piercing thorns leave their wounds in the four victims of Medea's sexual wrath.[8]

Aphrodite's son Eros too is linked to the rose. An epigram attributed to Plato describes a sleeping Eros, his bow and arrows hung on a tree, lying among rose blossoms. Even in this precious tableau, the quiver of thornlike arrows reminds us of how dangerous an awakened Eros can be. A rose is just a rose for us, but for the Greeks, living at a time when the image was still fresh and vivid, the rose's thorns signified the latent destructiveness of sexuality lurking beneath its fragrant beauty.[9]

. Fruit is another popular metaphor in Greek literature for describing the sexual ripeness of youth. Girls' breasts are often compared to apples, as when Theocritus's shepherd Daphnis gropes Acrotime's breasts and says, "I'm giving your downy apples their first lesson."[10] Copulation itself could be described as picking fruit. The suitors of the beautiful Hebe, daughter of Antaeus, desire "to pluck her blooming fruit." Greek brides ate a quince-apple before entering the bridal chamber, reflecting the same metaphor. The gift of an apple signified erotic interest, the source of the (nonbiblical) idea that Adam and Eve ate an apple in the Garden of Eden, the pagan love-apple reinforcing St. Augustine's sexualization of the Fall. Plato in an epigram uses this custom to make a point about the brevity of beauty: "I throw you an apple, and if willingly you love me, take it and share your virginity. But if you should think otherwise, take it anyway to see how short-lived beauty is."[11]

More important, fruit signifies abundance and fertility specifically in the context of agriculture, for fruit grows in the orchards created and nurtured with technological skill. This aura of joyful plenty created by human skill and labor is used by Aristophanes to communicate the hopeful happiness of the Athenians after the Peace of Nicias in 421 interrupted briefly the Peloponnesian War between Athens and Sparta. In the appropriately titled *Peace*, Aristophanes brings on stage Opôra, personifying the word meaning both "fruit" and "late summer," one frequently used to denote the sexual ripeness of girls. Aristophanes exploits both these meanings when his Trygaeus, who brought the virginal Opôra from heaven along with the two maidens Peace and Mayfair after riding to Olympus on a dung beetle, marries Opôra. Their wedding song at play's end celebrates the return of peace in terms of the fertility of the fields and sexual exuberance, both contained by the cultural orders of marriage and agriculture: rich harvests, granaries full of grain and wine, plenty of figs (sexual fruit par excellence), and wives who bear offspring. The Greek text is rife with double entendres linking eating, agriculture, and sex, as when the Chorus answers the question, "What shall we do with her [Opôra]?" with "We shall gather/strip her." The effect is a celebration of abundance, fertility, and peace strictly in terms of human social institutions and technologies that create the order in which both human and natural sexuality flourishes. Eros serves man, not vice-versa.[12]

As Plato's epigram shows, though, the metaphor of fruit is even more suggestive than flowers of a natural process ending in decay and death. For what makes fruit sweet is the decay that creates sugar. Its ripe blush is the blush of death. Fruit stands then as a powerful image of the ambiguity of human beauty, its sweetness dependent on loss and death. Aeschylus plays on this ambiguity of fruit beautifully in the *Suppliants*. By the end of this play the daughters of Danaus have won a temporary reprieve from their amorous cousins, for the king of Argos, Pelasgus, has given them sanctuary. Old Danaus, anxious for his daughters to comport themselves properly in their benefactor's land, advises them to beware of their sexual beauty's power: "Bring no shame upon me, having as you do the bloom that attracts men. The tender ripe fruit is hard to guard; beasts destroy it, and men—why not?—and creatures that fly and earth-treading ones. Aphrodite announces the dropping fruit." The fragility of the virgins' beauty, its subjection to mortality, the predatory nature of male sexuality, like that of their Egyptian cousins who will ultimately "gather" them as brides, all are suggested in this image, which reminds us that the sexual loveliness of youth is "beauty that must die."[13]

This depiction of the young girl's sexual beauty as ripe fruit destined to be consumed by a husband particularly reflected the experience of Greek upper-class girls, whose marriages were arranged by their fathers with older men the girls barely knew. A nubile young girl was often compared to a plant or a sapling, as Odysseus does twice when he is flattering the Phaiacian girl Nausicaa, claiming he is as amazed at her beauty as he was at the shoot of a palm tree growing beside the altar of Apollo. The image is not arbitrary filler: The byplay between Odysseus and Nausicaa follows from the implicit and explicit suggestions that she is ready to marry and that Odysseus would make a good husband.[14]

As well as locating the sexuality of girls in the context of cultural and social "cultivation," plant metaphors frequently depict the transition from their father's house to the alien world of their new husbands as a fall from natural innocence and happiness of girlhood, the "sweetest life known to mortals," as Sophocles' Procne describes it. The new world Procne must inhabit is particularly horrible, filled with sexual violence and cannibalism: Her husband Tereus rapes her sister Philomela, then cuts out her tongue to keep her from exposing him. Philomela, though, weaves the story into a robe, and Procne avenges her by killing Itys, her son by Tereus, and feeding the remains to her husband.[15]

The typical Greek girl didn't face such horrors in her married life, despite what some modern feminists may think, but the adjustment could have been hard for a girl in her midteens. Medea, working on the sympathy of the Corinthian women, evokes the difficulties of making the adjustment to a new household after an arranged marriage—a girl has to be a "prophet" to know what sort of man is her bedmate. In a fragment from a wedding song Sappho uses fruit imagery to evoke the delicate doomed innocence of the virgin's sexual ripeness destined to be consumed by a man, as well as the idyllic existence she must leave behind: "As the sweet apple blushes on the top branch, the top of the highest branch, the apple pickers have forgotten it; they haven't forgotten it, but they couldn't reach it." The image's poignancy comes from our knowledge that the apple is ripe and so must fall whether the pickers can reach it or not. Marriage for a girl is her "completion," the Chorus tells the daughters of Danaus, using a word that also means "death." The girl must die to her "natural" life protected in her father's house and enter the human cultural order, where her sexuality will serve the household and the city by bearing citizens and the mothers and wives of citizens. But remember, the Greeks would have found ripe fruit not picked a waste, as would be the woman whose sexual bloom faded before she provided any harvests.[16]

The fruit metaphor implicitly evokes the technology of agriculture to assert the necessity of subordinating the young girl's potentially destructive sexuality to the control of marriage. Farming for the Greeks was central to their lives in ways unimaginable to denizens of an urban world who take their food for granted, always assuming it will be waiting for them in the supermarket all wrapped up in plastic, the work, mess, and occasional danger associated with growing food kept safely distant. But the major activity for most of humanity before the twentieth century was hunting, gathering, and/or growing food. Today one farmer produces enough food for a hundred people; then ninety grew the food for a hundred. Even the self-consciously urban Greeks were intimately knowledgeable about farming, which makes agriculture the most powerful image for the relationship of humans to the natural world they must exploit to survive. As Socrates in Xenophon's *Oeconomicus* puts it, farming is "held in the highest repute" among the Greeks, for it creates "the best citizens and the most loyal to the community."[17]

The metaphor of plowing to describe conjugal sex makes the parallelism of marriage and agriculture explicit. The plowing image was part of the traditional wedding ceremony: "I give you my daughter for the plowing of legitimate children," the father of the bride would tell the groom. Among the Greeks, this formula was a commonplace shorthand for marriage, just as "for better or worse" signifies marriage for us. Related ways of referring to marriage included "sowing arable land" or calling the woman a "furrow," as when the Chorus of *Oedipus Rex* wonders how his "father's furrows [i.e., Jocasta] could bear" such an outrage as incest. The farming metaphor describing legitimate marital intercourse intensifies the horror of Oedipus's crime as well as pointing to its chaotic effects—the blight destroying the grain and the unborn of Thebes—by contrasting them with the orderly world of the farm.[18]

The most notorious—and ideologically loaded—example of this metaphor occurs in Aeschylus's *Eumenides*. Orestes, having killed his mother Klytaimestra for her murder of Agamemnon, is on trial for his life. His advocate, Apollo, must counter the argument of the snake-haired Furies, avenging pursuers of blood-violation, that the mother is the most important parent because the child is without doubt the mother's blood, whereas paternity is, as Joyce's Stephen Daedalus put it, a "legal fiction." The mother, Apollo argues in response, is not the parent but the "rearer of the new-sown embryo." The parent is the "mounter," the father, while the mother merely "preserves the sprout." Just as the farmer actively plows the earth and throws the seeds into the furrows, so the male mounts the passive woman, who then nurtures the seedling. One technology, agriculture, is used to legitimize another, marriage, both activities assuming that nature must be ordered and controlled for its creative energy to be exploited. In Apollo's reasoning, the cultural relationship created by marriage, paternity, takes precedence over the natural one, maternity.[19]

Inherent in all this imagery is the idea that the woman is earthlike, a source of natural fertility most productive when subjected to masculine rational control. This assumption informs Aeschylus's image we looked at earlier describing the masculine sky as impregnating the earth. Woman "imitates" the earth, as Plato put it, and so like the earth must be "cultivated" for her productivity to be maximized. Working from the same assumption, Aristotle explained why some children look like their mothers by noting that just as different kinds of soil affect plants differently, so women can alter the seed dropped in her womb by the man. Implicit in Aristotle's thinking is a paradigm in which the male, actively discharging seed during sex, imposes a form on the passive, matterlike woman, who does not discharge her semen. Thus the male, actively generating in another, is like the heavens and the sun, whereas the woman, generating in herself, is like the earth.[20]

This is a loaded dichotomy, of course, for as we have seen, reason and culture are privileged over the body and nature, the former pair making human identity possible through its control of the latter pair. Thus the power of agricultural metaphors: They evoke an activity that every day demonstrated to the Greeks, most of whom were farmers, the control of the mind and its skills over a natural world whose fertile sexual powers were inherently unstable and indifferent to humans. And women, closer to that natural world than men, likewise had to have their sexual energy subjected to the cultural order of marriage, as we will see in more detail in Chapter 7.

Plato in the *Laws* calls on these traditional agricultural metaphors when he describes the regulation not just of female but of all human sexuality in the Athenian Stranger's utopia. Concerned about minimizing the disorder eros causes in the state, the Athenian Stranger wants to regulate sexuality so that "procreative intercourse" is used "according to nature." This means banning homosexuality and abortion and "not sowing seeds on rocks and stones, where it will never take root and be fruitful, and staying away from all female fields in which you would not want your seed to spring up." Later, focusing on homosexuality and extramarital sex, he again prohibits "sowing bastard seeds and the sterile seeds of men against nature." As the agriculture imagery shows, the "nature" Plato has in mind is not the untouched wild but the nature of the farm, where the sexual energy of plants and animals is controlled and confined to reproduction. This order provides a model for the whole society, in which the volatile power of male and female eros is strictly limited, its energy directed not toward irrational pleasure—the sterile "rocks and stones" of sodomy and adultery—but toward the productive sowing of legitimate children. Like the Cyclopes' island, eros must be "cultivated" to make it useful for humans and to lessen its destructiveness.[21]

The Technology of Ritual

Agricultural metaphors worked implicitly to assert the need of culture to control and exploit the sexual energy of humans and nature. In ancient Greek society numerous religious festivals had as their explicit public purpose the harnessing of natural and human fertility for the benefit of the city. Even later, when state control of festivals meant they became sophisticated urban expressions of political ideology, the major festivals still had at their core a collective sacred ritual designed to enlist the power of a deity to ensure the fecundity of people, animals, and crops. In this sense festivals were a "technology," for just as a mill exploits the energy of wind or water to do work, so ancient religion harnessed the force of a deity for the material benefit of the community. Worship in these terms is much more calculated and practical than in, say, Christianity, where God is supposed to be worshipped because he is God, perfect moral good and creator, not because the worshipper wants to exploit his power—though of course many Christians at prayer are as pragmatic as any ancient hopefully leading an ox to sacrifice. Moreover, there was no "separation of church and state" in ancient Greece such as we are accustomed to. Religious ritual was literally political, as much the business of the polis as holding office or voting, and participation in the festivals was a civic, not a private act.

From girlhood to old age, women played an important role in many festivals and rituals. About a hundred girls younger than ten would be chosen to become "bears of Artemis," a mysterious procedure marking the transition to puberty from the "wild" natural life of girlhood. In the Anthesteria, a spring festival celebrating the opening of the new wine, the wife of the Archon Basileus, the magistrate in charge of religious festivals and celebrations, was "married" to the god Dionysus, probably represented by her disguised husband. She also officiated along with fourteen other carefully chosen women at the secret sacrifices whose purpose was the prosperity of the city. The festival celebrated the fertility of the vine and the political community and the renewal of both. But of the many festivals celebrated by the Greeks, perhaps the Thesmophoria illustrates best the conjunction of female sexuality with fertility and the life-cycle of nature in which death and decay figure prominently—all controlled by and subordinated to a cultural and social organization that at once acknowledges and exploits this necessary power.

The Thesmophoria is related to the central fertility myth of the Greeks, the story of Demeter and her daughter Persephone. Demeter is the mother-goddess, the power that makes the grain and other earthly life flourish. While gathering flowers in a meadow, her daughter Persephone was kidnapped by Hades, god of the Underworld and the dead, and taken below the earth to be his bride. When Demeter learned of her daughter's outrage, she withheld her fertilizing power from the earth, causing the grain to wither as soon as it sprouted. Faced with the extinction of mankind and the loss of sacrifices, Zeus ordered Hades to give the girl back. Unfortunately, she had already eaten some pomegranate seeds in the Underworld, and so she had to stay with Hades for four months a year. During these winter months nothing grows, for Demeter is mourning her daughter. But when her daughter returns, her joy covers the earth with the fertile beauty of spring.

Even this bald summary reveals the central point to the myth—the life-cycle of grain, which flourishes, is cut down, and then "buried" until it sprouts again in the spring, just as Persephone must "die" for four months and then return to her mother. The fate of Persephone, though, links the natural life-cycle to the woman's sexual life, her springlike life as a virgin brought to an end when the girl must marry and become fertile, a death to an old life and a rebirth into the role of wife and mother, integrated into the social structure of the household. The myth asserts the continuity of human, especially female, sexuality and natural fertility, powers that must be subordinated to cultural controls.

Much remains mysterious about what went on at the Thesmophoria. It is clear from what we do know that the festival reenacted certain details of Demeter's adventure and likewise asserted the city's ritualistic control over the potent sexual power of women and the earth. The festival took place in late October at the olive harvest, the last of the year, when the abundance of the earth ensured there was enough grain to last the winter and to provide the seed for next year's crop. This is a time when people who live closely with the rhythms of the earth are reminded daily of the reality of death and its intimacy with life. Only citizen-wives participated in the festival—men, children, concubines, prostitutes, and virgins were excluded—which took place over three days, during which time sexual abstinence was required of the participants. To strengthen their resolve, the women ate garlic. Because of the sexual ban, men especially were absolutely forbidden to witness the goings-on. Aelian tells the story of Battos, the mythical king of the North African colony of Cyrene who was castrated by the women after he insisted on viewing their secret rites.[22] Already we can see that not just female sexuality but *controlled* female sexuality is important to the festival; the sexual energy limited by marriage is further limited by the ritual itself, so that all sexual power is concentrated on fertilizing the next year's crop of grain and the next generation of citizens. Significantly, the women who participated in the Thesmophoria were called "Bees of Demeter," the chaste bee emblematizing the ideal wife, as we saw in Chapter 3.

On the first day, called Anodos, "The Road Up," the white-clad women assembled at the Thesmophorion, an open-walled space located south of the Pnyx, the hill in Athens across from the Acropolis, where the orators harangued the Assembly. Since the women camped out away from home for the three days, building huts in which they slept, the first day must have been consumed in trucking up all the building materials, pigs to be sacrificed, and other implements and in getting everybody organized and the mini-city of huts laid out and built. In fact, the women duplicated the political organization of the city from which normally they were excluded, complete with magistrates chosen by the women, a Council that passed decrees, and an Assembly—more evidence that procreative power was being integrated into the political patterns of the polis.[23]

The second day saw the suspension of the normal public business of the city. The law-courts closed, and the Council didn't meet. The women in their shadow city fasted, sitting on the ground on mats made of *agnus castus*, an anaphrodisiac that also was supposed to promote menstrual flow. The sexual energy of the women is being conserved to promote the fertility of the crops. Also, by sitting on the ground and fasting the women imitate Demeter, who during her search for Persephone refused to eat or to sit in a chair. Another practice deriving from the myth was the obscene abuse and insults and scourging that the women (no doubt grumpy from the lack of food) inflicted on each other, duplicating the behavior of Iambe, a servant in the household of Celeus where the goddess rested during her search for Persephone. Iambe spread a fleece on a chair that finally convinced Demeter to sit and cheered up the grieving goddess with her mockery and dirty jokes. The events of the myth that ends with the refructifying of the earth form a pattern the repetition of which ensures another renewal. Also, obscenity is a standard feature of most fertility rituals, a sort of sympathetic magic that by speaking of matters sexual encourages sexual potency. Part of the Greek wedding ceremony was the singing of obscene songs at the door of the bridal chamber, as in Sappho's fragment that advises the carpenters to raise the roof because the bridegroom is "much bigger than a big man"—and she's not talking about his height.[24]

At some point, perhaps at the end of the second day, the central act of the festival took place, the "bearing forth of the things laid down," which is what Thesmophoria means, and the sacrifice of the pigs, animals connected to Demeter because of their fecundity. These "things laid down" were an unpleasant melange of rotting sacrificed pigs mixed with dough-models of male and female genitals and snakes. The pigs and models had earlier been thrown into caverns, possibly during another festival that excluded males, the Skira, which took place at the grain harvest before midsummer. This throwing of pigs into caverns recalls the fate of the swineherd Eubouleus and his pigs, who were swallowed up in the cavern Hades opened up to rape Persephone. During the Thesmophoria this stuff was brought out in buckets by "Balers," women who had to maintain a state of sexual purity for three days before the festival, and then laid on the altars in the Thesmophorion. This compost would later be mixed with the seeds of next year's grain crop, for the festival took place before the wheat was sown. Every detail of this rite—the rotting flesh, the models of genitalia, the suggestion of human sacrifice in the fate of Eubouleus, the snakes—points to the concern with fertility both vegetable and human, as well as recognizing the fructifying role of death in the cycle of natural life. But that frightening ambiguity of nature's preserving and destroying power is here subject to the structure of a ritual performed by women, those humans closest to nature's power.

Little is known about the third day, Kalligeneia, the day of "beautiful offspring," but after the fasting of the second day it must have been a day of celebration, not just of the grain but of the children the women were expected to bear. All fecundity—of animals and plants and women—is connected, for all is the expression of one natural fertile power. Thus the ritual, through abstinence and sympathetic magic, focuses the women's sexual energy at a critical moment, when the seed for next year's food must be fertilized and sown—a time also to ensure that the women themselves, whose life experiences are reenacted in the myth of Demeter and Persephone, are as fruitful in providing the new citizens necessary to continue the life of the state for more than the present generation. Yet this harnessing of sexual power is strictly controlled and organized by the civic ritual that delimits and defines it, ensuring that the power wielded serves not nature's needs but the needs of the "unnatural" state. Indeed, Demeter Thesmophoros eventually became "the bringer of order, the order of marriage, civilization, and of life itself."[25]

That this responsibility is entrusted to women recognizes their power and the civic role they had to play despite the fact that they couldn't hold office or vote. Moreover, Greek women's role in such rituals belies the characterization of them as cowering weaklings that some modern scholars impose upon them, scholars whose assumptions are shaped by bourgeois liberal political ideals: All power resides in the right to participate in political machinery, and religion should be excluded from the political process. A Chorus member of the *Lysistrata* contradicts this same idea, spoken in the play by an old man, that the women have nothing to do with the business of the city, when she responds with a list of all the civic festivals and rituals she had participated in since girlhood. "Am I not obliged to offer something useful to the city?" she asks, since she has served it all her life through civic ritual and the birthing of male citizens and soldiers. This unnamed woman is staking a claim for civic recognition based on the sexual power she wields and manages for the fertility of the state.[26]

Putting Aphrodite in Her Place

Aphrodite embodies the sheer force of sexuality whose procreative dimension is the purview of Demeter. As we saw in Chapter 2, like her mother the sea Aphrodite has an awesome power that subjects to itself everything that lives and breathes. But like all natural forces represented by anthropomorphic gods, Aphrodite also was controlled by the technology of worship and ritual. Earlier in Chapter 2 we noted her status as maritime tutelary deity, worshipped by sailors as the "Watcher from the Cliffs" or the "Giver of Fair Winds." Throughout the Greek world she inhabited myriad temples in which she was induced through the gifts of sacrifice into turning her sexual power to the benefit of the worshiper. We mentioned earlier the Heavenly Aphrodite, worshipped in Athens, and the Aphrodite Pandemos, whose sanctuary was purified with the blood of doves and who along with Peitho—Persuasion, a good ally in both love and politics—was celebrated in late July during the Aphrodisia as the force of affection binding the people into a political community.

Also at Athens was the temple of Aphrodite in the Garden, which reflected the goddess's connection with flowers, trees, and vegetation. It was there that the festival of the Arrephoria took place in midsummer, a ritual connected both with the olive tree, one of the most important crops for the ancient Greeks, and with the initiation of citizen-girls into puberty. The myth believed to be the origin of the ritual reveals the same interlinking of human, civic, and agricultural fertility that the festival celebrates. Hephaistos, the lame and ugly blacksmith god, desired to possess the virgin goddess Athena. Horrified by his advances, the goddess ran away, but not before Hephaistos ejaculated on her dress. Athena wiped the semen off with some wool and threw it on the ground, whence sprung Erichthonios, one of the early kings of Athens. Ashamed at this offspring, Athena put the infant in a basket, which she entrusted to the daughters of Cecrops, the half-snake first king of Athens, ordering them not to look inside it. Of course two of the girls have to look and, horrified by the snakes guarding the infant, hurl themselves from the Acropolis. The obedient girl, Pandrosos, whose name contains the word for "dew," is given the honor of tending Athena's sacred olive tree.

The emergence of political and agricultural order out of a monstrous prehistory of half-snake kings and men sprung like plants directly from the earth is celebrated in this festival. The Assembly would choose four girls between the ages of seven and eleven from a list of noble families. For nine months, the girls would be given the task of helping with the weaving of Athena's robe, which was given to the goddess each year at the Panathenaea. At the time of the Arrephoria, two of the girls, dressed in white robes, bear on their heads secret objects that they carry via an underground passage, discovered by modern archaeologists on the north slope of the Acropolis, leading from the temple of Athena to the nearby temple of Aphrodite in the Garden. Without peeking at their burdens, like the faithful Pandrosos, they leave whatever it is they are carrying and take some other equally mysterious objects back to the temple of Athena. The exact import of this mysterious ritual is still debated, but the young girls, the domestic duties in the temple of Athena, the symbolic death in the underground passage, and the nighttime journey to the temple of Aphrodite all suggest a fertility function—perhaps connected with the nurturing dew and the olive, which during the fall months depends on dew for the fruit to develop—connected to a rite of passage for girls approaching puberty. Remember, too, that the sacred olive of Athena growing on the Acropolis—"terror to foreign spearmen, nurse of young citizens," according to Sophocles—embodied the life-force of the Athenian people, who fancied themselves "autochthonous," "sprung from the soil" like their ancestor Erichthonios, whose sequestration in a basket the "Dew Carriers" reenact. An anecdote in Herodotus confirms this link of the olive to the collective political soul of the Athenians. After the Persians burned the Acropolis during their invasion of 480–479, the scorched sacred olive sprouted a new shoot, emblematizing the survival of the Athenian people. Thus the Arrephoria functioned to harness the fecundating power of Aphrodite so that the olive and the Athenian people alike, especially its girls, were fruitful and multiplied.[27]

On the other end of the sexual spectrum from presexual girls, prostitutes were particular devotees of Aphrodite and benefited from her power, as we saw in Chapter 2. If the fundamental act of worship of the goddess, that is, of recognizing and acknowledging her power, was sex, then prostitutes were her most devout worshipers. Some temples of Aphrodite literally had prostitutes as priestesses, the most famous being at Corinth where more than a thousand women, in Pindar's words "stranger-loving girls, servants of Peitho [Persuasion]," were allowed by Aphrodite to "pluck without scandal on lovely couches the fruit of the delicate spring." Having such an enormous claim on Aphrodite's power, the prostitutes were considered potent allies in the affairs of the city: Whenever Corinth had to pray to the goddess on important state business, it enlisted as many prostitutes as possible to help them win over Aphrodite's goodwill. Even prostitutes not attached to a temple saw Aphrodite as their presiding deity. Greek poetry is filled with epigrams noting the offerings of aged prostitutes to Aphrodite: mirrors, lamps, jewelry, combs, fans, hair nets, veils, the mysteriously titillating "things men can't talk about" and other seductive accoutrements of their trade that old age is bringing to an end. Our sexual neuroses and idealism make it nearly impossible for us to imagine sex with a prostitute as an act of worship, but in ancient Greece prostitutes clearly functioned as mediators of Aphrodite's power, their sexual skills a sort of "technology" that canalized her potent force.[28]

A festival that reflected the purely carnal force of Aphrodite celebrated by prostitutes, but which nonetheless was circumscribed by the larger cultural order, was the Adonia. This rite centered on the youth beloved of Aphrodite, Adonis, who was born from an incestuous relationship between his mother Myrrha (or Smyrna) and her father. The girl visited her father's bed for twelve consecutive nights until her father found out her identity and she was turned into the myrrh tree before he could kill her. After the boy's birth from the tree, Aphrodite entrusted him to Persephone, but the Queen of the Underworld was also taken by his beauty and refused to give him back. The two goddesses compromised, with Aphrodite getting the boy eight months of the year. The other four he stays in the Underworld with Persephone.

The mingling of illicit sex and death, and the cyclic quality of Adonis's death and rebirth, all suggest a ritual whose purpose is to come to terms with chaotic sexual power, fertility, and natural renewal. The festival of the Adonia, though, was concerned not so much with fruitfulness as with the power and enjoyment of sexual pleasure for its own sake, the beauty of youthful sexuality embodied in Aphrodite's role as "postponer of old age." The rite took place in mid-July, on the rooftops of private homes rather than in a public civic space, during Dog-Days summer, when Sirius the Dog Star rose with the sun, a phenomenon the ancients thought to be responsible for certain diseases. Men and women both participated, especially prostitutes, courtesans, and their lovers: women, that is, whose sexuality was its own pleasurable end rather than directed to the procreative needs of the city, as was the case with the chaste citizen-wives of the Thesmophoria. The celebrants drank, told dirty jokes, feasted, burned spices, and made love.[29]

An important part of the festival was the growing of "Adonis Gardens," pots and baskets and pottery shards in which wheat, barley, lettuce, and fennel were planted. In eight days the plants sprouted quickly in the July heat then withered just as quickly, after which they were thrown into the sea; all the while the women mourned and bewailed the death of Adonis. The plants obviously represent Adonis, the "shoot of Aphrodite," as an anonymous lyric poet calls him, but not as the fruitful grain that humans must cultivate in the earth, cut down, and bury to survive. Rather it represents Adonis as youthful erotic beauty that dies before it bears fruit, just as Adonis dies without issue—hence an "unnatural" sexuality, as Aristotle notes when he compares a youth's rapid maturity due to precocious sexual experience to Adonis Gardens. The rites celebrate and mourn sex not as procreative force but as its own end, a sterile pleasure useless to the city and hence short-lived—several ancient proverbs compared useless, sterile, or worthless people to Adonis Gardens. The city, though, has the last word, simply by virtue of tolerating this circumscribed expression of private illicit sexual pleasure, a pleasure that like the Adonis Gardens flourishes quickly but soon passes away, leaving nothing for the future.[30]

The Adonia occupies one end of a spectrum of ritual technology whose other end is the Thesmophoria. Whereas the latter strictly circumscribes the sexual power of legitimate wives in order to ensure the fruitfulness of the grain and the women themselves, the prostitutes and mistresses of the Adonia give expression to the private pleasures of sex and emotion, pleasures ultimately that are their own end. But the city's allowance of this expression of sexual power is ultimately testimony to the city's control over sexuality, just as the prostitutes themselves were taxed and registered. The wailing of the women might disturb the Assembly while it deliberates its business, as the Proboulos in the *Lysistrata* complains, but the business goes on all the same.[31]

The exploitation of Aphrodite's power to serve cultural institutions, however, can most readily be seen in the important role that she plays in marriage. As early as Homer her purview is described by Zeus, after she has been wounded by Diomedes, as the "desirable works of marriage." Andromache's bridal veil was a personal gift from Aphrodite. Sappho speaks of a bridegroom transfigured by love as honored greatly by Aphrodite. Later poets give her such epithets as "fruitful," "lover of bridegrooms," and "provider of weddings." These poetic conceits reflect a widespread worship of Aphrodite in connection with marriage. There was an Aphrodite of the Bridal Chamber, an Aphrodite Joiner, an Aphrodite of the Nuptial Rites. The name of her daughter by Ares, Harmonia, from the word "join," reflects this conjugal function. Maidens and widows about to remarry sacrificed to Aphrodite, and widows still waiting prayed to her for a husband.[32]

The reason for enlisting her power in marriage is obvious. For a marriage to function for the benefit of the community it must be strong and fruitful, which means that husbands and wives need to desire one another sexually. That's where Aphrodite comes in. As we saw when Hera seduced her husband Zeus in the *Iliad*, Aphrodite provides the seductive power that makes Zeus desire his wife, for she loans Hera her breastband embroidered with the charms of desire. If marriage is a cultural "technology," then the energy it uses is the sexual power of Aphrodite, the mutual desire of husband for wife and wife for husband that strengthened the household. Readers familiar with the current received wisdom that Greek husbands didn't even like their wives and found emotional and sexual gratification elsewhere in mistresses and homosexual amours may wonder why Aphrodite would have been given a role at all in such loveless marriages.[33]

Apart from her subordination to the civic ritual of marriage, Aphrodite in Greek literature is put in her place in other ways, the scope of her power limited even as it is recognized. As we've already seen, in the *Iliad* Aphrodite's cold chastisement of Helen reveals the sudden, frightening force of the goddess when Helen tries to resist her command to join Paris in their bed. And her role in Hera's seduction of Zeus also asserts her power—although in the context of marriage, as we saw earlier, and at the behest of the tutelary goddess of marriage, Hera. But the *Iliad* gives us another episode in which Aphrodite is humiliated at the hands of a mortal man, humiliation and shame in Homer's world a way of establishing superiority and power over another. After the Greek champion Diomedes has wounded Aeneas, Aphrodite's son, crushing his hip socket with a stone, Aphrodite comes to her son's rescue, sweeping him up in her arms and rushing from the fray. But Diomedes, on instructions from Athena—he wouldn't dare attack a god, even the nonmartial Aphrodite, otherwise—pursues Aphrodite and wounds her slightly on the wrist, taunting her with the charge to stay out of the war and be satisfied with beguiling cowardly women. The goddess shrieks and drops her son, leaving Apollo to finish his rescue, and then dashes off to Olympus in the chariot of Ares. There her mother Dione comforts her, but the other gods all laugh and mock her, Zeus repeating Diomedes' advice to stay out of war and to stick to the "desirable works of marriage."[34]

The wounding of Aphrodite is one of those comic interludes in the *Iliad* when the suffering and death of mortals are rendered all the more heartbreaking by being juxtaposed with the trivial misadventures of the silly serene gods, who neither suffer nor die. But the scene works also to set a limit on the influence of Aphrodite, relegating her to a female sphere of marriage and maternity—after all, she enters the battle to save her son, although we should remember that the gods' interest in their children's fate usually reflects their concern with the risk of dishonor because they couldn't protect their own. In addition, the laughter and mockery Aphrodite endures serve to circumscribe her power, for those who suffer the mockery of others do so because they are powerless to stop it. Aphrodite, of course, will have her revenge: She gets back at Diomedes by making his wife take lovers and plot against him. But for the moment, the power she displayed earlier in her confrontation with Helen is here given its absolute limit, the world of male martial violence. Hector, right before he is killed in a duel with Achilles, juxtaposes poignantly Aphrodite's realm of courtship and lovemaking with the grim brutality of war, likewise asserting their incompatibility. Waiting for Achilles outside the walls of Troy, Hector momentarily considers stripping himself of his armor and offering Helen and treasure to Achilles to make the peace. But Hector quickly realizes that Achilles would simply kill him "like a woman," unarmed or not, and he says bitterly to himself, "I cannot dally with him as a youth and a maiden, a youth and a maiden dally with one another." In the world of heroic killing, the wiles of Aphrodite and her companion goddess Peitho, Persuasion, are useless.[35]

Laughter and humiliation put Aphrodite in her place in the *Odyssey* too. The story is sung by the blind bard Demodocus at the feast the Phaiacians give for Odysseus, who has been washed up on their island. Ares, god of war, was secretly visiting Aphrodite's bed while her husband Hephaistos, the god of craft and technology, was away. However, the sun-god Helios, who sees everything, tattled on the two. Hephaistos then set about his revenge. He forged unbreakable bonds as fine as spider webs, which he then hung around his bed. After he pretended to visit the island of Lemnos, Ares came to his house and he and Aphrodite started frolicking again. Immediately they are trapped in the nets, and Hephaistos calls on the gods to witness this outrage. All the gods gather to mock Aphrodite and Ares as they lay naked and tangled in Hephaistos's cunning nets, the roguish Hermes swearing he would endure three times as many bonds and laughter from all the gods and goddesses if he could sleep with Aphrodite. Finally the cuckolded husband sets them free, his anger mollified by the shame the two suffered and by the recompense Poseidon promises Ares will pay.[36]

As well as using humiliation to limit Aphrodite's power, this story asserts the dominance of technology over the natural energy of sex and of physical violence embodied in the war-god Ares. The lame, misshapen Hephaistos triumphs in the end because of his skill and craft that thinks up the trick and then forges the subtle nets. For all that Aphrodite "cannot control her passions," she nonetheless is literally constrained by metallurgical skill. Ultimately this constraint serves to validate the claims of legitimate marriage, as mind, technology, and the social institution of marriage triumph over the chaotic force of illicit passion.[37]

The use of shame and culture to establish the limits of Aphrodite's power characterizes as well the *Hymn to Aphrodite*. As we saw in Chapter 2, the *Hymn*, about the goddess's seduction of the Trojan Anchises, is one of the most important assertions of Aphrodite's nature and power that we have in Greek literature. But it is as well a statement of the absolute limits of that power. Indeed, the *Hymn* is structured by a pattern in which descriptions of Aphrodite's might alternate with descriptions of her constraints. The result is a complex picture of Aphrodite's complete meaning, her awesome power placed in a controlling context that ultimately gives the victory to Zeus and the male cultural order he represents.

The proem or introduction to the *Hymn* contains perhaps the best description of Aphrodite's power that "subdues the tribes of mortal men and flying birds and as many creatures as the dry land rears and as many as the sea." But immediately afterward the exceptions to her power are enumerated: Athena, goddess of war, technology, and the woman's household crafts; Artemis, goddess of the hunt, the lyre, and dancing; and Hestia, goddess of the hearth "in the middle of the house"—in other words, goddesses of culture and technology, of the household, of ritualized male violence like hunting and war. A space has been delimited in which Aphrodite's power is curtailed, a space defined by male culture.[38]

This alternating pattern structures the rest of the *Hymn*. Aphrodite's power over Zeus is asserted, her ability to "lead him astray" and mate him with mortal women, betraying his wife Hera. But Zeus reasserts his power by appropriating Aphrodite's—he "casts sweet desire" on her to be mated with a mortal man so that she cannot mock the other gods for their déclassé human amours. Aphrodite will be checked by being subjected first to her own power, sexual desire against her will, next to the shame at having lowered herself to mate with a mortal. Aphrodite herself says to Anchises that because of him she will have "great reproach" among the gods, and she memorializes her shame by instructing Anchises to name the child she will bear Aeneas, from the word meaning "awful," because she felt awful grief for lying in a mortal's bed.[39]

As the principle of cosmic order, Zeus cannot afford to have a power out there challenging that order. The *Hymn* recognizes the very potent force of sexual desire but does so in a context that marks its boundaries by excluding from her power the three culture-goddesses—Athena, Artemis, and Hestia—and by subordinating it to Zeus's rule, which is potent enough to turn Aphrodite's own power against her. In addition, the birth of a half-mortal son to Aphrodite implicates her in the contingent world of human suffering that now checks her freedom. Significantly enough, Aphrodite disguises herself before Anchises as a shy young virgin kidnapped by the messenger-god Hermes and deposited at Anchises' hut because she is destined to be his wife. Remember too that she is shamed and wounded by Diomedes because she tried to rescue her son Aeneas. Zeus asserts his power over Aphrodite by subjecting her to the same institutions that control mortal female sexuality. Marriage and motherhood, the fruit of woman's sexuality, also transform it by subjecting a woman to larger responsibilities, the nurturing of the child that limits the exuberance of sexual pleasure. This contrast is similar to the contrast between the Thesmophoria and the Adonia, the former a ritual of legitimate procreation and civic order, the latter a celebration of illicit, sterile sexual pleasure. Aphrodite, in a sense, has left nature—where her mere presence makes the animals copulate—for history, the human world of cultural order in which her scope is limited. Zeus has put her in her place.[40]

Perhaps the most subtle attempt to come to grips with Aphrodite can be found scattered in the fragments of Sappho's poetry. The late-seventh-century poet from Lesbos has been the victim of mischaracterization for 2,500 years. On the Greek comic stage she was the erotomaniac throwing herself off a cliff for unrequited love. In the nineteenth century she was transformed into a combination of Miss Jean Brodie and foursquare housewife, chastely instructing upper-class girls in the feminine arts and preparing them for marriage. These days she's a feminist heroine, the *fons et origo* of reciprocal lesbian love. The fragmentary remains of her poetry and the paucity of reliable evidence about her life make all these Sapphos to some extent caricatures that fulfill some need in their creators, but they tell us nothing about the poet herself. In the discussion that follows, no claim is being made that Sappho presided as high priestess over an actual cult of Aphrodite into which nubile aristocratic girls were initiated. I will be talking about poetic image and metaphor, not about biography or history.

Even in Sappho's fragments we can see that one of her major poetic interests was the power of sex and the ways humans come to terms with this power. She wrote epithalamia, wedding songs, which makes sense for someone interested in eros, for as we have seen (and will see in Chapter 7), marriage for the Greeks was one of the most important "technologies" for controlling sexuality. Given the important role in marriage played by Aphrodite, Sappho's concern with marriage includes acknowledging the place of Aphrodite in creating and sustaining the marriage bond. But in the surviving fragments Aphrodite also appears frequently in contexts outside of marriage. Enough evidence survives for us to piece together a complex of ritual imagery that functions as an alternative "technology" to marriage. The effect of Sappho's "ritual" is to put Aphrodite and her power into a meaningful conceptual structure that gives coherence to her chaotic volatility. In contrast to the male perspective in Homer or the *Homeric Hymn*, which seeks to control Aphrodite through limitation by force, Sappho wants rather to control the goddess through *understanding*, by justifying Aphrodite's ways to men and women. We will still suffer from Aphrodite's force, but at least we will know *why* we are suffering, for we will have a larger perspective that makes our misery more endurable. In short, Sappho's approach is part theological and part philosophical.[41]

Religion and the imagery of cult and festival provide useful metaphors for Sappho, for as we saw with the Thesmophoria, cult-ritual provides a "technology" for organizing and understanding the force the god represents. The only complete poem of Sappho, the so-called "Hymn to Aphrodite" (a modern title), is a good example of her poetic method. The poem follows the structure and conventions of prayers to the gods: Aphrodite is addressed directly, she is invoked with descriptive epithets similar to those used in cult, her parentage is noted, she is reminded of past services, and the immediate need is expressed. The suffering that Sappho goes on to describe, in traditional erotic imagery of disease and madness, is thus subordinated to the larger framework of the mortal's ritualistic relationship to the deity, the obligation imposed on the goddess by her acceptance of ritual gifts.[42]

After the prayer, Aphrodite appears to the poet and asks why she is suffering, why she is calling, what her "maddened heart" desires, whom she is to persuade to become her friend. "Who does you injustice, Sappho? If she runs away, soon she will pursue. And if she won't accept gifts, yet she will give them. And if she does not love, soon she will even if she's unwilling." What exactly Aphrodite promises Sappho is debated by interpreters. Is Aphrodite promising Sappho erotic reciprocity, that she will persuade the girl to enter a mutually sustaining sexual and emotional relationship with Sappho? That may be what Sappho and some modern commentators want, but I don't think that is what Aphrodite promises. Aphrodite doesn't say, "I'll make her want you as much as you want her." If that were the case, why would the girl have to "pursue" a willing Sappho or court her with gifts? Rather, with the amused solicitude of a mother comforting a child, the goddess explains the intellectual *context* of Sappho's suffering: the rhythm of sexual attraction, its constant oscillation between satiety and lack, the two species of pain

Sappho identifies in the first stanza. To the suffering human trapped in time, the pain seems unendurable. But a smiling Aphrodite, like Keats's urn "all breathing human passion far above," instructs Sappho that the pain will end, as it has many times in the past. For erotic pain is not a continuous experience but a repetitious cycle of gratification and lack—three times Aphrodite repeats the adverb "again," reminding Sappho that she has suffered erotically for other girls and still survived. Indeed, rather than reciprocity, the goddess seems to promise some revenge for the aristocratic Sappho, some recompense for the "injustice" she has suffered. Soon the girl will "pursue," court with gifts, and Sappho will "flee": The two women will change roles in the alternating rhythm of desire, Sappho repelled by satiety, the girl now pursuing in her pain of lack.[43]

Aphrodite offers Sappho the consolation of knowing that the suffering will end, even if it will be followed by a different kind of pain, the pain of getting what you want and not wanting it anymore. Aphrodite has given Sappho a conceptual control over sexuality by explaining to her the larger context the speaker maddened with desire cannot comprehend. The destructive passion that Aphrodite embodies and Sappho recognizes is now rendered meaningful and endurable. It is not a cataclysm fixed at one point in time—it is the curve of a cycle defined and valorized by its very transience. The power Sappho exercises over Aphrodite is philosophical power, the power of knowledge.

In some of Sappho's other fragments the imagery of cult locates human sexuality in the realm of a beautiful nature nonetheless organized by the structure of ritual that provides a controlling context for sex. Fragment 2 describes an invitation to Aphrodite to appear at a temple, where there are a "charming apple grove and altars smoking fragrantly with frankincense." Other details depict a lovely natural setting reinforcing the erotic suggestiveness of apples and perfume: a cool brook, roses, a meadow in which horses, emblems of sexuality, graze and flowers bloom and breezes blow. But this is no untouched nature—there are the temple, the altar, the chalices of the women's ritual, all accoutrements of cult technology that create a controlling framework for Aphrodite's epiphany and for the sexuality she represents. This is very different from the sudden anger of Aphrodite toward Helen in the *Iliad* or the revelation of her divinity to Anchises that frightens the mortal so much. Here, in contrast, Aphrodite's power is bound by the reciprocal obligation the gifts of ritual sacrifice impose upon her, so that Sappho can invite the goddess to serve the women by pouring the wine for their celebration.[44]

Another fragment seems to suggest that sex between the women is part of Sappho's poetic ritual. I say seems, for the papyrus on which fragment 94 was discovered is badly mutilated, a fact readers of modern translators of Sappho should remember, for some translations shamelessly fill in the gaps without clearly alerting the reader that the translators are essentially writing Sappho's poem for her. The poem records a parting between Sappho and a tearful girl grieving the loss of her friends and lovers. Sappho tells her to remember the good times, the "wreaths of violets and roses," the "woven garlands made from flowers," the perfume, the shrines, the dances. All these details suggest the cult imagery of fragment 2. But another detail seems more sexually explicit. Sappho reminds the girl of the "soft beds" on which she would "satisfy [her] longing . . . tender"—here the papyrus is riddled with tantalizing holes.[45]

But this broken sentence could easily be referring to sex acts the girl experienced. If so, sex is being made part of the cult metaphor, and hence is being given a controlling structure that serves to limit and define it by placing sexuality in the larger realm of nature's sexual beauty emblematized by the wreaths and garlands of flowers—the flowers that will fade and die, just as the girl has "died" to her erotic life with Sappho and her friends, perhaps because she has married and moved far away. Remember too that these are aristocratic girls who *will* marry, whose sexuality will be redefined in terms of the social institution of the household and its procreative imperative. What Sappho memorializes, then, as does the Adonia, is the flowerlike bloom of a girlhood sexuality that is limited by its very brevity, its transience, and that in Sappho's poem is organized by the imagery of cult technology. What this imagery describes finally is a transitional order between the chaos of indiscriminate natural eros and the circumscribed social structure of marriage that Sappho celebrated in her epithalamia.

For all her celebration of nature and sex in her fragments, Sappho still subordinates both to the technology of cult-ritual. In this she resembles the festival of the Adonia, and one wishes that the poems Pausanias told us she wrote of Adonis had survived. In both the festival and Sappho's poetry the brief beauty of young sexuality is celebrated and related to the flourishing of plants and flowers. But in both too the limit to this sexual exuberance is asserted. The flower must become the fruit, the fruit ripen and fall; the girl must become a wife and mother, as was Sappho herself, and take her place in the order of the city. Only the poetry—another cultural artifact—remains, even in its fragments a memorial to the transient loveliness of young girls in flower.[46]

Cultivating the Cyclopes' Island

The Greeks recognized the sexual beauty of the natural world, but they never lost sight of the destructive natural forces intimately connected with that beauty. They realized that the procreative powers of nature were volatile and chaotic, and so like the Cyclopes' island they had to be subjected to the order of culture. The flowers and fruit of the natural world, while symbolizing the exuberance of youthful sexuality, suggested also the decay and death that are the warp to the weft of natural beauty. Agriculture provides the paradigm for coming to terms with this terrible ambiguity, this mingling of life and death. Through the ordering of the earth with furrows, some measure of control can be gained and the fertile power of nature tapped, just as marriage exploits the procreative power of women to provide citizens for the city. The ritual of festivals works to the same effect, binding sexual power in a communal civic order, even in a private festival like the Adonia: The mourning for the Adonis Gardens thrown into the sea is an admission that unfulfilled youthful sexual beauty is a dead end, that the alternative to conception is death. In all these erotic technologies the awesome power of Aphrodite is channeled and limited, subjected to a larger order—the order of Zeus, the control of technology, or the cult-metaphors of Sappho's poetic artifice.

This attitude toward nature presupposes an intimacy with it that most of us urban moderns lack. For us, nature is scenery or the weather, kept at bay with technology, idealized as a lost home in which most of us wouldn't last five minutes. Few of us grow food or butcher animals, and so we have no firsthand experience with nature's callous intimacy with the death on which life feeds. In an age of corporate farms worked with machinery and chemical fertilizers and pesticides, agriculture as a metaphor cannot move us. The meat will always be in the store, neatly sealed in plastic, the blood and guts and dung completely erased. The fruit grown these days for glossy appearance rather than taste will not remind us of the sugar of decay. The flowers available all year round cannot suggest to us the brevity of sexual youth, and so our popular myths tell us that sexual exuberance cancels out the destructiveness of eros. And in an age of secularism and an organized religion leeched of its communal ritual, the collective civic rites that for the Greeks confronted and ordered the power of sex can only strike us as quaint superstitions. Made arrogant by Romantic idealism and technology alike, we blindly patronize the monster waiting to devour us.

SEVEN

Wives and the Order of the House

EARLY IN EURIPIDES' PLAY, Medea emerges from the house to which her husband Jason is bringing a new, younger wife. Speaking to the Chorus of Corinthian women, she bitterly recounts the evils of arranged marriages—the dowry with which the husband must be "bought," the girl's ignorance of his character and habits, the hard job she has of adjusting to a new household, the confinement at home where she undergoes the risk of childbirth. "Three times I would rather stand in the front line of battle, than bear one child," she declaims, reflecting the dangers of childbirth in the ancient world. For us moderns this passage provides a summary indictment of patriarchal marriages: They are arranged by fathers with no regard for the wishes of the girl. Like a piece of property, she is transferred from one male to another.[1]

As we saw earlier, though, Medea is speaking somewhat disingenuously here, working on the sympathy of the Corinthian women whose experience her speech describes more accurately than it does her own. Medea, remember, did not have an arranged marriage: She fell passionately in love with Jason and ran off with him, betraying her father and her homeland. For her, passion, not the father's economic or social interest, was the basis of her marriage. In short, Medea married for the reasons we marry today—because we fall in love, that is, we sexually and emotionally desire someone. Moreover, for us the quality and intensity of that sexual desire are seen as signs of the quality and intensity of the couple's emotional attraction, an attraction so intense and fulfilling that they want to spend the rest of their lives together. Any opposition, particularly of parents and a larger society, is taken as a validation of the unique, private worth of the relationship. Marriage is personal, a concern of the couple whose passion, not society's laws, legitimizes it, and so societal disapproval often draws the lovers even closer. The great founding myth of this view of marriage is, of course, Shakespeare's *Romeo and Juliet*, written at the end of the sixteenth century, when marriage custom was shifting away from arrangement by parents toward a greater recognition of the wishes of the couple and of the need for love between them, if only to cut down on adultery, the bane of arranged marriage. In that play all the components of Romantic Marriage are in place: love at first sight, a powerful sexual attraction that expresses the value and worth of the couple and their spiritual relationship, an opposing social order, and the climax of death freezing forever the couple's passion at its peak of intensity. One can hardly imagine a paunchy Romeo and a sagging Juliet celebrating their fiftieth wedding anniversary.

This ideal of Romantic Marriage, which we in the West take for granted as the most desirable kind even as some of us marry for more pragmatic reasons, is foreign to the ancient Greeks, with the exception, some would argue, of the Hellenistic period, when changing social and cultural circumstances and the erosion of the old polis brought about a shift toward a greater consideration of love as a precondition for marriage apparently similar to our modern views, as we will have occasion to discuss later. Thus although our ideals of Romantic Marriage make us applaud Medea's indictment of so barbaric and sexist a practice as arranged marriage, for Euripides her story shows the danger of basing *any* social institution on the volatile force of passion. For when circumstances change, as they must and do, passion becomes a force of destruction and death. Thus the sexual passion of Medea culminates in the obliteration of the household, her sons killed by her own hand. Rather than a private relationship, marriage for the Greeks is a cultural construct. Its main purpose is to harness and control the force of eros, particularly female sexuality. Marriage exploits women's procreative power to provide citizens for the city and distribute property while also limiting the scope of eros by focusing it on a socially sanctioned object. In short, marriage is a "technology," an order whose physical space is the household.

By describing Greek marriage this way, however, I don't mean to endorse the current received wisdom that sees ancient Greek marriage as "less than bliss," "rarely . . . a focus of love for either party," to quote a recent nonspecialist, always the best source of the received ideas that have trickled down from the academy.[2] Leaving aside the problem raised at the beginning of this book, that of moving from fragmentary written documents to actual lives, one can nonetheless discover in the surviving evidence praise of wives and marriage to counterbalance the misogyny we documented in Chapter 3 and to suggest the existence of affection and love between husbands and wives. Odysseus's father Laertes grows old before his time, grieving not only for his lost son but also for his dead wife Antikleia, a devotion that bespeaks strong ties of love and affection. Hesiod, who as we have seen has some nasty things to say about women, grouses that nothing's worse than a bad wife—but adds too that nothing's better than a good one. Semonides, Hesiod's equal in misogyny who gave us the female bestiary, says exactly the same thing. Theognis, retroaristocratic extoller of boy-love, the alleged ancient venue of romantic sexual passion, strengthens it to "nothing is sweeter than a good wife," indicating that the sentiment had all the unquestioned truth of a proverb. Statements like these would be meaningless unless conjugal affection existed between men and women and unless men found some measure of fulfillment in their emotional and sexual relationships with their wives.[3]

Consider the scene at the end of Xenophon's *Symposium*, a fictional recreation of a dinner party attended by Socrates. After the philosophical conversation, two actors come into the room and reenact the marriage of Ariadne and the god Dionysus, who fell in love with the Cretan maiden after she had been abandoned by Theseus on the island of Naxos during their flight from Crete. The actors do such a good job of passionately kissing and declaring their love for one another that the men at the dinner party are sexually aroused, with the result that "the unmarried men swore that they would marry, while the married men mounted their horses and rode home to their wives, so that they could find pleasure with them." This detail would be unconvincing to Xenophon's readers if at least some men did not find an exclusive emotional as well as sexual gratification from their wives.[4]

Equally meaningless would be the whole plot of the *Lysistrata*, in which the Greek men are blackmailed into ending the Peloponnesian War by their wives' refusal to have sex with them. The standard model would have us believe that boys and prostitutes offered the main source of sexual gratification for Greek men. If that's true, why don't those guys in the play just grab a boy or a prostitute and alleviate their sexual pressure? The answer is that there is often a big difference between sex with someone you love and who loves you and sex with an acquaintance or a stranger. As Lenny Bruce used to say, no matter how powerful the man, there's some woman whom he would beg on hands and knees just to touch it. Or as Aristotle explains it, receiving affection is preferable in love to sexual intercourse, and so intercourse is an end relative to receiving affection. Aristophanes' play depends on his audience's shared assumption that men desire not just sex but *affectionate* sex with their wives, an affection resulting from the intimacy of a shared life. That's why Lysistrata advises the women to show a sullen disinterest if their husbands force them to have sex, "for a husband never enjoys himself if he isn't getting along with his wife." This power to withhold affection from sex gives the wives a psychological hold over their husbands. If Athenian men found this sexual affection exclusively in homosexual amours or with courtesans, Aristophanes' plot would collapse.[5]

Recognizing conjugal affection and passion among the ancient Greeks should not, however, lead us to assume that their marital relations were "just like ours." Rather, we need to acknowledge a greater complexity and variety to those ancient relations than the current orthodox interpretation allows. Finally, though, the quotidian reality of conjugal relationships in ancient Greek households, what they were "really" like, is pretty much unrecoverable. There is too little evidence, especially of the sort most useful for answering such a question—private diaries and letters. We must remember, too, that "Greek marriage" covers a broad histori-cal spectrum, from the feudal aristocratic household complexes of the early Dark Age, through the agrarian and urban households of late-fifth-century city-states, to the more private suburban marriages of the Hellenistic period of the sort re-flected in Theocritus and Herodas, with their gossiping housewives complaining about their husbands and bullying the slaves. And the scanty evidence we have re-flects generally a narrow social class, the aristocracy. We know little of the lives, married or otherwise, of the bulk of the population that didn't have the leisure to leave even a fragmentary record of their existence. Once more, we are not trying to recover marriage as it "really" was for the ancient Greeks (although occasion-ally we will be describing actual social conditions), but we are attempting to de-scribe the *meaning* of marriage and its idealizations as evidenced in the literary re-mains, from which so much of our current beliefs about the Greeks emerges.

Sowing Heirs and Citizens

Looked at from the perspective of its cultural meaning, Greek marriage functions as an important element of the social order that controls sexuality and organizes the natural impulse of humans to reproduce. Children and sex are at the heart of Greek marriage to an extent that we, with our obsession with the careerist couple, our religion of self-fulfillment, and our dependable birth control, no longer rec-ognize. Hesiod, after describing the creation of Pandora and the "race of women" that are such an evil to men, goes on to say that they are nonetheless necessary, for from women come the heirs who will tend the man's old age and inherit his property. Given the harsh Iron Age, harsher still to the old man weakened by time, the family is a necessary institution for offsetting those natural contingencies. The natural sex drive is thus directed toward an end useful for men. As the early-fifth-century philosopher Democritus put it, having children is a necessity of life, an imperative of natural law from which men then try to find some profit to offset the trouble and pain that children (and their mothers) bring with them.[6]

This "profit" consistently involves in Greek literature the Hesiodic idea that children will tend the parent when he is old and feeble, without the pensions and social safety nets our modern aged people depend on. Phoinix, Achilles' old tutor who because of his father's curse could not have children of his own and so con-sidered Achilles his son, tries to coax him back into the fighting by appealing to the obligation Achilles has to Phoinix. Phoinix had taken care of him when he was a helpless child who needed his food cut up and who spit up on his tutor: "I made you my child, godlike Achilles, so that you would save me from shameful ruin." Fathers go to so much trouble—and put up with women—so that when weak and aged they will have children who will be obliged to reciprocate and so take care of the parents who gave them life and took care of them in their weak infancy. Medea reveals the same somewhat calculated but understandable attitude toward children when she is agonizing over her decision to kill her two sons to avenge herself on Jason. She mourns her wasted labor pains, since her sons will not be there to "cherish [her] old age and lay [her] out when [she] is dying, a happiness envied by all human beings." This universal desire for children makes the man as dependent on the woman as he is on nature, as Aristotle noted, and as the frustrated rhetorical cry of a Jason or a Hippolytus—"Why isn't there some other way of getting children?"—confesses.[7]

This natural desire to bear children who would tend one's old age was complicated in the city-states by the issue of citizenship. In Athens after the mid–fifth century citizenship was narrowly confined to those whose parents were both Athenians. Since only citizens could inherit property or participate in state religious rituals and cults, the issue of legitimacy was extremely important and explains the Greek male's obsession with adultery and female chastity as much as the suspicion of female sexuality does. Without the wife's chastity, no one could know who really belonged to the household or whether a child was a legitimate citizen. The high value of chastity can be seen in a treatise attributed to a Pythagorean community in Italy, which calls chastity the "greatest glory" and "foremost honor" a woman can have, for the adulteress "provides her family and home not with its own offspring but with bastards."[8] Likewise Euphiletus, in his defense-speech for murdering his wife's lover, argued that the law allowed a husband to kill an adulterer because the latter violated the conjugal affection that solidified the household. He caused uncertainty about who was the father of the children, thus threatening the stability of the larger society, which is structured by kinship. Control of the wife's sexuality is directly related to the issue of legitimacy, for the wife was the supplier not just of legitimate children but also of wealth through dowries and inheritance.[9]

Among the ancient Greek orators one finds courtroom speeches in which the issue of adultery and sexual laxness is inevitably intertwined with those of citizenship and property. The late-fifth-century orator Isaeus's third oration is an extremely complicated case of inheritance and perjury. The case turns on arguing that a girl, Phile, whose husband is making a claim for her alleged father's estate, is not legitimate, since her mother was a notorious debauchee whom no decent man would marry. As the speaker of the oration put it, "Since she was common to anyone who wished her, how could she reasonably be thought to be a wedded wife?" The categories of "wife" and "promiscuous woman" are mutually exclusive, since a wife by definition is a chaste woman providing for her husband *legitimate* children who alone have the right to inherit property.[10]

This same assumption underlies the oration attributed to the fourth-century orator Demosthenes, *Against Neaira*. Apollodorus and his brother-in-law Theomnestus bring an indictment against Neaira for posing as a legitimate citizen and wife of one Stephanus, against whom the two litigants carry a grudge for a pair of earlier indictments Stephanus had brought against Apollodorus. Neaira is accused, among other things, of being the shared mistress of two men, of working as a prostitute in Corinth, and of attending drinking parties with men—something only courtesans would do. She even went so far as to sleep with the serving men. When she set up house in Athens, she charged more for her sexual services because of her customers' added relish of having sex with a citizen-wife. Her "husband" Stephanus ran a scam on the side, threatening wealthy customers with the sanctions against adulterers, which as we have seen could include death, unless he was paid off. Neaira's whole checkered sexual career is graphically detailed by the litigants in order to make the point that such a publicly promiscuous woman could not possibly be a legitimate wife, sharing in the religious and civic privileges of Athenian citizen-wives. In fact, the litigants ask the jury to imagine what they would tell their own wives if they acquitted Neaira: Those wives of "most self-control/chastity" would be angry at them for allowing such a woman to participate, in the same way as legitimate wives, in the public ceremonies and religious rites of the city. And those women without sexual self-control would consider that no limits exist anymore on their sexual appetites, since the privileges of citizenship accrue to the strumpet and the chaste wife alike.[11]

This oration makes explicit the public and social context for controlling a potentially destructive female eros, for everyone's identity as citizen is threatened unless the status of legitimate wives, which is to say women of sexual self-control, is protected and reinforced by the city-state. The speaker of the oration makes the centrality of legitimacy to marriage explicit when he says, "This is what it means to set up a household with a woman, with whom one has children, and one introduces the sons to the clan and deme ['parish' or 'borough'], and betroths the daughters to men as one's own. Courtesans we have for pleasure, concubines for the daily care of our bodies, and wives to bear legitimate children and to be the trusty guardians at home." This passage, by the way, is often cited as evidence that bearing legitimate children was the *only* function of a wife, romance and daily companionship being the purview of mistresses or prostitutes. But clearly the functions of the last category, wife, are *inclusive*, not *exclusive* of the functions of the other two. Otherwise, the speaker would be saying that men get no sexual pleasure from their concubines or that wives don't take care of their husbands on a daily basis. Nonetheless, their role as bearers of legitimate children and caretakers of the household is the defining one for Athenian wives.[12]

The Most Important Possession: A Chaste Wife

The importance of legitimate children adds another dimension to the need to control women's sexuality. In Part 1, we encountered situations in which a chaotic female passion led to destruction. Now the procreative consequences of that passion demand a moral code that ensures the legitimacy of the offspring. In our society, the stigma of illegitimacy has nearly faded away, and no political or economic penalties afflict the illegitimate child—indeed, economic rewards, in the form of public aid, may accrue to the out-of-wedlock child. Our indifference to illegitimacy makes it is easy to miss the significance of legitimacy for the ancient Greeks and its centrality to their thinking about female sexuality. This anxiety about legitimacy means the qualities the Greeks sought in wives center on self-control, particularly of a sexual passion that in women is extremely volatile and prone to disorder. Without that self-control, the women through their sexual excesses will bring into the household children who don't resemble their fathers, whereas the good woman's chastity ensures that the children will look like their father. The resemblance of children to fathers is part of the standard praise of a good wife. Theocritus, in a panegyric to Ptolemy Philadelphus, the Macedonian emperor of Egypt in the late third century, praises the emperor's mother Berenice for loving her husband and giving him legitimate children and an orderly household, whereas the faithless wife bears offspring that don't favor their father.[13]

We have seen already an extreme image of this ideal of female sexual self-control, the good wife as asexual hardworking bee. In Semonides' misogynistic bestiary, remember, the good wife was the bee that avoids "sex-chatter" and makes her husband's property increase, chastity here specifically linked to the economic well-being of the household. This emphasis on the woman's self-control was another reason to distrust marriages based solely on passion, presumably because female sexuality is by nature indiscriminate. We have already seen that this is a point of Euripides' *Medea*, in which a marriage based on extreme sexual passion degenerates into violence and death. This distrust of basing marriage on passion apparently wasn't confined to myth. The orator Isaeus, appealing to a received wisdom he assumes the jury shares, remarks that young men who married disreputable women out of passion usually ruined themselves with their mindlessness, such marriages seldom lasting. But mostly we see the concern with wifely chastity in the one virtue consistently praised as the most important for a wife to possess: "self-control/temperance/chastity," the *sôphrosunê* we discussed in Chapter 5 and defined as the rational control of appetite, particularly sexual appetite. In other words, for the woman to function efficiently in marriage she must display a mental control over her appetites that reinforces the social control of the household, that is, she must be less like a woman, passionate and given to appetite, and more like a man.[14]

Sometimes this mental virtue can be expressed by describing the ideal wife as one "well-fitted to the man's mind," as Hesiod puts it. Or the key element of the good wife will involve some other mental power, such as in Menander's statement that a good marriage depends on a woman with "sensible/prudent character."[15] But mostly *sôphrosunê* will be the womanly virtue deemed most necessary for a successful marriage, since the woman's eros is the most potentially destructive force. "Self-control" (*sôphrosunê*) is the wifely virtue that is "the most common of all tributes inscribed on memorial reliefs and tombstones,"[16] and it recurs over and over in literary discussions of wives and marriage. It is the highest ideal of the wife: As Sophocles says in a fragment, "Nothing is better than a chaste/temperate wife." The fifth-century comic poet Epicharmus elaborates on this quality: The chaste/temperate woman "will not commit an injustice against her husband," for adultery violates the reciprocity owed to the husband as partner in the household. The unfortunate Euphiletus of Lysias's oration, whose wife has cuckolded him, sadly admits to the court that he mistakenly thought his wife was "very self-controlled." And as we've just seen this is the word the speakers of the *Against Neaira* use to describe the jurymen's wives who would be angry at the jury for acquitting Neaira.[17]

Euripides in *Iphigeneia at Aulis* gives us a particularly rich example of the way this virtue defined the wife's role. Klytaimestra, having heard of Agamemnon's intention to sacrifice their daughter Iphigeneia to mollify Artemis and so unlock the winds holding back the Greek fleet, establishes her credentials as a good wife and thus one worthy of having her voice heard by her husband. Agamemnon had violently stolen Klytaimestra from her first husband Tantalus, murdering him and his child by Klytaimestra. Despite that crime, Klytaimestra says she reconciled herself to her new lord and was a "wife without reproach, showing self-control regarding sex, and increasing [his] household"—such a wife is a "rare prey" for a man to find. This speech drips with irony, of course, since every Greek in the audience would know that Klytaimestra ends up as the epitome of the *bad* wife, taking as lover her husband's enemy Aegisthus and murdering Agamemnon on his return from Troy—adultery that her son Orestes will describe as a "strange/peculiar wedding without self-control." Orestes defines Klytaimestra's relationship with her lover Aegisthus as an antimarriage, "strange/peculiar" since it lacks by definition the key quality a woman must bring to a legitimate marriage, sexual self-control.[18]

This ideal of sexual control underlies some of the imagery describing marriage, as we saw in Chapter 6 with the imagery of the plow and furrow. Another agricultural image, that of the yoke, occurs frequently and is particularly revealing of the way ancient marriage was seen as a "technology" for harnessing and exploiting the sexual power of men and women, just as the yoke controlled the muscle power of oxen so that they could drag a plow or a cart. We see a distant descendent of this image in our folksy slang term for marriage, "getting hitched." In Greek literature "to be yoked in marriage" was a common locution for marrying, as in the *Oedipus Rex*, when Oedipus remembers the oracle's prophecy that he would be "yoked in marriage to his mother and slay his father." The Chorus of the *Hippolytus*, remembering other women destroyed by eros like Phaedra, calls Iole, before Heracles violently takes her as a bride, an "unyoked colt" whom Aphrodite then "yokes" to Heracles. Another image, not so common, uses "reins" to describe the male's control of the woman, a metaphor like the yoke that highlights marriage as a technology that uses and limits the natural power of sex as symbolized by the horse. Helen's daughter Hermione, plotting to kill her husband's concubine Andromache, justifies her intent by saying it is not "noble for one man to hold the reins over two women." Our related images such as "being tied down" often signify the oppressive limitations of marriage for the self. For the Greeks, however, these images define marriage in terms of necessary cultural-technological controls. And these social limitations parallel the control over passion of a rational virtue like *sôphrosunê*, which exploits the energy of the passions in the individual soul the way the reins or yoke exploit the muscle energy of the animal.[19]

Preserving the Household

This concern with the control of female sexuality has contributed to the recent feminist view of ancient Greek marriage as an instrument of patriarchal oppression in which the woman remained always a child, the father's power over her transferred to the omnipotent husband who kept her locked away, barefoot and pregnant. From our perspective of a sharp division between public and private, and of power defined solely in terms of individual political rights and autonomy, this is an understandable interpretation, though it still exaggerates the extent of female powerlessness and underestimates the power that sexual attractiveness can wield. But from the Greek perspective, the wife and her sexuality had to be understood in the context of the household, the social and political structure that formed the basic building block of the whole culture. Plato makes this link between female self-control and the management of the household explicit in the *Meno*, when he says that the woman's *sôphrosunê* is manifested in her running of the household.[20]

When we speak of the ancient Greek *oikos* or household, however, we shouldn't think about a modern single-family dwelling containing a nuclear family. We're talking about a much larger enterprise: The household comprised extended family and slaves and was the site where most of the family's goods were stored and produced.[21] Unlike our stereotypes of the "housewife," whether a rich Victorian matron lounging on her fainting couch in the parlor or a modern American wife with her electric can opener and microwave oven, the ideal Greek wife had much more extensive responsibilities. She had to manage and dispense the household goods; oversee the production of necessities, especially the spinning of wool and weaving of cloth; and keep an eye on the slaves and teach them their tasks, as well as tending and nurturing the children. Moreover, the important rituals of marriage, birth, and death were the responsibility and purview of the wife. She was, in short, the supervisor of a mini-factory, responsible for the spiritual and material well-being of the house, and had to exercise considerable organizational and managerial skills to keep it running smoothly. That is why when Socrates in Xenophon's *Oeconomicus* asks Critobolus whether "there is anyone to whom you entrust more of your important affairs than to your wife," Critobolus says no.[22]

Unlike our "homes," then, which we feel should function as havens in which we escape the complexities of the heartless public world, as private refuges from the larger social, political, and economic structures "out there," the Greek household was an integral part of those structures. To assign to women the household

as their space was to give them a much more important social function and significance than is allowed by our unfair caricature of the "mere" private housewife hypnotized by daytime television while her appliances do all the work. The
larger importance of the household is why in Aristotle's treatise on government,
the *Politics*, he starts with a discussion of the household. By necessity, the joining
together of male and female for purposes of procreation creates the first political
and social and economic unit from which the larger society is constructed. Elsewhere Aristotle calls humans "pairing creatures" by nature, who cohabit to reproduce but also because their capacities and natures complement one another, making up for each other's deficiencies. This rudimentary division of labor prefigures
the more complex one that creates the state. Thus man and wife form a "common thing," a joint enterprise greater than the sum of its individual members,
just like the state. Back in the *Politics* he specifies what each sex's talents consist of:
The male is good at acquisition, the female good at nurturing and preserving what
is acquired.[23]

The oration of Lysias written for the defense of Euphiletus, accused of murdering his wife's lover, gives us an example of marriage as a joint enterprise in
which the household was the woman's domain. Perhaps apologizing to the all-
male jury for not supervising his wife more strictly, Euphiletus describes how after
the birth of a son he trusted his wife to run the household, putting "all [his] affairs
into her hands" because she was "most domestic," a word in Greek formed from
the word *oikos*, meaning "household" (*oikeiotêta*). Praising her household skills
some more, he says she was clever and frugal and kept everything in good order,
using two more words derived from *oikos* (*oikonomos, dioikousa*). The defendant is
justifying why he turned the house over to his wife—she displayed the orderliness
and managerial skills the wife should have to control the household, as well as fulfilling her duty to bear him a son and heir. That's why he thought she was "very
chaste/self-controlled" and he was justified in allowing her considerable leeway in
the house and in not questioning the behavior that he only later realized was covering her adultery—for example, letting her lock herself in her quarters on the
pretext of quieting the baby, when in reality she had her boyfriend hiding there.
Clearly he is appealing to a cultural norm in which women oversaw the running
of the household and exercised within it some measure of autonomy.[24]

Other evidence for this supervisory role of the wife is found early in Greek literature. The early-seventh-century *Hymn to Demeter* describes how the goddess
approaches a city in her search for her kidnapped daughter Persephone; the
young girls of the households assure her that she will receive a proper welcome
from their mothers, for they "manage/arrange the household." A related sentiment in the playwright Hippothoon adds a value judgment to this description
when he says the woman "preserves the household." The sixth-century poet
Phocylides, in his catalogue of beast-women similar to Semonides', defines the
bee-woman as a good *oikonomos*, "housekeeper." In Aristophanes' *Women at the
Assembly*, his fantasy about what would happen if women seized political control,

Praxagora practices a speech in which disguised as a man she justifies surrendering control of the city to women because "in our own households we make use of them as stewards and managers."[25]

Aristotle, drawing parallels between household governance and political systems, sees the ideal household as resembling an aristocracy, where the man rules in matters suitable to him and hands over to his wife those affairs suitable to her while still retaining the ultimate authority. When the man controls everything, then the household resembles the degenerate form of aristocracy, oligarchy—a condition, by the way, that also arises when the woman rules, as apparently was the case if she was an heiress and thus had some indirect financial clout, for a husband had to return a dowry with 18 percent interest if he divorced his wife. Strepsiades, the bumpkin in Aristophanes' *Clouds* who sends his son to Socrates' "Thinkery" to learn how to help his father escape his debts, starts the play with a complaint about his aristocratic, wealthy wife's extravagance that has nearly bankrupted him. Even if a woman wasn't a rich heiress, her status as manager of the house could make her unbearable. A fragment of the work *On Marriage*, attributed to Theophrastus, Aristotle's successor as head of the Academy, complains that if you give a wife control of the house she'll make you her slave. A wooer of a reluctant maiden in one of Theocritus's *Idylls* offers this wifely authority as an inducement to matrimony. When Acrotime protests, "Women fear their husbands," Daphnis responds, "On the contrary, they always rule. Why should they be afraid?"[26]

Rather than the beaten-down recluses some modern scholarship has imagined, then, ancient Greek well-off women of the Classical period exerted considerable authority and control over the household, the sphere allotted to them in the division of labor that most efficiently exploited for a common enterprise the different capacities of the sexes. Their organizational and managerial household skills were publicly evident in their running of civic religious rituals, such as the Thesmophoria, and are what make plausible the plots of Aristophanes' *Lysistrata* and *Women at the Assembly*, both of which are parodies of male fantasies of what could happen if women were to exercise those skills at the political level. It is this division of labor that explains the cultural ideal of assigning women the "inside" space and men the "outside." This division of space by sex has led some modern commentators to believe that women were kept locked away in the house. Usually they'll cite a passage such as the following, in Aeschylus's *Seven Against Thebes*, a play about the civil war between Oedipus's two sons, Eteocles and Polyneices. When the latter attacks Thebes with an army and besieges the city, the Chorus of women start hysterically praying to the gods. Eteocles rails at their emotional panic and tells them to "keep quiet and stay inside the house." Likewise a fragment from a comedy of one of the Apollodoruses (there were two comic poets with this name) has a wife lecturing her husband about marital harmony. It results, she says, from the man doing his work outside the house and the wife doing hers at home, like the queen bee that doesn't leave the hive yet works nonetheless, tending what the other bees bring back. Thus Plutarch explains the significance of the tortoise on which the sculptor Phidias has his "Aphrodite of the Eleans" resting a foot: The woman should stay home and keep quiet.[27]

But this feminizing of "inside" does not mean that Athenian women never left the house, shackled in some Hellenic purdah. Associating women with the "inside" represents a cultural ideal, a demarcation of the symbolic space where women exerted a significant measure of authority and control, outside of which they were not given either one, with the exception of religious ritual and ceremony. Even given the difficulties of moving from fragmentary literary evidence to actual life, the plays of Aristophanes, as well as other literary sources, offer plenty of evidence that women could and did get outside the house for a variety of reasons. These could include at times cuckolding their husbands, as was the case with Euphiletus's wife. Her lover Eratosthenes first saw her when she went to her mother-in-law's funeral, and she used the occasion of the Thesmophoria, when wives kept themselves apart from their husbands, to meet her lover.[28]

The authority of women in the household is a source of pride and honor for them, and so any attack on the household's integrity, including their husbands' infidelities, is a source of dishonor and shame. That is why women can become deadly when their status or that of their children is threatened. As recounted earlier, Euripides' Phaedra leaves her damning suicide letter claiming her husband's son Hippolytus raped her. She did this partly to avenge his sexual dishonoring of her, but also to protect her children from their illegitimate half-brother, who she thinks would try to usurp their position in Theseus's house when she was not around to protect them. Likewise Medea is incensed with Jason's taking a new bride not only because of sexual jealousy and wounded honor but also because such an act compromises her own household and children, as two members of her household, the Nurse and the children's tutor, both assert. The integrity of the sexual relationship is directly linked to the integrity of the household, so a compromise of one is a threat as well to the other. This fierce protectiveness toward her children and her status as their mother and supervisor of the household explain as well the animus of the stepmother toward her husband's child from another woman. As we just saw, Helen's daughter Hermione plots to kill Andromache, the concubine of Hermione's new husband Neoptolemus. When Creusa's husband wants to bring Ion into the house—he thinks Ion is his son from a woman he impregnated while drunk—an old servant advises Creusa to kill the usurper, for he is an "enemy of the house." It's a good thing Creusa doesn't take the crone's advice, for Ion is her own son by the god Apollo.[29]

Just as the adultery of the woman compromises the household, the sexual infidelities of men pose a threat to the integrity of the home by dishonoring the wife. As we have seen, several stories from ancient Greek literature show the destructive consequences of male infidelity. Jason loses his old household and his new when Medea murders his children and his new bride; Agamemnon's open parading of his concubine Kassandra adds fuel to the fire of Klytaimestra's rage;

Heracles' lust for Iole destroys himself and his household; and the men of Lemnos, by taking concubines, incite their wives to murder them.

This recognition of the destructive effects of male sexual excess does not mean that men were as limited in their sexual activity as women. Men's sexual behavior was not nearly as strictly regulated as women's, as long as they left alone the wives of other citizens. Yet despite this double standard, some evidence suggests that men were expected to honor their marital relationship and their sexual responsibilities if they were concerned about the integrity of their households and the honor of the wives who ran it. Odysseus's father Laertes honored the slave Eurycleia as much as his wife, but he never lay with her in love, for he feared the anger of his wife, whom he loved so much that her death sent him into premature old age.[30]

We also see this expectation that men respect their wives' status in condemnations of male adultery. Aristotle's utopian legislation regarding marriage condemns male adultery in any circumstances. Similarly, Plato's legislative ideal would forbid extramarital sex to husbands. Euripides' Hermione asserts that men too should be monogamous if they want their household to thrive. She attempts to realize this sentiment by plotting the murder of her husband's concubine Andromache, whom Hermione accuses of making her barren with spells and plotting to take her place. This expectation of sexual attention from husbands underlies Theophrastus's complaints about the wife's annoying demand that her husband only look at her and never at another woman. Since Theophrastus's tirade comprises a tissue of stock misogynist complaints recognizable by anyone, the wife's expectation of sexual exclusiveness must have been common, even if sometimes it went unfulfilled. We should remember, however, that such condemnations are rare compared to the numerous complaints of female sexual fickleness. Given the lack of dependable contraception and the obsession with legitimate children, female chastity was always more highly valued and rigorously enforced than was that of the male.[31]

This sentiment that men should find at least their primary sexual fulfillment in their wives reinforces the role of Aphrodite in marriage we noted in Chapter 6. The mutual sexual attraction between husband and wife is the centripetal energy that holds the household together. Diogenes Laertius records that Pythagoras, in a trip to Hades, reported seeing the souls of men being tortured because they did not have sex with their wives. As Plato in the *Laws* puts it, marital sexual exclusiveness, if it could be universally achieved, would ensure that husbands were "loving and close [*oikeious*] to their own wives." Thus the need for reciprocity, what Theocritus in his literary wedding song for Helen and Menelaus calls "equal love"—wishful thinking for this couple, of course, since we all know about Helen's destructive adultery. Theocritus seems to reflect a common ideal. Xenophon mentions in passing a newly married man, Niceratos, who "loves/desires sexually his wife and is loved back." When Hecuba, her son Polydorus treacherously murdered by his guardian Talthybius, begs Agamemnon for revenge, she calls on the obligation he owes because of his lovemaking with Hecuba's daughter Kassandra, who is merely his concubine: "A great claim for thanks" is imposed by sharing someone's bed. A shared sexual life imposes reciprocal obligations, which in the case of a legitimate wife who manages a household and bears legitimate children would be much greater than those owed a concubine. This ideal of mutual love and obligation surfaces also in a fragment from a Hellenistic comedy, in which a daughter is trying to convince her father not to remarry her to a relative (a right a father or guardian could exercise in order to preserve family property). "There is a covenant between man and wife," she pleads; "he must love her, always, until the end, and she must never cease to do what gives her husband pleasure."[32]

Hellenistic comedy brings us to a vexed question in ancient Greek social history, the question whether something like romantic love and marriage is evidenced in the fragments of the comic poets or not. The individualism of the Hellenistic period fostered a concern with private emotion and passion that can lead to sexual idealism, the predicating of happiness on the quality and intensity of the sexual attraction between man and woman. This concern with erotic attachment in turn would militate against arranged marriages. Some have seen in the comedies of Menander, the late-third-century playwright considerable fragments of whose plays have been discovered this century on papyruses, evidence of a growing emphasis on sexual attraction as a prerequisite for marriage. The most complete play of Menander to survive, and indeed the only Hellenistic comedy in Greek to survive nearly intact, the *Misanthrope*, concerns a rich young man named Sostratos who falls in love at first sight with the daughter of a grumpy old farmer, Knemon. At one point in the play Sostratos's father says, "I want you to marry the girl you love, and I say you ought to. . . . I know that a young man's marriage will be secure if he is persuaded by love." Clearly the father is voicing the widespread sentiment that a marriage is stronger the more the boy and girl love each other.[33]

The importance of love for strengthening a marriage can be seen also in a fragment from another play. In the *Shield*, the bad guy Smikrines is trying to exercise his legal right and obligation to marry a much younger rich niece whose father has died without a male heir. Such a girl was called an *epikleros*, and the law stipulated that she should marry the father's oldest male relative, preferably an uncle, so that the family would have another chance at male heirs and the property remain in the household. If the male relative holding that right did not wish to exercise it, he was then obliged to arrange for the girl's marriage and provide a dowry. In Menander's play, the girl's other uncle remonstrates with his older brother Smikrines, protesting that he's too old for the girl and that she is already engaged to Smikrines' nephew Chaireas, who's grown up with his cousin. The implication is that the proposed arranged marriage is objectionable because it would keep apart two people who love each other and who will be unhappy if separated, as the downcast Chaireas reveals when he says, "I thought my life was going to be happy, I very much thought that I had reached the goal, and now I won't even be able to see her anymore." That Smikrines loses out and Chaireas gets his girl, following Menander's notorious penchant for giving his audiences what they wanted, suggests that the spectators would have been rooting for the young couple and against the mercenary Smikrines and the cold socioeconomic motives of arranged marriages.[34]

These snippets from Menander clearly indicate a recognition that in Hellenistic Greece, at least among the middle class reflected in comedy, love should have been or at least often was a precondition for marriage. But to say that husband and wife should desire one another is not the same thing as saying they should "love" one another in our idealized sense of the word, which implies a sexual attraction signifying an exclusive and ennobling emotional or spiritual attraction as well. In the absence of any other corroborating evidence, the fragments of Menander cannot support the attribution of "romantic love" or "romantic marriage" to the Hellenistic Greeks. Does the Greek verb translated "love" in the above examples carry our idealizing force, or does it just mean "desire sexually"?[35] How would an audience have reacted to a Sostratos or a Chaireas? As examples of their own romantic sexual ideals? Or as young rich men, like the "juveniles" of vaudeville, silly enough to marry a girl just because they want to sleep with her? At any rate, Hellenistic comedy does offer evidence that mutual and reciprocal sexual attraction was linked to marriage, corroborating the role of Aphrodite in marriage that we documented earlier. The power of eros was exploited to provide the energy that kept the household strong.

The place of Aphrodite in marriage (that is, the need for husbands and wives to desire and to find their sexual fulfillment in each other) represents of course an ideal, one that no doubt did little to curb predatory male sexuality, a constant in human history, as the evolutionary biologists keep telling us. But just the articulation of such an ideal testifies to a recognition of the potential destructiveness of male as well as female eros, and so to a need for the sexuality of husband and wife to be directed toward each other rather than indiscriminately toward others. Such reciprocal eros works as another form of erotic control, reinforcing the social institution of the household. This is how Isocrates has Nicocles, the fourth-century king of Cyprus, rationalize his own marital fidelity: Not only does it show respect for a relationship "more intimate and important" than any other, but it also avoids "factions and division" in the household.[36]

In the remainder of this chapter we will see how these various dimensions of marriage are exemplified in the adventures of some famous Greek literary wives. But first we will examine another philosophical treatise that defines marriage in terms of a cultural order in which human sexuality is exploited and controlled.

Home Economics

Xenophon's *Oeconomicus* is one of the most important documents for understanding the nature of marriage and the role of wives in Greece of the fourth century, at least among the class of landowning citizens. For as well as discussing wives and households, the dialogue also talks about farming, which is why its title is often translated "The Estate Manager." Here we're concerned with a conversation between Socrates and Ischomachus, a young man who has recently married and who describes to Socrates how he has handled his young bride so that she is an efficient and productive wife contributing to the flourishing of the household. There's a certain amount of what strikes us as sexist condescension to Ischomachus's remarks, but we should remember that his bride when he married her was not yet fifteen, whereas he was probably at least thirty, so his patronizing of her reflects age as well as sex.

The need to train a bride in her household duties and responsibilities is established earlier in the treatise, in a conversation between Socrates and Critobolus, one of those Socratic stooges whose job is to keep the discussion going with stupid answers to Socrates' questions. Working from his typical assumption that human behavior and activity should be rationally managed on the basis of knowledge instead of haphazard opinion, Socrates finds it odd that Critobolus admits to entrusting his most important business to his wife while also confessing that there is no one with whom he speaks less. Socrates thinks this domestic apartheid dangerous, for "the wife who is a good partner in the household is equivalent to the man in respect to its good." This domestic parity imposes on the husband an obligation to work closely with his wife to make sure she has the skill and values conducive to the household's good, which is to say its efficient functioning to achieve the end suitable to a household. Socrates goes on to justify this assessment on the basis of the complementary qualities of each sex: "The property/wealth come to the house through the man's exertions, but the dispensing depends mostly on the economy of the woman." They are partners, albeit unequal ones, whose abilities and qualities are organized by and subordinated to the larger structure of the household.[37]

Ischomachus's description of his wife's training expands on Socrates' analysis of the household in these terms, and in the process it touches on many of the same ideas about wives and their role that we have traced in other Greek literature. He starts by telling Socrates what he told his wife, that soon they will have children who will be the "best allies and tenders of old age," and that this is a "common good" for them. The need for children to support their parents, which we saw articulated as early as Hesiod, is here too made a central component of the household. But for now, Ischomachus says that the "household is our common thing." The word Ischomachus uses several times in this section, *koinos*, often communicates the idea of a shared political and social organization greater than the individuals who compose it, and its use here reinforces the Greek sense of the household as a unit of the larger state, a political, social, and economic enterprise to which the man and woman subordinate themselves and contribute everything that they have, she her dowry and management skills, he his income.[38]

The girl responds to this statement of her importance and responsibility by saying that she learned from her mother only that chastity/self-control (*sôphronein*) was her main duty. Ischomachus acknowledges this common wisdom and says his father told him the same thing, that is, that *sôphronein* was *his* main duty. Here the necessity of the female to practice self-control, which we would expect, is coupled to the *male's* need for the same quality, reflecting the sentiment we saw earlier that male sexuality also ought to be subordinated to the household. In fact, Ischomachus's offhand reference to his father's advice suggests that it was something of a banality, a piece of received wisdom bespeaking a widespread belief that men too needed to focus their sexuality on their wives.[39]

But Ischomachus goes further, defining "self-control" in such a way that its moral value is linked to the material success of the household: "Self-control [*sôphronôn*] in a man and a woman is acting in such a way that their property will be the best possible, and that as much property as possible shall be justly and fairly added." The link between the control of eros and the economic order of the household is made explicit in Ischomachus's formulation. Sexual self-control is part of a larger rational control over the appetites, one conducive to the flourishing of the household. This same need to control the appetites determines an important criterion for selecting a housekeeper and an overseer of the farm—such workers need to control their desires for sex, eating, drinking, and sleeping.[40]

To describe the important function of the wife in the house, Ischomachus repeatedly uses the bee metaphor we have encountered several times before, particularly significant because of the bee's supposed chastity. Like the "queen bee" in its hive, he tells his bride, she must apportion the labor of the slaves, keep track of their production, dispense the stores, oversee the weaving, nurture the children until it is time for them to leave the home, tend the sick slaves, teach them their tasks, and see to their moral improvement. In short, as we said earlier, she must be a good manager and organizer. And she accomplishes this feat by understanding the qualities specific to her as a woman, the part she must play in the division of labor that by exploiting the complementary abilities of men and women keeps the household running and makes it successful. Thus Ischomachus explains what we saw earlier in Aristotle, the idea that men and women by nature possess different qualities that complement each other—the man physically stronger and braver and so fit to acquire property outdoors, the woman fit to be "indoors" because she is physically weaker, more affectionate toward children, more fearful and hence more careful in nurturing the stores. But both men and women are alike in their powers of memory and diligence and in their capacity for "self-rule"—a somewhat emancipated statement by Ischomachus, given the more common assumption in Greek thought (Plato occasionally is an exception) that women are less capable of controlling their appetites than are men.[41]

The whole thrust of Ischomachus's program for training his wife is the creation of order, for as he says, "There is nothing as useful or good for humans as order." He then proceeds to an encomium of order, praising the organization of a chorus, an army, a ship, and finally the city itself, all linked to the household, which also must be ordered so that it can function as efficiently as possible. Even pots and pans are beautiful when ordered properly, he enthuses. We have perhaps no better statement of the rational control of raw human nature than Ischomachus's praise of the well-organized house as one part of a continuum of public human order that includes armies and ships and the city. Moreover, this order depends on the minimizing of natural appetite, particularly the sexual. That is why when Ischomachus's wife appears one day with white-lead makeup and rouge on her face and wearing high-heeled shoes he tells her to forgo those artificial sexual accessories, since what makes their "partnership of bodies" gratifying is her natural healthy beauty that results from her vigorous attending to her household duties. The woman's natural eros here is completely dependent on her function in the cultural construct of the household, her sexual energy exploited not just for procreation but also for production. The harder she works, the sexier she is to her husband.[42]

The good woman and wife, in Xenophon's dialogue, is clearly one whose innate appetitive disorder has been rationally ordered, that is, she has become more like a male and less like a female. As Socrates enthuses about Ischomachus's wife, she has a "masculine mind." But despite the authority and power given to the wife in the household, she is still subordinated to the man, serving ultimately his interests. And she is also obviously considered, to a degree the man is not, something like a colt or a calf that must be "broken" and trained to accept the "yoke," as we saw earlier in the yoke imagery and the epithet "unbroken" for an unmarried girl. This parallel is made obvious by Socrates in his observation to Critobolus: When a sheep turns out bad the shepherd is blamed, and when a horse is vicious we hold the rider responsible. In the same way, when a wife turns out bad we blame the husband for not training her properly. As we've seen repeatedly and as Socrates' analogies suggest, woman more so than man is a natural creature that must be ordered by culture so that her energy, particularly her erotic energy, can be exploited and her destructiveness curbed. A man also must control his appetites and subordinate them to the cultural orders, but his greater rational powers make this less a problem. That is why he still retains the ultimate authority in a marriage. But remember: The husband is at least thirty, his moral education complete; the wife, in contrast, is considerably younger, her socialization not yet finished.[43]

Another ancient treatise on household management, the *Oeconomica* attributed to Aristotle but not by his hand, adds little to what we learn from Xenophon's work, except that pseudo-Aristotle does not admit as much equality between husband and wife nor allow the wife as much authority over the management of the household. One passage of interest here elaborates on the sexual dimension of marriage and the need for controlling conjugal eros. A much greater issue is made of male fidelity: "A virtuous wife is most honored if she sees her husband observing chastity for her benefit and not caring for any other woman." Adultery on the male's part is specifically defined as an injury to his wife's honor, a giving to others of what is due only to her, whereas in Xenophon Ischomachus seems casually to refer to the husband's sexual access to slave women, although it's not clear he's speaking specifically of himself rather than generally. To pseudo-Aristotle, such fidelity on the male's part has the added benefit of setting an example for the wife, who will be more inclined to chastity herself if her husband doesn't stray. As for the woman's sexuality, the writer suggests a moderate passion, so that wives neither importune their husbands nor are agitated when they are gone, equally content whether they are at home or away. The anxiety about eros, even between married people, surfaces in these suggestions for limiting and controlling its expression. We have started down the road that leads from Socratic moderation of desire to Jerome's condemnation of marital sexual pleasure as fornication.[44]

Andromache

The first "good wife" in Greek literature is the *Iliad*'s Andromache, the wife of the Trojan champion Hector. She appears in one of the epic's most affecting scenes, a conversation between her and Hector after the hero has briefly left the fighting so that he can instruct the Trojan women to implore Athena's help for the beleaguered Trojans. The tender exchange between husband and wife reveals to us the importance marriage and the household had for the wife, as well as the qualities that define the good wife and the place she has in her husband's affections.

Worried about Hector because of the Greeks' temporary success, Andromache when she sees him pours out a simple but moving explanation of how central he is to her life. Her mother and father and brothers are all dead: "You, Hector, are my father and my regal mother and my brother, and you are my stalwart husband." The complete dependence of the wife on the husband is poignantly expressed here by Andromache. Her life depends on his, her whole identity is predicated on her status as wife and mother to his children. Nor is this dependence one-sided. As Hector, in a brief moment of prophetic insight, imagines the fall of Troy and the death of his family, he is moved not by the future grief and suffering of his mother and father and his brothers, but by contemplating Andromache's fate, the miserable life she will have as a slave and concubine to some Greek hero once Hector is not alive to protect her. Andromache, however, is not as central to Hector's life as he is to hers. Part of Hector's tragedy is the conflict between his desire for heroic honor and glory and his role as protector of Troy and his family. When the crisis comes in the duel with Achilles, Hector chooses to die gloriously, even though he knows this means the destruction of Troy and the enslavement of Andromache, for Troy lives only as long as Hector does. Yet that tragedy is sharpened by the love he has for Andromache, making his choice all the more painful, the price of glory all the more grievous.[45]

Hector's love for Andromache, then, does not create an equal partnership by any means. Andromache's advice to Hector on how to conduct the city's defense is answered by Hector's reminder of what her place is: "But you go to the house and tend your tasks, the loom and the distaff, and order the handmaids to busy themselves with their work. War is for men." Andromache is sent back to her sphere of influence, inside the house, practicing the wifely skills that keep the household flourishing—weaving and supervising the slaves. The world outside the house is the purview of men, and a woman's word is out of order in that space.[46]

Several key qualities of the ideal wife are embodied in Andromache. She is devoted to her husband and their relationship, she subordinates herself to him, and she is defined by the household and its tasks for which she is responsible. Thus later in the epic, when the news comes of Hector's death, Andromache is found weaving "in the recesses of the house," and she orders a cauldron set to boil for Hector's bath. The impact of his death is heightened here by the poet's reminding us of how it will destroy Andromache's identity, which is predicated on her role as Hector's wife, the role she is faithfully fulfilling when the first intimations of his death reach her. After she runs to the wall and sees Achilles dragging her husband's corpse behind his chariot, she faints, first tearing from her head the veil and headgear Aphrodite had given her on her wedding day. When Hector dies she "dies" and throws away her role as wife, for that role *is* her life. A woman has meaning only in the context of marriage.[47]

Andromache's function as exemplary wife totally dedicated to her husband and her role as wife reappears nearly three centuries later in Euripides' *Andromache* and *Trojan Women*. As we have already had occasion to mention, the former play concerns the attempts of Hermione, the daughter of Menelaus, to assassinate Andromache—Neoptolemus's concubine, a "spear-won bride" taken from the spoils of Troy—and her son Molossus because Hermione has not yet borne a child to her husband Neoptolemus and so is torn by jealousy and insecurity over her status. Part of the play's concern is to detail the suffering of an exemplary noble wife who has lost her husband and now must find some sort of meaning in the exploitative and demeaning role of concubine and slave. Several times Euripides evokes for us this shift in Andromache's status. The yoke image that commonly signifies marriage now symbolizes her status as slave; she is called an "all-wretched bride," the adjective pointing to the sad inaccuracy of the noun; and in a deft nod to the *Iliad*'s description of Andromache tearing off her bridal veil when she sees the mutilation of Hector, Euripides' Andromache cries, "I have thrown around my head a hateful slavery." Losing the role of honored wife, in which the woman's sexuality is integrated into a household over which she is mistress, entails putting on the role of slave-concubine, or pseudowife. Outside the household the woman is nothing more than sexual property.[48]

Yet though Andromache's status has changed drastically, she still knows what makes an ideal wife. The ideology of the good wife is developed in an early scene pitting the petty, vain daddy's girl Hermione against the older and wiser Andromache. Noting the girl's finery and beauty, Andromache advises her that virtue/nobility, not beauty, is what delights a husband. The marital bond is strengthened not by the sexual attractiveness of the bride, her problematic seductive powers, but by her virtue, her ability to control those powers. Women may be more prone to erotic "disease," Andromache says, but they can control themselves because of honor and shame. Later she attributes Hermione's anger to her excessive sexual appetites, *philandria*, her "lewdness" inherited from her mother Helen that causes "Aphrodite's disease," jealousy because she has to share her husband's sexuality with a reluctant concubine. Hermione correctly reads this as an accusation of lack of "self-control/chastity," the key quality that we have seen defines the good wife. The good wife controls her sexuality, does not make it the central issue in the marriage apart from the bearing of legitimate children, as opposed to the seductive Hermione, who like us moderns based her whole marriage on her and her husband's sexual relationship. When children—the purpose of that sexuality—are not conceived, then the integrity of the marriage is threatened, as Hermione rightly feels hers to be.[49]

Next Andromache articulates the wifely ideal of complete loyalty and fidelity to the husband, a quality she herself exhibits at the play's beginning, which finds her lamenting still the loss of Hector. The wife, she lectures Hermione, should be content with her husband, even if he is baseborn, and should separate herself from her father's household. This is a hit on Hermione, who has enlisted her daddy Menelaus to help her get rid of Andromache and her child. Once married, the girl's loyalty should be first and foremost to her husband's household, not her father's, to which she has "died." Andromache gives what to our ears is an extremely craven expression of such loyalty when she says she herself nursed Hector's bastards when "Aphrodite tripped him up," her nobility/virtue binding him to her all the closer. Though this abject endorsement of the double standard offends us, in the context of Greek marriage and its emphasis on legitimate procreation as the primary end of sex, it makes more sense. Andromache can display a noble magnanimity because she is assured of her place and authority as mother of Hector's legitimate son and mistress of his household.[50]

The qualities of the good wife are also detailed by Andromache in the *Trojan Women*, set among the Trojan women waiting to sail to Greece as concubines in the immediate aftermath of the sack of Troy. Andromache, contemplating the disgrace of her imminent sexual subjugation to Neoptolemus, describes the wifely excellences that make such a subjugation so painful: She was chaste, staying at home to avoid even the faintest hint of infidelity; she held her tongue; and she knew the limits of her sphere of influence and authority in the household. The key qualities of sexual self-control and subordination to the household lie at the heart of Andromache's wifely excellence. Sexual fidelity is particularly important—she scorns bitterly the woman who can forget one man and love another. "Not even the mare, unyoked from her stall-mate, easily drags the yoke." This is the essence of Andromache's misery: Her sexual integrity, the basis of her wifely excellence, will be destroyed when she is forced into the bed of her master Neoptolemus.[51]

Back in the *Andromache*, the complete absorption of the woman's identity in her role as wife is made explicit by Menelaus, completely oblivious to Andromache's feelings when he says that a woman who loses her husband loses her life. Menelaus says this to justify his meddling in Neoptolemus's household, but Andromache knows firsthand the bitter truth of his statement. As she herself says, when she offers her life in exchange for her son's, she died when Hector died. All she has left is her child by Neoptolemus and her role as mother for which now she will give her life. Motherhood validates the procreative and nurturing function of woman central to the wifely ideal, so even if the role of wife is lost, the role of mother can still testify to Andromache's status as a good woman. But Andromache is spared her own and her child's death. The sea-goddess Thetis, great-grandmother of Andromache's child Molossus, intervenes at play's end and gives this exemplary wife her just reward: She will marry Hector's brother, Helenus, and found the kingdom of the Molossians—whose most famous descendent, by the way, will be Alexander the Great. Though her household and husband are lost forever, Andromache nonetheless achieves the closest thing to them—a new household with her husband's brother. Wifely virtue has its rewards.[52]

Alcestis

Alcestis gets her just rewards too, though she has to die first. Euripides' *Alcestis* concerns a man named Admetus, who is given the privilege of having someone die in his place because he was a good host to Apollo once when the god was banished from Olympus. No one, including his aged father and mother, would volunteer to die for Admetus except his wife Alcestis, "the best/noblest woman under the sun," as the Chorus calls her.[53]

Alcestis represents the furthest extreme of wifely devotion to her husband and her household and shows as well that the possibilities for heroic honor and glory for a woman derive from her role as wife. Just as the male hero dies for glory, so the wife achieves renown by dying for her husband, honoring him and herself at the same time. As heroic wife, Alcestis is described in terms that point to her exemplary wifely qualities and to her nobility both of birth and of character. Thus she is the beloved manager of the household, a mother to the slaves, the mistress of the house whose death "destroys the household." The epithets given her emphasize both her household qualities and the self-control that allows those qualities to flourish: She is "diligent, trusty" and "self-controlled/chaste [*sôphrôn*]." But also she is characterized in terms that emphasize her heroic nobility: She is the "best," a word denoting the heroic warrior's nobility in both senses of the word (*aristê*), and "noble/good," another word combining social status with moral goodness (*esthlês*), as does "worthy/estimable." Her life is "most famous," and she is the "noblest woman of all." The superlative glory and honor the male hero wins through violence on the battlefield is available to the woman who completely submerges her identity into her role as wife, to the point that like Alcestis she will give up her life for his.[54]

The importance of such a wife to her husband is made clear by Admetus's grief at her loss, despite his own selfishness and cowardice, his "ignobility" that makes him fear death so much. In fact Euripides is playing with gender expectations, making the woman calm and noble, at least in public, concerned about her children most of all even as she is dying, whereas he depicts Admetus as almost hysterical. Yet Admetus's cowardice does not lessen the sincerity of his grief for Alcestis's death. His final words to her reveal a love for his wife almost romantic: "When you die, nothing is left. In you we [he and the children] exist, both to live and not to live, for we reverence your love." He promises her that he will never remarry and that he will mourn her a whole year. He banishes from his house all banquets and singing, all flute- and lyre-playing, and says, with a vague creepiness redolent of Edgar Allan Poe, that he will have a statue of her fashioned to lie on his bed. Finally, when he dies he will be buried side-by-side with her so that he will never be apart from his "only faithful" wife. No doubt the Greek audience thought Admetus protested too much, particularly since his own cowardice was killing his wife. And probably his display of emotion struck them as unmanly, just as Alcestis's fortitude and bravery were akin to that of the male hero. Yet unless the scene depicting Admetus's grief was meant to be comic, for it to be convincing to the audience there must have been men who dearly loved their wives, who found in their shared life in the household emotional as well as physical gratification.[55]

Alcestis, of course, like Andromache represents an ideal. The woman who controls her appetites, particularly her sexuality, who manages the household effectively, and who subordinates herself completely to her husband can achieve a meaningful life worthy of remembrance, can transcend her innate female worthlessness. Such a woman will create in her husband love and devotion. And she will have her reward, as Alcestis does. For just as Death arrives to take her soul away, Heracles, in the midst of one of his labors, arrives at Admetus's house. Wanting to help his friend and needing some cheerful hospitality, he wrestles with Death and liberates Alcestis, whom he then disguises and offers to Admetus in a bit of sadistic horseplay whose effect is to prove Admetus's devotion to his wife. In another version recorded in Plato, the gods bring Alcestis back to life because they are impressed with her nobility. Either way, the message is clear: The woman who defines herself in terms of her cultural and social role as wife wins her husband's devotion, heroic honor and glory, and a triumph over even death itself.[56]

Like Aeschylus's *Oresteia*, the *Alcestis* shows the superiority of the cultural bond over the natural: The blood-relatives refuse to die for Admetus; the wife doesn't. As Plato's Phaedrus says about the story, "She [Alcestis] through love so surpassed [Admetus's mother and father] in affection, that she showed them to be aliens to their son and kinsmen in name only." The bond of mere blood is what animals have. True human kinship is the natural bond of love expressed in and contained by the context of the social institution, marriage. The *Alcestis* shows that the importance and meaning of the woman and her sexuality are ultimately dependent on her subordination to this cultural order. And it shows as well that women in their "confined" role as housewife could, to the Greeks, be better, more heroic than men, proving that within each gender's sphere questions of character and worth were personal rather than predicated solely on gender.[57]

Circumspect Penelope

Marriage is one of the *Odyssey*'s most important ways of developing its concern with human identity, and in the epic's treatment of marriage we can see the way culture and nature intersect to create humans. As we have seen throughout, humans are natural creatures, defined by the "controlless core," the bestial body with its hunger, suffering, sexuality, and death. Yet they are human because they possess the "fancied sway"—social institutions and customs that mediate the destructiveness of their material, appetitive bodies, just as technology controls and exploits the energy of nature. In the *Odyssey*, the potentially destructive power of eros is evident in the suitors' sexual infatuation with Penelope that blinds them to the outrageousness of their behavior. Yet that illicit eros cannot prevail over the order of marriage that is revalidated by the suitors' destruction and the reunion of Odysseus and Penelope.

As a cultural institution, then, marriage is an important part of Odysseus's identity, and his wife, his son, and his household are all components of what he is both as a human being and as Odysseus. Thus marriage as defined by his world, as well as the quality of his wife's character, have to be understood in order for us to know exactly what Odysseus is: a material human being with a unique character created by the way his cultural practices such as marriage make sense of both the alien natural world and the appetites of his body. Odysseus is who he is because of his personal qualities of cunning and endurance, qualities necessary to survive in a savage environment, but also because he is Penelope's husband and Telemachus's father, that is, part of a household. He is not completely "home," completely Odysseus, until he has returned to those roles.

Odysseus himself defines the essence of the ideal marriage, embodied as we will see in his own marriage with Penelope, in his conversation with the Phaiacian princess Nausicaa, who discovers the naked and battered Odysseus when she goes with her handmaids to wash the household's clothes by the shore. Holding an olive branch over his privates, Odysseus first flatters the girl to gain her sympathy and then, in exchange for her help, wishes for her a good fortune particularly suited to a nubile girl: "A husband and a household, and noble like-mindedness. For nothing is more powerful or greater than this, when a husband and wife, being like-minded in their thoughts, hold the household." Other uses of this word "like-mindedness" (*homophrosunê*) imply qualities such as cooperation, honesty, and communication as well as affection and shared values. In the *Hymn to Hermes*, about how the infant Hermes, god of thieves and trickery, stole some cattle belonging to Apollo, Zeus mediates the quarrel by advising the two to have "like-minded hearts" and together search for the cattle. He particularly tells Hermes to reveal "with an innocent mind" where he hid the animals, linking "like-mindedness" to the soul's rational powers. Honest communication is also stressed when Persephone and her mother, Demeter, after they have been reunited and Persephone tells truthfully what befell her in the Underworld, are described as having "like-minded hearts." Pindar's description of a father's wedding toast for his new son-in-law specifically links this quality to the sexual life of the bride and groom when he praises their "like-minded bed." Notice that Odysseus bases a strong household and marital relationship on a *mental* virtue, a similarity of values and qualities, an agreement about what's important and significant, a willingness to heed one another, which unite the couple into a mutually affectionate whole and underwrite their sexual life, whereas our modern ideals of romantic marriage base a strong relationship on the intensity and reciprocity of passion.[58]

This quality of "like-mindedness" is illustrated in the *Odyssey* by the marriage of Penelope and Odysseus, a marriage whose excellence is made possible by Penelope's character. All her epithets stress her mental powers of control over her passions that in turn make her trustworthy, trustworthiness being one of the most important attributes of the good wife. During Odysseus's trip to the Underworld, he speaks with the ghost of the murdered Agamemnon, now an expert on good and bad wives. Agamemnon tells Odysseus of his own murder by Klytaimestra, then praises Penelope as the antithesis of his treacherous wife: Penelope is "very wise/of sound understanding," she "knows well counsels/arts in her mind," and she is *periphrôn*, "prudent/of good sense," one of her most common epithets, a word like *sôphrôn* formed from the word for "mind." The chief suitor, Antinoos, whose name means "antimind," signifying his lack of mental control over his sexual and material greed, nonetheless recognizes those mental powers in Penelope— he grudgingly praises her for her "good mind" and her "astuteness" and her "shrewd devices." If the bad woman like Klytaimestra is defined by the power of her destructive appetites, the exemplary wife is defined by *mental* powers controlling those appetites, particularly sexuality, just as Penelope has controlled her sexuality for twenty years. That's why one of the women in Aristophanes' *Women at the Thesmophoria*, castigating Euripides for writing about bad women like Phaedra, asks him why he never writes about a "chaste/self-controlled [*sôphrôn*] woman" like Penelope.[59]

The power of rational self-control makes Penelope the embodiment of the ideal wife, as she shows in her actions throughout the epic. She is closely linked with spinning and weaving, the representative activities of the wife who supervises the household. The Hellenistic poet Leonidas connects Penelope's weaving with her sexual fidelity when he says that a weaving shuttle was the "guard of her bed." Her trick with Laertes' shroud also illustrates the value of weaving as symbol of the faithful wife, as well as showing Penelope's Odyssean craftiness. Importuned by the suitors, Penelope promised she would choose one of them after she finished weaving a burial shroud for her aged father-in-law, Laertes. But what she wove during the day she unwove at night, managing this way to stall the suitors for three years, until a treacherous maid ratted on her. By busying herself with the wifely task of weaving she managed at least to put off betraying her husband and her household.[60]

Penelope's fidelity and craftiness help make her marriage strong because she is "like-minded" to Odysseus, who of course is known as the man "of many devices/tricks/stratagems." His approval of her trickiness, so like his own, is seen when Penelope beguiles gifts out of the suitors. While the disguised Odysseus looks on, Penelope chastises the suitors for taking gifts from the woman they want to marry, unlike the old days, when suitors vied with one another in gift-giving. Immediately all the suitors start showering her with gifts, and Odysseus "rejoiced, because she tricked them out of gifts and charmed their hearts with soft words." It takes a trickster to know one.[61]

His other quality, endurance, is also possessed by Penelope, who has had to endure his twenty-year absence as well as the importunities of 108 aggressive men who have taken over her household, aided and abetted by her own treacherous maids. But "like-mindedness" is also shown by the similarity of *values*, by the way Penelope and Odysseus respect the same important cultural and social institutions, especially their marriage and household. Penelope, of course, has been faithful for twenty years, struggling to maintain the integrity of her household and her marriage with Odysseus, even though she doesn't know whether he is alive or dead. And Odysseus too has struggled to get back home and, once there, suffers more indignities when, disguised as a beggar, he is abused in his own house.

That Penelope is central to what he longs to return to is clear in an exchange the hero has with the goddess Calypso. Having agreed after seven years of detaining him on her island to let him return home, the goddess tries one last bribe to get him to stay: She will make him a god, eternally young, her consort forever, "for all your desire to see your wife, for whom always you long all the days." Surely his wife can't be more attractive than the goddess. Of course not, Odysseus answers, but he wants to go back to her anyway, no matter how much he has to suffer. Modern readers, by the way, who see a double standard in Odysseus's having sex with Calypso and Circe while Penelope remains chaste should remember that the former two are *goddesses*, and you don't say no to a goddess touchy about her power and honor, especially when your chances for returning home are in her hands. Notice that after he's back home and is reunited with Penelope he doesn't hesitate to tell her about his sexual relations with the two goddesses—but he doesn't mention Nausicaa, whom he never touched. Because he respects his wife he leaves out the young nubile girl who posed a much greater threat to Penelope than the goddesses ever did. At any rate, Odysseus longs to return home and be reunited with Penelope because he wants to be Odysseus, which entails being Penelope's husband, living in a contingent world of suffering that makes necessary institutions such as marriage and the household. Any other life, including the life of a god, would be meaningless, literally inhuman.[62]

Odysseus and Penelope's "like-mindedness," their shared values and qualities, is what ultimately brings about the destruction of the suitors and the restoration of their marriage and household. For Penelope is not the immobile, helpless woman, passively waiting for her husband to take care of business. It is she who makes possible the destruction of the suitors, who have intruded into her domain. Remember Odysseus' problem: There are 108 armed men occupying his house, and he has only three fighting allies, including his son Telemachus, to whom he has already revealed himself, and those are odds even Odysseus has to be concerned about. The solution to his dilemma is provided by Penelope, during a conversation she has with the disguised Odysseus, a conversation in which she intimates that the beggar before her is actually her husband.

Acting to test her suspicion, she proposes a contest to be held the very next day. Whoever of the suitors can string Odysseus's bow and send an arrow through twelve lined-up axes, whose heads had some sort of hole in them, Penelope will marry. Odysseus's response to his wife's announcement that she will marry another man? "No longer put off this contest in the halls. For crafty Odysseus will be back here before these men, handling this polished bow, shall stretch the string and shoot an arrow through the iron." Why is Odysseus so delighted? Because he knows—and he knows Penelope knows—that no one but he can string the bow and, more important, that his wife has just devised a stratagem that possibly can put into his hands the one weapon needed to offset superior numbers—the bow. If this beggar is Odysseus, he'll figure out some way to get his hands on the weapon—which is precisely what happens. The suitors fail to string the bow. Odysseus, aided at a critical moment by Penelope, gets his hands on it, and then he sends the first arrow through the neck of Antinoos. The Odyssean cunning of Penelope has created the circumstances in which her husband can destroy the suitors and restore their household.[63]

Such working together toward a good valued by both husband and wife illustrates the kind of marriage Odysseus wished for the young Nausicaa. Because of their cunning and endurance, and especially because of Penelope's mental powers of control over her sexuality, their marriage is restored and reconsummated during a night of love that Athena lengthens to accommodate the passion of Odysseus and Penelope. Here we see a reversal of our modern expectations. We predicate the strength and integrity of a marriage on its passion; Homer shows us passion predicated on "like-mindedness," a similarity of character and values. Odysseus and Penelope's bed itself is the final symbol of this ideal marriage, its cornerpost a living olive tree whose roots still cling to the earth, an amalgam of culture and nature like the unmovable marriage of Odysseus, like the rational self-control of Penelope, the good wife.[64]

The Rehabilitation of Helen

The story has it that the early-sixth-century poet Stesichorus had written poems critical of Helen, who as we saw in Chapter 3 was the premier exemplar of destructive female sexual beauty. Because of his blasphemy, the poet was stricken with blindness. Once he realized his error, he wrote a palinode, a "song resung," in which he claimed that Helen never went to Troy—her phantom went while she sat out the war in Egypt under the care of the shape-shifter Proteus. After he composed his retraction the goddess Helen restored his sight.[65]

Given the immense literary authority of Homer, Stesichorus's revision of his famous plot was somewhat audacious. Imagine a poet a hundred years after Shakespeare writing a play in which Hamlet's father isn't killed by Claudius but is hiding out in England while his son vainly torments himself over his inability to exact revenge. Two intellectual developments perhaps explain Stesichorus's daring. First, a growing dissatisfaction with the Hesiodic and Homeric anthropomorphic descriptions of the gods and their sins is evident around the same time Stesichorus wrote. For example, the poet-philosopher Xenophanes, roughly contemporary with Stesichorus, complained about the poets who drag the gods down to the level of mortals and their passions. "Homer and Hesiod have attributed to the gods everything shameful and a reproach among humans—theft, adultery, and lying." Plato and others later would repeat the charge, reflecting a long-developing conception of the gods as concerned with moral goodness and rational order.[66]

This denial of the gods' moral failings and the evolving conception of their moral significance help explain Helen's rehabilitation, for as we saw in Chapter 3, without question she was a goddess, worshipped particularly at Sparta, Menelaus's kingdom in epic legend. Pausanias describes her shrine at Sparta and tells how an appearance of the goddess once deterred an attack on that country. Her wedding with Menelaus was celebrated every spring at Sparta by girls who hung garlands on a plane-tree and poured olive oil on the ground around its trunk. Her powers of natural fertility are apparent also when she is invoked along with Aphrodite at the end of the *Lysistrata* by the Spartan women celebrating the return of peace and sexual relations with their husbands. Her powers extend to the sea as well as to the earth. At the end of Euripides' *Orestes*, a plot-tidying Apollo appears to announce that she will become, again like Aphrodite, a maritime deity, worshipped by sailors, like her brothers Castor and Polydeuces, the Gemini of the horoscope. Moreover, Apollo's rationale for Helen's apotheosis—that she is a daughter of Zeus—links her divinity to the increasing role of Zeus as chief upholder of moral as well as cosmic order.[67]

The second reason for Helen's rehabilitation follows from her status as most beautiful of women, and hence a goddess of beauty. Her divine powers included the power to beautify. Herodotus tells the story of the Spartan king Demaratus's mother, who was an unfortunately homely child. Her nurse, troubled that the girl's parents were unhappy, took the child every day to the shrine of Helen at Therapne near Sparta, where Menelaus and Helen were buried. One day when she was leaving the temple a woman, actually the goddess Helen in disguise, asked to see the child. Stroking its head, she predicted the girl would be the fairest woman of all the Spartans. After that day, the girl's appearance began to improve, fulfilling the goddess's prophecy. But more important than these practical consequences of her beauty, the connection of beauty and goodness, one of Plato's most persistent themes, militated against the idea of the most beautiful woman in the world also being its most degenerate strumpet. This veneration of beauty is one of Isocrates' and the Sophist Gorgias's themes in their defenses of Helen, two late-fifth-century examples of the power of rhetoric to "make the worse argument the better." Helen, Isocrates reasons, is good because of her beauty, the love of beauty being the "most venerated, most precious, most divine" love mortals have. Thus there is no shame in succumbing to it. Likewise Gorgias praises her godlike beauty, which inspired lofty goals of honor and victory. These two rhetorical exercises illustrate the persistent ambiguity of Helen. Both reflect the idea then current that divinity and beauty should not be associated with something as sordid as adultery and promiscuity, yet both also depend on Helen's reputation as notorious femme fatale, for why else would it be a challenge to argue in her behalf?[68]

The late-fifth-century distrust of an amoral rhetoric like Isocrates' and Gorgias's, though, rather than her beauty and divinity, explains the various rationalizations of Helen's crime found in Euripides' plays. Isocrates' excuses—that Helen inspired Homer, that the war she caused was a venue for glory, or, giving a nod to the growing Panhellenism Alexander would later exploit to justify his brutal plundering of Persia, that she united the Greeks against the barbarians—sound as feeble as the special pleading of Helen herself or the uxorious Menelaus. In Euripides' *Trojan Women*, set in the immediate aftermath of the city's sacking, Helen pleads her case before her vengeful husband. She claims that if Paris hadn't chosen Aphrodite and thus gained Helen, Hera would have given the lordship of Greece to the barbarian as his reward for choosing her as the fairest. Menelaus ultimately agrees with his wife, once his anger is forgotten at the sight of her breasts. When Menelaus attempted to assassinate Andromache and her son, he was stopped by the boy's grandfather Peleus, who accused him of weakness toward women and of overindulging Helen. Menelaus exculpates his wife by arguing that Helen was forced by the gods—the excuse that Helen uses in the *Odyssey* and that Gorgias makes the gist of his defense. Menelaus adds that it was a good thing, too: Because of her the Greeks learned to be good fighters. These speeches, like Jason's shameless rationalizations of his betrayal of his family in the *Medea*, illustrate the late fifth century's awareness of how language could be perverted by a rhetorical technology that removed considerations of what was true, or what was just, from the art of persuasion.[69]

In his later play the *Helen*, though, Euripides endorses Stesichorus's rehabilitation of Helen into a paragon of goodness whose shameless phantom causes all the trouble. But Euripides goes even further—he turns Helen into a second Penelope, an epitome of wifely virtue. Perhaps this explains too the change in Helen's reputation: the need to assert the role of sexual beauty and attractiveness in the good marriage. If Helen, embodiment par excellence of a dangerous female sexual beauty, can be turned into a good wife, then sexual attractiveness has been validated as an important force in holding marriage together—and marriage has been validated as a cultural institution with the power to control the natural force of eros. Euripides would then be presenting us with a very idealized view of eros in marriage, an eros his other plays suggest is uncontrollable.

Euripides' play begins seventeen years after Helen was whisked away to Egypt and seven years after the fall of Troy. Helen is a suppliant at the tomb of Proteus, her guardian while he was alive, because his son Theoclymenus now wants to marry her, a thought that horrifies her—quite a change from that other Helen, who at Troy marries Deiphobus while Paris's corpse is still warm. Soon a ship-wrecked Menelaus appears, having left the phantom Helen in a cave with his men. When he sees the real Helen, he's understandably confused. Then a messen-ger comes to tell him the phantom Helen has disappeared, after conveniently ex-plaining the deception wrought by Hera. The queen of the gods wanted to pun-ish both Paris and Aphrodite because Paris picked Aphrodite as the fairest. Menelaus and Helen have a tearful and joyful reunion, then begin figuring out a way to escape from Theoclymenus. Helen comes up with a plot—Menelaus will disguise himself as a shipwrecked beggar who brings the news of Menelaus's death. Helen will then agree to marry Theoclymenus after she has performed the burial rites for Menelaus at sea. Theoclymenus falls for the plan and gives her and Menelaus a ship. Menelaus's men attack it and kill Theoclymenus's sailors, and Menelaus and Helen sail back to Greece.

Even in a bare summary, the play resembles the *Odyssey* in many respects. Like Odysseus, Menelaus disguises himself as a beggar and rescues his wife from an im-portunate suitor. Like Penelope, Helen rejects the suitor and plots with her hus-band to effect their reunion. Moreover, like Penelope Helen is characterized in terms that emphasize her sexual purity. For seventeen years she has been sexually faithful, almost as long as Penelope's twenty-year stint of chastity. She has come as a suppliant at the tomb of Proteus so that she might "preserve [her] bed for her husband and [her] body not incur shame." Later too she will assure Menelaus that she has remained "unsullied," and her cutting off her hair and scratching her cheeks, the signs of mourning used when she feigns Menelaus's death, also are re-pudiations of her sexual beauty. In this she contrasts with the "other" Helen, who in Euripides' *Orestes* cuts off only the tips of her hair in mourning for her sister Klytaimestra. In the *Helen* her chaste character is emphasized specifically in con-trast to the shameful phantom. The Greek hero Teucer conveniently shows up early in the play to tell Helen about the fall of Troy, Menelaus's disappearance, and the suicides of her mother and brothers. At first Teucer thinks she is the hated Helen, but after hearing her sober speech he says, "You have a body like Helen's, yet you don't have the same kind of mind, but one very much different." The key difference is her self-control, the rational virtue that characterizes Penelope and that makes Aphrodite Helen's enemy rather than her especial protector. Even Theoclymenus, reconciled to losing Helen by the timely appearance of her divine twin brothers, Castor and Polydeuces, praises her fidelity to her husband that re-flects a "most noble understanding, a thing not many women have."[70]

Helen's sexual purity is specifically linked to her dedication to her marriage with Menelaus. When she mistakenly thinks he is dead, she decides to kill herself rather than marry someone else. After she has been reunited with her husband, she tells him that if their escape plan fails, she will die with him. But the scene describing their reunion reaches almost romantic proportions in the tender joy both experience—Helen weeping and embracing Menelaus, just like Penelope when she finally accepts that Odysseus is really Odysseus. Helen calls her husband "dearest of humans," and he uses the same superlative, addressing her as "dearest person." Helen exclaims, "My husband, mine, I have, I have, for whom I waited, I waited," emotion making her redundant, and Menelaus responds, "I am yours, and you are mine." Their mutual love clearly reflects the strength of their marriage, a love reinforced in both by their control over their sexuality. One wonders how this scene would have struck the Greeks watching the play if their own marriages were as loveless as current received wisdom believes they were.[71]

The similarity of Helen and Menelaus's marriage to Odysseus and Penelope's is reinforced by the similarities of plot. As we have noted, like Penelope, Helen is besieged by a suitor; like Odysseus, Menelaus is a shipwrecked wanderer in a strange land, is thought to be dead, and has to disguise himself to rescue his wife. Just as Penelope helps plan the destruction of the suitors, Helen plots to help her husband and effect their escape. Helen claims that Menelaus can recognize her by certain "tokens" only those two share; Penelope tells Telemachus after the slaughter of the suitors that she will know Odysseus by "signs" secret to those two. And just as the wedding celebration ordered by Odysseus to hide the slaughter of the suitors also serves to celebrate the "remarriage" of Odysseus and Penelope, so Theoclymenus orders a wedding feast that ultimately celebrates the "remarriage" of Menelaus and Helen. All these parallels serve to refashion Helen into a good wife on the model of Penelope, with Helen's sexual power, once the worst example of eros's destructiveness, now subsumed into the structure of marriage, which that power strengthens rather than destroys.[72]

The Technology of Marriage

Helen's integration into the social order of marriage asserts the place of sexual attractiveness in that institution, as well as the way marriage contains and exploits the energy of female eros. In this she again resembles her divine double, Aphrodite, whose power is necessary for a marriage to flourish. Once more to the Greeks the "fancied sway" of the cultural order contains and organizes the volatile, destructive natural force of eros, which can then transform itself into the mutual love of Menelaus and Helen or Odysseus and Penelope. In contrast to our myth of Romantic Marriage, in which the quality of passion transforms and legitimizes the social institution that otherwise poses a threat to that passion, the message of the *Odyssey* or the *Helen* is that passion is legitimized and transformed into love by the conjugal values and rational virtues reinforced by the social order.

Helen, Penelope, Alcestis, Andromache, Ischomachus's wife all represent the wifely ideal in ancient Greek literature: female eros subordinated to the household, the order in which women find their meaning, their arena of glory and honor. Here is where they serve the state, by managing its fundamental building block and providing the future citizens who will inherit the city's property and political machinery. Moreover, the household parallels on the social level the rational virtue of *sôphrosunê*, rational self-control, on the individual level, a virtue we earlier saw associated with the male. If "maleness"—and being human—means greater rational control over the appetites, and "femaleness" greater appetitive control over reason, then the cultural order of marriage allows a woman to become more "male" and human; it is the "yoke" that transforms eros into a reciprocal conjugal love and affection whose energy bears fruit in legitimate offspring. Like reason, like agriculture, like civic religious cult, marriage is a "technology" in which the chaotic forces of nature are put to work for the benefit of human beings.

EIGHT

Eros the Pedagogue

THE SIXTH-CENTURY ATHENIAN Solon was one of that city's most important statesmen. His reforms broke the political and economic hold the aristocracy had on the people, laying the groundwork for the full-blown democracy of the fifth century. He was numbered among the ancient world's Seven Sages, according to legend once advising the fabulously wealthy King Croesus of Lydia not to trust in happiness, a lesson Croesus ruefully remembered when he was on the brink of being burned alive by the Persian Cyrus. Solon also wrote poetry, in which he justified his reforms and expounded his political philosophy. Here the distance between ancient Greece and modern America begins to appear immense—can anyone imagine a twentieth-century president or senator defending his political program in highly finished hexameter verses? Many of our politicians can't even write their own dull speeches.

But stranger still are the verses among Solon's fragments that tell of loving a "boy in the lovely flower of youth, desiring his thighs and sweet mouth." Now the difference between ourselves and the ancient Greeks becomes nearly incomprehensible. Any public figure, let alone a politician, in contemporary America who voiced such sentiments would be branded a pervert worthy of opprobrium and ostracism, even if the youth was in his teens, the age of the objects of ancient Greek boy-love. As the modern political folk adage has it, "Don't get caught in bed with a dead woman or a live boy." Pedophiles, along with rapists, are one of the last minorities it is still respectable to despise and insult. Our cult of sentimental, exculpating tolerance has no room for them. We give two cheers when the mother of a molested boy pumps five bullets into the head of his molester. Just the allegations of pederasty impel Michael Jackson to spend $15 million killing the investigation of the accusation. The Gay Establishment welcomes sadomasochists and transsexuals but keeps a careful distance from the North American Man-Boy Love Association, whose members fancy themselves the true heirs of Socrates and Plato.[1]

The chasm between ourselves and the ancient Greeks is as much of our own making as it is a result of the strangeness of the Greeks. As we saw in Chapter 4, our own confusion about homosexuality and its origins complicates our attempts at understanding Greek pederasty, or "boy-love." Contributing as well to our difficulty is the distinct aristocratic and militaristic aura that clings to ancient pederasty, given that America has never had an aristocracy and that the advent of a mercenary army means very few of us experience military life and values anymore. But Greek myth consistently associates pederasty with the nobility. In Chapter 4 we noted the "origins" of pederasty in the myth of King Laius, the father of Oedipus who kidnapped and raped the boy Chrysippus, for which violation Hera sent the Sphinx to destroy Thebes. The king of the gods, Zeus, likewise is enlisted as an originator of pederasty, for he fell in love with the beautiful Trojan boy Ganymede and snatched him up to be his cupbearer in Olympus.[2]

These mythic and divine aristocrats have their historical parallels. We saw earlier in Chapter 4 the origins of pederasty located among the Dorians, the best known of whom, the Spartans, were the most militaristic people in the ancient world. Aristocratic elitists supported by a suppressed majority of helots, serfs who worked the land, Spartan citizens devoted most of their time to military training.[3] All of male Spartan life was structured by a military order in which from an early age boys lived together in barracks under the supervision of an adolescent boy. They were constantly under the surveillance of older men as well, for whom they displayed their talents, whose approval they eagerly sought and disapproval fearfully shunned, and who were responsible for the mettle of their beloved— Plutarch reports that a youth who screamed in pain during battle got his admirer punished by the state. No wonder the Spartans supposedly sacrificed to Eros before every battle. In this male world of aristocratic martial values, of shared meals and naked exercising, of boys eagerly seeking the approval of older males, pederasty could easily flourish. That is the opinion of the Athenian Stranger in Plato's *Laws*, who blames homosexuality on these Dorian institutions.[4]

The fourth-century historian Ephorus records a custom in Crete, settled by Dorian Greeks, illustrating the extent to which pederasty was ritualized in Dorian culture. An older man would inform the family of a boy he fancied of his intentions. If the family considered the wooer worthy, they pretended to resist, but he would succeed in making off with the boy and hiding out with him for two months. Afterward the couple returned to the city, the boy receiving presents of armor, an ox, and a cup and considerable prestige at being so chosen. This connection of homosexuality and Spartan militarism was something of a commonplace by the time of Plato, especially among pro-Spartan Athenians. Plato's Phaedrus in the *Symposium* claims an army of lovers would be unbeatable, for they would do nothing shameful in the presence of their lovers. The famous Sacred Band of Thebes, 150 pairs of lovers killed to a man by Philip of Macedon at the battle of Chaeronea in 338, were supposedly just such an army.[5]

Several anecdotes from Greek history and legend demonstrate the power of pederasty to instill aristocratic values like martial courage and loyalty. Though Achilles, aristocratic hero par excellence, and his buddy Patroklos, whom he dies avenging, are both explicitly heterosexual in the *Iliad*, by the early fifth century they had been turned into a pederastic couple, though there was argument over who was the older and who the younger partner. Xenophon, in his tale of the Greek mercenaries who journeyed to fight for Cyrus, pretender to the Persian throne, recounts the story of Episthenes, who offered to die in the place of a beautiful boy prisoner. The most important pederastic *exemplum*, however, was the love of Aristogeiton and his boy-love Harmodius. As Thucydides tells the story, in 514 the latter was amorously pursued by Hipparchus, brother of Hippias, the tyrant of Athens. After Hipparchus was rebuffed he insulted Harmodius's sister by claiming she was unworthy to be a "basket-bearer" in the Panathenaic festival because she wasn't a virgin. Doubly dishonored, the two formed a conspiracy to assassinate Hipparchus. They were successful, and the subsequent repression ultimately led to the downfall of the tyranny. Significantly, two Spartan invasions helped facilitate Hippias's overthrow. The two lovers were thereafter celebrated as the liberators of Athens, a statue of them standing in the agora.[6]

Harmodius and Aristogeiton were particularly important role models for aristocrats. Their jealous regard for honor, their willingness to risk their lives for revenge—Harmodius died on the spot, and Aristogeiton after being tortured—and their bravery recalled epic heroes like Ajax and Achilles. Aristotle tells a story that shows Aristogeiton's pride and courage. After the assassination, Hippias was torturing Aristogeiton to find out the names of other conspirators. Aristogeiton gave him the names of Hippias's supporters. When Hippias demanded more names, Aristogeiton agreed and asked for the tyrant's right hand as a pledge. But when he had grasped Hippias' hand, he taunted Hippias with shaking hands with his brother's killer. Hippias was so enraged he killed Aristogeiton on the spot. This antipathy of most aristocrats toward the tyrants was a consequence of how the latter came to power. Remember, the tyrant's rule often resulted from his championing the people against the aristocrats, so the latter were usually the tyrants' most vehement opponents. Pausanias in Plato's *Symposium* voices this traditional opposition in terms of boy-love when he opines that tyrants, like barbarian despots, try to suppress pederasty because it engenders noble ideals that threaten their power, as the story of Harmodius and Aristogeiton illustrates.[7]

Boy-love, then, was not a private pleasure or relationship but a part of the social structure of the polis, one of its "technologies" for controlling the powerful force of eros. Eros in ancient Greek thought, some philosophers aside, is "polymorphously perverse," flowing out toward any object. But if those objects are citizen-boys or men, then the dangers of eros are magnified, for as we saw in Chapter 4, the citizen who submits to anal penetration opens his soul up to a compulsive appetite destructive of the social and political order embodied in and upheld by male citizens. Thus the very real sexual attraction to boys of those among the ruling elite is even more volatile than heterosexual eros. The citizen-wife who is corrupted is not violating her essential feminine nature. She is under the sway of her irrational passions anyway, necessitating the control of marriage and husbands. But the male is supposed to be more rational, more in control of his appetites—that is why he runs the city. The "technology" of boy-love, then, requires a delicate balancing act between acknowledging the power of homosexual eros without corrupting the boy who is its object, turning him into the dreaded *kinaidos*. This explains the numerous, almost ritualistic controls surrounding and organizing boy-love and the anxious caution with which it is treated in the ancient sources.

Let me once more remind the reader that I am not describing the behavior or proclivities of the "average Greek." Pederasty in the Greek literary remains (mostly Athenian from the late fifth to fourth centuries) is clearly an aristocratic institution; the high-proletarian "good ol' boys" and small farmers of Aristophanes certainly see it as the hoity-toity pastime of the nobles and those who ape their fashions, as in the *Wasps*, where long hair, a Spartan fashion, is linked to homosexual depravity. And since the majority of the Greek population in most *poleis* worked the soil, pederasty was not a well-known experience to most Greeks.[8]

The Heterosexual Paradigm Revisited

We saw in Chapter 4 that the boy-love is assimilated to the woman in a number of ways, particularly in the high value placed on his lack of facial and body hair and his "smoothness" and "softness." Girlish behavior was likewise desirable in the boy. Anacreon simultaneously praises and complains about an aloof young boy with a "virginal glance." Shyness and blushing were equally charming. The good-looking Lysis, in Plato's dialogue named for him, impresses Socrates because he is too shy to approach the philosopher though he wants to join in his conversation, and the equally attractive Hippothales charms him with his deep blush when Socrates seeks to discover the name of his beloved. There were other ways in which the man-boy relationship was patterned on the male-female relationship. Boys were courted with gifts, like women, except that girls were wooed indirectly, using family males as intermediaries. Just as numerous laws protected virgins and married women from sexual corruption, similar laws had as their aim the protection of citizen-boys, whose legal and political status was parallel to that of women, both being subordinated to older male relatives and both devoid of political rights. The orator Aeschines, in his speech prosecuting Timarchos for prostituting himself, refers to these laws. Some forbade the teacher or head of the gymnasium from opening their establishments before sunrise or keeping them open after sunset, so that no darkness was available for the corruption of the boys. Older boys were forbidden from fraternizing with the younger, and the producer of the choruses of boys, the *choregus*, had to be over forty years old, since that was considered the time of life when a man was most "self-controlled/chaste."[9]

In Plato's *Symposium*, Pausanias remarks on the less formal means fathers use to protect their sons, such as assigning a slave to watch over the boy and keep him away from any pursuers. Peer pressure as well would act as a safeguard, friends "reproaching," with the encouragement of the older men, boys who were too attentive to wooers. Reflecting this same general disapproval, Xenophon remarks that a wooer of a boy kept his intentions secret from the boy's family. Plato's Pausanias goes on to rationalize this obvious suspicion of boy-love as a means of separating good from bad lovers, that is, those concerned with the betterment of the boy's soul from those interested only in bodily satisfaction, who presumably would be more easily discouraged by these impediments. But Pausanias, remember, is described by Aristophanes as exclusively homosexual, still a partner of his boy-love Agathon—excoriated by Aristophanes in his plays as an effeminate passive homosexual—though the latter is around thirty at the dramatic date of the dialogue. Plato's Agathon, in fact, apparently confirms Aristophanes' appraisal when he defines the god Eros in terms that recall the ambiguous qualities of "softness" characterizing the boy and the *kinaidos*—since the god Eros "seizes always by the foot and every way onto the softest parts of the softest men, it is necessary for him to be the most delicate creature." Almost with defiance, Agathon twice uses as positive references forms of the word *malakos* that elsewhere in Greek literature consistently characterizes the physical effeminacy and moral degeneracy of the passive homosexual. Pausanias's rationalization of paternal impediments against pursuing boys—that they are really a means of sorting out good and bad lovers—may be special pleading. Such explanations are an attempt to cloak the socially despised exclusive homosexual relationship in the garb of the less threatening institution of boy-love.[10]

Just as the young girl and her sexual force were subordinated to her role as wife in the household, so the boy and his sexual power were channeled into teaching him his proper role as "good and beautiful/noble" citizen. The sexual beauty of the boy and the older man's attraction to it created the intimate energy for the boy's training and education—hence Eros was, in Euripides' fragment, the most important instructor of wisdom and inspirer of virtue. Alexis, a comic poet, adds that no teacher was more diligent or attentive. In Xenophon's *Memorabilia*, Socrates says this pedagogical function of pederasty is "customary" among the Athenians, for the man who attaches himself to a boy and teaches him virtue and goodness is acting the part of a noble/virtuous and good citizen. Plato's Phaedrus explains the psychological mechanism by which the boy learns the proper values. Because the beloved wants to impress his lover, he is ashamed at any behavior not noble and admirable: He feels "shame toward shameful things, and the love of honor toward noble things, for without these it is impossible for a city or a private person to perform great and noble deeds." Thus he is filled with courage, willing even to die rather than shame himself before his admirer, as we saw earlier in the story of Harmodius and Aristogeiton, which Pausanias cites as an example. Plato often has speakers in a dialogue rehearse received wisdom before Socrates takes the stage to set them straight, and Phaedrus here clearly is voicing a rationale for boy-love that any Athenian aristocrat would approve. The justification of erotic attraction to boys is found in the service it provides to the city by training citizens in the manly virtues necessary for the city's success.[11]

The pedagogical function of pederasty also involves the ethical ideal of reciprocity, which provides another rational control for pederastic eros. Much of Greek everyday ethics was based on the *do ut des*, "I give so that you may give," model. Gods were worshipped, given gifts of sacrifice and offerings, so that their power would be turned to the mortal's benefit. We saw that parent-child relationships could be structured by this paradigm: Parents give life to children and tend them when they are weak so that the children can tend parents when *they* are weak and bury them. Aristocratic values were particularly reflective of reciprocity based on an absolute identity of "friends" and "enemies." The standard definition of aristocratic justice was "help friends, hurt enemies," a formulation ubiquitous in Greek literature.[12] If you gave benefits to those who gave them to you, or injuries to those who injured you, that was justice. If you gave injury to those who benefited you, that was an injustice that inflicted dishonor. Thus the high value placed on revenge—it is the paying back of injury for injury. Achilles' killing of Hector for Hector's killing of Patroklos illustrates this ethical value, for Achilles "helps" his friend by injuring the man who injured him. Likewise Medea proves her aristocratic worth by injuring Jason, the "friend" she had benefited but who had paid her back with dishonor: To injure a friend is the height of injustice.

The person to whom one owed such help was a *philos*, "friend/dear one," and the pederastic relationship, like marriage, was a subspecies of this friendship. As Aristotle defines the *philos*, he is "one wishing or accomplishing good things or what seem to be good things for the sake of the friend." The service or benefit or "help" or other "good things" the lover gave to the beloved was flattering attention and education in the proper role and behavior expected of a man, particularly an aristocrat. What the beloved gave the lover was exclusive attention and some level of physical gratification, though exactly what that gratification consisted of will be dealt with later. We can see this ideal of pederastic reciprocity in some lines of Theognis that chastise a boy for his lack of faithfulness, his failure to reciprocate the attention and love the speaker bestowed on him: "Now you hold another friend; but I, the one who did well for you, lie neglected." Significantly, forms of the key word *philos* appear five times in these eight lines, indicating that Theognis understands the pederastic relationship in the larger context of aristocratic reciprocal friendship. Indeed, many of the lines in the Theognidean corpus are addressed to the boy Cyrnus, giving him advice and instruction in how to be a good, "virtuous" aristocrat. Plato's Pausanias, ever the font of received wisdom, calls on this ideal as the justification for the boy's physical gratification of the lover—it's acceptable as long as its purpose is "virtue/excellence" and the lover will make the beloved wise and good, that is, reciprocate a benefit for a benefit received.[13]

Reciprocity, however, doesn't necessarily imply equality. The lover and beloved are as proportionately unequal as the husband and wife. But the role of reciprocity in pederasty suggests another similarity to marriage, an institution also based on mutual benefits provided by partners one of whom is subordinated to the other. The heterosexual paradigm, then, is the key social order for controlling eros. Just as marriage harnesses the erotic energy of females to provide citizens for the city and managers for the household, so boy-love exploits the erotic energy of boys to create the citizen-elite who will fight in its armies and hold its offices.[14]

The Drinking Party

It is no coincidence that two ancient Greek dialogues concerned with eros should be set at a *sumposion* or "drinking party." The symposium was one of the most important institutions of Athenian civil society, particularly for the late-fifth-century nobility whose warrior function and political hegemony had diminished under the democracy. Through the symposium aristocratic values could be perpetuated and celebrated, poetry extolling its ideology performed, drinking songs recalling the deeds of other aristocratic heroes sung. The most popular *skolia* or "drinking songs" recounted the deeds of Harmodius and Aristogeiton: "I will carry my sword in a branch of myrtle, like Harmodius and Aristogeiton," a popular version of a drinking song went, the myrtle sacred to Aphrodite signifying their love. The presence of these famous lovers points us to the connection between pederasty and the symposium: Both were aristocratic cultural institutions whose function was to exploit pederastic eros for the inculcation of aristocratic values. During the fifth century this function became particularly important since the democracy in Athens had given power to nonnobles who also had access to political office and magistracies. The symposium thus became an alternative political organ energized in part by the sexual attraction of older males to young aristocratic boys.[15]

This sort of rationalized context for pursuing eros is evident in the highly structured and organized nature of the idealized symposium, although in actual fact the drinking party could become quite riotous, an expression of unbridled appetite rather than its control, making the symposium for Plato an apt metaphor for a hedonist's heaven. The participants—exclusively male, since citizen-wives could not attend—reclined on low couches, drinking and singing in due order under the direction of an elected "symposiarch" or leader, who oversaw the mixing of the wine. Ancient wine was diluted with water, so the tone of the drinking party could be set by how weak or strong the wine was mixed. After the meal a libation to the gods would be poured and a hymn sung to Zeus. Then the banqueters would converse or alternate singing, each singer reciting some verses of a poet, then giving a twig to another reveler who had to continue the poem. A game called *kottabus* would be played, in which the players flung drops of wine from a cup and tried to strike some sort of target, usually a small metal disk balanced on a pole. The object was to make the little disk clang onto another metal plate below it. Depending on the proclivities of the diners, entertainment in the form of actors, acrobats, flute girls, or dancing girls would be provided, and prostitutes of both sexes might be available. Particularly excessive drinking parties could continue in the streets, with lovers serenading their beloved to the annoyance of neighbors, or the drunken symposiasts accosting strangers. The famous incident of the mutilated herms—posts decorated with the face and erect phallus of Hermes and set up in front of houses—on the eve of the ill-fated Athenian expedition to Sicily in 415 was seen by the people as typical of aristocratic excess fueled by the symposium.[16]

The idealized symposia of literature, however, emphasized a strictly controlled context for the intellectual expression of eros. Socrates in the *Protagoras* mocks the riotous drinking parties of nonnoble men trying to ape their betters, boors who must have flute girls and prostitutes since they cannot entertain themselves with intellectual conversation. Xenophanes, the late-sixth-century critic of Hesiod's and Homer's anthropomorphic gods, says the participants should drink only to the point that they can still walk home without the aid of a servant. Rather than an excuse for sensual indulgence, then, the ideal symposium should be the occasion for the expression simultaneously of moderation and erotic beauty and power.[17]

The dialogues of Plato and Xenophon are obvious evidence for the centrality of eros to the symposium for which they are named, as is the sexual availability of hetaerae, flute girls, and servants of both sexes at more hedonistic drinking parties. No wonder, then, that Callimachus named Aphrodite and the Erotes or Loves the presiding deities of the symposium. Even the *kottabus* game had sexual connotations, for a kiss from a serving girl or serving boy was often the prize for the winner. At actual symposia this erotic ambiance no doubt led to sexual excess, as in the symposium Demosthenes describes where a woman was assaulted after the men became "heated" with wine, or the one mentioned earlier where Neaira is accused of having sex with the serving-men.[18]

But in the idealized symposium, this sexually charged atmosphere was often the backdrop for a celebration of the rational virtue of moderation. We have seen Xenophanes counsel moderation in drinking. Theognis also advises taking it easy with the wine, for "whoever exceeds the measure of drinking, that man no longer is ruler of his tongue and mind." The ideal is to drink enough to relax and enjoy the pleasure of wine, but not so much that the mind and its controlling powers are impaired. The Athenian Stranger in the *Laws* considers this exposure to the temptations of wine and sex at the symposium a good builder of character, since one can more easily resist the temptations to which he has had exposure. This rational control of the appetite for wine will, as we will soon see, have its erotic parallel in the virtue most important for pederasty, *sôphrosunê*. Just as the erotic energy of women is subordinated to the household and to self-control, so the erotic energy of boys and their lovers will be controlled and channeled into shaping aristocratic manly character through the key virtues of self-control and moderation. Like marriage, then, pederasty is a cultural institution exercising a "fancied sway" over homosexual eros.[19]

The flowers present at symposia represent this subordination of nature to culture. Flowers, as we saw in Chapter 6, represent the transient sexual beauty of youths. But at the symposium the flowers were made into garlands worn either as crowns or around the neck. In other words, human skill has shaped them into artifacts used in the quasi-ritual of the drinking party. Meleager exploits these associations in his image of blossoming boys Eros has woven into a "soul-beguiling garland." So it was with aristocratic youth—their sexual bloom was woven into the aristocratic masculine ideal perpetuating the social and political power of the nobility.[20]

Outrage, Shame, and "Just Eros"

In Chapter 4 we learned that sexual excess, particularly homosexual, was defined in terms of "outrage" and "shame." The seduction of a citizen-wife or daughter was a crime of "outrage" (*hubris*) that shamed the male responsible for her. Euphiletus, the man we met in Chapter 7 who murdered his wife's lover, defined Eratosthenes' seduction as an "outrage" against him (*hubrisen*). Likewise the man who submitted to anal penetration shamed himself because he abandoned his soul to appetite, violating a communal standard of self-control. He also allowed himself to be outraged by another, treated as an object for the gratification of another's appetite and pleasure. Sexual outrage, then, was the abandonment of the soul to one's own or another's appetite, a loss of rational control that shamed the victim because he did not uphold his society's most important order—the control of the passions and appetites by the mind and its social projections, law and custom.[21]

This obsession with sexual outrage and shame creates an obvious contradiction in the ritual of pederasty. For if the boy is to reciprocate for the benefits he has received—flattering attention and education in nobility, not to mention the more mundane material gifts—how can he do so? If he submits to physical gratification, particularly anal penetration, he has allowed himself to be outraged, and he has drawn perilously close to the *kinaidos*, the male sexual bogey. This contradiction explains the anxiety that permeates discussions of pederasty in our sources. One resolution works by extolling the same virtue used to define the good wife, whose sexuality likewise is problematic if not kept within the bounds of the household. Self-control/chastity, *sôphrosunê*, becomes the saving virtue that attempts to neutralize the ever-present possibility of outrage and shame.

Ancient discussions of pederasty continually move between the two poles of outrage/shame and self-control, the former abhorred and the latter extolled as a "just" love, one that confers benefits for benefits received, not the unjust outrage of physical lust. The sixth-century poet Anacreon, the celebrated lover of boys and habitué of the symposium who once said that boys were his gods, said as well that "just deeds" are beautiful to Eros and that children could appreciate his songs, presumably because they were not celebrations of physical lust. The fifth-century philosopher Democritus explicitly defines this "just" love as one that avoids outrage: "Just love is to pursue the beautiful without outrage [*anubristôs*]." These early formulations are consistent with what we find in Xenophon, Aeschines, and pseudo-Democritus, where the "just" or "chaste" lover will also be defined in terms of self-control/chastity and opposed to the physical gratification that leads to outrage.[22]

Xenophon's *Memorabilia* and *Symposium* both discuss the proper behavior of lovers in a pederastic relationship. Socrates in the *Memorabilia*, Xenophon's recollections of the philosopher's conversations, represents an extreme ascetic view of pederasty. He won't even allow kissing, for it leads to "harmful pleasures." That's why the boy with a noble soul won't allow himself to be kissed. In a conversation with the hedonistic Sophist Antiphon, Socrates defends his wisdom, which Antiphon questions because Socrates won't take money for his teaching. Socrates argues that his wisdom is intimately related to his sense of reciprocal justice that would be besmirched by accepting money as the "benefit." He then uses the pederastic relationship as an analogy. The boy who offers his beauty for money is a prostitute, whereas the boy who becomes the friend of a "noble/virtuous and good man" is considered "self-controlled/chaste" (*sôphrona*). Socrates' pedagogy is based on this model, as an ennobling activity kept separate from any material benefits, either money or physical gratification. A little later he elaborates on pederasty in precisely the same terms. Ideal friends are those who honor the same chaste behavior and who are moderate in their appetites, so that "though they delight in the sexual pleasures of blooming youths, they control themselves, so that they don't cause pain to those they shouldn't." The reciprocal code of pederasty—the obligation to give benefits for benefits received—clearly depends on the prohibition of physical gratification as a benefit. Physical gratification would shame the boy and hence be an injustice to one to whom a benefit is owed. Self-rule is the virtue that allows the relationship to function properly, that is, "justly," without shame.[23]

The idealization of self-control as defining the "just" pederastic eros is apparent as well in Xenophon's *Symposium*. One of the guests at this drinking party is the beautiful teen Autolycus, an athlete who at the dramatic date of the dialogue (421) had just won a prize competing in the fierce pancratium, a combination of wrestling, boxing, and kicking, sort of like modern kick-boxing. Autolycus, by the way, was a real person, subject of a comedy by Eupolis and ultimate victim of the Thirty, the terrorist junta installed by the victorious Spartans after they defeated Athens in the Peloponnesian War. The admirer of Autolycus, Callias, hosts the dinner fictionally recreated by Xenophon. But it is not the occasion for any physical seduction of Callias's beloved, for Autolycus's father is present also, and the boy modestly sits beside him. The chastity of both Autolycus's character and Callias's love is made explicit by the narrator when he comments that Autolycus's beauty was "kingly," particularly because it was joined to "a sense of shame/sobriety and chastity/self-control" (*sôphrosunês*), and that Callias's demeanor was admirable because it reflected a "chaste Eros" (*sôphronos Erôtos*). Socrates later seconds this appraisal when he attributes Callias's love to the "Heavenly Aphrodite," which is for the "soul and friendship and beautiful/noble deeds" and is so innocent that Callias invites Autolycus's father to the banquet. Here the two qualities admired—a sense of shame and self-control—are precisely the opposite of the two associated with the physical lust of the *kinaidos*, shamelessness and outrage.[24]

Socrates' later description of Autolycus reinforces this distance between the idealized boy-love and the monstrous *kinaidos*. Whereas the latter is characterized by effeminacy and "softness," both physical and moral, Autolycus is explicitly not "corrupted by softness/effeminacy" (*malakia*, the same word the homosexual fop Agathon defiantly uses to praise his homosexual Eros). Rather, he displays "bodily strength, endurance, manliness, and self-control/chastity" (*sôphrosunên*). The male ideal of rational control over the appetites so displaces the possibility of the shaming outrage of physical gratification that Autolycus is forbidden the girlish softness other pederasts find desirable. Xenophon clearly creates here a pederastic ascetic ideal in which the threatening power of *kinaidos*-like eros is completely banished. Thus not even a kiss is allowed the "self-controlled/chaste" lover.[25]

The fourth-century orator Aeschines' prosecution of Timarchos as a prostitute who should be barred from political activity plays on the same contrast between the *kinaidos* and the "just" or "chaste" eros. As we saw in Chapter 4, Aeschines casts Timarchos as the typical degenerate *kinaidos* and, like Aristophanes, connects uncontrolled sexual appetite to political corruption. That's how he interprets the intent of the law banning prostitutes from addressing the assembly: "He who has sold his own body for others to outrage, would easily sell the common interests of the city." But Aeschines carefully distinguishes between a Timarchos, creature of unbridled physical lusts, and the "just" or "chaste" lover, the participant in a high-toned pederastic relationship. He does this for strategic reasons. One, he himself has been active in pederastic courtship, so he must head off any counterattack along the lines of the pederastic pot calling the kinaidic kettle black. Two, since he must cultivate the goodwill of the several hundred male jurors and play to their prejudices, he has to acknowledge the shared cultural ideal of pedagogical pederasty. Thus he heads off the accusation that he is beginning a "fearsome decline of the education of youth." This in turn means protecting the integrity of pedagogical pederasty by reinforcing how far it is from the dreaded passive homosexual. Finally, he plays to another prejudice by unmasking those who would use pederasty as the camouflage for homosexual lust, and so gratifies those jurors who, like the characters in Aristophanes, think that boy-love often is just high-toned buggery.[26]

In defending pederasty, Aeschines indulges every cliché found in Xenophon and Plato, sounding over and over the "self-control/chastity" note, the talisman that wards off the outrage of physical gratification. He admits the praise of beauty, but only if it is found with self-control (*sôphrosunês*). He defines the "just lover" (*erôta dikaion*) in terms consistent with the cultural ideal we've been tracing: The just lover is in love with the "beautiful/noble and chaste" (*sôphronôn*), and he loves in an "uncorrupted" manner. The fact that a citizen pursued a boy with such noble intent was a "witness to chastity," and such a wooer was himself the "greatest guard of chastity" (*sôphrosunês*), presumably because he displaced more unscrupulous wooers. The usual suspects Harmodius and Aristogeiton are trotted out, their love defined as "chaste and lawful" (*sôphrôn*). Such love, Aeschines claims (quoting Euripides), is one of life's most beautiful experiences, and he finishes with a list of contemporary couples who were "the most chaste" lovers (*sôphronestatôn*). Aeschines' repetition of *sôphrosunê* (chastity/self-control) and words derived from it functions to keep at bay even the hint of physical gratification in idealized pederasty.[27]

Such physical gratification would be a shaming "outrage," and Aeschines continually contrasts his "just lover" with the *kinaidos*-like Timarchos and his ilk, who submit to anal penetration, the ultimate sexual "outrage" for a man. His first definition of the "just lover" works by contrasting him with the "wanton [*hubristou*] and uncultured man" who is so debased he hires his body out for others to outrage. A little later, again the "chaste" lovers are contrasted with those who are "without self-rule and wanton [*hubristas*]," that is, those who "outrage" their own bodies by allowing other males to perform sexual acts on them. As we saw in Chapter 4, the *kinaidos* is defined in precisely the same terms, as one who will "outrage" his own body, that is, allow others to penetrate him anally and use him for their pleasure. Aeschines here is rescuing the cult of boy-love from any suggestions of such horrifying, womanlike behavior. The chaos of eros, window into the myriad destructive appetites of the soul, is here contained and controlled by the social ideal of pederasty and its key virtue, rational self-control: Pederasty is to sodomy as marriage is to adultery.[28]

The author of the "Erotic Essay" wrongly attributed to Demosthenes follows the same procedure in his defense of idealized pederasty. The "just lover" is defined as one who would not do anything shameful, and his "justice" is several times attributed to his "self-control/chastity" and contrasted with "shame." The boy too, like Xenophon's Autolycus, is characterized in these ideal terms—his glance is "manly and chaste," and he behaves "chastely" toward his lover, favoring behavior that is "just and beautiful/noble" rather than "shameful." Such a boy is a "son of Excellence/Virtue sired by Eros." Once more we see the aristocratic value system informing pederasty: To seek physical gratification from the beloved would be a shaming "outrage," an injury to a friend, the height of injustice. The "just lover" should rather seek to reciprocate by giving the boy instruction in manly, noble virtue, a development of the mind and character that control the chaotic passions of the body.[29]

The descriptions of pederasty in Xenophon, Aeschines, and pseudo-Demosthenes provide us the background for understanding what Pausanias is up to in Plato's *Symposium*. As we noted earlier, he rehearses the received ideas about boy-love. He starts by contrasting "chastity" and "outrage" in terms of the "Heavenly" and "Vulgar" Aphrodite, the former partaking only of the male and "untinged with outrage [*hubreôs*]" because the male has "more mind." But the "vulgar" lovers of the body and pleasure create the scandal for pederasty, leading people to think it "shameful to gratify lovers" since they see the "vulgar" lovers' "impropriety and injustice." So far Pausanias is in line with the standard interpretation of ideal pederasty, a love of the mind and soul kept distant from physical gratification. But Pausanias—who was what we would call a homosexual, remember, according to Aristophanes in this same dialogue—begins cleverly to exploit this dichotomy to justify physical gratification. Whatever is done "lawfully and in an orderly manner" is above reproach; thus Pausanias bases "shame" and "outrage" not on the acts themselves, as in our other pederastic apologists, but on the purpose, the manner, and the object of the act. It is noble or shameful not in and of itself, but if shamefully or basely done—shamefully if one gratifies a worthless man in a worthless way, nobly if one gratifies a noble man in a noble way. Is "noble way" to be understood as "without physical gratification"? It seems unlikely, since the verb Pausanias uses over and over—"gratify" (*charizesthai*)—clearly is a euphemism for sex. Such gratification is justified if it is for the purpose of virtue and if the lover will make his beloved "wise and good," contributing to his "intellectual and other excellence/virtue." Pausanias has found a way to valorize an otherwise despised relationship by sneaking it into the accepted pederastic ideal. No wonder those rubes in Aristophanes figured pederasty was a highfalutin pretense for buggery.[30]

Having surveyed these encomia of "just" or "chaste" eros, the modern reader no doubt wonders exactly what these pederastic couples were doing under their cloaks. Were the 150 couples of the Theban Sacred Band sodomizing one another on the eve of Chaeronea? Was Solon celebrating buggery in his poetry? One modern school of interpretation seems to think so, the prohibition on sodomy lifted for those in an exclusive pederastic relationship, its full force felt only by those citizen-males who accepted money for anal sex or had more than one partner or weren't part of a pederastic couple. Given the general vitriolic disgust at passive buggery that we saw in Chapter 4, and given the continual anxious harping on "shame" and "outrage" found even in apologists for pederasty, this seems highly unlikely.[31]

A more widely accepted view is that the pederastic lover had "intercrural" intercourse with his beloved—he rubbed his penis between the boy's thighs while both were standing. Postures of lovers on vase-paintings seem to support this idea, as do the few references to thighs in pederastic poetry. We saw Solon "desiring the thighs" of young boys, and fragments from Aeschylus's lost play about Achilles and Patroklos as pederastic lovers, the *Myrmidons*, show Achilles bewailing the "holy reverence of thighs."[32] Such intercourse presumably avoided the shame of penetration and thus avoided the charge of "outrage" while allowing the older active partner to achieve orgasm. This evidence, however, is slight and depends on reading into the fragments their lost context. And I see no reason why the lovers on vases couldn't be practicing sodomy, though others more expert than I will have to determine whether the postures shown on vases are physically compatible with buggery. So what did those Greek boy-lovers do in the shadowy margins of the gymnasium or on the couches of the symposium? The answer to this question depends on the great variety of character, imagination, and proclivities of those men and boys actually involved in such a relationship, and that is information we don't have. Some men, by natural inclination homosexual, obviously enjoyed being sodomized; others on occasion may have sought out a male passive partner; the majority perhaps found anal sex taboo. At any rate, the question cannot be answered irrefutably with the evidence at hand. Modern generalizations about what sort of sex, if any, was practiced in boy-love, or about the rigid active and passive roles assumed in pederastic intercourse, are ultimately speculations dependent upon an oversimplification of human behavior.

In the idealized pederasty of the literary remains, however, the answer is clear: Physical consummation is taboo. And the rational virtue of self-control/chastity gives pederasty its power to distance itself from the chaos of eros and its mind-obliterating pleasure. As such it functions as another "technology," a tool for controlling nature's force and directing it to ends beneficial for the citizen and state. Cercidas, the third-century philosopher and poet, brings out this dimension of self-control beautifully in his image of the "twin winds" of Eros, the one mild and gentle, leaving the "sea of love" calm, the other stormy with the "wind-storms of passion." But even the mild sea requires the soul to sail it with the "oar of self-control/chastity" (*sôphroni*). Just as the technology of sailing exploits the energy of wind and sea, so the rational virtue of self-control navigates the deeps of eros. This cultural ideal of an erotically energized pederasty divorced from sexual gratification is the background for Plato's *Phaedrus* and Socrates' discourse on Eros in the *Symposium*, the most highly developed examples of pederasty as a vehicle for the triumph of the rational soul over the shifting natural world of change and decay.[33]

Taming the Horses of the Soul

Plato's *Phaedrus* imagines a conversation between Socrates and a handsome young man, Phaedrus, outside the city walls on the banks of the river Ilissus one bright summer's day. Such a pastoral setting, as well as the flirtatious byplay between the young Phaedrus and the older Socrates, is fitting for a conversation about idealized pederastic eros, but sexual passion is just one of the dialogue's concerns. Socrates spends more than half the time talking about rhetoric, the power of language to conceal as well as reveal truth, and about the mind's power of categorization and definition. Despite the natural beauty of the riverbank, then, with its grass and breezes and willows and chirping cicadas, the dialogue is about the rational control the "unnatural" mind, the truly human aspect of our being, should wield to learn the truth of existence and human good. And it is about how the natural force of eros must be exploited, not just controlled, in order to provide the energy that propels the rational soul to its apprehension of that good and the genuine reality transcending this shifting material world of nature.[34]

The conversation begins with the recitation of a speech Phaedrus heard from the orator and politician Lysias. The gist of it is the sophistical paradox that the beloved should prefer the lover who is not himself in love to the one who is in love. Lysias's logic follows from the accepted attitudes toward eros and pederasty that we have traced in Xenophon, Aeschines, and pseudo-Demosthenes. Since the lover is controlled by passion, Lysias argues, he is diseased and insane, and so incapable of rationally determining what is best for the beloved. The nonlover, conversely, freed from the mental chaos wrought by eros, can rationally consider what is best for the boy's development and education, as well as protect him from the shaming slander and public disruptions caused by the jealous passionate lover. In short, the nonlover will be able to reciprocate properly for the physical favors received. He will keep in mind the boy's future needs while not publicly injuring him. The passionate lover, out of jealousy or wounded pride or some other erotically stoked emotion, will injure his beloved—perhaps even publicly.[35]

As Socrates himself says, the speech is pretty much full of received wisdom. If the pederastic relationship is based on reciprocity—education returned for physical gratification—then the man whose mind is not disturbed by passion will be able to see clearly what will improve the boy's character and make him good and noble. Socrates also faults the speech's repetitiousness as well as its obvious argument, and so, after some prodding by Phaedrus, he offers his own version of the same thesis. He starts by more carefully defining the nature of eros, which he numbers among the "inborn desires for pleasures" and to which he opposes the "opinion that strives for the best." These two principles of the soul are often at war. When "opinion leads through reason to the best" this is called self-control/chastity, our old friend *sôphrosunê*. But when "desire irrationally drags us toward pleasures" this is called "outrage," *hubris*. Eros, then, is the force of desire that conquers rational opinion and leads the soul to the enjoyment of the beauty of bodies.[36]

Once more we are on familiar ground: The opposition between self-control and outrage defines idealized pederasty, an idealization made necessary by eros's destructive power. Socrates continues in the same vein of received ideas. The lover who is a slave to his passions will want a boy weak and inferior and so better suited to the gratification of his lusts. Thus he will injure the boy by committing outrage against his body and turning him into a *kinaidos*, "soft/effeminate," unaccustomed to manly work and sweat, living a "delicate and unmanly" life, using makeup like a woman and indulging in behavior Socrates would rather leave unmentioned. Also he will keep the boy from improving his character, from marrying and siring children, so that the boy remains the socially stunted tool of the lover's private pleasure rather than taking his place in the social and political life of the city and so living up to the role idealized pederasty is supposed to prepare him for. In other words, the passionate lover cannot respect the ideals of pederasty, for he will not treat the boy as a "friend," reciprocating benefits in the form of education, but will injure and "outrage" him because of irrational appetite for bodily pleasure. Thus he "loves" the boy the way a wolf loves a lamb—as the result of a violent natural force ultimately destructive to the boy's soul.[37]

So far Socrates has given us a sort of reverse justification of pederasty by focusing on the bad lover who uses boy-love as an excuse for gratifying his lust, inflicting "outrage" on his unfortunate victim. But Socrates, on the brink of heading back to the city, suddenly intuits that he had made an error and blasphemed against the god Eros. Now he must make restitution by singing a palinode, a retraction, like Stesichorus's apology in song for his insult to Helen. Just as Stesichorus must recognize the positive power of female sexual beauty by exculpating a divine Helen from the depravity of her shameless phantom double, so Socrates now must redefine Eros as a beneficial force driving the soul not just to the improvement of character but to the apprehension of ultimate reality itself, the knowledge that will allow one to know virtue and the good, the best foundation for a truly noble and good character. The power of the irrational should not just be controlled and limited and kept from being destructive but now must be tapped and exploited as the energy that the soul will use to transcend the natural world.[38]

Socrates begins by rejecting the old dualism of the destructive irrational and the positive rational. Madness, for example, is not all bad. There is the madness of prophecy, like the prophetess at Delphi, or the "fine frenzy" of the poet. Eros, too, inflicts a madness of this sort, sent by the gods as the energy that can assist the soul in discovering the true good the possession of which creates happiness. This recognition of the irrational's positive potential follows from the soul's structure, which is not dualistic, a godlike reason controlling bestial appetites and passions, but tripartite. Socrates uses the image of the chariot to describe this soul when it is outside the body, a chariot steered by a charioteer, reason, who guides two winged horses: a "beautiful/noble and good" one and the other "quite the opposite." The wings represent the immortal soul's innate desire to ascend to the heavens and leave behind the material world of change and decay.[39]

These wings are nourished and made to grow by contemplation of divine beauty, wisdom, and goodness and are destroyed by the opposite qualities. The soul desiring to ascend on its wings, however, is held back by the bad horse, which drags it back to the natural world and away from the heaven of true reality, which is "colorless, formless, and intangible," the true object of knowledge that only the rational mind can see. If the soul attains this vision of true reality, it will nourish its wings on the sight of absolute justice, self-control/chastity, and knowledge rather than on the smudged simulacra of these virtues we see in the shifting material world. This vision is difficult to achieve, however, for the bad horse clouds the soul's sight and distracts it from reality until, its wings broken and lost, it descends into material bodies, the quality of its earthly incarnation dependent on how much of eternal reality its soul has seen.[40]

What has eros to do with all this? The fallen soul can be reawakened to its former vision of absolute goodness through the beauty irradiating a handsome boy, so that the soul once again desires transcendent beauty and its wings start to grow again. Those on earth who cannot see (that is, rationally comprehend) the absolute beauty that inspires their sexual desire turn to lust and "outrage" and "pleasures contrary to nature," which can only refer to homosexual sodomy. They remain in the world of nature and its chaotic forces. But the soul whose passion is inspired by the glimpse of a remembered absolute beauty begins to feel a pain and irritation as its wings begin to grow again. Now the traditional imagery of erotic madness and disease creates a picture of the impact of beauty on the soul. The fire of eros, which usually communicates its destructiveness, Socrates now uses metaphorically to describe the growth of the wings, and the goad, image of eros's compulsive power, becomes a metaphor for the action of the burgeoning feathers painfully opening up passages long closed. Socrates transforms the traditional imagery of eros's destructiveness into metaphors for the stimulating effect sexual beauty has on the immaterial soul and its yearning for absolute knowledge.[41]

Now we have a whole new context for idealized pederasty and its contrast between self-control/chastity and outrage. The good horse of the soul is defined as a "lover of honor along with self-control/chastity [*sôphrosunês*] and shame/modesty" and is guided not by the whip but by reason. The bad horse, in contrast, is the "companion of outrage [*hubreôs*] and boastfulness," hardly controlled by the whip and the spur. When the soul begins to heat with the sight of divine beauty shining forth from the boy, the good horse pulls backs and restrains itself, but the bad horse leaps forward, forcing the soul to approach the beloved and seek the "favors of sexual pleasure." The charioteer and the good horse recoil from such "awesome and unlawful things"—again, a probable reference to sodomy—but nonetheless nearly give in until the vision of absolute beauty standing "with self-control/chastity on a pure/chaste pedestal" shames it into retreat. The charioteer then pulls back hard on the reins, thus chastising and training the bad horse until it too, broken after many such attempts at mounting the beloved, sees him in "reverence/shame and fear." Even if the beloved should consent to sex, the lover will oppose gratification out of "modesty and reason." Those who achieve this ideal will live a life of happiness and harmony on earth, and after death their souls will escape the round of material reincarnation.[42]

Socrates' poetic fancy masks a relentless expropriation of the energy of the body's sexual passion. Just as the cultural artifact of the chariot and the technology of horse-breaking exploit the horse's muscle energy, so the mind will exploit the force of physical eros. But it will not push eros to the point where shame and outrage will compromise the souls of the lover and the beloved by indulgence in a physical act, although if the lovers do falter, they won't necessarily be denied an ultimate vision of reality. Moreover, the invention of the "good" horse, a part of the irrational innately conducive to reason's control, marks another inroad of the mind into the powerful force of the appetites and passions. The pretensions of reason are obvious here, in Socrates' vision of a soul that turns the irrational against itself, that paradoxically exploits the energy of sex to ascend to an immaterial sexless world far above the shifting chaos of the body's passions.[43]

The Ladder of Erotic Beauty

Though its ultimate aim is to bring the rational soul to possession of that abstract reality beyond the material world, eros in the *Phaedrus* is still saturated with the physical reality of sexual passion. Despite the expected disapproval of sexual intercourse between lover and beloved, such consummation delays but does not bar the aspirant soul from its ultimate return to the immaterial heaven and escape from the round of material reincarnation. Even the language of the dialogue is sexually charged, its imagery of "streams" and "fount," of feathers burgeoning with warmth and moisture nearly functioning as metaphors for intercourse.[44] In the speech of Diotima from the *Symposium*, however, the abstraction of eros is more complete and sexual energy is more thoroughly drained of its physicality. Here we see Plato's remarkable gambit, one that has profoundly influenced Western idealizations of sexuality: A reality defined as immaterial, rational, eternal, and absolute—that is, everything the natural world of matter and sex is not—will be *rationally* apprehended using the energy of sexual desire, which is an *irrational* function of a material, time- and space-bound physical body.

The exposition that Socrates puts into the mouth of the mysterious Diotima— most likely a ventriloquist's dummy for Socrates himself—begins by disavowing the materialistic attributes earlier speakers, particularly Agathon, had given love. Eros is neither good nor beautiful, neither divine nor mortal, but something in between: a spiritual agency that mediates between the world of the gods—that is, the world of ultimate reality, not Homer's braggarts and lechers—and the shadow-world of mortals. It is a connecting force, an energy for bridging the gap between the "real" world and its deformed, mutable simulacra that we with our mortal bodies must inhabit. And because our rational souls live in exile from that world, we suffer from desire, an absence of those immortal unchanging virtues— wisdom, beauty, especially the good—the possession of which would fulfill and complete us and make us happy.[45]

But how can one describe this erotic process in action? Diotima must have recourse to the world of nature and, in so doing, performs a remarkable appropriation of the most messy and physical of natural processes, birth—that quintessentially female experience that links women to the world of beasts and sex to the processes of nature. All men are "pregnant" and desire to give birth, Diotima asserts, and this yearning is stimulated by apprehension of beautiful bodies, which promise deliverance from the labor pangs. But the bodies themselves are not what the travailing soul desires—it is rather the *good* that the soul wants to possess forever, the immortal absolute good intimately interrelated with absolute beauty and reflected in the beauty of the boy. In other words, as Diotima says, "Eros is of immortality." Animals and lesser men "pregnant in terms of the body" fulfill this longing by begetting mortal offspring. But those pregnant in soul long to bear those things fitting for the soul to bring forth: "practical wisdom/prudence" or the more divine "self-control/chastity and justice," that is, *sôphrosunê*, the pederastic virtue par excellence.[46]

The man who is pregnant with these virtues will seek to develop them in a beautiful boy, and *this* is the rationale for pederastic pedagogy. The lover who happens on a soul "beautiful and noble and graceful" becomes adept at speaking of virtue and everything that makes for good character and takes in hand the boy's education, nurturing virtue in his own as well as in the boy's soul. This familiar educational function of pederasty, however, is just the beginning of a much longer and more significant journey. No longer is the issue simply one of inculcating noble values socially and culturally useful in this shifting material temporal world, but rather of *transcending* this world altogether, along with its physical bodies and passions. Engendering virtue in one beautiful body should be only the starting point for an ascent of the "ladder of beauty." For the acknowledgment of beauty in one body should rationally lead to the recognition of the beauty in all bodies, as all partake in the abstract form of beauty that allows one to recognize and conceptually identify its presence in material things. At this point the lover will now look down disdainfully on the physical erotic beauty of the one beloved, for all his desire, still presumably charged with the energy of sex, will be for the *idea* of beauty that all beautiful bodies share.[47]

Thus the first rung of the ladder. Next the lover steps from the beauty of bodies to the beauty of souls, then from there to the beauty of laws and customs, then to the beauty of all the branches of knowledge. Every step increases his distance from the "slavery" of an attachment to a "petty" and "cheap" instantiation of beauty. This physical, contingent, material example of beauty now is disdainfully dismissed. The lover who makes it this far in his transcendence of the world in which we happen to live will be vouchsafed a vision of the "sea" of beauty—absolute essential Beauty, immortal and unchanging—of which the various instances of beauty in this world partake. But the final goal is to see that "pure and unmixed" form of Beauty that is not "infected with the flesh and mortal colors and much other mortal nonsense," to see Beauty directly and immediately, not with the body's eyes but with the immaterial rational soul that will ultimately achieve immortality.[48]

The gist of all this is that Diotima has managed to desexualize sex. She uses the metaphors of eros's destructiveness—disease and slavery—to describe not just the disorder of sexuality but the chaos of the material temporal world. The problem with sex, in other words, is that it is physical, bodily, contingent—disorderly. But her attempt to dematerialize sex leaves us with a strange paradox. All the attributes of the divine, absolute, "really" real Beauty that inspires eros are direct opposites of those that define human sex, which is an issue of the body and its passions. Somehow—exactly how remains a mystery—the *energy* of sex has been distilled from the body and given to the rational soul. We see here a vision of same-sex relations light-years from the modern gay experience, in which physical and emotional gratification are seen as central to the couple's relationship—a physical gratification, moreover, that most Greeks would find disgusting. And we find in Plato's homoerotic metaphysics the most extreme instance of the mind's attempt to control the body's most volatile appetite by appropriating and exploiting its energy to fuel the transcendence of this messy, chaotic world of change, suffering—and sex.

The Fancied Sway

We end Part 2 where it started, with a divine reason asserting its power over the formless chaos of the natural world. In the individual, the mind orders and limits the bestial appetites and passions of the soul, directing their energy to ends determined by the rational mind and conducive to its harmony. In the larger social world, projections of the mind, "technologies" exploiting and ordering the energy of nature, work to create a habitable space for human beings, one in which the depredations of a fickle nature are minimized, thus allowing society to flourish. Agriculture is the best model for this activity, altering as it does the natural world to increase and rationalize its fertility. In civic religion, cult and ritual collectively organize the divine forces of fertility both natural and human, subjecting them to political control. Likewise with marriage and pederasty. Just as the dangerous procreative power of women is channeled through marriage into the creation of legitimate children, the future citizens who will inherit the city, so the erotic beauty of boys is subordinated to a social ritual whose goal is the creation of noble and good citizens.

But Plato goes even further. His visions of eros as the fuel propelling the rational soul beyond the contingent world is ultimately unconcerned with the city or society, despite the obligatory nods toward the political utility of knowing the good. His concern is almost salvational: the immortality of the individual soul, soaring in its chariot through the empyrean or swimming in the sea of Beauty. Plato represents the most extreme attempt to conquer a material world of change, decay, and death whose disorder is so frightening—and yet his yearning is betrayed by the central role eros must play in the soul's liberation, the way our blood must be the blood of paradise. And so he takes us back to this book's epitaph from *Don Juan* and its cheeky dismissal of such naive dreaming. The world and the body and their passionate forces, as Byron recognizes, are not so easily controlled, and our "sway" over them is merely imagined. Only in death do we escape the dialectic of mind and body, culture and nature, reason and eros.

Conclusion:
Dissing Eros and Aphrodite

Moonlight and love songs, never out of date,
Hearts full of passion, jealousy and hate,
Woman needs her man, man must have his mate,
This nobody can deny.

                                   —*As Time Goes By*

Romance is mush.

                                   —*Lush Life*

SEXUAL IDEALISM AND SEXUAL PESSIMISM—these are the ancient Greek axes of the grid on which Western attitudes toward sex have been plotted for 2,500 years. Even the developments that received wisdom tells us were most un-Hellenic—the Christian hatred of the sexual body and the modern invention of Romantic Love—have their distant roots in the conceptions and meanings of eros created by a handful of ancient Greeks.

Anyone attending to the Greeks' relentless negative characterizations of sexuality documented in Part 1 will no longer lay the blame for a wary distrust of eros on Christianity. That many still do so results from the longevity of the turn-of-the-century European reaction against the Victorians. Those sunlit pagan Greeks indiscriminately and uninhibitedly delighting in the sexual body were created by late Victorians and Edwardians to be used as sticks with which to beat their "repressed" Victorian fathers and *their* myth of the Greeks as staid marmoreal burghers and honorary Christians. But when the Hellenized Jew Paul says, "It is better to marry than to burn" (I Cor. 7:9), both the thought and the fire metaphor would not have struck either Euripides or Plato as strange, although they might have disagreed about marriage as the best prophylactic against eros's disorder.

Important differences, however, do arise in Christianity. The ascetic ideal of making oneself a eunuch for the kingdom of God's sake, of taming the body until its appetites, especially the sexual, were irrelevant, of refining it in the fire of the will until those physical passions and needs literally disappeared, is one alien to the Greeks. Plato in the *Republic* imagines a superrace of philosophers whose rational minds have absolute control over their appetites—just as his mentor Socrates supposedly had, resisting as he did the seductive wiles of Alcibiades—but those appetites never disappear. Humans are defined by the necessities of bodily drives, needs, and passions, and rational control, not eradication, of them is the best mortals can hope for in this life. And pessimists like Euripides don't admit even the possibility of controlling eros, as the fate of his Hippolytus shows.

Asceticism remained a powerful ideal in Christianity, strewing the deserts of Egypt with hermits and, as late as the Middle Ages, sending long lines of autoflagellants wandering the medieval landscape. But virginal asceticism was always an ideal more honored in the breach than in the observance, too exalted for the silent majority of Christians. Most continued to marry and bear children, following the common sense of Jovinian, the fourth-century former ascetic who denied that celibacy was holier than marriage, rather than his radical critic Jerome, who considered even legal conjugal sexual pleasure fornication. More significant for subsequent Western sexual pessimism was St. Augustine's raising of the stakes of erotic disorder by linking it to the *spiritual* chaos central to the drama of salvation history. For St. Augustine reinterpreted the Fall as resulting in the betrayal of the will and reason to the tyranny of sexual desire. Before the Fall Adam was not a slave to desire. He could even control his erections with his mind and will: "Their [Adam and Eve's] members did not know how to fight against their will."[1] Consequently, sex was relegated strictly to procreation. But the Fall surrendered the soul to the control of sexual desire, every instance of which thus becomes a reminder of the divided soul's alienation from God. The disorder of eros now takes on cosmic dimensions, becomes a sign of the soul's continual disobedience, its fallen nature transmitted to each new generation in the semen discharged in the act of sex.

The Christian drama, however, is a "comedy," not a tragedy. And the happy ending is the result of love—God's love of his creation that leads to his taking on human flesh and dying in expiation of our continual disobedience, thus healing the wounded soul so that its innate love of God can now be fulfilled. This idealization of love in Christianity, though of course redefined as a rarefied asexual "charity," nonetheless retains as in Plato a faint but recognizable sexual charge. The Christian marriage metaphor used to describe the relation of Christ to the church is obviously a sexual one. And what is Dante's vision of Paradise, of souls simultaneously desiring God and having their desire eternally gratified, if not a description of a perpetual spiritual orgasm, infinitely superior to the paltry pleasures of the flesh, whose desire and gratification are mutually exclusive, the one killing the other? As in Diotima's vision, the intense pleasure of sexual gratification has been filched from the body and given to the immaterial soul—as though that pleasure could ever be separated from the flesh and its nerves and hormones.

Here, in a Christian sexual idealism influenced by Platonism, is one origin of Romantic Love that locates this supposedly new idealization of eros in earlier Greek thinking. The originators of so-called Courtly Love in twelfth-century southern France and their subsequent imitators borrowed Christianity's idealized erotic structure and its vision of love's salvational power but substituted for God the Lady, before whom the knight groveled and to whom he prayed for the improvement of his soul, "Dumbly adoring her, / Humbly imploring her," as the troubadour Bernard de Ventadour put it.[2] It was scandalously—and arousingly—blasphemous. And the presence of a flesh-and-blood, tangible Lady now meant that the body and physical passion were restored to erotic idealism, the worshipped Lady simultaneously Beatrice, Dante's lady who in the *Divine Comedy* symbolized God's wisdom, and Francesca, who was Dante's epitome of carnal lust. The result was an exciting tension between the lust of the flesh and the spiritually improving power of love, a circling dance of body and soul, flesh and spirit, in which the intensity and quality of desire, rather than of sex, became the goal—as in the fifteen-year ordeal of the harelipped thirteenth-century knight and courtly exemplar Ulrich von Lichtenstein, who chopped off his finger, waded in a lake, and was thrown from a window before his lady deigned to let him (maybe) enjoy her favors. What drove Ulrich was the "love of love," the lust for the *feelings* of sexual desire, rather than for the necessarily deflating letdown of sexual consummation.

The origins of this strange cultural ideal that so influenced our own attitudes are of course manifold, from Islamic love poetry to Celtic vegetation myths to Manichean heresy. But the combination of intense physical desire with a spiritually improving erotic power, the paradox of sexual energy without physical sexual gratification, goes back to Plato. And the idea that eros can make the soul more noble and brave or propel it to a vision of ultimate reality resembles the pedagogical function of eros in ancient pederasty. It is something of a paradox that Romantic Love, the great modern heterosexual myth, is ultimately homosexual in origins.

So neither Christianity nor Romantic Love gave the West any brand-new ideas about eros but elaborated on assumptions first recognized by the Greeks. Likewise with the two modern intellectual movements that profoundly shaped and continue to shape our world. The Enlightenment's ideal of rational understanding and mastery over the forces of nature was, of course, a rebirth of Greek rationalism. If the world is mere matter in motion, an intricate machine following rational laws, then eros too can be identified, analyzed, and ultimately controlled. Kraft-Ebbing's *Psychopathia Sexualis*, with its Latinate taxonomy of the exotic flora and fauna of human sexual deviancy, embodies these pretensions. And Freud does too, though his thought is riven by the contradiction between an almost Euripidean acknowledgment of eros's irredeemable destructiveness and a faith in the power of therapeutic technology to rechannel sexual energy into the personally and socially useful work of maturity.

The other shaping movement of the modern era, Romanticism, continues the idealization of eros found in Courtly Love. Now, however, it is connected to the radical individualist quest for meaning and autonomy to be discovered in the quality and intensity of emotional experience. Eros becomes the liberating force of the individual, the breaker of repressive social bonds that chain the individual's unique sensibility to the dreary morality of middle-class culture and its life-denying rationalism. Goethe's Werther is the first modern example of sexual passion as the validator of a superior sensibility, of an Aeolian harp so sensitively tuned that the force of passion destroys it even as eros inspires its most beautiful music. No reader of *The Sorrows of the Young Werther* would rather be the dull prig Albert, with his torpid Hellenic sermons against excess, than the incandescent Werther dying of love for Lotte. Even the destructiveness of eros, seemingly suggested by Werther's madness and suicide, in the end serves to deepen and charge with a stirring pathos the exquisite feeling, the depths of his soul Werther reveals to a swooning Lotte. Indeed, suffering and death in Romantic literature become important intensifiers of erotic feeling. This sexualization of terror will dominate the Gothic, the old Greek linking of sex and death that once signified the destructiveness of eros now serving to heighten the sexual charge.

Our own contemporary attitudes in America have become a confused welter of the contradictions wrought by these various historical antecedents. Sexual pessimism is decidedly out of fashion today, at least in our public discourse. Only Christian fundamentalists still rail against the evils of eros, unenlightened avatars from the sexual stone age who suffer from "repression" and so drape their fear of sex in the grim robes of Christianity, à la Jim Bakker and Jimmy Swaggert—or so most of the so-called "sexually liberated" imagine. But sexual pessimism has surfaced as well in some unlikely venues. The "recovered memory" fad, in which long-repressed memories of childhood sexual abuse resurface in therapy, is driven in part by the old view of sex as the root of all evil. The date-rape hysteria often reflects as well the ancient fear of eros as much as it addresses real social pathologies. Young college girls, raised with naive sexual idealism, confront the frightening, dark possibilities of eros in themselves and in men and recoil in fear, retreating into the radical feminist cant of patriarchal oppression, the ideological magic wand that can by the next morning turn otherwise consensual sexual intercourse with an insensitive, predatory, and rude partner into "rape." Thus young women preserve their sexual idealism. Since mainstream culture gives them no vocabulary with which to talk about the threatening mystery of sex or the dangers of surrendering the intellect to passion, feminist ideology fills the void, scattering bluelit emergency phones across America's universities where rape is much less prevalent than in other environments.

This same fear of erotic power drives as well the feminist attack on pornography. By definition and intent "porn" reduces sex to its bare physical minimum of groping, rubbing, and ejaculation, to an assertion of bestial appetite even sophisticated intellectuals cannot bear to confront when they are armed only with the frail shield of sexual idealism or therapeutic scientism. Hence they attribute female powerlessness and victimization and objectification to a medium in which *everybody*, male and female, gay and straight, is dehumanized and in which women most often are shown wielding all the frightening sexual force the old Greek jurymen recognized in the bared breasts of the courtesan Phryne, "attendant and expounder" of Aphrodite.

But mostly our attitudes reflect various modes of sexual idealism, all of which are profoundly, and dangerously, disrespectful of Eros's and Aphrodite's power. The Enlightenment dream lives on in the research of sexologists who still look upon eros as a natural force like electricity or gravity, to be quantified and anatomized and analyzed and ultimately tamed with knowledge and technology, whether they study sex as a physiological or a psychological phenomenon. "Undoubtedly, the future will bring major progress in our understanding of the mechanisms and development of sexuality," Simon LeVay confidently asserts, begging the question of just how much good this knowledge will bring us when we are storm-tossed on the sea of eros.[3] Soon the breakthrough will come, the liberating knowledge will surface in the research institute, and the technological intervention—whether chemical or therapeutic—will vault us all into a sexual paradise in which the dark side of eros will disappear in the bright light of science. Hence the shelf after shelf of self-help sex manuals like *The Joy of Sex*, crammed with techniques and recipes for the perfect orgasm, the guilt-free liberating affair, the mastery of sex akin to expertise in tennis or sales. But eros, that "unspeakable evil thing," as Apollonius of Rhodes calls it, is more frighteningly mysterious, more darkly complex; it lurks beyond the reach of mere reason and science, not with impunity to be trivialized into sport or recreation.

Then there are the pitiful remnants of Romantic Love, mass-produced in the debasing images of advertising and pop music and movies and supermarket Gothic romance. There the age-old dreams of eros as "therapeutic energy"[4] for the fulfillment of the self, the expression of a genuine personal identity that has been stunted by the grim repressive rules of society, are tarted up and commodified and put to the service of consumer culture. The sleek gamine lounging by the BMW, the buff stud pouting in his Calvin Klein underwear, the MTV diva grinding her hips in minutely calculated choreography, the dreary predictable rhymes of pop crooners, the countless happy endings of countless movies, like *Pretty Woman* with its fairy-tale prostitute, in which eros is an instrument for sweeping away the impediments to the marriage of true hearts and minds: All are oblivious to the destructive power of eros, its madness and disease, violence and fire. No better was the sixties dream of political liberation through sexual license, the naive belief that sexual democracy and freedom would create their political equivalents. This dream was a barely more sophisticated version of the wacky Wilhelm Reich's beliefs that sexual liberation would cure heart disease and leukemia, clean up smog, and end inner-city crime. The sixties dream found its realization in the frantic promiscuity of the gay bathhouse, the onetime sexual "city on a hill" now quickly becoming a necropolis. As Camille Paglia says, everybody who preached free love is responsible for AIDS, grim Eros's answer to sexual idealism. Nor should heterosexuals feel smug—they have herpes, genital warts, new strains of syphilis, gonorrhea, and chlamydia, not to mention the psychological costs of our so-called "sexual liberation."

Finally there is the quaint idea of Romantic Marriage, the strange belief that marriage—a social institution invented by culture for the benefit of society and the children it must absorb—can somehow be private and personal, a validation of the couple's passion, meaningful in its own unique terms. Euripides in the *Medea* put that illusion to rest: Not even the powerful structure of ancient Greek marriage was able to withstand the force of Medea's sexual rage. How much more frail a prop, then, is modern American marriage—predicated on romantic idealism and weakened by the dissolution of the taboos against adultery, divorce, and illegitimacy—for supporting the eventual disillusionment romance must suffer after the knight has shared a bathroom with his lady, after the lady has heard her knight flatulating in his Barcalounger. The old troubadours knew better. That's why there were very few examples of courtly love between husband and wife and why sexual consummation was so often delayed or forgone altogether—to avoid the contempt sexual familiarity eventually breeds. Romance demands a willing suspension of disbelief, a misty distance requiring heroic efforts if one is to maintain it in the quotidian, scruffy intimacy of marriage and childrearing. Homer's "like-mindedness," the shared qualities and values underlying Penelope and Odysseus's marriage, is a much more sensible foundation for conjugal bliss than are shifting sands of passion.

So it is that we, who have abandoned shame and who ridicule tradition, are deaf to the wisdom of the Greeks, blithely failing to respect Aphrodite's and Eros's power. Our scientists and therapists scorn Aphrodite and her son, believing them to be mere physical forces soon to fall beneath the sway of knowledge, to be more finely calibrated and mapped in the circuits of the brain. The advertiser and the screenwriter and the pop lyricist keep peddling their heap of broken images, promising us fulfillment and happiness if only we can achieve the orgasm born in our imaginations—and in the cars and perfumes, the records and videos that are supposed to arouse us. All of them slight the dark chaos of eros, its destructive power that left the plains of Troy strewn with corpses or murdered Medea's children or kept the suitors bound to their fates in Odysseus's halls. Nor do we believe any longer in the strong social and cultural institutions, the "technologies" of ritual or marriage, that the Greeks cultivated to contain and exploit that natural force. Indeed, our cultural ideals and institutions are saturated with Romantic sentimentalism and Enlightenment arrogance, an unholy alliance inciting us to a profound disrespect for and trivialization of eros, a disrespect whose wages we now see in illegitimacy and its frequent effects—crime, random violence, poverty, and social barbarism. About the only voice these days warning of eros's power is that of Camille Paglia, who continues the tradition of Sade, Nietzsche, Lawrence, and Freud that recognizes the "cruel energies"[5] of eros that society must contain and channel. But the defensive resistance to her message reflects just how ingrained our worn-out sexual idealism is, even among our supposedly more sophisticated intelligentsia. No wonder Christian fundamentalist and New Age feminist alike find her sermon terrifying.

In July 1995 Susan Smith was convicted of strapping her two little boys into their carseats and then rolling the vehicle into a lake, drowning them. In her confession Smith told the world why she did what she did: "I was in love with someone very much," someone who didn't want her extra baggage of children. The media examined Smith's life to discover what possibly could have driven her to such a crime, and the media rounded up the usual suspects sanctioned by our therapeutic society: two adolescent suicide attempts, a father who killed himself when she was six, a stepfather who had been molesting her since she was fifteen, a string of affairs. But if, like Aristophanes' Dionysus in the *Frogs*, we could journey to Hades and question the shade of Euripides about this crime, perhaps he would merely shrug and quote the Chorus of his compatriot Sophocles' *Electra*—"Eros was the killer."

Abbreviations

MODERN EDITIONS

C	D.A. Campbell, *Greek Lyric* (London and Cambridge, Mass., 1982–1993)
DK	Hermann Diels and Walther Kranz, *Die Fragmente der Vorsokratiker* (Berlin, 1960)
E	J.M. Edmonds, *Greek Elegy and Iambus* (London and Cambridge, Mass., 1931)
E-W	Hugh G. Evelyn-White, *Hesiod, the Homeric Hymns, and Homerica* (London and Cambridge, Mass., 1914)
FrGrH	Felix Jacoby, *Die Fragmente Grieschischen Historiker* (1922; Leiden, 1968)
GA	W.R. Paton, *The Greek Anthology* (London and Cambridge, Mass., 1916–1918)
K	Theodor Kock, *Comicorum Atticorum Fragmenta* (Leipzig, 1880–1888)
N	August Nauck, *Tragicorum Graecorum fragmenta. Supplementum continens nova fragmenta Euripidea et Adespota apud Scriptores Veteres reperta, adiecit Bruno Snell* (Hildesheim, 1964)
P	J.U. Powell, *Collecteana Alexandrina* (1925; Oxford, 1970)
PMG	D.L. Page, *Poetae Melici Graeci* (Oxford, 1962)
S	Sir John Sandys, *The Odes of Pindar* (London and Cambridge, Mass., 1919)
T	C.A. Trypanis, *Callimachus* (London and Cambridge, Mass., 1975)
W	M.C. West, *Iambi et Elegi Graeci*, 2d ed. (Oxford, 1989)

ANCIENT AUTHORS AND WORKS

A.	Aeschylus	
	A.	*Agamemnon*
	Ch.	*Libation Bearers*
	Eu.	*Eumenides*
	Pr.	*Prometheus Bound*
	Supp.	*Suppliants*
	Th.	*Seven Against Thebes*
Achae.	Achaeus	
Acus.	Acusilaus	
Adesp.	Anonymous	
Ael.	Aelian	
	NA	*The Nature of Animals*
Aeschin.	Aeschines	
Alc.	Alcaeus	

Alc. Mess.	Alcaeus of Messenia
Alcm.	Alcman
Alex.	Alexis
Anacr.	Anacreon
Anaxandr.	Anaxandrides
Antag.	Antagoras
Antipho.	Antiphon the Sophist
Antiph.	Antiphanes
Antip. Sid.	Antipater of Sidon
Antip. Thess.	Antipater of Thessalonika
Antisth.	Antisthenes
Apollod.	Apollodorus
Apollod. Com.	Apollodorus Comicus
A.R.	Apollonius of Rhodes
Ar.	Aristophanes

	Ach.	*Acharnians*
	Av.	*Birds*
	Ec.	*Women at the Assembly*
	Eq.	*Knights*
	Lys.	*Lysistrata*
	Nu.	*Clouds*
	Pax	*Peace*
	Pl.	*Wealth*
	Ra.	*Frogs*
	Th.	*Women at the Thesmophoria*
	V.	*Wasps*

Arch.	Archias
Archil.	Archilochus
Arist.	Aristotle

	Ath.	*Constitution of the Athenians*
	de An.	*On the Soul*
	EE	*Eudemian Ethics*
	EN	*Nichomachean Ethics*
	GA	*Generation of Animals*
	HA	*History of Animals*
	Metaph.	*Metaphysics*
	MM	*Magna Moralia*
	Ph.	*Physics*
	Pol.	*Politics*
	Pr.	*Problems*
	Rh.	*Rhetoric*
	Somn. Vig.	*On Dreams*

[Arist.]	pseudo-Aristotle

	Oec.	*Economics*
	Phgn.	*Physiognomy*

Asclep.	Asclepiades
Ath.	Athenaeus

Aug.	St. Augustine
	C.D. *City of God*
Autom.	Automedon
Axionic.	Axionicus
B.	Bacchylides
Call.	Callimachus
	Aet. *Aetia*
	Ap. *Hymn to Apollo*
	Epgr. *Epigrams*
	Iamb. *Iambi*
Canthar.	Cantharus
Carm. Conviv.	*Drinking Songs*
Cerc.	Cercidas
Chaerem.	Chaeremon
Cic.	Cicero
	N.D. *On the Nature of the Gods*
	Tusc. Disp. *Tusculan Disputations*
Chrysipp. Stoic.	Chrysippus the Stoic
Cypr.	*Cypria*
Clearch.	Clearchus
Cratin.	Cratinus
D.	Demosthenes
[D.]	pseudo-Demosthenes
Democr.	Democritus
Dicaeog.	Dicaeogenes
Diocl.	Diocles
Diog. Apoll.	Diogenes Apolloniates
Diosc.	Dioscorides
D.L.	Diogenes Laertius
D.S.	Diodorus Siculus
E.	Euripides
	Alc. *Alcestis*
	Andr. *Andromache*
	Ba. *Bacchae*
	Cyc. *Cyclops*
	El. *Electra*
	Hec. *Hecuba*
	Hel. *Helen*
	Heracl. *Children of Hercules*
	HF *Hercules Mad*
	Hipp. *Hippolytus*
	IA *Iphigeneia at Aulis*
	Ion *Ion*
	IT *Iphigeneia Among the Taurians*
	Med. *Medea*
	Or. *Orestes*
	Ph. *Phoenician Women*

	Supp.	*Suppliants*
	Tr.	*Trojan Women*
Emp.	Empedocles	
Ephor.	Ephorus	
Epich.	Epicharmus	
Epicur.	Epicurus	
Epigr.	Epigram	
Eub.	Eubulus	
Eup.	Eupolis	
Even.	Evenus	
Gorg.	Gorgias	
h. Cer.	*Homeric Hymn to Demeter*	
h. Merc.	*Homeric Hymn to Hermes*	
h. Ven.	*Homeric Hymn to Aphrodite*	
Hdt.	Herodotus	
Hedy.	Hedylus	
Hellanic.	Hellanicus	
Hermesian.	Hermesianax	
Hermipp.	Hermippus	
Heraclit.	Heraclitus	
Herod.	Herodas	
Hes.	Hesiod	
	Op.	*Works and Days*
	Th.	*Theogony*
Hier.	St. Jerome	
	Adv. Jov.	*Against Jovinian*
Hippon.	Hipponax	
Hom.	Homer	
	Il.	*Iliad*
	Od.	*Odyssey*
Hp.	Hippocrates	
	Epid.	*Epidemics*
Ibyc.	Ibycus	
	Dithy.	Dithyrambs
Il. Parv.	*Little Iliad*	
Il. Pers.	*Sack of Ilium*	
Ion Lyr.	Ion of Chios, Lyrics	
Isoc.	Isocrates	
Is.	Isaeus	
Leon.	Leonidas	
Lyc.	Lycophron	
Lychophronid.	Lycophronides	
Lys.	Lysias	
Mel.	Meleager	
Men.	Menander	
	Asp.	*Shield*
	Dys.	*Dyskolos*

Metag.	Metagenes
Mimn.	Mimnermus
Mosch.	Moschus
Myrin.	Myrinus
Nicharch.	Nicharchus
Ovid	Ovid
	Am. *Amores*
Parm.	Parmenides
Paus.	Pausanias
Phan.	Phanocles
Pherecr.	Pherecrates
Pherecyd. Syr.	Pherecydes of Syria
Philem.	Philemon
Philetaer.	Philetaerus
Philet.	Philetas of Samos
Philol.	Philolaus
Phld.	Philodemus
Phoc.	Phocylides
Pi.	Pindar
	O. *Olympian Odes*
	P. *Pythian Odes*
Pl.	Plato
	Alc I *Alcibiades I*
	Ap. *Apology*
	Chrm. *Charmides*
	Cra. *Cratylus*
	Ep. *Letters*
	Euthd. *Euthydemus*
	Grg. *Gorgias*
	La. *Laches*
	Lg. *Laws*
	Ly. *Lysis*
	Mx. *Menexenus*
	Men. *Meno*
	Phd. *Phaedo*
	Phdr. *Phaedrus*
	Phlb. *Philebus*
	Prt. *Protagoras*
	R. *Republic*
	Smp. *Symposium*
	Tht. *Theaetetus*
	Ti. *Timaeus*
[Pl.]	pseudo-Plato
	Ax. *Axiochus*
Pl. Com.	Plato Comicus
Plin.	Pliny
	Nat. *Natural History*

Plu.	Plutarch	
	Alc.	*Life of Alcibiades*
	Alex.	*Life of Alexander*
	Lyc.	*Life of Lycurgus*
	Per.	*Life of Pericles*
	Thes.	*Life of Theseus*
Polystr.	Polystratus	
Posidip.	Posidippus	
Prodic.	Prodicus	
Rhian.	Rhianus	
S.	Sophocles	
	Aj.	*Ajax*
	Ant.	*Antigone*
	El.	*Electra*
	O.C.	*Oedipus at Colonus*
	O.T.	*Oedipus the King*
	Tr.	*Women of Trachis*
Sapph.	Sappho	
Semon.	Semonides	
S.E.	Sextus Empiricus	
Simon.	Simonides	
Sol.	Solon	
Stesich.	Stesichorus	
Str.	Strabo	
Th.	Thucydides	
Theoc.	Theocritus	
Theophil.	Theophilus	
Theopomp. Hist.	Theopompus	
Thgn.	Theognis	
Thphr.	Theophrastus	
Timae.	Timaeus	
Timocl.	Timocles	
X.	Xenophon	
	Ages.	*Agesilaus*
	An.	*Anabasis*
	Cyr.	*Cyropaidia*
	Lac.	*Constitution of the Spartans*
	Hier.	*Hiero*
	Mem.	*Memorabilia*
	Oec.	*Estate Management*
	Smp.	*Symposium*
Xenarch.	Xenarchos	
Xenoph.	Xenophanes	

Notes

A full citation for modern works also cited in the Critical Bibliography will be found there.

PREFACE

1. Winkler, *The Constraints of Desire*, 45.
2. Winkler, 19.
3. In "Manners, Morals, and the Novel," 200.
4. Green, "Sex and Classical Literature," 130.
5. Bernard Knox, "The Oldest Dead White European Males," in *The Oldest Dead White European Males* (New York, 1993), 33–34.
6. Maynard Mack, *Everybody's Shakespeare* (Lincoln, Neb., 1993), ix.

INTRODUCTION

1. Hdt. 3.38, trans. de Sélincourt.
2. Eup. Fr. 91K; E. *Hec.* 599–600; Th. 3.82; Antipho. DK 87 Fr. 44; E. Fr. 920N.
3. Cic. *N.D.* 2.81–82.
4. Critias DK 88 Fr. 25; [D].25.15; Pl. *Ti.* 46c-d.
5. Camille Paglia is one of the few modern writers who understands nature in these terms: "Society is an artificial construction, a defense against nature's power. Without society, we would be storm-tossed on the barbarous sea that is nature," in *Sexual Personae*, 1.
6. Nicharch. GA 9.330; *Od.* 5.63–73, 171–79; *h. Cer.* 5–10.
7. *Eoiae* 19E-W; E. *Ion* 887–96; Ibyc. Fr. 286C; Theoc. *Idylls* 5.87; 13.39–42; A. *A.* 741.
8. E. *Ba.* 677–768.
9. *Od.* 9.191–92, 9.215, 9.414, 9.383–94.
10. A. *Eu.* 905–08, trans. Lattimore.
11. A. *Pr.* 437–504; Pl. Com. Fr. 136K; S. *Ant.* 332; other passages describing progress in these terms include E. *Supp.* 201–13; Moschion Fr. 6N; Critias DK 88 Fr. 25; Pl. *Prt.* 320c ff.; cf. also X. *Mem.* 1.4.13.

CHAPTER 1

1. A.R. 3.111–66.
2. Hes. *Th.* 116–20; Acus. DK 9 Fr. 1; Fr. 198C; Alc. Fr. 327C; Fr. 575C. See also Acus. DK 9 Fr. 3; Parm. DK 28 Fr. 13; Antag. apud D.L. 4.28; Pl. *Smp.* 178b, 203b; Theoc. 3.15; Mel. GA 5.177.

3. E. *Hipp.* 1274–80; X. *Smp.* 8.1; *Lg.* 644e; E. Fr. 430N, Fr. 136N. See also Archil. Fr. 124E, Pl. *Smp.* 186b, S. *Tr.* 443, *Ant.* 781, E. Frs. 816N, 895N, 269N; Philem. Fr. 479K, B. 9.72; Achae. Fr. 6N; Adesp. Fr. 186N; Call. GA 12.150; Crates Fr. 17K; Men. Frs. 235K; 449K, 209K.

4. E.g., *Il.* 1.469, 24.227.

5. *A.* 341–42; *Ba.* 812.

6. Hdt. 5.32; Th. 6.24; Isoc. 10.22; also A. *Th.* 688; E. *IT* 1172, *Med.* 700, *Supp.* 137, *Alc.* 715, *Ion* 67, Adesp. Fr. 129N, Agatho Fr. 7N, Th. 2.43.

7. *Il.* 14.316.

8. E.g., *Il.* 23.655, *Od.* 4.637, *Il.* 18.432.

9. *Od.* 6.109, 228; Sapph. Fr. 102C. Also Hes. *Th.* 122, Pi. *O.* 1.41, S. *Tr.* 432, Thgn. 1350, 1308, Anacr. Fr. 357C. Adesp. GA 5. 168.

10. A.R. 3.275–98, trans. R.C. Seaton (London and New York, 1930).

11. *Il.* 17.737–39.

12. Prodic. DK 84 Fr. 7. Philosophers of all stripes characterize sexual passion as madness. See, e.g., Pl. *Smp.* 213d, *R.* 403a; Arist. *EN* 1147a, 1152b, *EE* 1229a; Gorg. DK 82 Fr. 11.19; Chrysipp. Stoic. apud D.L. 7.113; Epicur. apud D.L. 10.118.

13. *Hipp.* 38, 141–44, 203–31, 214, 232, 241.

14. Pi. *P.* 2.26; Theoc. 2.48–51; Arist. *HA* 572a, 577a; Theoc. 2.136; Fr. 446C. Also "woman-crazy," Hom. *Il.* 3.39; Archil. Fr. 103E: passion "stole his soft brains"; Sapph. Fr. 1.18C: the poet prays for relief for her "maddened heart"; cf. also A. *Supp.* 109–11; S. *Tr.* 988–99, 1142; Anacr. Fr. 359C, 398C, Herod. 1.57–60.

15. *Il.* 19.137, 91.

16. Pi. *P.* 3.24; Thgn. 1231; *Il. Pers.* Fr. 1E-W, also E. *Tr.* 77.

17. A.R. 3.798, 4.62, 4.412.

18. *Od.* 12.40–46, 18.21; *Ba.* 404, Adesp. 3P; *Tr.* 354–55; A.R. 3.4, 86. Also A. *Pr.* 865, E. *Hipp.* 1274.

19. S. *Tr.* 582–87; also Apollod. 2.7.6.

20. E. Fr. 433N; Pi. *P.* 4.216; Adesp. GA 5.205; cf. X. *Mem.* 3.11.12.

21. Theoc. 2.18–62, 2.159–60, Theoc. 2.12–13; A.R. 3.251, 738 E. *Med.* 395–97.

22. Pi. Fr. 123S; Theoc. 1.66, 82; A.R. 3.1019–21. See also Ibyc. Fr. 282(xiv)C; A. *Pr.* 590; Theoc. 7.76–77, 11.14, 14.26; Asclep. GA 5.210; Mel. GA 12.72.

23. *Od.* 18.158–61; A. *A.* 1204, cf. *Il.* 3.362. Also Sappho Fr. 31.6C: passion "shakes my heart"; Fr. 47C: "Eros shook my heart like wind attacking mountain oaks"; E. *Med.* 639–40: the Chorus sings "never may a terrible Aphrodite strike my heart with passion for a strange bed."

24. *Ba.* 221–25; *Ion* 550–52; Men. Fr. 920K.

25. E. *Ph.* 21–22; Anacr. Fr. 376C; also 389C.

26. *Am.* 1.9.21–26; Pl. *Smp.* 193d; S. *Ant.* 781.

27. *Il.* 1.113–15, 9.336, 19.297–98.

28. S. *El.* 197, 562; A. *A.* 1446–47.

29. Hdt. 1.1–5; Duris apud Athen. 560d; Ar. *Ach.* 526–28; Pl. *Phd.* 66c.

30. Ar. *Lys.* 250–51, 254ff, 424–30, 430–32.

31. Lyc. 999–1001.

32. Archil. Fr. 103 E; *Il.* 16.344; A.R. 3.962–63.

33. *Il.* 13.412; *Od.* 18.212; *Od.* 18.238; *Od.* 14.69.

34. Hes. *Th.* 120–22; Sapph. Fr. 130C; also: Alcm. Fr. 3.61C; Archil. Fr. 85E; Metag. Fr. 4K; Hedy. GA 11.414.

35. Alc. 380 C; Alc. Fr. 287 C; Ar. *Ec.* 963–64; *Hipp.* 527, 542.

36. E. *HF* 160–61; *Il.* 3.29–37; *Il.* 4.104 ff.

37. Th. 4.50; E. Fr. 161 N.

38. Plu. *Alex.* 63; Hp. *Epid.* 5.98, trans. Guido Majno, *The Healing Hand* (Cambridge, Mass., 1975), 193; Hp. *Epid.* 5.47; *Il.* 4.151–52.

39. Archil. Fr. 84E; *Il.* 5.399.

40. A. *Supp.* 1003–05; cf. too *Pr.* 649; *Med.* 632–34; *IA* 548–51; *Tr.* 577ff, 672ff, 749ff. Also Pi. *P.* 4.213; Anacr. Fr. 445C; Simon. Epigr. 56C; A. *A.* 741; B. Epigr. 10.42–43; E. *Tr.* 255, *Hipp.* 530–34.

41. Apud Ath. 534e; Pl. *Smp.* 219b; Pl. *Alc.* 7; Theoc. 23.5; A.R. 3.279; *Il.* 15.451.

42. A.R. 3.286–87; Mel. GA 5.214, GA 12.76. Other arrow images can be found at Theoc. 2.82, 3.17, 7.118, 11.16; A.R. 3.26–27, 3.153, 3.764–75; Hermesian. Fr. 7.64P; Leon. GA 5.188; Posidip. GA 12.45; Phld. GA 5.124; Asclep. GA 5.189, 5.194; Mel. GA 12.109, 12.144, 5.177, 12.48, 12.49, 12.47, and many more.

43. A. *Pr.* 649–50; Sapph. Fr. 31.9–10; A.R. 3.296–97; *Il.* 5.461.

44. Mel. GA 12.63, GA 12.110.

45. Mel. GA 12.119, GA 5.160. Erotic fire imagery abounds in Greek poetry and prose. Pindar's Medea is "burning in her mind" with passion for Jason, *P.* 4.219; Heracles is "kindled with desire" for Iole, S. *Tr.* 368. See also Thgn. 1359–60; A. Fr. 243N; S. Frs. 153N, 320N, 433N; Pl. *Chrm.* 155d; X. *Mem.* 1.3.9, *Smp.* 4.24, *Cyr.* 5.1.16; Theoc. 3.17, 7.56, 7.102, 23.24, among many; Call. *Ap.* 42, also *Epgr.* 27, 45, *Aet.* Fr. 67.2, *Iamb.* 195.23; Hermesian. Fr. 7.91P; Phld. GA 5.124, 131; Posidip. GA 5.211; Leon. GA 5.188, Asclep. GA 5.209; Mosch. 1.22–23.

46. E. *Alc.* 788–91; Ath. 512e; Ath. 556f, also Paus. 9.27.6.

47. S. *Tr.* 431–33.

48. *Tr.* 445, 544, 767–87, 1053–56.

49. Sapph. Fr. 1.3–4C, Fr. 31C; Theoc. 2.82–90, 2.106–10.

50. *Hipp.* 131–32, 765–66.

51. *Smp.* 207a; *Lg.* 714a; *Tim.* 91b, 86d, 73c.

52. Other examples of erotic disease imagery: E. *Med.* 1364, Frs. 400N, 428N; Democr. DK 68 Fr. 32; Eub. Fr. 67K, 41K; Theoc. 11.69, 14.3–6, 23.24, 30.1; Call. *Epgr.* 32; Men. Fr. 541K.

53. *Il.* 15.381–83; Hes. *Op.* 687, 236–37, 247: Cf. Archil. Fr. 97aE, where the two worst evils the poet can wish on an enemy are shipwreck and slavery; Alc. Fr. 6C.

54. Ibyc. Fr. 286C; *Hipp.* 315, 767–68; Cerc. Fr. 5P.

55. GA 10.21; Thgn. 457–60; apud D.L. 3.31. For other sailing/sea imagery see Anacr. Fr. 413C, 403C; Ion Lyr. Fr. 744C; Pi. Fr. 123S; Asclep. GA 5.209, Adesp. GA 5.53; Theoc. 3.42; Men. Fr. 536K, Adesp. GA 12.156.

56. Ar. *Lys.* 59–60; Ar. *Ec.* 38–40; Diosc. GA 5.54; E. *Tr.* 159–60. See also Pl. Com. Fr. 3K, Theophil. Fr. 6K, Autom. GA 11.29, Mel. GA 5.204.

57. Mel. GA 12.157, GA 5.190, GA 5.156.

58. X. *Mem.* 1.3.9–1.4.

59. Arist. *Pr.* 880a, *EN* 1118a; Sapph. Fr. 130C; Pl. *Smp.* 4.28, *Ti.* 70d.

60. Plu. *Th.* 30.

61. Anacr. Fr. 417C; Ar. Fr. 703K. Other equine erotic metaphors at Thgn. 1267–70, 1249; Eub. Fr. 193K; Anacr. Fr. 360C, 346C; Hermesian. Fr. 7.83–84P; Mel. GA 12.158.

62. *Hipp.* 1219–41; Call. *Iamb.* Fr. 195T.

63. *Od.* 19.447–54.

64. Ibyc. Fr. 287C; X. *Mem.* 2.1.4; Rhian. GA 12.146; Theoc. 23.10; Mel. GA 12.92. Other hunt imagery: Dicaeog. Fr. 1N; Lyc. 405, 104; Mel. GA 5.177; Mosch. 6.7; E. *Ba.* 459; Pl. *Chrm.* 155d, *Phdr.* 241d; Theoc. 8.56, 27.17. Passion as "birdlime," a substance used to catch birds: Adesp. GA 5.100, Mel. GA 5.96; Rhian. GA 12.93.

65. Pl. *Ap.* 30e; A. *Pr.* 640–86, 877–86.

66. *Ba.* 795; Simon. Fr. 541C; Pl. *Ti.* 91b-c.

67. A.R. 3.275–77, trans. Seaton. The goad/gadfly image for sexual and other appetites is very common. See also A. *Supp.* 109–11; E. *IA* 547, *Hipp.* 39, 1300; Pl. *R.* 573a; Lyc. 405; Herod. 1.57–60; Adesp. GA 10.120.

68. Anacr. Fr. 346[2]C, Fr. 396C; S. *Tr.* 441–42.

69. Pl. *Smp.* 217c; S. Fr. 855.13N; *Hipp.* 5–6.

70. Arist. *Pol.* 1254b.

71. Anacr. Fr. 346[2]C; Arist. *Pol.* 1253b; Pl. *Phdr.* 258e.

72. X. *Mem.* 4.5.3–5; D.L. 6.66. Other examples of passion as enslaving: Pl. *Smp.* 183a, *Lg.* 838d, *Ep.* 7, 335b; X. *Mem.* 1.3.9, *Cyr.* 5.1.12; Adesp. GA 5.100, GA 12.160; Men. Fr. 611K.

73. Sol. Fr. 32E; Arist. *Pol.* 1295a.

74. E. Fr. 136N; *Hipp.* 538–44; Pl. *R.* 577c-e, *R.* 573d; apud Pl. *R.* 329c.

75. A.R. 4.445–47. Examples: *schetlion*: Simon. Fr. 575C, *h. Ven.* 225, Thgn. 1231; "awesome, terrible": Alc. Fr. 327C, S. Fr. 781N, E. *Hipp.* 28, *Eoiai* 76, S. *Tr.* 476, E. Fr. 850N, 1054N, Mel. GA 5.176; "harsh": Sapph. Fr. 1.25–26C, Thgn. 1337, 1308, 1332, 1384, Chaerem. Fr. 787N, Call. *Epgr.* 32T; "bitter": Pl. apud D.L. 3.29, E. *Hipp.* 727, Theoc. 1.93, Asclep. GA 12.50, Bion 10.7; "violent, heavy": Eub. 178K, 41K, Aristopho Fr. 280K, Alc. Mess. GA 5.10; "pain": Sapph. Fr. 172C, Thgn. 1323, 1295, 1338; E. *Hipp.* 775, 348, Fr. 136N, Pl. *Phlb.* 47e, Theoc. 3.12, 2.39, Mosch. 6.7; "oppressive": Eub. Fr. 41K, Theoc. 3.15, Mel. GA 12.48; "rough": A.R. 1.613; "cruel": A.R. 3.296–97, Mosch. 7.2; "remorseless": Call. *Epgr.* 47.10; "wild": Mel. GA 5.177, GA 5.178, Bion 10.5; "sharp": Call. *Aet.* Fr. 75, Pl. *R.* 403a; "man-slaughtering": Diosc. GA 12.37.

76. In *Life Against Death* (Middletown, Conn., 1959), 308.

77. *Eros and Civilization* (Boston, Mass., 1955), 197.

CHAPTER 2

1. *h. Ven.* 5.182–90.

2. S. Fr. 855N; E. Fr. 26N; *h. Ven.* 153–54.

3. *h. Ven.* 5.1–6. Other statements of Aphrodite's power: Hom *Il.* 14.199, E. *Hipp.* 1–6, 1280–82, Fr. 898N, 648N, S. *Tr.* 498, Fr. 855.9–12N. E. *Hipp.* 360–61; Hdt. 1.105; Mimn. Fr. 22E, Lyc. 612–15; A.R. 1.609–19; E. *Hipp.* 6.

4. Paus. 8.6.5; Phryne: Paus. 10.15.1; Athen. 588c, 590e.

5. *Il.* 5.349, 3.405; *Il.* 14.217: For Aphrodite's cunning cf. also Sapph. Fr. 1C, Alc. Fr. 42C, Simon. Frs. 541C, 575C; Thgn. 1386; B. 5.175C; A. *Supp.* 1036–37; E. *IA* 1301, *Hel.* 1103.

6. E. *Andr.* 289; Paus. 8.31.6; Sapph. Fr. 200C; Paus. 1.22.3. Aphrodite and Peitho linked also at A. *Supp.* 1039–40, Ibyc. Fr. 288C, Pi. Fr. 122S.

7. Sapph. Fr. 1C, Fr. 15C, 202C; E. *Hel.* 238, 1102. Other negative characterizations of Aphrodite: See also Hom. *Il.* 14.218, *h. Ven.* 5.1, Thgn. 1308, Asclep. GA 12.50, Ibyc. Fr. 287C and *Dithy.* 17.10C, E. *Hipp.* 563, *Med.* 640, Pi. *P.* 4.213, Theoc. Epigr. 1.96, 100, 101.

8. Mimn. Fr. 1.1E.

9. *Cypr.* 6E–W; Pi. *O.* 7.11; Hes. *Th.* 910–11; *Od.* 18.192–93; E. *Hel.* 364–66.

10. Hes. *Th.* 200; S. *O.C.* 693; Ibyc. Fr. 282C; "Golden" Aphrodite: Hom. *Il.* 9.389, Mimn. Fr. 1.1E, Hes. *Th.* 980, 1008, *h. Ven.* 5.9; "coy-eyed": Hes. *Th.* 16; P. Fr. 123.5–10S; Hes. *Th.* 206.

11. E. *Alc.* 790–91; *Il.* 14.215–17; Hes. *Th.* 205–06.

12. For foam as "semen" cf. Archilochus, who describes a fellating woman with "much foam around her mouth," Fr. 44W.

13. Hes. *Th.* 116–206. Other origins for Aphrodite emphasize as well her primal nature. The sixth-century Cretan philosopher Epimenides makes her the daughter of Cronos and sister of the Fates and the Furies, the latter goddesses also forces of fertility, as in Aeschylus's *Eumenides* (DK 3 Fr. 19; cf. also an inscription recorded by Pausanias that calls Aphrodite the oldest of the Fates [1.19.2]).

14. Mel. GA 5.180.

15. Paus. 1.1.5, 2.34.11; Ath. 675f–676a.

16. *Il.* 3.372; Dione: *Il.* 5.370–71; Hes. *Th.* 353, 353, 136.

17. Mel. GA 5.180; Mimn. Fr. 23E; Hephaistos as fire: *Il.* 2.426; *Il.* 21.330–82; *Il.* 5.890; Ares' children: *Il.* 13.299, 15.119, Hes. *Th.* 934.

18. Paus. 3.17.5, 2.5.1, 3.15.10, 3.23.1, 2.19.6. See also the epigrams in the *Greek Anthology*, 16.171–77, 9.320–21.

19. Laïs: *Moralia* 768a, Athen. 589a; *Il.* 4.441; Arist. *Pol.* 1269b.

20. Paus. 6.20.6, 6.25.2, 1.105, 1.131; Pandemos: Paus. 9.16.3, 8.32.2, 1.22.3; Philemon apud Athen. 569d.

21. Paus. 6.25.1; three names: Paus. 9.16.3–4; Philetaer. Fr. 5K; Theoc. Epigr. 13.

22. Pl. *Smp.* 8.10, *Smp.* 181b–d. Note the same dialogue's Eryximachus, who speaks also of a Heavenly and Vulgar Eros, the latter sprung from Polyhymnia, or "various song," and associated with excess and debauchery, 187e.

23. *Il.* 3.392.

24. *Il.* 3.64–65.

25. *Il.* 3.396–97, 3.158, 3.399–412.

26. *Il.* 3.414–17.

27. *Il.* 3.442, 446.

28. *Il.* 14.198–99, 14.214–17.

29. *Il.* 14.316–28, 14.353.

30. *h. Ven.* 5.68, 5.69–74.

31. *h. Ven.* 5.86–90, 5.91–106.

32. *h. Ven.* 5.143, 5.158–60.

33. Feeble: *Od.* 10.521; *h. Ven.* 5.288, 218–38.

34. Sapph. Fr. 1.2–4C; Fr. 1.18, 25–26C; *poikilophron*: Fr. 1.1C.

35. Sapph. Fr. 1.7–12C; Fr. 1.14C.

36. Diomedes' prayer: *Il.* 5.15–20; Sapph. Fr. 1.28C.

37. *Hipp.* 360.

38. *Hipp.* 1–5; cf. 1267–82.

39. *Hipp.* 102, 106; Phaedra's lust: 28, 38–40; Semele; 545–64.

40. *Hipp.* 358–59.

41. *Hipp.* 79–81.

42. *Hipp.* 75–77, 563–64.

43. *xunôn, homilias: Hipp.* 17, 19; 118, 616–68.

44. *Hipp.* 165–69; Artemis and animals: cf. A. *A.* 140–43; arrows: *Hipp.* 167, cf. 530–34; 148–50. The goddesses are linked in other ways: A statue of each is present on stage; Aphrodite opens the play with a speech, Artemis closes it with one; Artemis is as callous toward the death of Adonis she will bring about in revenge as Aphrodite is about Phaedra's and Hippolytus's suffering.

45. *Hipp.* 209–31.

46. *Hipp.* 415, 443, 470. The image of sea-storms as disaster recurs throughout the play. See also 139–40, 315, 447–48, 767, 822–24.

47. *Hipp.* 1206–48, 1239–40, 1236.

48. *Hipp.* 1267–69.

49. Theoc. 1.93, 1.95–96, 1.97–98, 1.100–01.

50. A.R. 3.36–166.

51. A.R. 3.284–90. This imagery of mental disorder, disease, and fire continually is used to describe Medea's passion. See also 3.446, 452, 417, 616–35, 664.

52. A.R. 4.421–81.

53. S. Fr. 855N; *h. Ven.* 10.2.

CHAPTER 3

1. Hes. *Th.* 570–613, *Op.* 54–89.

2. Hes. *Th.* 600–01; Semon. Fr. 7.115E; plague: S. Fr. 187N, E. Fr. 496N; Ar. Fr. 10K; Men. Fr. 535K. Other examples of misogyny are easily found. Cf. A. *Th.* 187–90; E. *Hipp.* 616–68, *Med.* 575, *Andr.* 353–54 Frs. 808N, 1059N; Pl. Com. Fr. 98K; Men. Frs. 532K, 803–04K, etc.

3. Ar. *Th.* 392–94; Hes. *Op.* 374; Xenarch. Fr. 14K. For women's garrulity see also E. *Ph.* 198, 200–01, Semon. Fr. 7.105E, Men. 302K, Pl. *R.* 549d-e.

4. Democr. DK 68 Fr. 274; S. *Aj.* 293, Arist. *Pol.* 1260a; Th. 2.45; Pl. *Mx.* 236b; Plu. *Per.* 28.

5. Emp. DK 31 Fr. 62; *Med.* 928; *Andr.* 181; Pl. *R.* 469d, 359d-e, 549d-e; Pl. *Phd.* 117d; Arist. *HA* 608b.

6. S. Fr. 742N; *Hipp.* 616. The faithlessness of women is a common complaint. See Hes. *Op.* 375, Semon. Fr. 7.109–11E, Xenarch. Frs. 5K, 6K, Antiph. Fr. 251K, E. *IT* 1298, Fr. 671N, Men. Fr. 746K, 801K.

7. Hippon. Fr. 68W. E.g., from the fourth-century tragedian Chaerem. Fr. 32N, to the sixth-century A.D. Palladius, GA 11.38. Antimarriage sentiment runs rife in Greek comedy. See Adesp. Frs. 296–97K, Antiph. Fr. 221K, Alex. Fr. 146K, Men. Fr. 650K, etc. Sometimes, though, marriage is condemned because it compromises a man's autonomy by giving him "hostages to fortune," as in the fifth-century Sophist Antiphon, DK 87 Fr. 49, or the Hellenistic poet Posidippus, GA 9.359.

8. Hes. *Op.* 373–74; A. *Ch.* 597–601; Ar. *Lys.* 12–13, 25, 107–10; *pagkatapugon*: *Lys.* 137; *Lys.* 708, 715.

9. Ar. *Th.* 472ff, 491–92; *Ec.* 613–20, 1015–20.

10. Adesp. GA 10.120; *Melampodia* Fr. 3E-W; Herod. 6.

11. Democr. DK 68 Fr. 214; apud X. *Mem.* 2.1.21–22; Arist. apud D.L. 5.7; Arist. *EN* 1109b.

12. Pl. *Ti.* 69e–70a; Arist. *Pol.* 1260a, also 1254b, 1277a; for the Athenian law see, e.g., D. 46.14.

13. Ar. Fr. 596K. Women and wine: e.g., Pherecr. Fr. 143K, Axionic. Fr. 5K, Antiph. Fr. 56K, Pl. Com. Fr. 174K, Alex. Fr. 167K.

14. Ar. *Lys.* 196–97, 230–35. Aristophanes frequently makes jokes about women and wine. See also *Lys.* 395, 465–66, *Th.* 34–37, 630ff, *Ec.* 14–15, 43–45, 224–28.

15. [D]. 59.33.

16. E. Fr. 400N; Democr. DK 68 Fr. 110; *Hipp.* 640–44; *Med.* 285–86, 407–09; Men. Fr. 702K.

17. *Il.* 1.31; Hdt. 2.35, S. *O.C.* 339–41; E. *Ba.* 514, 1236.

18. Nicharch. GA 6.285; Ar. *Av.* 829–31. Other examples of weaving as signifying woman's role: *Il.* 6.490–92, *Od.* 1.356–60, Pl. *Alc. I* 126e, *Ly.* 208d, *R.* 455d.

19. *Il.* 3.128; A. *A.* 908–13, 1381–83; Sapph. Fr. 1.2.C. As we will see, Heracles' wife Deianira destroys him with a woven fabric, the shirt dipped in the blood of Nessus, cf. S. *Tr.* 1050–52, 832. Note also that the two dangerous goddesses in the *Odyssey*, Calypso and Circe, are shown weaving (*Od.* 5.62, 10.222). Medea destroys her rival Glauke and her father Kreon by means of a poisoned robe (*Med.* 786ff). Cf. also E. *Andr.* 66, *Ion* 1278ff.

20. Hes. *Op.* 582–87, also Alc. Fr. 347aC, Arist. *HA* 542b; Hes. *Op.* 519–25.

21. Alex. Fr. 302K, cf. Men. Fr. 488K; Arist. *HA* 572b; Hermipp. Fr. 10K; Ar. *Lys.* 683; *Ach.* 764ff.

22. Semon. Fr. 7E; cf. also Phoc. Fr. 3E.

23. Semon. Fr. 7.108–11E; Ar. *Th.* 787–99; Arist. *GA* 553a; Ael. *NA* 5.11; Plu. *Moralia* 144d; Semon. Fr. 7.83–95E.

24. Empusa: cf. Ar. *Ra.* 293; Arist. *Pr* 879a, also Arist. *GA* 775a; Diog. Apoll. DK 64 Fr. A19.

25. Ar. *Eq.* 1284–86; mirrors: Arist. *Somn. Vig.* 459b–460a, Plin. *Nat.* 7.64–66. According to the Stoic philosopher Chrysippus, all animals including women have an easy birth at the full moon, apud schol. *Il.* 21.483.

26. For the Hippocratic sources see Mary R. Lefkowitz and Maureen B. Fant, *Women's Life in Greece and Rome*, 89–91, 93–96.

27. Pl. *Tim.* 91c. In fairness to the Greek doctors, though, we should note that there is a disease, endometriosis, caused by uterine tissue, perhaps discharged by menstrual backflow through the fallopian tubes, implanting itself on other organs, where it bleeds during menstruation and causes severe pain.

28. Arist. *GA* 775a, 767b, 765b; Democr. DK 68 Fr. 110. Cf. also Philem. Fr. 132K, E. *El.* 932, Fr. 463N, Men. Fr. 484K.

29. S. *Ant.* 484, 525.

30. Arist. *Pol.* 1269b–1270b; cf. Pl. *Lg.* 637c.

31. Str. 11.5.1; Plu. *Thes.* 26–28, A. *Eu.* 685–90; Isoc. 12.193.

32. A.R. 1.609ff. See also Pi. *P.* 4.251–54, Hdt. 6.138; "Lemnian": e.g., A. *Ch.* 631–34.

33. Hes. *Op.* 90–105, 109–20.

34. Hes. *Op.* 61, *Th.* 571; *Th.* 576–84, *Op.* 75; *Op.* 63, *Th.* 572; *Op.* 66; *Op.* 78.

35. Hes. *Op.* 67; Hom. *Od.* 17.290–327; Clearch. apud Ath. 611d; *Il.* 1.4–5; *Il.* 22.66–76; *Od.* 18.338, 19.91.

36. Hes. *Op.* 57, *Th.* 585; *Op.* 61–62.

37. Hes. *Th.* 592–95; *Th.* 604; *Op.* 96–97.

38. Semon. Fr. 7.115–18E; Critias DK 82 Fr. 11.2.

39. Hom. *Od.* 4.569; *Od.* 4.561–69; Leda's egg: Sapph. Fr. 166C, Paus. 3.16.1; *Eoiae* 66E-W, 68.8–9E-W; Nemesis: *Cypria* Fr. 8E-W, Paus. 1.33.1.

40. Hom. *Il.* 3.156; *Eoiae* Fr. 68.5E-W; E. *IA* 391–92, 53–54, Stesich. Fr. 190PMG; *Eoiae* 68.89–97E-W, Paus. 3.20.9.

41. E. *Tr.* 1055–57; *Il. Parv.* Fr. 13E-W: Also Ar. *Lys.* 155–56, E. *Andr.* 629–31, *Or.* 1287.

42. Ibyc. Fr. 296C; Stesich. Fr. 201C; E. *Cyc.* 180–81. A more "rationalist" explanation for Helen's sexual looseness is given in Euripides' *Andromache* (595ff)—her behavior reflects that wantonness of Spartan girls that earlier we saw Plato and Aristotle remark on.

43. Stesich. Fr. 191C; *Eoiae* Fr. 67E-W; *Il. Parv.* Fr. 1E-W; statue: Paus. 3.15.11; E. *Or.* 521; *Or.* 521.

44. *Il.* 3.180, 6.356, 6.344, *Od.* 4.145. Also E. *Andr.* 630, Lyc. 87.

45. Lyc. 142–43; Hellanic. *FrGrH* 4 Fr. 134. For Theseus see also Alcm. Fr. 21C, Hdt. 9.73.2, Isoc. 10.18ff.

46. Plu. *Thes.* 31; Theseus and sodomy according to the ninth-century A.D. lexicographer Photius; Spartan sodomy: Ath. 602d; *Cypr.* Fr. 11E-W; Plu. *Thes.* 34. Pausanias, obviously working from a tradition that makes Helen older at the time of her kidnapping and omits the sodomy, has a child born of her adventure with Theseus, Iphigeneia, Agamemnon's "daughter" whom he sacrificed for a fair wind to Troy, 2.22.6.

47. *Eoiae* 68.100–06E-W; *Cypria* Fr. 1E-W; Lyc. 171–73; Paus. 3.19.13. In her literary afterlife Helen maintains her penchant for getting herself kidnapped—in Nikos Kazantzakis's *The Odyssey: A Modern Sequel* it's Odysseus's turn to make off with Helen.

48. Sapph. Fr. 16.7–11C; Hom. *Il.* 6.356, *Od.* 4.261. Other descriptions of Helen's behavior: Alc. Fr. 283C, A. *A.* 408, 1455, E. *IA* 1253, *El.* 1027. Penelope and Andromache, those exemplary wives, agree with Helen's own assessment (*Od.* 23.223, E. *Andr.* 103).

49. *Od.* 4.240–64.

50. *Od.* 4.265–89.

51. E. *Tr.* 919–65; *deinon* 968; e.g., Pl. *Ap.* 17a.

52. Hom. *Od.* 14.69; Alc. Fr. 42C; A. *A.* 689; E. *Hel.* 136, 142; *Or.* 1131–52. See also Alc. Fr. 283C, Ibyc. Fr. 282C, A. *A.* 749, E. *Hec.* 443, *Tr.* 368–69, 892–93, 768–69, 771, *El.* 213, *Hel.* 73, *IT* 525.

53. *Stugerên*, *Il.* 3.404; *okruoessês*, *Il.* 6.344, war so described at 9.64; *rhigedanês*, *Il.* 19.325, of a lion at 11.383, cf. also 24.775; plague: *Il.* 3.50; bitter: E. *IA* 1316; spat upon: E. *Tr.* 1024; hated: E. *Hel.* 72; without justice, etc.: E. *Hec.* 1148; hated by the gods: E. *Or.* 19; she-dragon: Lyc. 114.

54. *Il.* 3.39–40; E. *Andr.* 298; Lyc. 102, 1143.

55. Paus. 3.19.9–11.

56. *Od.* 11.438–39; A. *A.* 716–36.

57. *Od.* 11.424–28; A. *A.* 606–08, 1228–29.

58. A. *A.* 1233–36; *A.* 1492, *Ch.* 249; *A.* 1258.

59. Pi. *P.* 11.22–25; A. *A.* 1432; *A.* 1447; *A.* 1237, *Ch.* 430. For both Sophocles and Euripides, Klytaimestra's daughter Electra dismisses the issue of Iphigeneia's sacrifice as mere camouflage for her adultery, S. *El.* 562, 439, E. *El.* 481.

60. A. *Eu.* 459, E. *El.* 481; snare: Hom. *Od.* 4.92, 11.439; A. *A.* 1116–17.

61. A. *A.* 11; *A.* 1125–28; *Ch.* 889–90; *Ch.* 585–92.

62. *Med.* 1339–40.

63. Hes. *Th.* 956–62. The later historian Diodorus Siculus makes Circe and Medea sisters, 4.46. *Med.* 395–97, A.R. 4.50–52; moon: A.R. 3.528–30; Simon. Fr. 548C.

64. E. *Med.* 556.

65. Pi. *P.* 4.218–19; E. *Med.* 8; *Med.* 330; *Med.* 569–73; Chorus: *Med.* 627–30; *Med.* 38, 103; *Med.* 319, 859.

66. A.R. 4.391–93; Pelias: *Med.* 9–10, 486–91, D.S. 4.50–52; E. *Med.* 796.

67. Plu. *Thes.* 12–14, Apollod. 1.6; Achilles: Ibyc. Fr. 291C, A.R. 4.814–15; E. *Med.* 1279–80, 187–88, 1407; Scylla: *Med.* 1347, Hom. *Od.* 12.85–92; *Med.* 1079–80.

68. *Med.* 24–29, 97, 144–47; marriage: *Med.* 230–58; Pi. *O.* 13.53–54; *Med.* 807–10; Hom. *Il.* 1.1–2.

69. *Med.* 889–90.

70. E. *Hipp.* 243–46; *Hipp.* 399, 420; *Hipp.* 407–09.

71. E. *Hipp.* 649, 728–30.

72. E. *Hipp.* 730–31.

73. S. *Tr.* 9–23, 507–30; *Tr.* 476; good wife: *Tr.* 27–48, 103–11; *Tr.* 542.

74. *Tr.* 555–81. For Nessus see also *Eoiai* 98eE-W, B. 16.23–35, Archil. Fr. 286W, S. *Tr.* 1050–52; blood: Apollod. 2.7.6.

75. Ath. 594e–595a; Antisth. apud D.L. 6.4.

CHAPTER 4

1. Pl. *Grg.* 491e–92a, *Grg.* 494e.

2. Pl. *Chrm.* 155d; *Smp.* 182a, d.

3. The age of the *eromenos* or "boy-love" could fall in a range between twelve and seventeen, if we can believe the second-century A.D. poet Strato, who put together an anthology of pederastic verse (GA 12.4). Aristotle states that puberty, defined as the ability to produce semen, began at fourteen (*HA* 581a); Solon says that during the third seven years, i.e., fourteen to twenty-one, the boy's chin is "downy" (Fr. 27E). Given that the widespread aversion to hair refers to the full-grown beard, not adolescent peach fuzz, and given that twenty-one was the standard age at which the beard was supposed to be in, a range of fourteen to twenty-one appears to be the suitable age for a boy-love. Other references suggest an age closer to eighteen as typical. Agathon was the boy-love of Pausanias at that age (Pl. *Prt.* 315d-e), and Meleager writes of a dream in which he embraced a seventeen-year-old (GA 12.125). In this chapter and in Chapter 8 "boy-love" denotes a youth who has reached puberty but is still legally a "minor," not a prepubescent boy, who was protected by law against sexual abuse.

4. Simon LeVay, *The Sexual Brain*, 120; in *The Erotic Traveler*, 28.

5. Cic. *ND* 2.128.

6. *R.* 358e–360d; Lys.3.4.

7. Peisandros, *FrGrH* 16 Fr. 10. The surviving ancient details about Chrysippus, his death, and Laius's role in it are murky. See Timothy Gantz, *Early Greek Myth*, 488–91. Another tradition, recorded in the Hellenistic poet Phanocles, makes Orpheus the inventor after he loses his wife Eurydice, for which affront to fertility the Maenads, devotees of Dionysus, dismember him (Fr. 1P).

8. Pl. *Lg.* 836b-c; *Phdr.* 254b, 250e–51a.

9. E. Fr. 840N.

10. See Jeffrey Henderson, *The Maculate Muse*, 218 n.37, for examples.

11. For olive oil cf. Th. 1.6.5, Pl. *Tht.* 162b.

12. Pl. *Lg.* 636b-c, 836c–840e; X. *Lac.* 2.12–14, also *Smp.* 8.35.

13. Arist. *Pol.* 1272a; Hdt. 1.61; E. *Med.* 490–91; Hdt. 1.135; cf. Pl. *Smp.* 182c.

14. For Diogenes cf. D.L. 6.69; S.E. *P.* 3.245–49.

15. Arist. *EN* 1148b.

16. Arist. *Pr.* 879b–80a. Aeschines likewise describes the depraved youth of Timarchos to account for his adult homosexuality (1.11). This linking of homosexuality to anal-genital deformity had a long life. Richard Francis Burton mentions Mantegazza, who claimed that the nerves of the genitals and rectum were abnormally connected in the pathic, *The Erotic Traveller*, 31.

17. [Arist.] *Phgn.* 808a.

18. Jeffrey Henderson, *The Maculate Muse*, 207.

19. Pl. *Smp.* 189c–193e, 181a-c. This idea that there are homosexuals who are born that way is found also in an anonymous Hellenistic poet who speaks of those who are "soft [that is, effeminate] by nature [*phusei*]," GA 9.38. For other examples of homosexual desire as a natural force see X. *Hier.* 1.31–33, Lys. 3.4.

20. Arist. *EN* 1162a; Cratin. Fr. 152K; Timocl. Fr. 25K.

21. Pl. *R.* 474d-e; Adesp. GA 12.123; Thgn. 1341, Mel. GA 12.94: used of maidens, e.g., at *h. Ven.* 5.14, Hes. *Op.* 519.

22. Polystr. GA 12.91, used of maidens A. Fr. 313N, S. *Tr.* 523; Anacr. Fr. 360C; apud Athen. 605d. Praise of girlish boys rife in Hellenistic poetry. See Adesp. Fr. 223K, Mel. GA 12.125, 133, Adesp. GA 12.136, Asclep. GA 12.161, Theoc. 7.105, 29.25, 5.90.

23. Theopomp. Hist. *FrGrH* 115 Fr. 225; Pl. *Prt.* 309a; Phan. GA 12.31; Alc. Mess. GA 12.30; Mel. GA 12.33, 41. Other condemnations of hairiness: Autom. GA 11.326, Adesp. GA 12.39, Diocl. GA 12.35.

24. X. *Mem.* 2.1.30; Pl. *Lg.* 836d.

25. Ar. *Lys.* 801–04; Alex. Fr. 264K. See also Anacr. Fr. 424C, Aeschin. 1.185, 195, Pl. Com. Fr. 3K, Ar. *Th.* 31ff, Fr. 407K.

26. Ar. *Nu.* 979; Arist. *EN* 1150a; Pl. *R.* 556c; Ar. *V.* 686–95. For "softness" and homosexuality see also Philetaer. Fr. 5K, Aeschin. 1.131, Myrin. GA 6.254.

27. Pl. *Smp.* 193c. For Pausanias and Agathon see also Pl. *Prt.* 315d-e, X. *Smp.* 8.32; Ar. *Th.* 97–98, 137, 191–92, 215–16, 204–05; things suffered: 200–01, cf. also 35, 50, 206.

28. Ar. *Ach.* 119; *Pax* 758; *Ra.* 423–24; *Th.* 574–75; *Lys.* 1092. For more on Cleisthenes see Ar. *Nu.* 355, *Av.* 829, *Ra.* 57.

29. Ar. *Ec.* 364–65; Cratin. 151K; Eub. Fr. 107K.

30. Pl. *Phdr.* 239c-d.

31. E.g., K.J. Dover, *Greek Homosexuality*, 143.

32. Ar. *V.* 1067–70; *V.* 687; *Ach.* 635. Other examples of these epithets: *euruprôktos*: Ar. *Ach.* 716, 843, *Eq.* 721, *V.* 1070, *Th.* 200; "gapers": *Eq.* 1263, 380–81, *V.* 1493; *katapugôn*: *Ach.* 79, 664, *Eq.* 638, *Nu.* 1023, *V.* 84, *Th.* 200, Fr. 130K, Cratin. Fr. 241K.

33. Cratin. Fr. 151K; Ar. *Pax* 11–12, 724; *Eq.* 638–42; *Th.* 316–17, 361–68.

34. Arist. *Rh.* 1383b, trans. W.R. Roberts (Princeton, N.J., 1984).

35. Ar. *Nu.* 909. Cf. *Pax* 762, where Aristophanes, speaking directly to the audience about his theatrical career, says that despite his success he never lurked about the wrestling schools bothering the boys.

36. X. *Smp.* 8.19, 8.27–28, 8.32–35; Pl. *Lg.* 836d-e.

37. Pl. *Smp.* 181d–182e, 183d; Aristophanes: 192a; Pl. *Phdr.* 251a.

38. [D] 61.1–2, 61.5.

39. Aeschin. 1.29.

40. Aeschin. 1.3. The charge of "shame" repeated at 1.28, 37, 129, 188. Shameful pleasures: Aeschin. 1.42. That Aeschines is accusing Timarchos of passive homosexuality is clear at 1.46 and 1.85. Aeschin. 1.95, 1.54, 1.160, 1.185, 1.85–86.

41. Aeschin. 1.70. "Beastly" also at 1.26, 38, 41, 60, 70, 180, 189, 192. Aristotle's famous definition of a human as a "social animal" at *Pol.* 1253a.

42. Theoc. 5.37–41; Ar. *Eq.* 364.

43. Arist. *EN* 1148b; Pl. *Phdr.* 253e, 254b; Aeschin. 1.15, 1.116, 1.185.

44. X. *Mem.* 1.2.29–30.

45. Call. *Iamb.* Fr. 695T; Diosc. GA 12.42; Ar. *Pl.* 153–59.

46. Aeschin. 1.191; Men. Fr. 363K.

47. Ar. *Nu.* 1020–21; Ar. *Lys.* 488–92, 652–55.

48. Ar. *Eq.* 167. K.J. Dover, in the Postscript to the 1989 edition of *Greek Homosexuality*, agrees with H.D. Jocelyn (*PCPhC* 206 [1980] 12–66) that the verb translated "fuck" more accurately means "fellate"—a sexual image communicating an even worse political corruption. Ar. *V.* 1299–1449; *Ra.* 1078–88.

49. Ar. *Nu.* 1085, 1088–1100; *Nu.* 1019; *Eq.* 963.

50. Ar. *Eq.* 423–26, 1242, 78, 875–80.

51. Ar. *Eq.* 736–40. Aristophanes may be parodying an image from Pericles' Funeral Oration delivered at the beginning of the Peloponnesian War, in which Pericles exhorted the Athenians to be "lovers of the city," Th. 2.43.1.

52. Ar. *Nu.* 979–80, 973–76, 990–92, 1016–19; *V.* 1068–80, 687–95.

53. Pl. *Ap.* 19b; Pl. Com. Fr. 186K; Ar. *Nu.* 1001–02, 1018; *Ra.* 1069–70; *Ec.* 112–14.

CHAPTER 5

1. The chimera is the monster made of a "lion in front, serpent in back, she-goat in the middle," according to Homer (*Il.* 6.181).

2. Pl. *R.* 588c–589a, 589a-b.

3. Philol. DK 44 Fr. 14; Emp. DK 31 Fr. 126; X. *Mem.* 3.11.9; Pl. *Phdr.* 250c, *Ti.* 69d–71e, *Phd.* 81d; Pl. *Phd.* 80B.

4. Arist. *Metaph.* 984b; Hes. *Th.* 116–25.

5. Pherecyd. Syr. DK 7 Fr. 3; Parm. DK 28 Frs. 12–13; Pl. *Smp.* 178b, 186a-b.

6. Emp. DK 31 Fr. 17; "adhesive" love: Frs. 19–20, 17; Fr. 17; Arist. *Metaph.* 985a.

7. Emp. DK 31 Frs. 21–22.

8. Emp. DK 31 Frs. 17, 27a; Frs. 17, 30; Frs. 128, 130.

9. Pl. *Phd.* 83d.

10. Democr. DK 68 Fr. 235; X. *Smp.* 8.15; Pl. *Phlb.* 31a.

11. Pl. *Grg.* 493b-c: Cf. the *Republic*, where carrying water in a sieve is the punishment of the "impious and unjust" in Hades, according to Orpheus (363d). Pl. *Grg.* 493e–494a. The fifty daughters of Danaus, who all except one murdered their husbands on their wedding night, are condemned in Hades to continually filling leaky jars with water (cf. [Pl.] *Ax.* 371e).

12. Antisth. apud D.L. 6.3; Heraclit. DK 22 Fr. 4; Epich. DK 23 Fr. 44a; Democr. DK 68 Fr. 31, Fr. 189; X. *Mem.* 4.5.3, *Smp.* 8.23.

13. S. *O. T.* 872; Pl. *R.* 403a, 577d; *R.* 553c, 589d.

14. Pl. *Phd.* 64d, 65d, 66d; *Ti.* 86b; *Lg.* 714a. Though he is not as radical an absolutist rationalist as Plato, Aristotle still views the pleasures of taste and touch as "slavish and brutish," belonging to our animal natures, *EN* 1118a-b, also 1119b, 1095b.

15. Cerc. Fr. 5P; Democr. DK 68 Frs. 214, 236; Pl. *La.* 191d; victory: *Lg.* 714a; Arist. *EN* 1179b, 1102b; Posidip. GA 12.120.

16. Democr. Frs. 40, 189; X. *Mem.* 1.6.10, 4.5.6, 10; Pl. *Ti.* 90b-c; Arist. *Pol.* 1260a, 1254b.

17. Pl. *R.* 588c-d; lion: *R.* 439e–441c; *R.* 440d; wolf: *R.* 441a; *R.* 589a.

18. Pl. *Ti.* 69c–70a. Aristotle's description of the soul in the *Ethics* likewise posits a part of the irrational soul that can participate in the rational, but he includes in it the appetites and desires. *EN* 1102a–1103a. Cf. also *de An.* 433a.

19. Pl. *R.* 485b-e.

20. Pl. *R.* 558d–559d.

21. Pl. *Lg.* 733b–734e.

22. Arist. *de An.* 433a. Cf. also the discussion at *EN* 1119b.

23. Epicur. apud D.L. 10.128–32; D.L. 10.118.

24. At *EN* 1140b, Pl. *Cra.* 411e–412a; Hom. *Od.* 23.11–13, cf. also Thgn 39–42, Hdt. 3.35; Ar. *Lys.* 781–96; *Ra.* 853. The meaning "having sense" very common. Cf. *Lys.* 1093, D. 58.56, 6.28, etc.

25. Pl. *Smp.* 219d, 220a–221b; Pl. *Grg.* 504d.

26. Pl. *R.* 389d-e, *Grg.* 491d; "leaky jar": Pl. *R.* 402e, *Grg.* 504e; Pl. *Phd.* 68c. Cf. also *Prt.* 332a, *Phdr.* 230a.

27. Arist. *EN* 1118a-b; *EN* 1119a; *EN* 1118b–1119a.

28. Antipho. DK 87 Fr. 58; D. 45.79–80; Isoc. 8.119.

29. Ar. *Nu.* 529; X. *Mem.* 1.3.8.

30. E. *IA* 543–57; *Hel.* 1105; *Med.* 630–36.

31. Antipho. DK 87 Fr. 59; Pl. *R.* 571d–572a; *Lg.* 635b-d.

32. E. *Hipp.* 79–80; *Hipp.* 358–59. Later, though, having witnessed the power of Phaedra's lust, the Nurse will conclude that Phaedra's *not* "temperate" and so can cure her disease only by having sex with Hippolytus (494).

33. Arist. *EN* 1152a. See also Aristotle's discussion at *MM* 1202a–1204a.

34. E. Fr. 840N; *Hipp.* 1304, 399, 380–81; *Med.* 1079–80.

CHAPTER 6

1. Hom. *Od.* 9.122–24.

2. *Od.* 9.131–41.

3. Hes. *Th.* 131 ff; Hom. *Il.* 14.346–50.

4. A. Fr. 44N, cf. also E. Fr. 898N; Paus. 2.19.6.

5. Thgn. 1277–78.

6. Mimn. Fr. 1.3–4E; Ibyc. Fr. 282C[i]C, cf. also Sol. Fr. 25E, Mel. GA 12.256; Neobule: Archil. Fr. 42W; Fr. 196a W.

7. Mimn. Fr. 2.3–7E; Sapph. Fr. 105c C. Other examples of floral imagery can be found at Chaerem. Fr. 786N; Pl. *Smp.* 196a; Alc. Fr. 45C, Fr. 296(b)C; Sol. Fr. 25E; Alcm. Fr. 3.66ff C; Anacr. Fr. 346C; Phld. GA 5.124; Asclep. GA 5.169; Mel. GA 5.144.

8. Rose as gift: e.g., Lycophronid. Fr. 844C; Mel. GA 5.136; Paus. 6.24.6; E. *Med.* 826–43.

9. Pl. GA 16.210, cf. also Ar. *Ach.* 991–92.

10. Theoc. 27.50. See also, e.g., Canthar. Fr. 60K, Crates Fr. 40K, Ar. *Ach.* 1199; Pl. *Lg.* 837b, where love of the body is called "hungering after [its] bloom, as it were that of a ripening peach."

11. Pi. *P.* 9.110, cf. also Frs. 122, 123S; Plu. *Moralia* 138d; Pl. GA 5.79.

12. *Opóra* for sexual ripeness: e.g., Pi. *I.* 2.4.5, Ar. Fr. 582K, Chaerem. Fr. 12N, etc.; Ar. *Pax* 706–8; *Pax* 1319–28; *Pax* 1336–39. The resumption of sexual relations between the Greeks and their wives in the *Lysistrata* after peace likewise is linked to a feast and agricultural plenty, cf. 1182–1215. Cf. also the ending of the *Birds.*

13. A. *Supp.* 996–1001, cf. also Ar. Fr. 582K.

14. Hom. *Od.* 6.162–67; also at 157.

15. S. Fr. 524N.

16. E. *Med.* 238–43; Sapph. Fr. 105[a]C; A. *Supp.* 1050–51: cf. Call. Fr. 401T.

17. X. *Oec.* 6.10.

18. Wedding formula: e.g., Men. Fr. 720K; sowing: A. *Th.* 754; S. *OT* 1210–11. These metaphors are very common in Greek literature. See also Alc. Fr. 120C; Thgn. 582; Pi. *P.* 254–55; A. Fr. 99N; S. *OT* 1257, *Ant.* 569, *Tr.* 32–33, *Aj.* 1293; Pl. *Phdr.* 251a, *Ti.* 91d; E. *Or.* 552–54, Fr. 215N, 1064N, *Ph.* 22, *Hipp.* 449.

19. A. *Eu.* 557–61.

20. Pl. *Mx.* 238a; Arist. *Pol.* 1335b; Arist. *GA* 716a, 765b.

21. Pl. *Lg.* 838e–839a, *Lg.* 841d.

22. Fr. 44 Herscher, in Marcel Detienne, "The Violence of Wellborn Ladies: Women in the Thesmophoria," 130.

23. Cf. Ar. *Th.* 372 ff.

24. Sapph. Fr. 111C.

25. Walter Burkert, *Greek Religion*, 246.

26. Ar. *Lys.* 639–51.

27. Arrephoria: Paus. 1.27.3; S. *O.C.* 699–700; Hdt. 8.55.

28. Fr. 122S, cf. Str. 8.6.20; Corinth: Athen. 573c; dedications: see, e.g., Pl. GA 6.1; Mel. GA 6.162; Antip. Sid. GA 6.206, 207; Philet. GA 6.210.

29. Postponer: Paus. 3.18.1, Adesp. Fr. 872C.

30. Adesp. Fr. 1029C; Arist. *Ph* 230a-b, cf. Pl. *Phdr.* 276b.

31. Ar. *Lys.* 390–98.

32. *Il.* 5.429, cf. also Pi. *P.* 9.13; *Il.* 22.470; Sapph. Fr. 112C; fruitful: S. Fr. 763N; bridegrooms: Phld. GA 10.21; weddings: Arch. GA 6.207; widows: Paus. 2.34.12, 10.38.12.

33. *Il.* 14. 214–21.

34. *Il.* 5.297–430.

35. *Il.* 22.127–28.

36. *Od.* 8.266–366.

37. *Od.* 8.320.

38. *h. Ven.* 3–5, 7–32.

39. *h. Ven.* 33–44, 45–52, 247, 198–99.

40. *h. Ven.* 107–41.

41. Aphrodite and marriage: cf. Sapph. Fr. 194C.

42. Sapph. Fr. 1.1–7C.

43. Sapph. Fr. 1.15–24; Fr. 1.3C; again: Fr. 1.15, 16, 18; Fr. 1.20.

44. Sapph. Fr. 2.1–3C; Fr. 2.5–11; Fr. 2.15–16.
45. Sapph. Fr. 94.12–29C; Fr. 9421–23.
46. Paus. 9.29.9; cf. Sapph. Fr. 140[a]C.

CHAPTER 7

1. E. *Med.* 230–51.
2. Diane Ackerman, *A Natural History of Love*, 24.
3. Hom. *Od.* 15.356–57; Hes. *Op.* 702; Semon. Fr. 6E; Thgn. 1225–26, cf. Antipho. DK 87 Fr. 49.
4. X. *Smp.* 9.7.
5. Arist. *Pr.* 68a-b, Cf. Epicurus also, who sees sexual love as a means of gaining friendship, its true end. Apud D.L. 7.130; Ar. *Lys.* 165–66.
6. Hes. *Th.* 590–612; Democr. DK 68 Fr. 278.
7. Hom. *Il.* 9.485–95; E. *Med.* 1033–35. See related sentiments at X. *Oec.* 7.12, *Mem.* 2.2.5–10, and Men. Fr. 325K. Arist. *Pol.* 1252a; E. *Med.* 573–75, *Hipp.* 618–24.
8. In Mary Lefkowitz and Maureen B. Fant, *Women's Life in Greece and Rome*, 104, trans. Lefkowitz.
9. Lys. 1.33.
10. Is. 3.11.
11. [D.] 59.34, 59.41, 59.113.
12. [D.] 59.122.
13. Theoc. 17.40–44.
14. Semon. Fr. 7.91E, cf. also X. *Oec.* 7.17; Is. 3.17, 29.
15. Hes. *Op.* 607, cf. also Antipho. DK 87 Fr. 49; Men. Fr. 646K.
16. Helen North, *Sophrosune*, 21. See n. 71 for supporting references.
17. S. Fr. 621N, cf. E. Fr. 545N, 909N; Epich. DK 23 Fr. 35; Lys. 1.10; [D.] 59.113.
18. E. *IA* 1148–63; E. *Or.* 558. Wives and *sôphrosunê*: cf. also E. Fr. 543N, 909N; Ar. *Lys.* 473; Arist. *Rh.* 1361a.
19. S. *OT* 825–26; E. *Hipp.* 546–54. Other examples: Hippothoon Fr. 3N; E. *El.* 99, *Tr.* 676, *IA* 907, *Med.* 242, *Alc.* 314, 342, etc., Fr. 781N; S. *Tr.* 536, Fr. 583N; E. *Andr.* 177–78, cf. Ar. *Av.* 1739, Plu. *Moralia.* 139b.
20. Pl. *Men.* 71e–73b.
21. I am speaking of the well-off households, mostly from Athens of the late fifth to fourth centuries, reflected in the literary evidence.
22. X. *Oec.* 3.12.
23. Arist. *Pol.* 1252a; *EN* 1162a, cf. Pl. *Lg.* 773a-d, Hom. *Il.* 9.134; Arist. *Pol.* 1264b.
24. Lys. 1.6, 1.7, 1.10, 1.11–14.
25. *h. Cer.* 156; Hippothoon Fr. 6N; Phoc. Fr. 3E; *Ec.* 211–12, cf. *Lys.* 567 ff, Pl. *Lg.* 805e.
26. Arist. *EN* 1160b–1161a, [D.] 59.52, cf. A. *Th.* 189, Men. Fr. 402K; Ar. *Nu.* 41–79; Thphr. apud Hier. *Adv. Jov.* 1.47; Theoc. 28.27–28.
27. A. *Th.* 232, cf. E. *Heracl.* 476–77, Fr. 521N; Apollod. Com. Fr. 13A Edmonds (*The Fragments of Attic Comedy After Meineke, Bergk, and Kock* [Leiden, 1957–1961]); Plu. *Moralia* 142d, also Paus. 6.25.1.
28. Lys. 1.8, 20.
29. E. *Hipp.* 717; E. *Med.* 77, 139, cf. 909–10; E. *Andr.* 39–48; E. *Ion* 843–46, 1291.

30. Hom. *Od.* 1.429–33.

31. Arist. *Pol.* 1335b–1336a; Pl. *Lg.* 841d; E. *Andr.* 179–80, also 469–70, 909, cf. also Isoc. 3.37, 40; Thphr. apud Hier. *Adv. Jov.* 1.47.

32. D.L. 8.1.21; *Lg.* 839b, cf. E. Fr. 823N, 1062N; Theoc. 18.51–52; X. *Smp.* 8.3; E. *Hec.* 828–32; comic fragment in *Women's Life in Greece and Rome*, 19, trans. Lefkowitz. Cf. also the fragment from Menander translated on 18, Fr. 15 Papyrus Antinoopolis.

33. Men. *Dys.* 786–90.

34. Men. *Asp.* 250–69, *Asp.* 294–97.

35. *Dys.* 786, *eras*; *Asp.* 288, *erôti peripesôn*.

36. Isoc. 3.40–41.

37. X. *Oec.* 3.12, 3.15.

38. X. *Oec.* 7.12, cf. also 19; "common thing": 7.13; *koinos*: 7.13.

39. X. *Oec.* 7.14.

40. X. *Oec.* 7.15; housekeeper: 9.11, 12.13–14.

41. Bee's chastity: e.g., Ael. *NA* 5.11; X. *Oec.* 7.32–41; nurturing: 7.23–25; "self-rule": 7.26–27.

42. X. *Oec.* 8.3; efficiency: 8.3–23; pots: 8.19; natural beauty: 10.4, 9–13.

43. X. *Oec.* 9.19; training: 3.11.

44. [Arist.] *Oec.* 3.2; cf. also 1.4; X. *Oec.* 10.9; [Arist.] *Oec.* 1.4.

45. Hom. *Il.* 6.429–30. Tecmessa, the "spear-won" bride of Ajax, says much the same thing about her dependence on her husband, *Aj.* 485–524. *Il.* 6.450–65.

46. *Il.* 6.490–93.

47. *Il.* 22.440–44; 22.468–72.

48. E. *Andr.* 98, 140, 110.

49. E. *Andr.* 207; honor and shame: 221; jealousy: 229–31; good wife: 235.

50. E. *Andr.* 213; nursing Hector's bastards: 222–27.

51. E. *Tr.* 648–56; yoke: 669–70.

52. E. *Andr.* 373–74; died with Hector: 456–67; role as mother: 409–10; Alexander: 1243–47.

53. E. *Alc.* 151.

54. Dying for husband: cf. E. *Alc.* 154–55; slaves: 769–70; household: 415; trusty: 99, 880; chaste: 182, 615; best: 83, 151, 235, 241, 324, 899; noble: 200, 418, 615, 1083; worthy: 370, 433; noblest: 623, 993.

55. "Your love": E. *Alc.* 277–79; cf. 242; year: 329–30, 336–37; statue: 343–54; faithful wife: 367–68.

56. Devotion: cf. E. *Alc.* 473–76; devotion: 1008 ff; Pl. *Smp.* 179c.

57. Pl. *Smp.* 179c.

58. Hom. *Od.* 6.181–84; *h. Merc.* 391–93; *h. Cer.* 434; Pi. *O.* 7.1–6. See also Thgn. 81, where "like-mindedness" is made a quality of true friends, or *Od.* 15.198, where the guest-host relationship is defined by "like-mindedness." Also Ar. *Av.* 632, *Od.* 9.456. For the importance of marital harmony see also Pi. *O.* 7.10; Democr. DK 68 Fr. 186; E. *Med.* 14–15; Antip. Sid. or Thess. GA 6.209.

59. *Od.* 11.445–46; devices: 2.117–18, 121; cf. also 24.194; Ar. *Th.* 548.

60. Leon. GA 6.289; *Od.* 2.96–110.

61. *Od.* 18.274–83.

62. *Od.* 5.209–20; Nausicaa: 23.310–43.

63. *Od.* 19.582–87.

64. *Od.* 23.241–46; bed: 23.190 ff.

65. Stesich. Fr. 192C. Herodotus also tells of Helen's sojourn in Egypt, leaving out the phantom, 2.112–20.

66. Xenoph. DK 21 Fr. 11; cf. also Frs. 14–16; e.g., Pl. *R.* 378b ff. For other passages condemning the attribution of evil to the gods see also S. Fr. 623N; E. *IT* 391, *Ion* 441–51, Fr. 292N, Fr. 606.

67. Paus. 3.15.3, 4.16.9; wedding: cf. Theoc. 18.45–48; Ar. *Lys.* 1314–15; *Or.* 1634–48, *Hel.* 1666–69.

68. Hdt. 6.61, cf. also Paus. 3.7.7. Note too that Plato in the *Republic* equates the real Helen of Stesichorus with intellectual pleasure of the rational soul, the phantom with the irrational pleasures of the body that throw the soul into a Trojan War (586c). Isoc. 10.54–55; Gorg. DK 82 Fr. 11.4.

69. Isoc. 10.65, 10.17, 10.67; E. *Tr.* 928–37; *Od.* 4.261; E. *Andr.* 679–84. Apollo in Euripides' *Orestes* gives us another exculpating reason: By causing the war, Helen helped relieve the earth of its excessive population (1640–43).

70. E. *Hel.* 65–67; unsullied: 795; beauty: 1087–89; E. *Or.* 128–29; *Hel.* 160–61; protector: 884; understanding: 1686–87. Menelaus traditionally is characterized by noteworthy chastity/self-control. Aristotle remarks on the fact that Homer does not show Menelaus sleeping with a concubine at Troy out of respect for Helen (Fr. 144 Rose), and Isocrates says he was awarded Helen's hand in marriage by Zeus because of his "chastity/self-control" (10.72).

71. Someone else: E. *Hel.* 299–303, 353–57; die: 837; weeping: 625–59; dearest: 625, 637; waited: 650–51; mine: 652.

72. E. *Hel.* 290–91; *Od.* 23.109–10; *Od.* 23.130–40; E. *Hel.* 1433–40.

CHAPTER 8

1. Sol. Fr. 25E.

2. Ibyc. Fr. 289C.

3. Dorian origins: Pl. *Lg.* 636b, Arist. *Pol.* 1272a, X. *Lac.* 2.12–14, Timae. *FrGrH* 566 Fr. 144, Athen. 602f, Plu. *Moralia* 761d.

4. Plu. *Lyc.* 18; eros: Ath. 561e; Pl. *Lg.* 636b-c.

5. Ephor. *FrGrH* 70 Fr. 149, also Str. 10.4.21; Pl. *Smp.* 178d–179a, also X. *Cyr.* 7.1.30.

6. Achilles: Pl. *Smp.* 179e; A. Frs. 135, 136N; X. *An.* 7.4.7–10; Th. 6.54–59; statue: Ar. *Ec.* 682.

7. Arist. *Ath.* 18.1 ff; Pl. *Smp.* 182c.

8. Ar. *V.* 1066–70.

9. Anacr. Fr. 360C; Pl. *Lys.* 207a-b, 204b-c; Aeschin. 1.9–11.

10. Pl. *Smp.* 183c-d; wooers: *Smp.* 183d, also *Phdr.* 255a; X. *Smp.* 8.19; Pl. *Smp.* 195e.

11. E. Fr. 897N; Alex. Fr. 289K; X. *Mem.* 1.6.13–14; Pl. *Smp.* 178d–179a. Cf. also Anaxandr. Fr. 61K; Pl. *Euthd.* 282b; X. *Lac.* 2.13; [D] 61.2.

12. Hurt enemies: cf. Archil. Fr. 65E, Sol. Fr. 13.5E, Thgn. 869–72, Pi. *P.* 2.83, E. *Med.* 809. Socrates in the *Republic* exposes the fallacies of this conception of justice, 335e. Sophocles' *Ajax* likewise explores the limitations of such a simplistic ethic.

13. Arist. *EN* 1166a. Cf. too Aristotle's definition of the verb *philein*: "wishing good things for someone" for his sake, and trying to bring them about (*Rh.* 1380b–1381a). Thgn. 1311–18; cf. also Theoc. 29; Pl. *Smp.* 184b-e.

14. Husband and wife: cf. Arist. *EE* 1238b, 1243b.

15. *Carm. Conviv.* 893C, also 894–96; Ar. *V.* 1225.

16. Pl. *R.* 363c-d; capping verses: cf. Ar. *V.* 1222–48, *Carm. Conviv.* Test. 1C; kottabus: cf. Ath. 665d–668f; neighbors: e.g., Call. GA 12.118, Adesp. GA 12.116, Mel. GA 12.117; strangers: cf. Ar. *V.* 1252–55.

17. Pl. *Prt.* 347c-e; Xenoph. Fr. 1.17–18E.

18. Call. Fr. 227T; prize: Call. Fr. 227T. Cf. also S. Fr. 255N, E. Fr. 631N, Ath. 667c; D. 19.196; [D] 59.33.

19. Thgn. 479–80, cf. also X. *Smp.* 2.25–26; Pl. *Lg.* 649d. The Sophist Evenus and the amateur philosopher Critias have more practical reasons for moderation in drinking—it makes sex better (Even. Fr. 2E, Critias DK 88 Fr. 6).

20. Garlands: cf. Xenoph. Fr. 1.2E; Mel. GA 12.256.

21. Lys. 1.4; pleasure: cf. Arist. *Rh.* 1378b.

22. Anacreon: Test. 1C, 7C; Anacr. Fr. 402C; Democr. DK 68 Fr. 73, cf. also Euripides, Fr. 388N, 672N. Aristotle sees even innocent pleasure that avoids "outrage" as ultimately breaking down the reciprocal nature of pederastic love, which can't last because the lover's and beloved's pleasures have different sources—the former's from gazing at the beauty of the boy, the boy's from receiving attention. Once the boy's beauty fades, the relationship ends—unless they have developed a love of each other's character. *EN* 1157a; cf. also *EN* 1164a.

23. X. *Mem.* 1.3.11; kissed: 2.6.32; chaste: 1.6.13; pain: 2.6.22–23.

24. X. *Smp.* 1.8–10; banquet: 8.10.

25. X. *Smp.* 8.8; chaste: X. *Smp.* 1.26. Xenophon also praises the Spartan king Agesilaus, who wouldn't even kiss his favorite Megabates, for his pederastic chastity (*Ages.* 5.4).

26. Aeschin. 1.29; black: 1.135; youth: cf. 1.132.

27. Aeschin. 1.133; just lover: 1.136; manner: 1.137; chastity: 1.139; lawful: 1.140; experiences: 1.151; lovers: 1.156.

28. Aeschin. 1.137; sexual acts: 1.142.

29. [D]. 61.1; chastity: 61.3, 4, 5, 7; shame: 61.5–6; chaste: 61.13; shameful: 61.20; Eros: 61.21.

30. Pl. *Smp.* 181b-c; injustice: 182a; noble way: 183d; virtue: 184b-c; excellence/virtue: 184d-e.

31. An anecdote suggesting that sodomy was practiced in a pederastic relationship is found in Aristotle, who tells how the tyrant Periander was plotted against by his favorite because he publicly asked the boy if he was pregnant yet (*Pol.* 1311a-b). The insult makes sense only if it was assumed that boy-favorites were habitually buggered. But then again, the boy could have been angered because the *untrue* implication of such "outrage" was so shaming, which in turn depends on sodomy being universally condemned, even between pederastic couples.

32. Sol. Fr. 25E; A. Fr. 135N, also 136N.

33. Cerc. Fr. 5P. Two other examples of idealized pederasty in Plato can be found at *R.* 403b, where sexual gratification is forbidden to those who would "love rightly." Thus they are restricted to kissing, spending time together, and touching as a father would a son. In the *Laws* the "two loves" again are contrasted. The lover of the soul considers bodily satisfaction an "outrage" and worships "chastity," "manliness," and "prudence" (*Lg.* 837b-d).

34. Pl. *Phdr.* 230b-c.

35. Beloved: Pl. *Phdr.* 231c-d; lover: 232a–233d; publicly: 233e–234a.

36. Wisdom: Pl. *Phdr.* 236a; "best": 237d-e; "outrage": 237e–238a; bodies: 238c.

37. Lusts: Pl. *Phdr.* 239a; unmentioned: 239c-d; idealized role: 240a; soul: 241c-d.

38. Pl. *Phdr.* 242c–243a.

39. happiness: Pl. *Phdr.* 244a–245c; "opposite": 246b.

40. qualities: Pl. *Phdr.* 246d-e; rational mind: 247d; soul has seen: 248a-e.

41. grow again: Pl. *Phdr.* 249d; "beast": 250e–51a; soul: 251b-c; closed: 251d.

42. reason: Pl. *Phdr.* 253d; spur: 253e; "pleasure": 254a; retreat: 254b; "fear": 254e; "reason": 256a.

43. Pl. *Phdr.* 256d.

44. reincarnation: Pl. *Phdr.* 256c-d; intercourse: 255c-d.

45. mortals: Pl. *Smp.* 202b-e; happy: 203b–206a.

46. "immortality": Pl. *Smp.* 206c–207a; pederastic virtue: 207d–209b.

47. soul: Pl. *Smp.* 209b-c; "beauty": 211c; share: 2210a-b.

48. Pl. *Smp.* 211e–212a.

CONCLUSION

1. Aug. *C.D.* 14.17.

2. Quoted in Morton Hunt, *The Natural History of Love*, 140.

3. *The Sexual Brain*, 137.

4. Lawrence Osborne, *The Poisoned Embrace*, xi.

5. Camille Paglia, "No Law in the Arena," 25.

Critical Bibliography

The following brief notes are not meant to be exhaustive or comprehensive, but rather to direct the interested reader to further discussion of ideas raised in the text, as well as to note debts I owe to the work of other scholars. Matters of textual disagreement or arguments over literary interpretation are omitted, and attention is particularly focused on issues currently the "flash points" of recent scholarship—most of which "flash points" will be found in the chapters on women, marriage, pederasty, and homosexuality. Readers who desire to delve further into those and other issues and who are interested in works in languages other than English should consult the bibliographies of the secondary works listed here or peruse the annual survey of classical scholarship, *L'Année Philologique*, under the rubrics "Histoire Sociale: civilisation Grecque" and "Generalia," or under those for individual authors. Readers interested in pursuing individual mythic and literary characters in more detail should see Timothy Gantz's exhaustive *Early Greek Myth: A Guide to Literary and Artistic Sources* (Baltimore and London, 1993). These notes are arranged by chapter and page number. Journal abbreviations follow those used in *L'Année Philologique*. For reprinted or translated books and articles, the date of original publication will precede place and date of publication of edition referred to.

Twentieth-century scholarship on ancient Greek sex starts with "Hans Licht," the pseudonym of Paul Brandt, *Sexual Life in Ancient Greece*, trans. J.H. Freese (1928; rpt. New York, 1993). This latest reprint, by the way, shamelessly omits the original date of the German publication and the English translation (1932). Moreover, the English translation is based on the abridged second German edition and leaves out most of Brandt's bibliographical footnotes and illustrations (Martin Kilmer, *Greek Erotica* [London, 1993], 134 n. 2). Just about every reference to sexuality in ancient Greek literature can be found in Brandt, who was an early advocate for sexual, particularly homosexual, liberation. Thus the frequent tone of special pleading in his book and the aura of jolly nymph-and-satyr hedonism. (See the introduction to *Before Sexuality: The Construction of Erotic Experience in the Ancient Greek World*, ed. David M. Halperin, John J. Winkler, Froma I. Zeitlin [Princeton, 1990], 10–12, for more on Brandt; cf. also 7–16 for other key early works on ancient sexuality.) Another available general survey, less comprehensive than Brandt's, is Robert Flacelière, *Love in Ancient Greece*, trans. James Cleugh (1960; New York, 1962). More recently K.J. Dover has written frequently about ancient sex. See "Eros and Nomos," *BICS* 11 (1964), 31–42; "Classical Greek Attitudes to Sexual Behavior," *Arethusa* 6 (1973), 59–73; *Greek Popular Morality in the Time of Plato and Aristotle* (Oxford, 1974), 205–16; *Greek Homosexuality* (1978; updated version Cambridge, Mass., 1989), especially 42–54 for a definition of eros. Though it's concerned with Attic red-figure pottery, Martin Kilmer's *Greek Erotica* provides pictorial evidence substantiating some of the conclusions reached in this book.

Two briefer surveys are sane and informative, particularly for the nonspecialist. Excellent is Peter Green's 1983 "Sex and Classical Literature," rpt. in *Classical Bearings: Interpreting Ancient History and Culture* (New York, 1989), 130–51. See also Jeffrey Henderson, "Greek Attitudes Toward Sex," in M. Grant and R. Kitzinger, eds., *Civilization of the Ancient Mediterranean: Greece and Rome* (New York, 1988), 1249–63. Anne Carson's refreshingly impressionistic, if at times vaporous, philosophical discussion of eros, *Eros the Bittersweet* (Princeton, N.J., 1986), explores the ambiguous meaning of eros in terms of desire as lack and its relation to the imagination and the definition of the self. Readers who enjoy high-octane Gallic intellectualizing should see two essays by Jean-Pierre Vernant, "One . . . Two . . . Three: Erôs," in *Before Sexuality*, 465–78, and "Dim Body, Dazzling Body," in *Fragments for a History of the Human Body*, ed. Michael Feher (New York, 1989), 18–47. Simon Goldhill's *Foucault's Virginity: Ancient Erotic Fiction and the History of Sexuality* (Cambridge, 1995) appeared after this book was finished. Finally, for a descriptive survey of some recent scholarship see Marilyn Arthur-Katz, "Sexuality and the Body in Ancient Greece," *Métis* 4 (1989), 155–79.

Nonspecialists who write of ancient Greek sex too often end up repeating the received ideas that have seeped out of the academy into widespread currency, e.g., that Greek women were locked away at home, that Greek men didn't like their wives, or that their only emotional interest was in courtesans or homosexual amours with teenaged boys (see note below on Chapter 3). So the reader should be careful with the following: Morton Hunt, *The Natural History of Love*, rev. ed. (New York, 1994), 15–55; Reay Tannahill, *Sex in History* (New York, 1980), 84–105; and the highly unreliable Diane Ackerman, whose rhetorical reach exceeds her intellectual grasp (*The Natural History of Love* [New York, 1994]), 17–28. See too Vern L. Bullough, *Sexual Variance in Society and History* (New York, 1976), 93–126, and Nigel Davies, *The Rampant God: Eros Throughout the World* (New York, 1984), 143–68.

Those who may associate Michel Foucault with the wanton theorizing and pretentious patois typical of Continental poststructuralists showing off for dull Americans will be surprised to find that his book on ancient Greek sex is usually quite readable, surveying the ancient evidence to make some good observations about the various techniques developed to control passion: "those intentional and voluntary actions by which men not only set themselves rules of conduct, but also seek to transform themselves, to change themselves in their singular being, and to make their life into an *oeuvre* that carries certain aesthetic values and meets certain stylistic criteria." *The Use of Pleasure*, trans. Robert Hurley (1984; New York, 1986), 10–11. In his choice of documents, though, Foucault limits himself to "prescriptive" and "practical" texts "offering rules, opinions, and advice on how to behave as one should"; thus he narrows his scope to fourth-century medical and philosophical works (12–13). Finally, highly recommended is Camille Paglia's wild and brilliant *Sexual Personae: Art and Decadence from Nefertiti to Emily Dickinson* (New York, 1991), 72–125. Even when she's wrong, Paglia is more interesting than any dozen poststructuralist clerks.

PREFACE

xi   James Redfield has made the same point about the absence of evidence that could reveal the Greeks' personal lives, in "Homo Domesticus," *The Greeks*, ed. Jean-Pierre Vernant (1991), trans. Charles Lambert and Teresa Lavender Fagan (Chicago and London, 1995), 153–54.

xii   Much of the recent work on ancient Greek sexuality reflects several developments in humanities scholarship of the last twenty-five years. Particularly important has been the interest in Continental theorists of various stripes, most of whom reflect a vaguely leftist radical social constructionism and antinaturalism, in which humans are epiphenomena of some submerged sinister power structure or other, combined with a self-conscious "advocacy" agenda in which the claims to social justice of historically excluded groups—in the comfortable, white, haute bourgeoise world of Classics, this means women and homosexuals—will be furthered by scholarly reinterpretations of ancient society. As a result, much tendentious, theoretically self-conscious "scholarship" on ancient sexuality has flooded the library shelves. For a discussion of these issues the reader should see Camille Paglia's brilliantly savage demolition of the new careerist scholarship's pretensions and shortcomings in "Junk Bonds and Corporate Raiders: Academe in the Hour of the Wolf," *Arion*, n.s., 1.2 (1991), 139–212; rpt. in *Sex, Art, and American Culture* (New York, 1992), 170–248. See also my "Idolon Theatri: Foucault and the Classicists," *CML* 12.1 (1991), 81–100; "Constructionism and Ancient Greek Sex," *Helios* 18.2 (1991), 181–93. For the role of opportunism and careerism in shaping classical scholarship see, in addition to Paglia, John Heath, "Self-Promotion and the Crisis in Classics," *CW* 89.1 (1995), 3–24.

     However, unlike what happens in academic criticism in English literature departments, where semiliterate subjectivity is unrestrained—since it's relatively easy to acquire the knack of interpreting literature written in one's native tongue—as a discipline Classics has a firmer empirical foundation: the actual texts and fragments that scholars must learn to read in the original language and that cannot with impunity be capriciously translated or tortured. This prerequisite skill imposes an absolute limit on fanciful speculation, though of course there are plenty of Greek- and Latin-reading dunces. In addition, classicists are trained to ground any argument directly on those texts and to locate it in the tradition of previous scholarship. These professional limits account for a lot of soporific pedantry, but they also mean that even the most ideologically or theoretically loaded argument will occasionally yield some nuggets of valuable information, if one has the patience to pan out the mud of jargon and ideology.

xii   We should heed Kilmer's caution about extrapolating "from the visual depictions left us by Greek painters to the everyday lives of the individuals whose activities they are normally assumed to be illustrating. The difficulties are particularly acute in the case of erotica. Some of the problems involved have to do with the fact that the illustrations of sexual activity on vases are likely often to have as much to do with fantasy as with ordinary life. There are further problems which pertain to the intentions of the artists—to amuse, rather than to inform, I should think—and still others having to do with the intended and actual clienteles. The fact that so many of the surviving vases come from Italy, and especially from Etruria, has a significance which is difficult to assess. How well does the sample represent the original production, and how much is it biased by Etruscan taste?" *Greek Erotica*, 170; see too 213–15.

xii   Lionel Trilling is worth quoting further on the "evanescent context" lost from past literature: "The voice of multifarious intention and activity . . . all the buzz of implication which always surrounds us in the present, coming to us from what never gets fully stated." "Manners, Morals, and the Novel" (1948), rpt. in *The Liberal Imagination* (New York, 1950), 200.

xii   The oddness of the Greeks has been long acknowledged. W.H. Auden made the same point about their strangeness in "The Greeks and Us," his preface to *The Viking Portable Greek Reader*, 1948, rpt. in *Forewords and Afterwords* (New York, 1974), 15. See also his comments on "The Erotic Hero," 22–25.

INTRODUCTION

1   A description and analysis of the *nomos/phusis* idea in Greek thought can be found in W.K.C. Guthrie, *A History of Greek Philosophy, Volume 3: The Fifth-Century Enlightenment* (Cambridge, 1969), 55–134. See also Charles Segal, "The Raw and the Cooked in Greek Literature: Structure, Values, Metaphor," *CJ* 69, no. 4 (1974), 289–300. With its interest in bipolar oppositions and their mediation, structuralism, when it hasn't lapsed into a mania for schemata medieval in its totalizing scope, has been fruitful in bringing out the tense contrast of culture and nature in Greek thought, for structuralism's "emphasis falls not so much upon the dominant, ideal values at the surface of the culture as on the subsurface tensions within the system, the dynamic pulls that the culture has to allow, resist, and contain in order to exist" (Charles Segal, "Greek Tragedy and Society," 1981, rpt. in *Interpreting Greek Tragedy: Myth, Poetry, Text* [Ithaca, N.Y., 1986], 22–23). One of the "pulls" comprises the forces of nature, including eros, that constantly impinge on the cultural orders created to control and exploit them.

2   The landscape of Greece itself helps to account for the ancient Greeks' ambivalence toward nature. Michael Grant notes that the Mediterranean area is a "paradox of fruitfulness and frugality, rich both in suggestions and obstacles. Conditions are exceptionally discouraging and exceptionally favourable at the same time. People must never relax their efforts to direct nature and correct and check it, and keep it under control." Hence the Greek concern with the control and exploitation of nature: "Nowhere is this effect of man on nature as inextricably all-pervading as in the Mediterranean." *The Ancient Mediterranean* (1969; rpt. New York, 1988), 313, 314. Cf. Victor Davis Hanson: "The agrarian ideology of self against nature is crucial to understanding the political and military mentality of agrarianism, and thus the entire cultural history of the ancient Greek *polis*," in *The Other Greeks* (New York, 1995), 155.

4–5   The ambiguity of the landscape in Greek literature has been analyzed in terms of the nature/culture contrast by Charles Segal, "Nature and the World of Man in Greek Literature," *Arion* 2 (1963), 19–53.

CHAPTER 1

12   A brief discussion of erotic imagery in lyric poetry can be found in David A. Campbell, *The Golden Lyre: The Themes of the Greek Lyric Poets* (London, 1983), 1–27. Also for images of eros related to its impact on the mind, see Ruth Padel, *In and Out of Mind: Greek Images of the Tragic Self* (Princeton, N.J., 1992), 114–37. Monica Silveira Cyrino's *In Pandora's Jar: Lovesickness in Early Greek Poetry* (Lan-

ham, Maryland, 1995) was published after this book was finished. Eros as sickness has a long history in the West, culminating in Freudian psychology and modern sex technicians like Dr. Ruth Westheimer. Particularly fascinating are the early "scientific" treatises such as Robert Burton's *The Anatomy of Melancholy* and Jacques Ferrand's *A Treatise on Lovesickness.* See the edition of the latter by Donald A. Blecher and Massimo Ciavoiella (Syracuse, N.Y., 1990), particularly 3–202 for the early modern *scientia sexualis.*

18   *Atê* is a complex concept in ancient Greek literature, and no doubt my definition here leaves much to be desired. Those interested in exploring the complexities of this idea should start with E.R. Dodds's discussion of *atê* in *The Greeks and the Irrational* (Berkeley and Los Angeles, 1951), 1–63. A recent critical survey of various interpretations is Matt Neuberg's "*Atê* Reconsidered," in *Nomodeiktes: Greek Studies in Honor of Martin Ostwald* (Ann Arbor, Mich., 1993), 491–504.

20   A photograph of a reconstructed *iunx* can be found in A.S.F. Gow's *Theocritus,* 2d ed., vol. 2 (Cambridge, 1952). See also his discussion on 41. The link between eros, magic, and violence is explored in Christopher A. Farrone, "The Wheel, the Whip, and Other Implements of Torture: Erotic Magic in Pindar *Pythian* 4.213–19," *CJ* 89, no. 1 (1993), 1–20.

23   This stark separation of sex and violence is still an unquestioned assumption in our culture. Cf. Bill Moyers, during an interview about a series on violence for PBS: "How have we come to tame that aggression [innate in humans] and channel it into work, sex, love, compassion, altruism?" *Fresno Bee,* 9 January 1995. A Greek would have been puzzled to see sex listed with altruism in contrast to violence.

23   For military erotic metaphors see Leah Rissman, *Love as War: Homeric Allusion in the Poetry of Sappho* (Konigstein, 1983). Violence and eros are discussed in Walter Burkert, *Homo Necans: The Anthropology of Ancient Greek Sacrificial Ritual and Myth,* trans. Peter Bing (Berkeley and Los Angeles, 1983), 58–82. Cf. 59: "Male aggression and male sexuality are closely bound up with one another, stimulated simultaneously and almost always inhibited together."

31   A brief survey of sexual fire imagery is in Jeffrey Henderson, *The Maculate Muse: Obscene Language in Attic Comedy,* 2d ed. (New York and Oxford, 1991), 177–78.

35   For a more detailed analysis of this belief in the detrimental effects of losing sperm see Aline Rousselle, *Porneia: On Desire and the Body in Antiquity,* trans. Felicia Pheasant (Oxford, 1980), 12–15.

35   The impact of the sea on the imagination of the ancient Greeks is enormous. See the brief discussion by Michael Grant, *The Ancient Mediterranean,* 144–47.

37   This point about the sexual implications of sailing imagery in Euripides' *Trojan Women* is made by Elizabeth Craik, "Sexual Imagery and Innuendo in *Troades,*" in *Euripides, Women, and Sexuality* (New York, 1990), 1–15. For comic sailing metaphors for sex see Henderson, *The Maculate Muse,* 162ff.

CHAPTER 2

49   An extensive description of the various incarnations of Aphrodite, her functions, and her symbols is in Lewis Richard Farnell's *The Cults of the Greek States,* vol. 2

(Oxford, 1896), 618–730. Readers should beware, though, of Farnell's late-Victorian Hellenic idealism that, for example, won't let him accept that temple prostitutes or physical sex were any part of Aphrodite's worship during the Classical period: "Although we have no proof of immorality being at any time a common characteristic of the worship of Aphrodite in the Greek states . . . yet we have signs of a degeneracy that belongs to the later period," 667. A substantial overview of Aphrodite's origins, literary incarnations, and meanings can be found in Paul Friedrich's *The Meaning of Aphrodite* (Chicago and London, 1978). Also helpful is Nicole Loraux's "What Is a Goddess?" in *From Ancient Goddesses to Christian Saints*, ed. Pauline Schmitt Pantel, trans. Arthur Goldhammer (1990; Cambridge, Mass., 1994), 11–45, vol. 1 of *A History of Women*, eds. Georges Duby and Michelle Perrot.

50   For a discussion of this "female disease" and its possible meanings see W.W. How and J. Wells, *A Commentary on Herodotus* (Oxford, 1912), *ad loc.*

52   See Friedrich's discussion of the epithet "laughter/penis-loving" in *The Meaning of Aphrodite*, 202–04.

53   The historical development and origins of Aphrodite are described in Friedrich, *The Meaning of Aphrodite*, 129–48.

53   See Friedrich, 201–02, for the etymology of Aphrodite's name.

55   For Aphrodite Pandemos see David Halperin, "The Democratic Body: Prostitution and Citizenship in Classical Athens," in *One Hundred Years of Homosexuality* (New York and London, 1990), 104–07.

59   My understanding of the *Hymn to Aphrodite* has been influenced by Charles Segal's "The Homeric Hymn to Aphrodite: A Structuralist Approach," *CW* 67.4 (1974). See also Jenny Strauss Clay, *The Politics of Olympus: Form and Meaning in the Major Homeric Hymns* (Princeton, N.J., 1989), 152–201. The general reader will get the most out of Peter Walcot's "The Homeric Hymn to Aphrodite: A Literary Appraisal," *GR* 38.2 (1991), 137–55.

60   As a woman and a poet who writes of erotic attachments to other women, Sappho bears two of the "fashionable stigmata," to borrow Wendell Berry's phrase, that excite modern "advocacy" critics. Hence the endless stream of interpretations that promote banal ideas such as the following: "Sappho's fragments [offer] an erotic practice and discourse outside of patriarchal modes of thought" and Sappho "constructs erotic experience outside male assumptions about dominance and submission" (Ellen Greene, "Apostrophe and Women's Erotics in the Poetry of Sappho," *TAPA* 124 [1994], 42). In words other than poststructuralist and feminist clichés, those bad boys just want to dominate, penetrate, and get back to the football game, whereas homosexual women are caring, sensitive, considerate creatures whose sexual practices are mutually gratifying—and Sappho is their ancient mother. This follows a particularly unconvincing interpretation of Sappho by John J. Winkler, in which her fragments are made to elicit the belief that they invite us to "think of the interconnection of all the parts of the body in a long and diffuse act of love, rather than the genital-centered and more relentlessly goal-oriented pattern of love-making which men have been known to employ" ("Double Consciousness in Sappho's Lyrics," *The Constraints of Desire: The Anthropology of Sex and Gender in Ancient Greece* [New York and London, 1990], 186). Such interpretations tell us a lot about New Age sentimental femi-

nism but very little about Sappho. Readers who want some sensible information about Aphrodite in Sappho Fr. 1 should start with Denys Page, *Sappho and Alcaeus: An Introduction to the Study of Ancient Lesbian Poetry* (Oxford, 1955), 3–18, 126–28. "Lesbian," by the way, refers to the island of Lesbos, home of Sappho and another great seventh-century Archaic poet, Alcaeus, not to female homosexuals. See too Leah Rissman's discussion of Sappho's use of Homeric diction and imagery to elaborate on the metaphor of love as war in Fr. 1C, in *Love as War: Homeric Allusion in the Poetry of Sappho*, 1–29. Margaret Williamson's *Sappho's Immortal Daughters* (Cambridge, Mass. and London, 1995), appeared after I completed this book.

61   My reading of Euripides' *Hippolytus* and Aphrodite's role in the play owes much to Charles Segal's important article, "The Tragedy of the *Hippolytus*: The Waters of Ocean and the Untouched Meadow," *HSCP* 70 (1965), 117–70.

63   For Hippolytus as representative of this type of late-fifth-century Athenian see L.B. Carter, *The Quiet Athenian* (Oxford, 1986), 52–56.

CHAPTER 3

The volume of scholarship on women in ancient Greece has increased exponentially in the last twenty-five years. Some very good work has been done, but unfortunately much tendentious "advocacy" research has contributed to the distorted views of ancient Greek women that pass for received wisdom these days. Despite some modern scholars' implied claims of giving ancient women a voice long silenced by sexist scholarship, ancient Greek women have been a topic of inquiry throughout the century, usually sympathetically, no doubt because of the influence of nineteenth-century feminism and J.J. Bachofen, whose theory of a prehistorical matriarchy is still alive in New Age feminism. (For a historical critique of the persistence of Bachofen's theory in modern classics see Mary Lefkowitz, *Women in Greek Myth* [Baltimore, Md., 1986], 15–29.) The dominant view of Greek women, and the one most current today, is that they were beaten-down recluses whose husbands despised them. Cf., e.g., Lawrence Stone, who recently described Greek women as "mostly cooped up at home for breeding purposes" ("The Use and Abuse of Herstory," *New Republic*, no. 4,137 [2 May 1994], 35).

This view, or at least its corollary that Greek men found romantic sexual satisfaction primarily with boys or prostitutes, can be found in E.F.M. Benecke, who surveyed the depictions of women in Greek literature in *Antimachus of Colophon and the Position of Women in Greek Poetry* (1896; Groningen, 1970). Benecke's thesis was that Greek literature doesn't refer to love between men and women before Antimachus of Colophon's poem *Lyde* of 400 B.C., all earlier erotic references hence homosexual. F.A. Wright, in *Feminism in Greek Literature: From Homer to Aristotle* (1923; Port Washington, N.Y., and London, 1969), describes the literary depictions of women, sternly disapproving of their treatment at the hands of depraved Greek men. He is rather extreme: "The Greek world perished from one main cause, a low ideal of womanhood and a degradation of women which found expression both in literature and in social life," 1. We can see in Wright too just how old is the received wisdom, still repeated today, that Greek women were sequestered drudges locked up in their quarters: "A woman's life at Athens in the fifth century B.C. was a dreary business. She was confined closely in the house, a harem prisoner. . . . An Athenian house was small, dark, and uncomfortable, and a woman's day was occupied with a long round of monotonous work. Occasionally she was allowed out of prison to walk in some sacred procession," 57–58.

Charles Seltman, in *Women in Antiquity* (London and New York, 1956), took exception to this view of Athenian women and correctly saw that it reflected the prejudices of scholars who saw women as weak creatures in need of close supervision, 111–14. Cf. 137: "The all-male life of the 19th-century public school and college inclined too many scholars to retro-spective wishful thinking. In their day-dreams they wanted to think of their beloved Atheni-ans as people unencumbered, like themselves, by femininity." Seltman, however, swings too far in the other direction, ignoring the very real anxiety aroused in men by the specter of a chaotic female eros. At any rate, the "seclusion" thesis remained lively, cropping up again in Robert Flacelière's *Daily Life in Greece at the Time of Pericles* (London, 1965), e.g., 55.

I have dwelt on these older surveys of ancient Greek attitudes toward women to make the point that the common feminist view of Greek women as secluded drudges, despite be-ing accompanied by claims of daring revision of sexist orthodoxy, has *itself* been the ortho-doxy since the nineteenth century. Sarah Pomeroy's survey, *Goddesses, Whores, Wives, and Slaves* (New York, 1975), though it usually describes the ancient evidence objectively, is still informed by this hoary feminist tradition. Thus we learn that women were kept at home in quarters that were "dark, squalid, and unsanitary," their work not letting them out of the house (79). And though "[w]omen of all economic classes went out for festivals and funer-als" (80), they "were usually secluded so that they could not be seen by men who were not close relatives," 81. Presumably all the men stayed indoors when the women participated in the numerous festivals celebrated throughout the Greek year. Eva Cantarella, *Pandora's Daughters: The Role and Status of Women in Greek and Roman Antiquity*, trans. Maureen B. Fant (1981; Baltimore, Md., 1987), follows in the same tradition: Greek women were "closed off in the internal part of the house to which the men did not have access"; their lives were "empty" and "deprived of interests and gratifications," 46. They were "excluded" from "love . . . which . . . found its highest expression in relationships between men," 177. This view of Greek women reaches its most extreme expression in Eva Keuls's *The Reign of the Phallus: Sexual Politics in Ancient Athens*, 2d ed. (Berkeley and Los Angeles, 1993). Greek women, vic-tims of a "phallic ethos" (34), now spend "their lives wrapped in veils, nameless, concealing their identity, and locked away in the dark recesses of closed-in homes," 97. Any reader of Aristophanes can see for herself the limitations of this interpretation.

Throughout this chapter I will refer to other works on ancient women that avoid the orthodox view of some modern feminists. Mary Lefkowitz's *Women in Greek Myth* is a good example of sound scholarship whose first allegiance is to the evidence, which on its own affords us ample grounds for criticizing the Greek estimation of women (see espe-cially 112–32, which finds the roots of Greek misogyny in the recognition of eros's volatil-ity). But the seclusion thesis has had remarkable staying power. For more temperate ver-sions see also W.K. Lacey, *The Family in Classical Greece* (1968; Ithaca, N.Y., 1984), 151–76; and J.P. Gould, "Law, Custom, and Myth: Aspects of the Social Position of Women in Clas-sical Athens," *JHS* 100 (1980), 38–59. For other writing on Greek women see Marilyn B. Arthur, "Early Greece: The Origins of the Western Attitude Toward Women," in *Women in the Ancient World: The Arethusa Papers*, ed. J. Peradotto and J.P. Sullivan (Albany, N.Y., 1984), 7–58; David Cohen, *Law, Sexuality, and Society: The Enforcement of Morals in Classical Athens* (Cambridge, 1991), especially 133–70; Roger Just, *Women in Athenian Law and Life* (London and New York, 1989); Raphael Sealey, *Women and Law in Classical Greece* (Chapel Hill, N.C., and London, 1990); Gillian Clark, *Women in the Ancient World* (Oxford, 1989); Margaret Williamson, *Sappho's Immortal Daughters*, 90–132; Martin Kilmer, *Greek Erotica*, 133–69; and the essays in Helene P. Foley, *Reflections of Women in Antiquity* (New York, 1981). The recently published *Women in the Classical World*, by Elaine Fantham, Helene Peet Foley, Natalie Boymel Kampen, Sarah B. Pomeroy, and H. Alan Shapiro (Oxford and New York, 1994), 1–206, discusses, usually fairly, most of the literary, visual, and archaeological evidence and is well illustrated. See too Nancy Demand, *Birth, Death, and Motherhood in Classical Greece* (Baltimore, Md., and London, 1994). Many key documents have been gathered and translated in Mary R. Lefkowitz and Maureen B. Fant, *Women's Life in Greece and Rome: A Source Book in Translation* (Baltimore, Md., 1982). Sue Blundell's ideologically correct *Women in Ancient Greece* (Cambridge, Mass., 1995), was published after I finished this book. Bibliographical surveys include S.C. Humphreys, *The Family, Women, and Death: Comparative Studies* (London, 1983), 33–57, and Sarah B. Pomeroy, "Selected Bibliography on Women in Classical Antiquity," in *Women in the Ancient World*, 315–72. See also Pomeroy's "The Study of Women in Antiquity: Past, Present, and Future," *AJPH* 112.2 (1991), 263–69.

69   The view of Greek women's isolation sketched above and taken to an extreme in Keuls's work has had its critics over the years. In addition to Seltman, A.W. Gomme, in "The Position of Women in Athens in the Fifth and Fourth Centuries," *CPh* 20 (1925), 1–25, argued against it. Cf. also C.D. Richter, "The Position of Women in Classical Athens," *CJ* 67, 1–8, and H.D.F. Kitto, *The Greeks* (Harmondsworth, Eng., 1951), 233–36. (Both Gomme [1] and Richter [1–2] provide even more examples of the ubiquity and persistance of the "seclusion" thesis.) More recently David Cohen has marshaled the evidence against seclusion in *Law, Sexuality, and Society*, 149ff. A balanced assessment of the ancient sources by Roger Just concludes: "Athenian women were not literally locked away. Nevertheless, the ideology of female seclusion, the degree of male oversight, and the workings of a morality of social distance all meant that women's legally subordinate and sheltered role was matched by the mores of daily life," in *Women in Athenian Law and Life*, 124; evidence surveyed at 106–25. In other words, women weren't *literally* locked away, but the effect *psychologically* was the same. This interpretation has the advantage of reconciling the "optimists" and "pessimists" but is weakened by the fact that we have no evidence for assessing the efficacy or nuances of the psychological effects wrought on the minds of Greek women by the "mores of daily life." Some women, no doubt, simply ignored them; some, perhaps most, like the women of Aristophanes, probably had the intelligence and strength to subvert them.

70   Gould, in "Law, Custom and Myth," 57, aptly summarizes Greek attitudes toward women: "Male attitudes to women, and to themselves in relation to women, are marked by tension, anxiety, and fear. Women are not part of, do not belong easily in, the male ordered world of the 'civilised' community; they have to be accounted for in other terms, and they threaten continually to overturn its stability or subvert its continuity, to break out of the place assigned to them by their partial incorporation within it. Yet they are essential to it: they are producers and bestowers of wealth and children, the guarantors of due succession, the guardians of the *oikos* and its hearth. Men are their sons, and are brought up, as children, by them and among them. Like the earth and once-wild animals, they must be tamed and

cultivated by men, but their 'wildness' will out." See Helene P. Foley, "The Conception of Women in Athenian Drama," in *Reflections of Women in Antiquity*, 127–63, especially 140–48, for a critical discussion of the view of ancient Greek women as "natural" versus "cultural" men.

70   The picture of women as controlled by appetite and vulnerable to their excessive passions is ubiquitous in the secondary literature. A recent descriptive survey is in Just, *Women in Athenian Law and Life*, 153–93.

70   Pericles' brief mention of women in his funeral speech is one of the standard pieces of evidence for the "silencing" of women. Recently Lisa Kallet-Marx has pointed out that Pericles addresses the war widows, not women in general, and is commenting on *their* public responsibilities deriving from their privileged status as wives of the slain. "Thucydides 2.45.2 and the Status of War Widows in Periclean Athens," *Nomodeiktes: Greek Studies in Honor of Martin Ostwald* (Ann Arbor, Mich., 1993), 133–43.

73   For ancient sex manuals see Holt N. Parker, "Love's Body Anatomized: The Ancient Erotic Handbooks and the Rhetoric of Sexuality," in Amy Richlin, ed., *Pornography and Representation in Greece and Rome* (New York and Oxford, 1992), 90–112.

73   Another piece of evidence in the indictment of Athenian male sexism is the presumed existence of "men's quarters" and "women's quarters," the former comfortable, facing the street, and the scene of male symposiastic camaraderie that was forbidden to the wives locked away in their dark and dank quarters. See Susan Walker, "Women and Housing in Classical Greece: The Archaeological Evidence," in *Images of Women in Antiquity*, ed. Averil Cameron and Amélie Kuhrt (Detroit, Mich., 1983), 81–91, who repeats the by now obligatory formula "cramped and dreary quarters," 82. More recently Michael Jameson has shown that little archaeological evidence survives to establish that there were indeed clearly segregated "men's" and "women's" quarters, "Private Space and the Greek City," in *The Greek City: From Homer to Alexander*, ed. Oswyn Murray and Simon Price (Oxford, 1990), 171–95, esp. 172. Sarah B. Pomeroy, in *Xenophon's Oeconomicus: A Social and Historical Commentary* (Oxford, 1994), 295–97 (see especially 295 n. 220), discusses the issue of women's seclusion more temperately than in her earlier work.

74   A brief description of ancient weaving, its connection with women, and the weaving of Athena's robe can be found in E.J.W. Barber, "The Peplos of Athena," in Jenifer Neils, ed., *Goddess and Polis: The Panathenaic Festival in Ancient Athens* (Hanover, N.H., and Princeton, N.J., 1992), 103–18.

76–77   See the survey of slang for the female pudenda in Jeffrey Henderson, *The Maculate Muse*, 131–33. For pigs specifically cf. Mark Golden, "Male Chauvinists and Pigs," *Echos du Monde Classique/Classical Views* 32, n.s., 7 (1988), 1–12.

77   Further discussion of Semonides is found in Hugh Lloyd-Jones, *Female of the Species: Semonides on Women* (London, 1975). Also see Nicole Loraux, "On the Race of Women and Some of Its Tribes: Hesiod and Semonides," 1978, rpt. in *The Children of Athena: Athenian Ideas About Citizenship and the Division Between the Sexes,* trans. Caroline Levine (Princeton, N.J., 1993), 72–110.

77–78   For the significance of bees and their relation to chastity see Marcel Detienne, "The Myth of 'Honeyed Orpheus,'" in *Myth, Religion, and Society: Structuralist Es-*

says by M. Detienne, L. Gernet, J.-P. Vernant, and P. Vidal-Naquet, ed. R.L. Gordon (Cambridge, 1981), 98–99.

78   Aristotle's speculations about female biology, and the medical writers' theories about menstruation and other reproductive processes, have both attracted a lot of recent attention, for obvious reasons: The various and somewhat zany—but, given the crudity of medical science, understandable—theories about women and reproduction provide more ammunition for the shelling of ancient Greek sexism. See Anne Carson, "Putting Her in Her Place: Women, Dirt, and Desire," in *Before Sexuality*, 135–69, and Ruth Padel, "Women: Model for Possession by Greek Daemons," in *Images of Women in Antiquity*, 3–19. For discussions of the image of female biology in philosophers and medical writers see Aline Rouselle, *Porneia*, 24–46; Lesley Dean-Jones, "The Cultural Construct of the Female Body in Classical Greek Science," in *Women's History and Ancient History*, ed. Sarah B. Pomeroy (Chapel Hill, N.C., 1991), 111–37; Ann Ellis Hanson, "The Medical Writers' Woman," in *Before Sexuality*, 309–38; Thomas Lacqueur, *Making Sex: Body and Gender from the Greeks to Freud* (Cambridge, Mass., 1990), 25–62; and Giulia Sissa, "The Sexual Philosophies of Plato and Aristotle," in *From Ancient Goddesses to Christian Saints*, 46–82.

79   Of all the sexist crimes of the Greeks, "hysteria" is one of the worst to feminists, for it tries to locate a perceived inferior female character in an unalterable fact of women's biology, thus legitimizing their subjection to men. See Aline Rouselle, *Porneia*, 67–77; Mary Lefkowitz, "The Wandering Womb," in *Heroines and Hysterics* (New York, 1981), 12–25; Helen King, "Bound to Bleed: Artemis and Greek Women," in *Images of Women in Antiquity*, 109–27; and Ann Ellis Hanson, "Continuity and Change: Three Case Studies in Hippocratic Gynecological Therapy and Theory," in *Women's History and Ancient History*, 73–110; Nancy Demand, *Birth, Death, and Motherhood in Classical Greece*, 33–70. Cf. Lesley Dean-Jones, "The Cultural Construct of the Female Body," 122–23: "The 'wandering womb' deprives a woman of control over her sexuality—a bestial or god-like creature seeking to dominate the seats of the soul" located in the heart, liver, and brain.

79–80   Just explains the interconnection of woman's perceived subjection to their natural appetites and their exclusion from political rule: "It is the opposition between those innately possessed of self-control, and those who lack it, that ideologically renders women's subordinated place within the structure of the *polis* a 'natural' one," 166. "Freedom referred not only to a logically defined status, but to a general condition of autonomy; autonomy meant freedom not only from the command of others, but also from bodily desires and emotions; freedom from the bodily desires entailed 'self-control,' the mastery of the rational self of those bodily desires and emotions which threatened to enslave it," 184.

81   For Prometheus and Pandora see J.-P. Vernant, "The Myth of Prometheus in Hesiod," in *Myth, Religion, and Society*, 43–56; Nicole Loraux, "On the Race of Women"; and Linda S. Sussman, "Workers and Drones: Labor Idleness and Gender Definition in Hesiod's Beehive," in *Women in the Ancient World*, 79–93.

82   The symbolism of dogs in ancient Greek literature is discussed in S. Lilja, *Dogs in Ancient Greek Poetry* (Helsinki, 1976).

83   A descriptive survey of Helen's character can be found in Linda L. Clades, *Helen: The Evolution from Divine to Heroic in Greek Epic Traditions* (Leiden, 1976). A more

recent study focusing on Helen's dual nature is Norman Austin, *Helen of Troy and Her Shameless Phantom* (Ithaca, N.Y., 1994). Nicole Loraux's "The Phantom of Sexuality" (*The Experience of Tiresias*, trans. Paula Wissing [Princeton, N.J., 1995], 194–210), came to my attention after the completion of this book, as did Robert Emmet Meagher, *Helen: Myth, Legend, and the Culture of Misogyny* (New York, 1995).

85   For Astyanassa see Holt N. Parker, "Love's Body Anatomized," 92.

91   Much has been written about Medea, but readers should start with Bernard Knox's "The *Medea* of Euripides," 1977; rpt. in *Word and Action: Essays on the Ancient Theater* (Baltimore, Md., and London, 1979), 295–322.

96   A recent analysis of Deianira's character can be found in Christopher A. Faraone, "Deianira's Mistake and the Demise of Heracles: Erotic Magic in Sophocles' *Trachiniae*," *Helios* 21.2 (1994), 115–35.

CHAPTER 4

Recent writing on homosexuality in ancient Greece is overwhelmingly influenced by K.J. Dover's *Greek Homosexuality*. Though an old-style empirical philologist, Dover excited the "advocacy" scholars with his thesis that the Greeks were indifferent to same-sex relations, indeed considered them perfectly normal as long as the participants observed certain protocols and conventions, particularly a dominance-submission paradigm that reflected the political status of the "boy-love" and the older male and that was sexually expressed in the act of penetration (in the case of pederasty, of the boy's thighs). This paradigm included ritualistic conventions such as the requirement that the boy be courted and play hard to get, that his reputation be protected, that he not be anally penetrated, that he not receive money, and that he not enjoy the "intercrural" sex—the older man's penis rubbing between his thighs. Any condemnation of same-sex relations derived not from a disapproval of such relations per se, but from a failure of the participants in such a relationship to respect these conventions, thus challenging the political power structure they reflected.

Dover was elaborated on, with a heavy dose of Continental theorizing, by David Halperin, "The Democratic Body: Prostitution and Citizenship in Classical Athens" (in *One Hundred Years of Homosexuality* [New York and London, 1990], 88–112), and John J. Winkler, "Laying Down the Law: The Oversight of Men's Sexual Behavior in Classical Athens" (in *The Constraints of Desire*, 45–70; for a generally sympathetic review of Dover, Winkler, and Halperin see Mark Golden, "Thirteen Years of Homosexuality [And Other Recent Work on Sex, Gender, and the Body in Ancient Greece]," *Echos du Monde Classique/Classical Views* 35, n.s., 10 [1991], 327–40; see too David Cohen, "Sex, Gender, and Sexuality in Ancient Greece," *CPh* 87.2 [1992], 145–60; for a critique of the social-constructionist interpretation of homosexuality see John Boswell, "Revolutions, Universals, and Sexual Categories," in *Hidden from History: Reclaiming the Gay and Lesbian Past*, ed. Martin Duberman, Martha Vicinus, and George Chauncey [New York, 1989], 17–36; Winkler and Halperin were brutally demolished by Camille Paglia in "Junk Bonds and Corporate Raiders").

Eva Cantarella pretty much follows the Dover line as well, although she claims (unconvincingly) that some of the restrictions Dover identified did not apply, e.g., that on anal intercourse between boy-love and lover (*Bisexuality in the Ancient World*, trans. Cormac O

Cuilleanáin [1988; New Haven and London, 1992], 3–93). Likewise Foucault built his analysis of the concern with moderation and excess out of the dominance-submission/active-passive paradigm (*The Use of Pleasure*, 46–47, 187–214, see especially 215). David Cohen, in *Law, Sexuality, and Society*, 171–202, has pointed out the oversimplicity and patness of the Dover model as elaborated by Foucault, the way it glosses over the anxiety and ambivalence surrounding same-sex relations in ancient Greece, as well as passing too lightly over or rationalizing away the very real evidence of disgust toward the passive homosexual irrespective of the presumed pederastic protocols. Cf. Cohen's remarks in another article: "The widely differing attitudes and conflicting norms and practices [of Greek homoeroticism] represent the disagreements, contradictions and anxieties which make up the patterned chaos of a complex culture. They should not be rationalized away. To make them over into a neatly coherent and internally consistent system would only serve to diminish our understanding of the 'many-hued' nature of Athenian homosexuality," in "Homosexuality in Classical Athens," *Past and Present*, no. 117 (1991), 3–21, quote on 21.

100   See note 3 in Chapter 4. See also E. Eyben, "Antiquity's View of Puberty," *Latomus* 31 (1972), 677–97, especially 691–95, for the distinction between adolescent down and the adult's full beard. Cantarella, in *Bisexuality in the Ancient World*, argues for seventeen or eighteen as the age ending "boy-love" status, but she depends mainly on Strato, who wrote four hundred years after the heyday of pederasty in Classical Athens (Cantarella, 36–42).

101   The culture/nature issue is discussed in Dover, *Greek Homosexuality*, 60–68; for Plato and Aristotle, see 165–70. Cf. also Winkler, "Laying Down the Law," 64–70.

102   For the myth of Chrysippus see Bernard Sergent, *Homosexuality in Greek Myth*, trans. Arthur Goldhammer (1984; Boston, 1986), 67–70.

103   The Dorians, Spartans, and homosexuality are discussed in Dover, *Greek Homosexuality*, 185–96, Paul Cartledge, "The Politics of Spartan Pederasty," *Proceedings of the Cambridge Philological Society*, n.s., 27 (1981), 17–36, and Sergent, *Homosexuality in Greek Myth*, 16–49. A popular explanation for pederasty relates it to initiation rituals that effect the boy's transition from the female-dominated world of childhood into the male warrior society, as occurs in some primitive societies such as the Aranda of Australia or the Marind-Anim of Dutch New Guinea. The "rite of passage" thesis is consistent with the marked aristocratic and militaristic aura that clings to pederasty in the Greek evidence (see Cartledge, 23–26, Cantarella, *Bisexuality in the Ancient World*, 4–8, J. Bremmer, "An Enigmatic Indo-European Rite: Paederasty," *Arethusa* 13 [1980], 279–98). Dover has criticized this interpretation in "Greek Homosexuality and Initiation," *The Greeks and Their Legacy* (Oxford, 1988), 115–34. Mark Golden offers a modified "rite of passage" interpretation: "Athenian male homosexuality (whatever its origins) was in part an institution of transition from the subordinate and quasi-servile status of boyhood to the status of adult free citizen; . . . certain conventions of Athenian male homosexuality marked the Athenian male off from the slaves with whom he was otherwise so closely associated," "Slavery and Homosexuality at Athens," *Phoenix* 38 (1984), 308–25, quote on 309. Finally, mention should be made of a briefly influential Freudian interpretation of Greek homosexuality and misogyny by Philip Slater, who linked both to the dominance of Greek boys by their mothers, since the latter presumably were the primary caretakers of male children until the age of

seven, while the father was off leering at the teenagers in the gymnasium (*The Glory of Hera: Greek Mythology and the Greek Family* [Boston, 1968], 3–74).

106   Cf. Cohen, *Law, Sexuality, and Society*, 187: "Sexual roles . . . were defined in terms of a male/female dichotomy and judged by norms that were felt by some to be at once social and natural."

106   For the rivalry of boys and women see the remarks of Cantarella, *Bisexuality in the Ancient World*, 88–91.

106   See Dover, *Greek Homosexuality*, 68–87, for the girlishness of the boy's appearance and behavior, particularly during courtship.

107   Henderson, *The Maculate Muse*, 219–20, documents the insults directed toward the effeminate man.

107   For the significance of hair in pederastic poetry from the *Greek Anthology* see S.L. Tarán, "*Eisi triches*: An Erotic Motif in the Greek Anthology," *JHS* 105 (1985), 90–107.

108   As Barber points out, saffron was a color particularly associated with women's garments, in "The Peplos of Athena," 116.

109   Henderson gives a list of pathics pilloried by the comic poets, 213–15.

110   Cohen, *Law, Sexuality, and Society*, 177–82, provides the evidence supporting the view that sodomizing a citizen-youth could fall under the law against *hubris* (contra Dover, *Greek Homosexuality*, 34–39). For a more detailed analysis see his "Sexuality, Violence, and the Athenian Law of Hubris," *GR* 38.2 (1991), 171–88. Cohen also links *hubris* to the issues of shame and honor: "The law of *hubris* was constituted by a complex normative repertoire which encompassed a variety of forms of aggressive sexual conduct which degrades, dishonors, or insults the victim," 184. An extensive analysis of shame and honor in Greek literature is Douglas L. Cairns' *Aidôs: The Psychology and Ethics of Honor and Shame in Ancient Greek Literature* (Oxford, 1993). Winkler, "Laying Down the Law," argues that the shame/honor paradigm regarding homosexual behavior had meaning only in the context of political participation; cf. 60: "It begins to look as if the entire procedure [of rigorous scrutiny of sexual behavior] had very little to do with sex and everything to do with political ambitions and alliances in the high-stakes game of city leadership according to the rules of honor/shame competition." This still begs the question of why receptive anal penetration per se, rather than, say, fellatio, should be so intensely marked as a disgusting, unnatural activity.

110   These homosexual insults are discussed by Henderson, 209–15; see also Cantarella, 46–48, Dover, 135–53.

CHAPTER 5

Modern philosophy has increasingly become a pseudoscience, with jaw-breaking jargon and complex, abstract arguments accessible only to initiates of the guild. (Cf. William Barrett's remarks on the unfortunate effects of modern philosophy's whoring after the gods of technique, in *The Illusion of Technique: A Search for Meaning in a Technological Civilization* [New York, 1978], 22–25.) Unfortunately, many who write on ancient philosophy assume it was identical to modern, and so write of Plato or Aristotle in the same mind-numbing style. But much of ancient philosophy, Plato in particular, was as much *literary* as it was philosophical. And most of it was particularly concerned with the genuine philosophical issues of what Cicero called the "discipline of living well" (*Disp. Tusc.* 4.3.6): what we should value, what makes for happiness, and what should motivate our choices. My discussion of the philosophers, then, is concerned with what they say about eros and the sorts of imagery they use to say it. Matters of argumentative nuance or fine-tuning are ignored.

The general reader wishing to become better acquainted with the philosophers and works discussed in this chapter should start with W.K.C. Guthrie's six-volume *History of Greek Philosophy*. For Plato and Aristotle on sex see A.W. Price, *Love and Friendship in Plato and Aristotle* (Oxford, 1989), 223–50. A brief and accessible introduction to Greek philosophy is Julia Annas's "Classical Greek Philosophy," in *The Oxford History of Greece and the Hellenistic World*, ed. John Boardman, Jasper Griffin, and Oswyn Murray (1986; Oxford, 1991), 277–305.

125   The fragments of Empedocles are translated and discussed in G.S. Kirk and J.E. Raven, *The Presocratic Philosophers* (1957; Cambridge, 1963), 320–61; cf. also 24–31 for earlier cosmogonies. See too W.K.C. Guthrie, *The History of Greek Philosophy, Volume 2: The Presocratic Tradition from Parmenides to Democritus* (Cambridge, 1965), 138–85.

126   Cf. Guthrie, *The Presocratic Tradition*, 248–49, for the Golden Age of Love.

127   This view of pleasure, particularly sexual, as a force tending to excess and thus requiring a rational and calculating control is elaborated by Foucault, *The Use of Pleasure*, 33–94; see summary at 91–92.

134   The standard treatment of *sôphrosunê* in Greek thought is Helen North, *Sophrosyne: Self-Knowledge and Self-Restraint in Greek Literature* (Ithaca, N.Y., 1966).

137–38 Euripides' scepticism about the rationalist claims of the new philosophy was analyzed in E.R. Dodds's "Euripides the Irrationalist," *CR* 43 (1929), 97–104. David Roochnik has recently analyzed rationalism in ancient Greek thought in terms of its "tragic" character: "Not only does logos have limits, but . . . it *must* collide with them. This implies that in its initial 'scene' logos does not know its limits. Like the tragic hero, logos has some sort of internal drive toward greatness; it is driven to go beyond the bounds of its legitimate efficaciousness and suffer a catastrophe." *The Tragedy of Reason: Towards a Platonic Conception of Logos* (New York and London, 1990), 13.

CHAPTER 6

140   The imagery from the natural world used to characterize female sexuality is discussed by Page DuBois, *Sowing the Body: Psychoanalysis and Ancient Representations of Women* (Chicago and London, 1988).

143   See Henderson, *The Maculate Muse*, 64–66, for the extensive sexual imagery at the end of the *Peace*.

144   The death imagery used to describe the bride's transition from girlhood to adult woman and mother is oversimplified by Eva Keuls: "Marriage is symbolized as the sacrifice of the bride to the system," *The Reign of the Phallus*, 131. More re-

cently cf. Rush Rehm, *Marriage to Death: The Conflation of Wedding and Funeral Rituals in Greek Tragedy* (Princeton, N.J., 1994), 11–29, where he notes the similarities between the wedding and funeral rituals.

144–45   The centrality and pervasiveness of agriculture in Greek life escape most modern scholars, who have no firsthand familiarity with the quotidian reality that permeated the lives of ancient peoples. Coupled with the fragmentary nature of the written evidence, most of which reflects a narrow urban elite, this ignorance of agricultural practice and experience lessens the force of farming imagery and obscures its meaning for many contemporary scholars. For a recovery of the importance of farming in Greek culture see V.D. Hanson, *The Other Greeks* (New York, 1995).

146   An overview of women's festivals in ancient Greek cities can be found in Louise Bruit Zaidman, "Pandora's Daughters and Rituals in Grecian Cities," *A History of Women*, 338–76.

147   Athenian women participated in nearly half of the some thirty festivals celebrated during the year. This does not mean, of course, that they enjoyed a "separate but equal" status with men, controlling the household and religious festivals while men held political power. Men dominated the celebration of religious festivals and rituals. For example, women were excluded from sacrificing the animal, the central act of most Greek religious ritual. Cf. Zaidman: "The oikos was the domain of women. What went on there went on under their control. But because the oikos was governed by the rules of society, the law of men, masculine law, was ultimately sovereign. Conversely, civic activity in its religious aspect could not ignore women entirely. The sacred required the presence of women because they alone possessed certain keys to the renewal of life and therefore to the perpetuation of the city. The gods spoke to women and expected to be served by women. A door had to be kept ajar for them: women were permitted to perform certain rituals, but only under the close surveillance of men," "Pandora's Daughters," 376.

147   For the Little Bears see Zaidman, 342–44. For the Anthesteria see Zaidman, 357–58, Walter Burkert, *Greek Religion*, trans. John Raffan (Cambridge, Mass., 1985), 237–42, and H.W. Parke, *Festivals of the Athenians* (Ithaca, N.Y., 1977), 107–120.

147   A brief description of the Thesmophoria can be found in Zaidman, 349–53; Walter Burkert, 242–46; and in H.W. Parke, 82–88. The archaeological evidence is considered in Erika Simon, *Festivals of Attica: An Archaeological Commentary* (Madison, Wis., 1983), 18–22. See too Marcel Detienne, "The Violence of Wellborn Ladies: Women in the Thesmophoria," in Marcel Detienne and Jean-Pierre Vernant, *The Cuisine of Sacrifice Among the Greeks*, trans. Paula Wissing (1979; Chicago, 1989), 129–47.

150   Cf. Burkert, *Greek Religion*, 245: "At the core of the festival [the Thesmophoria] there remains the dissolution of the family, the separation of the sexes, and the constitution of a society of women; once in the year at least, the women demonstrate their independence, their responsibility, and importance for the fertility of the community and the land."

150   For the Aphrodisia see Simon, *Festivals of Attica*, 48–51.

150   Details of the Arrephoria are found in Simon, 39–45; Burkert, 228–29; Parke, 141–43; Zaidman, 341–42.

151   For the Panathenaic festival see Jenifer Neils's introduction to *Goddess and Polis*, 14–27.

152   The Adonia is discussed in Burkert, 176–77; Zaidman, 371–372. An extensive analysis is Marcel Detienne's *The Gardens of Adonis: Spices in Greek Mythology*, trans. Janet Lloyd (1972; Hassocks, Sussex, 1977), especially 99–102.

153   The Thesmophoria and Adonia are specifically contrasted by Detienne, "The Myth of 'Honeyed Orpheus,'" 101–02; cf. too *The Gardens of Adonis*, 102ff. Cf. Robert A. Segal: "The myth of Adonis represents . . . the negation of practices without which the polis cannot be conceived: exogamy and reproduction. The myth dramatizes the consequences of rejecting those practices: barrenness and death," in "Adonis: A Greek Eternal Child," *Myth and the Polis*, ed. Dora C. Pozzi and John M. Wickersham (Ithaca, N.Y., and London, 1991), 64–85, quote on 85.

153   The function of Aphrodite in marriage is treated in Farnell, *The Cults of the Greek States*, vol. 2, 655–56; Friedrich, *The Meaning of Aphrodite*, 142–43; and Zaidman, 364–65.

155   For the limiting of Aphrodite's power in the fifth *Homeric Hymn* cf. Ann L.T. Bergren: "The *Hymn* will attempt to resolve the tension between a cosmos controlled by Aphrodite and a cosmos controlled by Zeus into a stable hierarchy in which the immortal male 'tames' the principle of sexuality as an immortal female, who herself 'tames' the mortal male," in "*The Homeric Hymn to Aphrodite*: Tradition and Rhetoric, Praise and Blame," *CA* 8.1 (1989), 1–41, quote on 7.

156   The ancient evidence about Sappho's life—most of it secondhand, late, and polemical—is meager, to say the least, and certainly unreliable. See Mary Lefkowitz, *Lives of the Greek Poets* (Baltimore, Md., 1981), 36–37, for just how little evidence there is. But this lack of evidence hasn't slowed down a mini-industry in classics turning out various speculations about Sappho's life and her relationship to the shadowy young girls whose names survive in her poetry and other ancient testimonia. A recent example is Holt Parker, "Sappho Schoolmistress," *TAPA* 123 (1993), 309–51; see too the response of André Lardinois, "Subject and Circumstance in Sappho's Poetry," *TAPA* 124 (1994), 57–84. The old slander that Sappho killed herself because of unrequited love for a ferryman named Phaon—balm to heterosexual men, evidence to modern feminists of incorrigible heterosexism—has been examined by Gregory Nagy, "Phaethon, Sappho's Phaon, and the White Rock of Leukas," *HSCP* 77 (1973), 137–78. For the ancient evidence see Sappho testimonia 3C, 4C, and 23C, and Fr. 211C. See too Friedrich, *The Meaning of Aphrodite*, 108–28.

157   For conventions of ancient ritual-prayer see Denys Page, *Sappho and Alcaeus*, 16–17.

CHAPTER 7

The volume of recent scholarship on marriage equals, obviously, that on women, with which it overlaps. Brief overviews from varying perspectives include W.K. Lacey, *The Fam-*

ily in Classical Greece, 100–18; J.-P. Vernant, "Marriage," in *Myth and Society in Ancient Greece*, trans. J. Lloyd (1974; New York, 1990), 29–54; Michel Foucault, *The Use of Pleasure*, 141–84; J. Redfield, "Notes on the Greek Wedding," *Arethusa*, 15 (1982), 181–201; Mary R. Lefkowitz, *Women in Greek Myth*, 61–79; Roger Just, *Women in Athenian Law and Life*, 40–104; Wm. Blake Tyrrell and Frieda S. Brown, "Patriarchal Mythmaking on Marriage," in *Athenian Myths and Institutions: Words in Action* (Oxford, 1991), 99–132; Cynthia Patterson, "Marriage and the Married Woman in Athenian Law," in *Women's History and Ancient History*, 48–72; James Redfield, "Homo Domesticus," in *The Greeks*, 153–83. The complexities of Athenian property, inheritance, dowry, and marriage laws are explicated by Claudia Leduc, "Marriage in Ancient Greece," in *A History of Women*, 235–95. For a more detailed study see A.R.W. Harrison, *The Law of Athens, Volume 1: The Family and Property* (Oxford, 1968). Raphael Sealey discusses the "Laws of Gortyn," twelve columns of text inscribed on stone from the fifth-century Cretan town of Gortyn. These laws provide invaluable information about marital law in ancient Greece (*Women and Law in Classical Greece*, 69–74). The Athenian wedding ceremony has been reconstructed from vase-paintings by John H. Oakley and Rebecca H. Sinos, *The Wedding in Ancient Athens* (Madison, Wis., 1993).

165 For adultery-anxiety and its relationship to citizenship see David Cohen, *Law, Sexuality, and Society*, 98–170; also Roger Just, *Women in Athenian Law and Life*, 68–70; W.K. Lacey, *The Family in Classical Greece*, 113–16. Cf. Cohen, 141: "Women are thought to embody a seething sexuality that can ignite an uncontrollable response in men. To preserve the social order, this potentially destructive force must be controlled and mediated through the institution of the family, which, when properly contained and channeled, it serves to reproduce. The male role, then, is to ensure the chastity on which men's reputation, in large part, depends."

165 A recent discussion of the *Against Neaira* can be found in Cynthia Patterson's "The Case Against Neaira and the Public Ideology of the Athenian Family," in *Athenian Identity and Civic Ideology* (Baltimore, Md., and London, 1994), 199–216. Patterson provides on 206 a helpful chronology of Neaira's intricate sexual career.

166 The connection of legitimacy and citizenship to control of female sexuality is summarized by Nancy Demand, *Birth, Death, and Motherhood in Classical Greece*, 147–54.

167 For women and *sôphrosunê* see Helen F. North, "The Mare, the Vixen, and the Bee: Sophrosyne as the Virtue of Women in Antiquity," *Illinois Classical Studies* 2 (1977), 35–48, as well as her more extended study *Sophrosyne*.

169 See Zaidman, "Pandora's Daughters," 365–71, for the woman's supervision of birth, marriage, and death rituals in the household.

170 For Lysias 1 see Edward M. Harris, "Did the Athenians Regard Seduction as a Worse Crime Than Rape?" *CQ* 40.2 (1990), 370–77.

174 This issue of whether or not something like romantic love is evidenced in Greek new comedy is addressed by P.G. Mcc. Brown, "Love and Marriage in Greek New Comedy," *CQ* 43.1 (1993), 189–205, who argues that the evidence does suggest a link between love and marriage. See also P. Walcot, "Romantic Love and True Love: Greek Attitudes to Marriage," *Ancient Society* 18 (1987), 5–33, who surveys the evidence before the Hellenistic period as well; and Niall Rudd,

"Romantic Love in Classical Times?" *Ramus* 10 (1981), 140–58. Cf. Rudd 155: "Romantic love was not unknown in antiquity; it was not confined to homosexual relationships, nor to couples who would not or could not marry. Granted, it did not represent the prevailing social ethos. . . . It was commonly mocked, denigrated, and feared. Yet it was undeniably there, and it was always assumed to be there until very recent times." Indirectly useful is David Konstan, "Premarital Sex, Illegitimacy, and Male Anxiety in Menander and Athens," in *Athenian Identity and Civic Ideology*, 217–35.

175   A useful and well-balanced introduction to the *Oeconomicus* can be found in Sarah B. Pomeroy's *Xenophon's Oeconomicus: A Social and Historical Commentary.*

182   For Alcestis as exemplary wife see C.A.E. Luschnig, "Euripides' *Alcestis* and the Athenian *oikos*," *Dioniso* 60.1 (1990), 9–39.

184   Penelope of late has become interesting to a subspecies of feminist classical scholarship that emphasizes the resourcefulness of ancient women in creating alternative social structures within the confines of patriarchal marriage. See John J. Winkler, "Penelope's Cunning and Homer's," in *The Constraints of Desire*, 129–61. See too Helene P. Foley, " 'Reverse Similes' and Sex Roles in the *Odyssey*," in *Women in the Ancient World: The Arethusa Papers*, 59–78, more recently, "Penelope as Moral Agent," in *The Distaff Side: Representing the Female in Homer's Odyssey*, ed. Beth Cohen (New York, 1995), 93–116. Two recent book-length studies include Marilyn A. Katz, *Penelope's Renown: Meaning and Indeterminacy in the Odyssey* (Princeton, N.J., 1991); and Nancy Felson-Rubin, *Regarding Penelope: From Character to Poetics* (Princeton, N.J., 1994).

187   The dual nature of Helen's character, Euripides' *Helen*, and Semonides' "Palinode" are analyzed in Norman Austin, *Helen of Troy and Her Shameless Phantom*. See also Ingrid E. Holmberg, "Euripides' *Helen*: Most Noble and Most Chaste," *AJPh* 116.1 (1995), 19–42. For Helen as goddess see M.L. West, *Immortal Helen* (London, 1975).

190–91   For the correspondences between the *Helen* and the *Odyssey* see Robert Eisner, "Echoes of the *Odyssey* in Euripides' *Helen*," *Maia* 32 (1980), 31–37.

CHAPTER 8

Dover's *Greek Homosexuality*, especially 39–109, provides the basic information for understanding pederasty, with the limitations noted above in note to Chapter 4. See too Dover's "Eros and Nomos." Cantarella has a brief overview, in *Bisexuality in the Ancient World*, 17–42, but her claims that pederasty provided "adult Greek males" a "normal, acceptable, natural alternative" flies in the face of the evidence, as well as begging the question of just who was an "adult Greek male," 42. Cohen, *Law, Sexuality, and Society*, 171–202, respects the complexity and ambivalence that surrounded pederasty. An early article by George Devereux discussed pederasty in terms of Freudian assumptions—e.g., "inadequate fathering" (70)—no longer valid even for modern homosexuality, in "Greek Pseudo-Homosexuality and the 'Greek Miracle,' " *Symbolae Osloenses* 42 (1967), 69–92. See too Foucault, *The Use of Pleasure*, 185–226, and Jan Bremmer, "Greek Pederasty and Modern Homosexuality," in *From Sappho to de Sade: Moments in the History of Sexuality*, ed. Jan Bremmer (London, 1989), 1–14. See also evidence from red-figure vases gathered by Kilmer in *Greek Erotica*. The articles by Golden, "Slavery and Homosexuality in Athens," and Cartledge, "The Politics of Spartan Pederasty," are also useful. Readers should see too Camille Paglia's discussion of the beautiful boy in Greek art, "a rebuke to mother nature, an escape from the labyrinth of the body, with its murky womb and bowels," and the "triumph of mind over matter," in *Sexual Personae*, 109–23, quotes on 116–17.

194   The surviving evidence for pederastic practice in the ancient world, especially the comedies of Aristophanes, support Peter Green's assessment that the "aristocratic-homosexual tradition . . . represented only a tiny elitist minority at any time," in "Sex and Classical Literature," 136.

195   For the homoerotic transformation of Achilles and Patroklos see Bernard Sergent, *Homosexuality in Greek Myth*, 250–58.

196   Courtship of boys as evidenced on vases is discussed in Dover, *Greek Homosexuality*, 91–99; cf. too Cohen, 193, for similarities to courtship of women.

198   For the definition of the *philos* relationship see Gregory Vlastos, "The Individual as Object of Love in Plato," 1969; rpt. in *Platonic Studies* (Princeton, N.J., 1973), 3–6. The issues of reciprocal friendship, homosexuality, and aristocratic values discussed in terms of Theognis's poetry appear in Daniel B. Levine, "Symposium and the Polis," in *Theognis of Megara: Poetry and the Polis*, ed. Thomas J. Figueira and Gregory Nagy (Baltimore, Md., and London, 1985), 176–96; and from the same volume John M. Lewis, "Eros and the Polis in Theognis Book II," 199–222.

199   For the aristocratic/homoerotic connections of the symposium cf. Oswyn Murray: "It is indeed the *symposion* which, with its daytime extension the *gymnasion*, explains both the origin and persistence of the aristocratic phenomenon of homosexuality in Greek society," in "The Greek Symposion in History," *Tria Corda: Scritti in onore di Arnaldo Momigliano* (Como, 1983), 257–72, quote on 264. See too Murray's "The Symposion as Social Organization," in *The Greek Renaissance of the Eighth Century B.C. Tradition and Innovation* (Stockholm, 1983), 195–99, and his description of the typical symposium in *Early Greece* (Stanford, 1980), 197–203; cf. too Chester Starr, *The Aristocratic Temper of Greek Civilization* (New York and Oxford, 1992), 35–36. For the pedagogical-pederastic function of the symposium see Jan N. Bremmer, "Adolescents, *Symposion*, and Pederasty," in *Sympotica: A Symposium on the Symposion*, ed. Oswyn Murray (Oxford, 1990), 135–48.

200   For a description of the *kottabus* and photographs of recovered ancient implements see Brian A. Sparkes, "Kottabos: An Athenian After-Dinner Game," *Archaeology* 13.3 (1960), 202–07.

201   The importance of *hubris* and shame is discussed and documented in Cohen, *Law, Sexuality, and Society*, 175–87. Cf. 183: "Indeed, that honor and shame define the normative boundaries of homoeroticism (and sexuality in general) is implicit, and often explicit, in all our sources from Plato, Aristotle, and Xenophon to the orators and drama. Sexual submission is shameful and slavish; it dishonors and humiliates a free male."

205   The question of what specific sex acts may have taken place between a lover and a boy-love is variously answered by the writers on pederasty. Dover, *Greek Homosexuality*, implies that "intercrural" sex was the norm, though his position is not consistent. Cf. 91: "Acceptance of the teacher's thrusting penis between his

thighs or in his anus is the fee which the pupil pays for good teaching, or alternatively, a gift from a younger person to an older person whom he has come to love and admire." Winkler, in "Laying Down the Law," seems to imply that they did whatever they wanted, including buggery, since the public prohibitions had to do with political activity, not personal behavior, and were not meant to prohibit actual sexual practices: "The texts we study are, for the most part, rather like men's coffeehouse talk. Their legislative intent contains a fair amount of bluff, of saving face: they regularly lay down the laws which are belied by the jokes those same men will later tell," 70. Unfortunately, since those "texts we study" are all the evidence we have, Winkler can only arrive at his position by means of an ingenious and unconvincing interpretation whose fundamental assumption (in the best tradition of the ancient Sophists) is that the Greeks never meant what they said and somehow were incapabable of saying what they meant. Finally, Eva Cantarella's assertion of unrestrained buggery—"anal penetration was normal in pederastic relationships"—works only by ignoring completely the abundance of evidence that anal penetration was marked by shame, dishonor, and disgust even among pederastic enthusiasts (*Bisexuality in the Ancient World*, 25).

206   Readers who wish to familiarize themselves with the *Phaedrus* should start with W.K.C. Guthrie, *Plato: The Man and His Dialogues: Earlier Period*, volume 4 of *The History of Greek Philosophy* (Cambridge, 1975), 396–433. For the issue of eros specifically see Richard Price, *Love and Friendship in Plato and Aristotle*, 55–102. Also valuable for the general reader, though in error about the physical dimensions to erotic attraction, is Irving Singer, *The Nature of Love, Volume 1: Plato to Luther*, 2d ed. (Chicago and London, 1984), 47–87. The very real presence of physical sexuality in the *Phaedrus* is emphasized by Gregory Vlastos, "Sex in Platonic Love," in *Platonic Studies*, 38–42. Vlastos reminds us too that we should recognize the distinctions between Platonic and Socratic eros—the latter lacking the former's transcendent pretensions—in *Socrates: Ironist and Moral Philosopher* (Ithaca, N.Y., 1991), 38–39. Finally, Martha Nussbaum makes an ingenious but ultimately unconvincing argument that Socrates in the *Phaedrus* at least briefly entertains the possibility of mutual erotic attraction between men, including a high valuation of the passive homosexual's sexual experience: "It would not be fanciful to see Plato as expressing . . . his complex attitude towards the passive and receptive aspects of his own sexuality, aspects which, for a proud Greek gentleman of this time, could not have been easy to accept. . . . Now it [the life of the *kinaidos*] appears as a metaphor for the good life. . . . What Plato is saying . . . is that the truly blessed life involves the proper cultivation of both activity and passivity, working in harmony and mutuality. A horror of passivity is what lies beyond his culture's (and his own) condemnation of the life of Ganymede [Zeus's boy-love]; he tells us that this hatred of openness leads to a life impoverished in value and knowledge," in "'This Story Isn't True': Madness, Reason, and Recantation in the *Phaedrus*," in *The Fragility of Goodness: Luck and Ethics in Greek Tragedy and Philosophy* (Cambridge, 1986), 200–33, quotes on 231. Apart from what the old New Critics used to call the "biographical fallacy," and apart from the problem of projecting modern New Age feminist sexual idealism back onto Plato, Nussbaum's reading depends on Plato's imagery and metaphorical language—in a dialogue one of whose major points is the potential duplicity and

danger of such rhetorical tricks. Socrates himself says his speech was a "tolerably credible and possibly true though partly erring myth," something "mostly playful" (*Phdr.* 265).

209   That Socrates means sodomy at 250e–251a is argued by Vlastos, "The Individual as Object of Love in Plato," 25 n. 76.

210   For the *Symposium* see Guthrie, *Plato: The Man and His Dialogues*, 365–95; Price, *Love and Friendship*, 15–54; Singer, *The Nature of Love*, 47–87; and Martha Nussbaum, "The Speech of Alcibiades: A Reading of the *Symposium*," in *The Fragility of Goodness*, 165–99, where the stable rationality of Socrates and Diotima and the contingent passion represented by Alcibiades are found to be mutually exclusive.

210   Cf. Vlastos on the *Symposium*'s "heterosexual paradigm": "What started as a pederastic idyl ends up in transcendental marriage," "Sex in Platonic Love," 42. See the analysis of Plato's birth imagery by Giulia Sissa, "The Sexual Philosophies of Plato and Aristotle," 47–51.

CONCLUSION

The volume of writing on sex is immense, as any reader who browses the HQ section of the local library can attest, and I make no claim here to refer to even a significant fraction of it. For sex after the Greeks the general reader should start with the surveys mentioned at the beginning of these notes: Morton Hunt, *The Natural History of Love*, Reay Tannahill, *Sex in History*, Vern L. Bullough, *Sexual Variance in Society and History*, Camille Paglia, *Sexual Personae*, and Nigel Davies, *The Rampant God*. See too volume 3 of Irving Singer's *The Nature of Love: The Modern World* (New York, 1984). Anyone wanting a trenchant and insightful analysis of our current sexual scene should see Camille Paglia, "No Law in the Arena," in *Vamps and Tramps: New Essays* (New York, 1994), 19–94.

213   For dismissals of the idea that Christianity was responsible for sexually repressing the West cf. Peter Green, "Sex and Classical Literature," 150. Foucault, *The Use of Pleasure*, 14–24, elaborates on the continuity and differences between ancient Greek attitudes toward sex and Chritianity's. Lawrence Osborne, from whom I filched the phrase "sexual pessimism," traces the equation of sexual love with death throughout Western culture. I'm not convinced by his argument that the roots of this attitude lie in Gnostic Christianity, but Osborne's book is informative and entertaining (*The Poisoned Embrace: A Brief History of Sexual Pessimism* [New York, 1993]). Osborne's concluding section is particularly fascinating in its documentation of the links between "sexual liberation" and early-twentieth-century totalitarianism.

214   The history and development of Christian asceticism are discussed by Peter Brown, *The Body and Society: Men, Women, and Sexual Renunciation in Early Christianity* (New York, 1988). On the difference between Hellenic and early Christian views of passion cf. 31: "Where second-century pagans differed most profoundly from the views that had already begun to circulate in Christian circles was in their estimate of the horizons of the possible for the body itself.... Like society, the body was there to be administered, not to be changed." Brown goes

on to quote the late-second-century Christian philosopher Clement of Alexandria, who said Greek philosophy "teaches one to resist passion, so as not to be made subservient to it, and to train the instincts to pursue rational goals." But the Christian ideal "is not to experience desire at all" (*Stromateis* 3.7.57, trans. Henry Chadwick).

214   For St. Augustine's sexualization of the Fall see Elaine Pagels, *Adam, Eve, and the Serpent* (New York, 1988), 98–126.

215   The following works deal with Courtly Love and its descendent, Romantic Love: C.S. Lewis, *The Allegory of Love: A Study in Medieval Tradition* (1936; Oxford and New York, 1958); Denis de Rougemont, *Love in the Western World*, trans. Montgomery Belgian (1940; Princeton, N.J., 1983); Maurice Valency, *In Praise of Love: An Introduction to the Love-Poetry of the Renaissance* (1958; New York, 1961); Irving Singer, *The Nature of Love, Volume 2: Courtly and Romantic* (New York, 1984).

215   Freud's theory of sexuality is briefly and clearly described by Gerasimos Santas, *Plato and Freud: Two Theories of Love* (Oxford, 1988), 97–115.

216   Katie Roiphe recognizes the fear of sexuality underlying the date-rape hysteria in *The Morning After: Sex, Fear, and Feminism on Campus* (New York, 1993), 8–84. See too the detailing of radical feminism's horror of sexuality by Rene Denfeld, *The New Victorians: A Young Woman's Challenge to the Old Feminist Order* (New York, 1995), 25–123.

216   Cf. Paglia on pornography: "In fact, pornography, which erupts into the open in periods of personal freedom, shows the dark truth about nature, concealed by the artifices of civilization. Pornography is about lust, our animal reality that will never be fully tamed by love. Lust is elemental, aggressive, asocial." "The Return of Carry Nation: Catharine MacKinnon and Andrea Dworkin," 1992; rpt. in *Vamps and Tramps*, 107–12, quote on 110.

217   In addition to scientists like LeVay, there are the surveys of sexual behaviors like Alfred Kinsey, Shere Hite, and the recent *Sex in America: A Definitive Survey*, ed. Robert T. Michael, John H. Gagnon, Edward O. Laumann, and Gina Kolata (New York, 1994). The writers' Enlightenment faith in the transforming power of knowledge, as well as their assumption that nature counts for very little compared to culture, can be seen in the following: "With an understanding of what the data can and cannot tell us, and with reliable data in hand, we can begin to understand how society shapes our sexual behavior. We can describe the ways in which social understandings, incentives, and networks combine to elicit the sexual behaviors that usually were attributed to untamed instincts or impulses. . . . With data we can trust, we can get beyond the myths and paradoxes and can start having an informed discussion," 40–41. For an exposure of this survey's methodological inadequacies see R.C. Lewontin, "Sex, Lies, and Social Science," *NYRB* 42.7 (20 April 1995), 24–29. And always, of course, we have the sex manuals, the classic of which is *The Joy of Sex*. A more recent addition to this ancient genre reflects as much as do the sex surveyors the assumption that knowledge of eros can be translated into ameliorating techniques. Cf. the following's tone of Baconian optimism: "I will regularly invite you [the reader] to examine your own peak erotic experiences and show you how to search gently for clues to

268 Critical Bibliography

your eroticism. You'll open new pathways to sexual satisfaction" (Jack Morin, *The Erotic Mind: Unlocking the Inner Sources of Sexual Passion and Fulfillment* [New York, 1995], 8). But who knows what else you will find behind that locked door?

Finally, nowhere is this Enlightenment faith in the power of knowledge more evident than in those who devise and promulgate sex-education programs. The naiveté of, say, famous sex technician Ruth Westheimer would be comic if its consequences weren't so destructive: "I think that a child knowing about his or her body will be able to deal with the pressure to have sex" (quoted in Mary Gibbs, "How Should We Teach Kids About Sex?" *Time* [24 May 1993], 60). One can only quote a much more acute psychologist, Euripides, when he has his Phaedra say, "We know the good and recognize it, but we cannot bring it to pass" (*Hipp.* 380–81). When the flames of Eros rage in the blood, knowledge, like Prospero's oaths, is just "straw for the fire."

About the Book and Author

Eros: The Myth of Ancient Greek Sexuality is a controversial book that lays bare the meanings Greeks gave to sex. Contrary to the romantic idealization of sex dominating our culture, the Greeks saw eros as a powerful force of nature, potentially dangerous and in need of control by society: Eros the Destroyer, not Cupid the Insipid, is what fired the Greek imagination.

The destructiveness of eros can be seen in Greek imagery and metaphor, and in their attitudes toward women and homosexuals. Images of love as fire, disease, storms, insanity, and violence—top 40 song clichés for us—locate eros among the unpredictable and deadly forces of nature. The beautiful Aphrodite embodies the alluring danger of sex, and femmes fatales like Pandora and Helen represent the risky charms of female sexuality. And homosexuality typifies for the Greeks the frightening power of an indiscriminate appetite that threatens the stability of culture itself.

In *Eros: The Myth of Ancient Greek Sexuality*, Bruce Thornton offers a uniquely sweeping and comprehensive account of ancient sexuality free of currently fashionable theoretical jargon and pretensions. In its conclusions the book challenges the distortions of much recent scholarship on Greek sexuality. And throughout it links the wary attitudes of the Greeks to our present-day concerns about love, sex, and family. What we see, finally, are the origins of some of our own views as well as a vision of sexuality that is perhaps more honest and mature than our own dangerous illusions.

Bruce S. Thornton is professor of classics and chair of the Department of Foreign Languages at California State University, Fresno.

Index